Professional Jakarta Struts

Professional Jakarta Struts

James Goodwill
Richard Hightower

Wiley Publishing, Inc.

MAY 0 3 2004
005.2762
G656p

Professional Jakarta Struts

Published by
Wiley Publishing, Inc.
10475 Crosspoint Boulevard
Indianapolis, IN 46256
www.wiley.com

Copyright © 2004 by Wiley Publishing, Inc., Indianapolis, Indiana

Published by Wiley Publishing, Inc., Indianapolis, Indiana

Published simultaneously in Canada

Library of Congress Cataloging-in-Publication Data is available from the publisher.

ISBN: 0-7645-4437-3

Manufactured in the United States of America

10 9 8 7 6 5 4 3 2 1

No part of this publication may be reproduced, stored in a retrieval system or transmitted in any form or by any means, electronic, mechanical, photocopying, recording, scanning or otherwise, except as permitted under Sections 107 or 108 of the 1976 United States Copyright Act, without either the prior written permission of the Publisher, or authorization through payment of the appropriate per-copy fee to the Copyright Clearance Center, 222 Rosewood Drive, Danvers, MA 01923, (978) 750-8400, fax (978) 646-8700. Requests to the Publisher for permission should be addressed to the Legal Department, Wiley Publishing, Inc., 10475 Crosspoint Blvd., Indianapolis, IN 46256, (317) 572-3447, fax (317) 572-4447, E-mail: permcoordinator@wiley.com.

LIMIT OF LIABILITY/DISCLAIMER OF WARRANTY: WHILE THE PUBLISHER AND AUTHOR HAVE USED THEIR BEST EFFORTS IN PREPARING THIS BOOK, THEY MAKE NO REPRESENTATIONS OR WARRANTIES WITH RESPECT TO THE ACCURACY OR COMPLETENESS OF THE CONTENTS OF THIS BOOK AND SPECIFICALLY DISCLAIM ANY IMPLIED WARRANTIES OF MERCHANTABILITY OR FITNESS FOR A PARTICULAR PURPOSE. NO WARRANTY MAY BE CREATED OR EXTENDED BY SALES REPRESENTATIVES OR WRITTEN SALES MATERIALS. THE ADVICE AND STRATEGIES CONTAINED HEREIN MAY NOT BE SUITABLE FOR YOUR SITUATION. YOU SHOULD CONSULT WITH A PROFESSIONAL WHERE APPROPRIATE. NEITHER THE PUBLISHER NOR AUTHOR SHALL BE LIABLE FOR ANY LOSS OF PROFIT OR ANY OTHER COMMERCIAL DAMAGES, INCLUDING BUT NOT LIMITED TO SPECIAL, INCIDENTAL, CONSEQUENTIAL, OR OTHER DAMAGES.

For general information on our other products and services or to obtain technical support, please contact our Customer Care Department within the U.S. at (800) 762-2974, outside the U.S. at (317) 572-3993 or fax (317) 572-4002.

Wiley also publishes its books in a variety of electronic formats. Some content that appears in print may not be available in electronic books.

Trademarks: Wiley, the Wiley Publishing logo, Wrox, the Wrox logo, the Wrox Programmer to Programmer logo and related trade dress are trademarks or registered trademarks of John Wiley & Sons, Inc. and/or its affiliates in the United States and other countries, and may not be used without written permission. [Insert third party trademark language]. All other trademarks are the property of their respective owners. Wiley Publishing, Inc. is not associated with any product or vendor mentioned in this book.

About the Authors

James Goodwill

James Goodwill is the co-founder and chief technology officer at Virtuas Solutions, LLC, located in Denver, Colorado. With over 10 years of experience, James leads Virtuas' Senior Internet Architects in the development of cutting-edge tools designed for J2EE e-business acceleration.

In addition to his professional experience, James is a member of the JSP 2.0 Expert Group (JSR-152.) He is the author of the best-selling Java titles *Developing Java Servlets, Pure JavaServer Pages, Apache Jakarta Tomcat,* and *Mastering JSP Custom Tags and Tag Libraries.* James is also a regular columnist on the Java community Web site, OnJava.com.

More information about James, his work, and his previous publications can be found at his company's web site, www.virtuas.com.

Rick Hightower

Rick Hightower (www.rickhightower.com) is a developer who enjoys working with Java, J2EE, Ant, Struts, Web Services and XDoclet. Rick is also the CTO of Trivera Technologies (www.triveratch.com), a global training, mentoring, and consulting company focusing on enterprise development. Rick is a regular contributor to IBM developerWorks and has written more than 10 IBM developerWorks tutorials on subjects ranging from EJB to Web Services to XDoclet to Struts to Custom Tags.

While working at eBlox, Rick and the eBlox team used Struts and J2EE to build two frameworks and an ASP (application service provider) for online ecommerce stores. They started using Struts long before the 1.0 release.

Rick recently helped put together a well-received course for Trivera on Struts that runs on Tomcat 4.x, Resin EE 2.x, IBM WebSphere 5.0 (WSAD), JBoss 3.x, and WebLogic 8.1. When not traveling around the country teaching the Trivera Struts course (our bestseller), speaking at conferences about Struts, or doing Struts consulting and mentoring, Rick enjoys drinking coffee at an all night coffee shop and writing code, writing about Struts and other Java, J2EE and XP topics, and writing about himself in the third person.

Credits

Authors
James Goodwill
Richard Hightower

Executive Editor
Robert Elliot

Production Editor
Vincent Kunkemueller

Technical Editors and Reviewers
Andy Barton
Erik Hatcher
Craig Pfeifer

Copy Editor
Elizabeth Welch

Vice President & Executive Group Publisher
Richard Swadley

Vice President & Executive Publisher
Robert Ipsen

Vice President & Publisher
Joseph B. Wikert

Executive Editorial Director
Mary Bednarek

Editorial Manager
Kathryn A. Malm

Compositor
Amy Hassos

Book Producer
Ryan Publishing Group, Inc.

Dedication

To my girls, Christy, Abby, and Emma

—James Goodwill

To my sons, Dante, Ryan, and Richard Jr., and my lovely first-born Whitney Marie.

And, to the memory of Dave Richardson and Lou Souza; mentors and friends

—Rick Hightower

Acknowledgments

I would like to begin this text by thanking the people who made this book what it is today. They are the people who took my words and shaped them into something that I hope will help you use and develop Jakarta Struts applications. Of these people, I would like to especially thank Tim Ryan, and Liz Welch. They both contributed considerably to what I hope is a successful book. I would also like to thank Rick Hightower for his incredible contributions of Chapters 5, 12, 13, and 21. He work is an invaluable addition to this text.

On a closer note, I would like to thank everyone at my company, Virtuas Solutions, LLC, for their support while I was completing this text. The entire "UNREAL" staff contributed by picking up my assignments when my plate was too full.

Finally, the most important contributors to this book are my wife, Christy, and our daughters, Abby and Emma. They are the ones who really sacrificed during the development of this text, and they are the ones who deserve the credit for this book. Without their support, this text would be a collection of words that made very little sense.

—James Goodwill

Thanks to James Goodwill and Tim Ryan for inviting me to the party (okay I begged Tim and James, but still). I really enjoyed reading James Goodwill's other books and it is a real pleasure working with him. Tim Ryan is an amazingly talented editor who makes me look much smarter than I am.

I'd like to thank the eBlox team (Andy Barton et al) who helped review my chapters. I learned Struts while working at eBlox. Pair programming with Nick Nicholas Lesiecki, Erik Hatcher, Andy Barton, Paul Visan, and more at eBlox helped us all learn Struts long before Struts 1.0. Special thanks to the famed XDoclet, Struts, and Ant expert, Erik Hatcher whose critical eye made my chapters much more detailed and accurate. It is good to have Erik as a friend.

Thanks to my wife Kiley and kids for sacrificing time with me so I could work on this book. Last but not least, I'd like to thank the Trivera Technologies Team and Kimberly Morello who gave me some schedule flexibility so I could work on this book. Thanks to our clients, where I learned a lot of new Struts tricks while training Struts, and mentoring and consulting on Struts projects. Okay one more: Thanks to the Struts contributors who provided a great framework to build J2EE web applications.

—Rick Hightower

Introduction

Throughout my experiences in server-side development, I have assembled many applications using many different technology combinations. Of all of these, I am most impressed with the Java server-side technologies, including servlets, EJBs, JSPs, and JSP custom tags.

This text focuses on a particular server-side Java framework, known as the Jakarta Struts project, or simply enough Struts. Struts combines two of the most popular server-side Java technologies—JSPs and servlets—into a server-side implementation of the Model-View-Controller design pattern. It was conceived by Craig McClanahan in May of 2000, and has been under the watchful eye of the Apache Jakarta open source community since that time.

The remarkable thing about the Struts project is its early adoption, which is obviously a testament to both its quality and utility. The Java community, both commercial and private, has really gotten behind Struts. It is currently supported by all of the major application servers including BEA, Sun, Caucho, and of course Apache's Jakarta-Tomcat. The Tomcat group has even gone so far as to use a Struts application in its most recent 4.0.4 release for managing Web applications hosted by the container.

This book covers everything you need to know about the Struts 1.1 project and its supporting technologies, including JSPs, servlet, Web applications, the Validator framework, the Tiles framework, and the Jakarta-Tomcat JSP/servlet container. We also cover best practices, discuss design issues, and warn of potential roadblocks with each technology. The goal of this text is to provide you with the foundation you need to design, build, and deploy Jakarta Struts applications with all of the Struts 1.1 features and techniques.

As I have stated with most of my book projects, there will be topics that I have not discussed but that are of interest to individual readers. If you run across such an issue or just have a question, please feel free to contact me at books@virtuas.com or Rick Hightower at rick_m_hightower@hotmail.com. In these e-mails, please be sure to place the text "Jakarta-Struts" in the subject line.

Thanks and good luck,

James Goodwill III

The Organization of the Book

The book you are about to begin is formatted as a tutorial describing the Jakarta Struts project. It is divided into 16 distinct chapters, beginning with an introduction of Struts and continuing with discussions about each of the major Struts components:

Chapter 1: Introducing the Jakarta Struts Project and Its Supporting Components lays the groundwork for the complete text. We introduce the Jakarta Struts project and discuss the Model-

View-Controller (MVC) design pattern that it's based on. We also define Java Web applications and explain how to construct and use them. In addition, we examine the Jakarta-Tomcat Web application container, the container used for all our examples.

Chapter 2: An Overview of the Java Servlet and JavaServer Pages Architectures contains a JSP and servlet primer. It is aimed at the Java developer who is not yet familiar with these two technologies. These topics are the foundation of Jakarta Struts projects, and you must understand them before continuing with the text.

Chapter 3: Getting Started with Struts is where we first encounter actual Struts code. This chapter covers the step-by-step process of building a Struts application by taking you through the development of a simple Struts application.

Chapter 4: Actions and the ActionServlet begins our first detailed discussions of an individual group of Struts components. In this chapter, we look at four distinct Struts Controller components: the ActionServlet class, the Action class, Plugins, and the RequestProcesser.

Chapter 5: Advanced Action Classes continues our Controller discussions with a look at some prepackaged Struts Action classes including the DispatchAction, ForwardAction, IncludeAction, LookupDispatchAction, and SwitchAction.

Chapter 6: Building the Presentation Layer discusses the Struts implementation of the View component of the MVC design pattern. This chapter covers everything you need to know when connecting JSPs to a Struts Controller. We also briefly discuss some of the tag libraries provided by the Struts framework.

Chapter 7: Debugging Struts Applications takes you through the process of configuring the Eclipse and IntelluJ IDEs for debugging Struts application. This chapter discusses both debugging your applications and stepping though the actual Struts framework.

Chapter 8: Working with Custom ActionMappings discusses the org.apache.struts.action.ActionMapping class, which provides the information that the ActionServlet needs knows about the mapping of a request to a particular instance of an action class. After describing the default ActionMapping, we go on to explain how you can extend the ActionMapping class to provide specialized mapping information to the ActionServlet.

Chapter 9: Internationalizing Your Struts Applications describes the Struts mechanisms for internationalized application development. Here, we examine each of the components used and provide an example of internationalizing a Struts application.

Chapter 10: Managing Errors looks at some of the methods available to you when you're managing errors in a Struts application. We begin by looking at the different error classes provided by the Struts framework, and we show how errors can be managed in both the Controller and Views of a Struts application by adding error handling to a sample application.

Chapter 11: Integrating the Jakarta Commons Database Connection Pool (DBCP) discusses how you can leverage the Commons Database Connection Pool's functionality to manage a DataSource connected to a sample database.

Chapter 12: Working with the Validator In this chapter, you will learn how to use Struts to validate form fields. We go a step further and cover best practices regarding validation, and then have you develop your own validator components.

Chapter 13: Using Tiles will describe the newly contributed Tiles templating mechanism and provide several examples of how Tiles can be used to give your application a common look and feel, while also saving you a tremendous amount of time on the presentation layer. We take the Tiles coverage further and show you how to create tile based visual components, managed tile scope and write tile controllers.

Chapter 14: Developing a Compete Struts Application takes you through the development of an entire Struts application. The purpose of this chapter is to tie all of the previous discussions together by creating a practical Struts application.

Chapter 15: The struts-config.xml File describes the struts-config.xml file, the Struts deployment descriptor. We tell you how you can add and configure each major Struts component in this file.

Chapters 16-20: The Struts Custom Tag Libraries describe the Struts framework's tag libraries. In these chapters, we examine each of the Struts tag libraries, including the Tiles, Bean, HTML, Logic, and Template tag libraries. We describe the custom tags in the library, look at their attributes, and provide examples of how they can be used.

Chapter 21: Struts Cookbook contains a wealth of advanced material that will enable you to get the most out of Struts and this book. Think of it as a cookbook for recipes that will help you solve common problems in your Web application development with Struts. We cover transaction tokens, dynamically changing locale, i18n enabled messaging, allow user to cancel an operation, Best Practices and much more. You may want to read the Best Practices section before you start your first Struts application. Then, for good measure, we throw in a list of related tools you should consider using when developing Struts applications namely JSTL (tags and API), Cactus, StrutsTestCase, and XDoclet.

Contents

1

Introducing the Jakarta Struts Project and Its Supporting Components

In this chapter, we lay the foundation for all of our further discussions. We start by providing a high-level description of the Jakarta Struts project. We then describe Java Web applications, which act as the packaging mechanism for all Struts applications. We conclude this chapter with a discussion of the Jakarta Tomcat JSP/servlet container, which we use to host all of our examples throughout the remainder of this text.

At the end of this chapter, you should have an understanding of what the Struts project is, be familiar with its packaging mechanism, and have an installed JSP/servlet container to run your Struts applications.

The Jakarta Struts Project

The Jakarta Struts project, an open-source project sponsored by the Apache Software Foundation, is a server-side Java implementation of the Model-View-Controller (MVC) design pattern. The Struts project was originally created by Craig McClanahan in May 2000, but since that time it has been taken over by the open-source community.

The Struts project was designed with the intention of providing an open-source framework for creating Web applications that easily separate the presentation layer and allow it to be abstracted from the transaction and data layers. Since its inception, Struts has received quite a bit of developer support and is quickly becoming a dominant factor in the open-source community. This book covers version 1.1 of the Jakarta Struts Project.

> **A small debate is going on in the development community as to the type of design pattern that the Struts project most closely resembles. According the documentation provided by the actual developers of the Struts project, it is patterned after the MVC, but some folks insist that it more closely resembles the Front Controller design pattern described by Sun's J2EE Blueprints Program. The truth is that it does very much resemble the Front Controller pattern, but for the purpose of our discussions, I am sticking with the developers. If you would like to examine the Front Controller yourself, you can find a good article on this topic at the Java Developer Connection site, http://developer.java.sun.com/developer/technicalArticles/J2EE/despat/.**

Understanding the MVC Design Pattern

To gain a solid understanding of the Struts Framework, you must have a fundamental understanding of the MVC design pattern, which it is based on. The MVC design pattern, which originated from Smalltalk, consists of three components: a Model, a View, and a Controller. Table 1.1 defines each of these components.

Table 1.1 The Three Components of the MVC

Component	Description
Model	Represents the data objects. The Model is what is being manipulated and presented to the user.
View	Serves as the screen representation of the Model. It is the object that presents the current state of the data objects.
Controller	Defines the way the user interface reacts to the user's input. The Controller component is the object that manipulates the Model, or data object.

We discuss each of these components in more detail throughout this chapter. Some of the major benefits of using the MVC are:

Reliability: The presentation and transaction layers have clear separation, which allows you to change the look and feel of an application without recompiling Model or Controller code.

High reuse and adaptability: The MVC lets you use multiple types of views, all accessing the same server-side code. This includes anything from Web browsers (HTTP) to wireless browsers (WAP).

Very low development and lifecycle costs: The MVC makes it possible to have lower-level programmers develop and maintain the user interfaces.

Rapid deployment: Development time can be significantly reduced, because Controller programmers (Java developers) focus solely on transactions, and View programmers (HTML and JSP developers) focus solely on presentation.

Maintainability: The separation of presentation and business logic also makes it easier to maintain and modify a Struts-based Web application.

The Struts Implementation of the MVC

The Struts Framework models its server-side implementation of the MVC using a combination of JSPs, custom JSP tags, and a Java servlet. In this section, we briefly describe how the Struts Framework maps to each component of the MVC. When we have completed this discussion, we will have drawn a portrait similar to Figure 1.1.

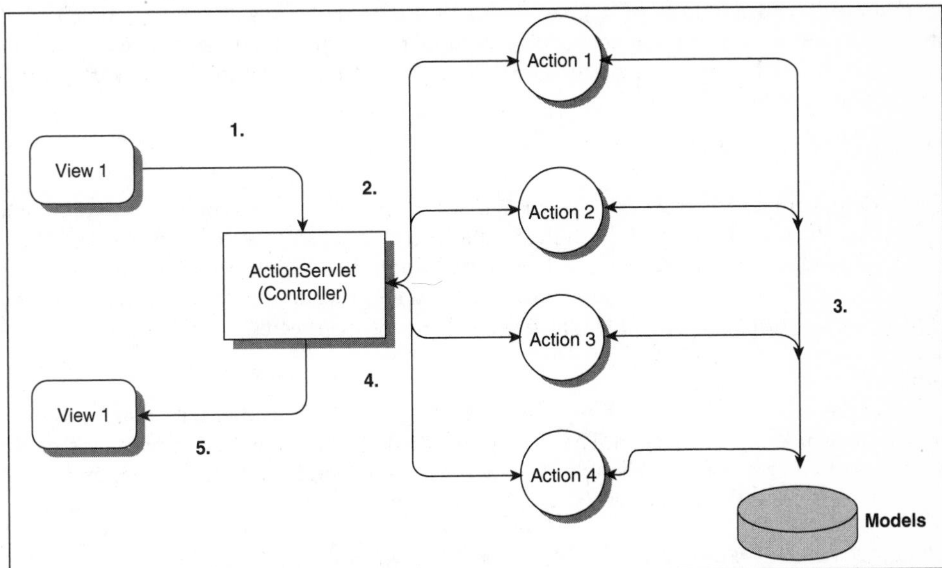

Figure 1.1 The Struts implementation of the MVC.

Figure 1.1 depicts the route that most Struts application requests follow. This process can be broken down into five basic steps. Following these steps is a description of the components involved in this sequence.

1. A request is made from a previously displayed View.
2. The request is received by the ActionServlet, which acts as the Controller, and the ActionServlet looks up the requested URI in an XML file (described in Chapter 3, "Getting Started with Struts"), and determines the name of the Action class that will perform the necessary business logic.
3. The Action class performs its logic on the Model components associated with the application.
4. Once the Action has completed its processing, it returns control to the ActionServlet. As part of the return, the Action class provides a key that indicates the results of its processing. The ActionServlet uses this key to determine where the results should be forwarded for presentation.
5. The request is complete when the ActionServlet responds by forwarding the request to the View that was linked to the returned key, and this View presents the results of the Action.

As you can probably surmise, the previous steps are a simplified representation of a Struts request. We cover these steps in much more detail, including a discussion on several other components, as this text progresses.

The Model

The Model components of the Struts Framework, as we stated earlier, represent the data objects of the Struts application. They often represent business objects or other backend systems and can be implemented as simple JavaBeans, Enterprise JavaBeans, object representations of data stored in a relational database, or just about anything that needs to be manipulated or presented using a Web application. We take a look at the Model component in greater detail in Chapter 11, "Integrating the Jakarta Commons Database Connection Pool (DBCP)."

The View

Each View component in the Struts Framework is mapped to a JSP that can contain any combination of HTML, JSP, and Struts custom tags. JSPs in the Struts Framework serve two main functions. The first is to act as the presentation layer of a previously executed Controller Action. This is most often accomplished using a set of custom tags that are focused around iterating and retrieving data forwarded to the target JSP by the Controller Action. This type of View is not Struts specific and does not warrant special attention.

The second of these functions, which is very much Struts specific, is to gather data that is required to perform a particular Controller Action. This is accomplished most often with a combination of Struts tag libraries and ActionForm objects. This type of View contains several Struts-specific tags and classes. The following code snippet contains a simple example of this type of Struts View:

```
<%@taglib uri="/WEB-INF/struts-html.tld" prefix="html">

<html:form action="loginAction.do"
  name="loginForm"
  type="com.wrox.loginForm" >

  User Id: <html:text property="username"><br/>
  Password: <html:password property="password"><br/>
  <html:submit />
</html:form>
```

As you can see, several JSP custom tags are being leveraged in this JSP. These tags are defined by the Struts Framework and provide a loose coupling to the Controller of a Struts application. We build a working Struts View in Chapter 3, and in Chapter 6, "Building the Presentation Layer," we examine the Struts Views in more detail.

While JSPs are the common presentation tool in a Struts application, they are not the only presentation method available. You can leverage many other tools, including template tools, the Jakarta Velocity Project, and XSLT, among others. For the purpose of this text, we focus on the default Struts presentation layer: JSPs.

The Controller

The Controller component of the Struts Framework is the backbone of all Struts Web applications. It is implemented using a servlet named org.apache.struts.action.ActionServlet. This servlet receives HTTP requests and delegates control of each request, based on the URI of the incoming request, to a user-defined org.apache.struts.action.Action class. The Action class is where the Model of the application is retrieved and/or modified. Once the Action class has completed its processing, it returns a key to the ActionServlet. This key is used to determine the View that will present the results of the Action class's processing. You can think of the ActionServlet as a factory that takes named requests for services and based upon these requests creates Action objects to perform the actual business logic required to complete these services.

The Controller is the most important component of the Struts Framework. We discuss the Controller in Chapter 3, "Getting Started with Struts," and in even greater detail in Chapter 4, "Actions and the ActionServlet."

Web Applications

All Struts applications are packaged using the Java Web application format. Therefore, before we continue, let's take a brief look at Java Web applications.

Java Web applications are best described by the Java Servlet Specification 2.2, which introduced the idea using the following description: "A Web Application is a collection of servlets, HTML pages, classes, and other resources that can be bundled and run on multiple containers from multiple vendors." In simpler terms, a Java Web application is a collection of one or more Web components that have been packaged together for the purpose of creating a complete application to be executed in the Web layer of an enterprise application. Here is a list of the common components that can be packaged in a Web application:

- Servlets
- JavaServer Pages (JSPs)
- JSP custom tag libraries
- Utility classes and application classes
- Static documents, including HTML, images, and JavaScript
- Metainformation describing the Web application

The Directory Structure

All Web applications are packed into a common directory structure, and this directory structure is the container that holds the components of a Web application. The first step in creating a Web application is to create this structure. Table 1.2 describes a sample Web application, named wroxapp, and lists the contents of each of its directories. Each one of these directories will be created from the *<SERVER_ROOT>* of the Servlet/JSP container.

Table 1.2 The Web Application Directory Structure

Directory	Contains
/wroxapp	This is the root directory of the Web application. All JSP and HTML files are stored here.
/wroxapp/WEB-INF	This directory contains all resources related to the application that are not in the document root of the application. This is where your Web application deployment descriptor is located. You should note that the WEB-INF directory is not part of the public document. No files contained in this directory can be served directly to a client.
/ wroxapp/WEB-INF/classes	This directory is where servlet and utility classes are located.
/ wroxapp/WEB-INF/lib	This directory contains Java Archive (JAR) files that the Web application is dependent on.

If you're using Tomcat as your container, the default root directory is *<CATALINA_HOME>*/webapps/. Figure 1.2 shows the wroxapp as it would be hosted by a Tomcat container.

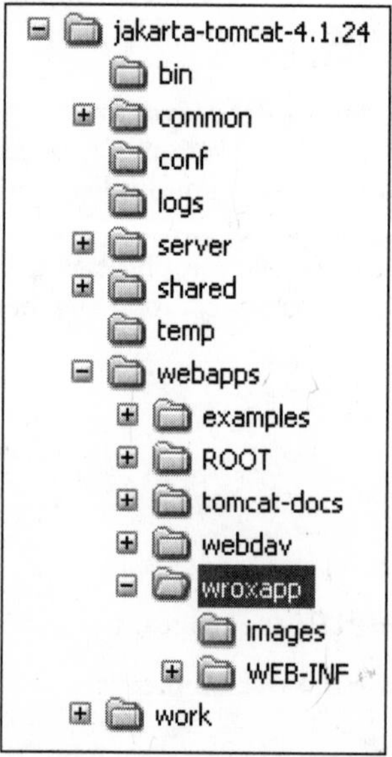

Figure 1.2 The wroxapp Web application hosted by Tomcat.

> **Web applications allow compiled classes to be stored in both the /WEB-INF/ classes and /WEB-INF/lib directories. Of these two directories, the class loader will load classes from the /classes directory first, followed by the JARs in the /lib directory. If you have duplicate classes in both the /classes and /lib directories, the classes in the /classes directory will take precedence.**

The Web Application Deployment Descriptor

The backbone of all Web applications is its deployment descriptor. The Web Application deployment descriptor is an XML file named web.xml that is located in the /*<SERVER_ROOT>/application-name*/WEB-INF/ directory. The web.xml file describes all of the components in the Web application. If we use the previous Web application name, wroxapp, then the web.xml file would be located in the /*<SERVER_ROOT>*/wroxapp /WEB-INF/ directory. The information that can be described in the deployment descriptor includes the following elements:

- ServletContext init parameters
- Localized content
- Session configuration
- Servlet/JSP definitions
- Servlet/JSP mappings
- Tag library references
- MIME type mappings
- Welcome file list
- Error pages
- Security information

This code snippet contains a sample deployment descriptor that defines a single servlet. We examine the web.xml file in much more detail as this text progresses.

```
<?xml version="1.0" encoding="ISO-8859-1"?>

<!DOCTYPE web-app PUBLIC
  '-//Sun Microsystems, Inc.//DTD Web Application 2.3//EN'
  'http://java.sun.com/dtd/web-app_2_3.dtd'>

<servlet>
  <servlet-name>SimpleServlet</servlet-name>
  <servlet-class>com.wrox.SimpleServlet</servlet-class>
</servlet>

</web-app>
```

Packaging a Web Application

The standard packaging format for a Web application is a Web Archive file (WAR). A WAR file is simply a JAR file with the extension .war as opposed to .jar. You can create a WAR file by using jar, Java's archiving tool. To create a WAR file, you simply need to change to the root directory of your Web application and type the following command:

```
jar cvf wroxapp.war .
```

This command produces an archive file named wroxapp.war that contains the entire wroxapp Web application. You can deploy your Web application by simply distributing this file.

The Tomcat JSP/Servlet Container

The Tomcat JSP/Servlet container is an open-source Java-based Web application container created to run servlet and JavaServer Page Web applications. It has become Sun's reference implementation for both the Servlet and JSP specifications. We use Tomcat for all of our examples in this book.

Before we get started with the installation and configuration of Tomcat, you need to make sure you have acquired the items listed in Table 1.3.

Table 1.3 Tomcat Installation Requirements

Component	Location
Jakarta-Tomcat 4.1.24 LE	http://jakarta.apache.org/
JDK 1.4.1 Standard Edition	http://java.sun.com/j2se/1.4/

Installing and Configuring Tomcat

Once you have Tomcat and the JDK downloaded, go ahead and install them according to their packaged instructions. For our purposes, we are installing Tomcat as a stand-alone server on a Windows XP operating system (OS). We are installing Tomcat in the directory C:\Tomcat 4.1 and the JDK in the directory C:\j2sdk1.4.1_02.

After we have Tomcat and the JDK installed, the next step is to set the JAVA_HOME environment variable. This variable is used to compile your requested JSPs. To do this under XP, perform these steps:

1. Open the Windows XP Control Panel.
2. Start the System Application, and then select the Advanced tab.
3. Click the Environment Variables button. You will see a screen similar to Figure 1.3.

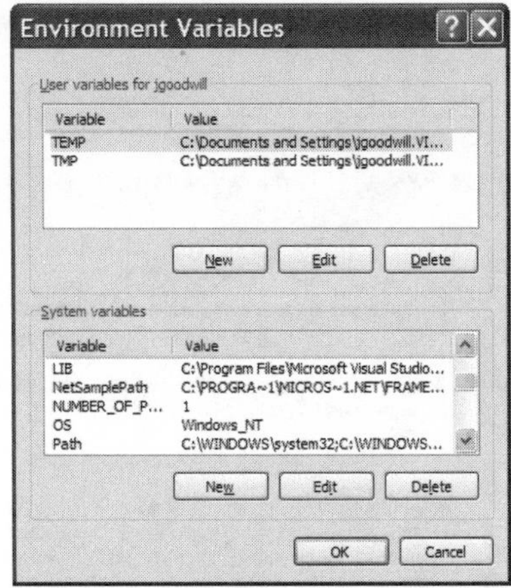

Figure 1.3 The Windows NT/2000 Environment Variables dialog box.

4. Click the New button in the System Variables section of the Environment Variables dialog box. Add a Variable named *JAVA_HOME* and set its value to the location of your JDK installation. Figure 1.4 shows the settings associated with our installation.

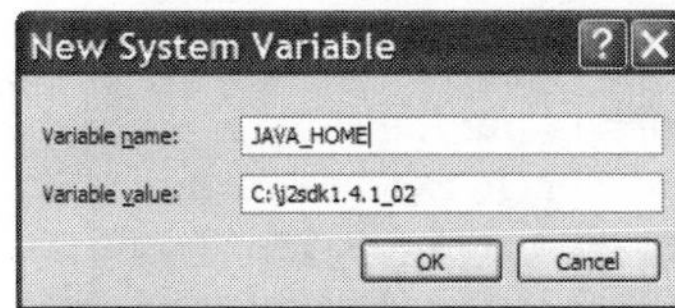

Figure 1.4 The JAVA_HOME environment settings for our installation.

That's all there is to it. You can now move on to the next section, in which we test the Tomcat installation.

Testing Your Tomcat Installation

Before continuing, let's test the steps we have just completed. To begin, first start the Tomcat server by typing the following command (be sure to replace *<CATALINA_HOME>* with the location of your Tomcat installation):

```
<CATALINA_HOME>\bin\startup.bat
```

Once Tomcat has started, open your browser to the following URL:

```
http://localhost:8080
```

You should see the default Tomcat home page, which is displayed in Figure 1.5.

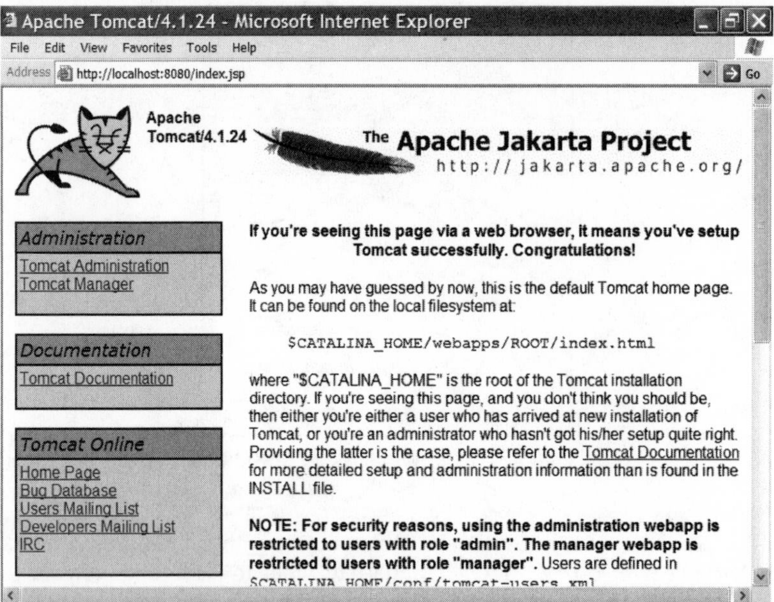

Figure 1.5 The default Tomcat home page.

The next step is to verify the installation of our JDK. The best way to do this is to execute one of the JSP examples provided with the Tomcat server. To execute a sample JSP, start from the default Tomcat home page, shown in Figure 1.5, and choose JSP Examples. You should see a page similar to Figure 1.6.

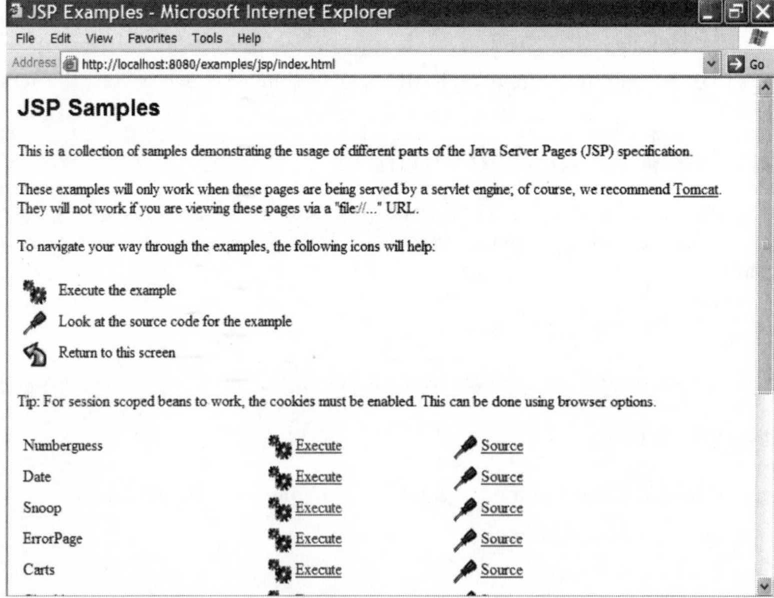

Figure 1.6 The JSP Examples page.

Now choose the JSP example Snoop and click the Execute link. If everything was installed properly, you should see a page similar to the one shown in Figure 1.7.

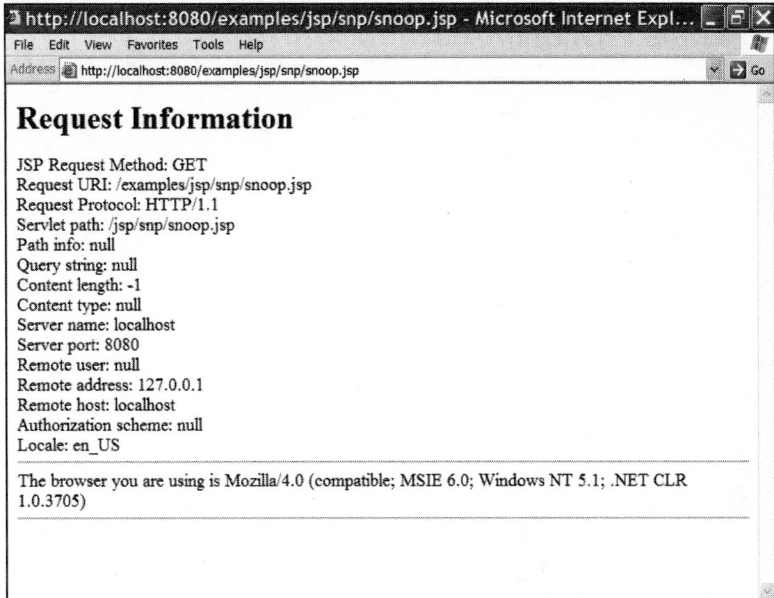

Figure 1.7 The results of executing the Snoop JSP example.

If you do not see the page shown in Figure 1.7, make sure that the location of your JAVA_HOME environment variable matches the location of your JDK installation.

What's Next?

Our next chapter is devoted to a brief tutorial of JSPs and servlets. The goal of this chapter is to provide you with the foundational technologies that you leverage throughout the remainder of this book. If you are already familiar with both of these technologies, you may want to skip to Chapter 3, "Getting Started with Struts."

2

An Overview of the Java Servlet and JavaServer Pages Architectures

In this chapter, we discuss the two technologies that the Struts Framework is based on: Java Servlets and JavaServer Pages (JSP). We begin by describing the servlet architecture, including the servlet lifecycle; the relationship between the ServletContext and a Web application; and how you can retrieve form data using servlets.

Once you have a solid understanding of servlets, we move on to discussing JSPs, which act as the View component in the Struts Framework. In our JSP discussions, we define JSPs and describe their components.

The goal of this chapter is to provide you with a brief introduction to the servlet and JSP technologies. At the end of this chapter, you should have a clear understanding of both servlets and JSPs and where they fit into Java Web application development.

The Java Servlet Architecture

A *Java servlet* is a platform-independent Web application component that is hosted in a JSP/servlet container. Servlets cooperate with Web clients by means of a request/response model managed by a JSP/servlet container. Figure 2.1 depicts the execution of a Java servlet.

Two packages make up the servlet architecture: javax.servlet and javax.servlet.http. The first of these, the javax.servlet package, contains the generic interfaces and classes that are implemented and extended by all servlets. The second, the javax.servlet.http package, contains all servlet classes that are HTTP protocol specific. An example of this would be a simple servlet that responds using HTML.

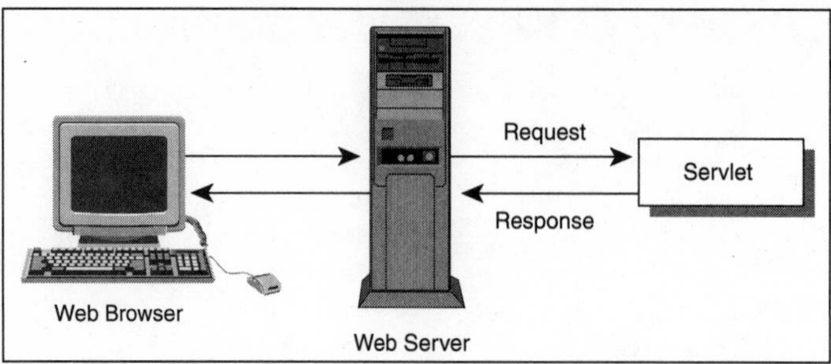

Figure 2.1 The execution of a Java servlet.

At the heart of this architecture is the interface javax.servlet.Servlet. It is the base class interface for all servlets. The Servlet interface defines five methods. The three most important of these methods are:

- the init() method, which initializes a servlet
- the service() method, which receives and responds to client requests
- the destroy() method, which performs cleanup

These are the servlet lifecycle methods. We describe these methods in a subsequent section. All servlets must implement the Servlet interface, either directly or through inheritance. Figure 2.2 is an object model that gives you a very high-level view of the servlet framework.

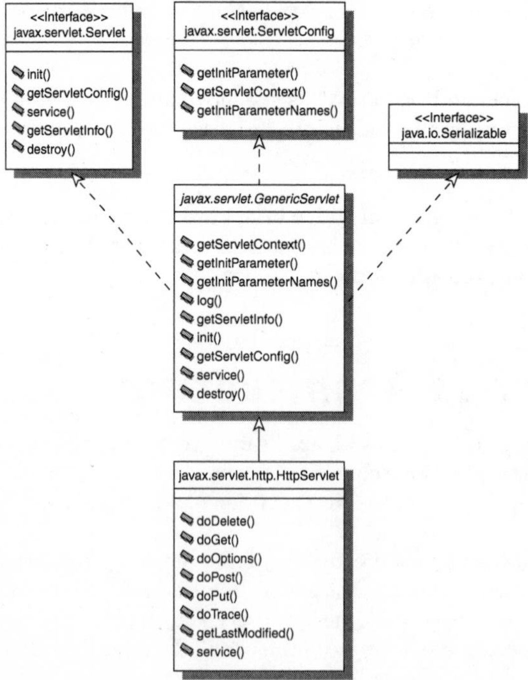

Figure 2.2 A simple object model showing the servlet framework.

The GenericServlet and HttpServlet Classes

The two main classes in the servlet architecture are the GenericServlet and HttpServlet classes. The HttpServlet class is extended from GenericServlet, which in turn implements the Servlet interface. When developing your own servlets, you will most likely extend one of these two classes.

When extending the GenericServlet class, you must implement the service() method. The GenericServlet.service() method has been defined as an abstract method in order to force you to follow this framework. The service() method prototype is defined as follows:

```
public abstract void service(ServletRequest request,
  ServletResponse response) throws ServletException, IOException;
```

The two parameters that are passed to the service() method are ServletRequest and ServletResponse objects. The ServletRequest object holds the information that is being sent to the servlet, and the ServletResponse object is where you place the data you want to send back to the client.

In contrast to the GenericServlet, when you extend HttpServlet you don't usually implement the service() method; the HttpServlet class has already implemented the service() method for you. The following prototype contains the HttpServlet.service() method signature:

```
protected void service(HttpServletRequest request,
  HttpServletResponse response)
  throws ServletException, IOException;
```

When the HttpServlet.service() method is invoked, it reads the method type stored in the request and determines which HTTP-specific methods to invoke based on this value. These are the methods that you will want to override. If the method type is GET, it will call doGet(). If the method type is POST, it will call doPost(). Five other method types are associated with the service() method, but the doGet() and doPost() methods are the methods used most often and are therefore the methods that we focus on.

The Lifecycle of a Servlet

The lifecycle of a Java servlet follows a very logical sequence. The interface that declares the life-cycle methods is the javax.servlet.Servlet interface. These methods are the init(), the service(), and the destroy() methods. This sequence can be described in a simple three-step process:

1. A servlet is loaded and initialized using the init() method. This method is called when a servlet is preloaded or upon the first request to this servlet.
2. The servlet then services zero or more requests. The servlet services each request using the service() method.
3. The servlet is then destroyed and garbage-collected when the Web application containing the servlet shuts down. The method that is called upon shutdown is the destroy() method.

The init() Method

The init() method is where the servlet begins its life. This method is called immediately after the servlet is instantiated and is called only once. The init() method should be used to create and initialize the resources that it will be using while handling requests. The init() method's signature is defined as follows:

```
public void init(ServletConfig config) throws ServletException;
```

The init() method takes a ServletConfig object as a parameter. This reference should be stored in a member variable so that it can be used later. A common way of doing this is to have the init() method call super.init() and pass it the ServletConfig object.

The init() method also declares that it can throw a ServletException. If for some reason the servlet cannot initialize the resources necessary to handle requests, it should throw a ServletException with an error message signifying the problem.

The service() Method

The service() method services all requests received from a client using a simple request/response pattern. The service() method's signature is shown here:

```
public void service(ServletRequest req, ServletResponse res)
  throws ServletException, IOException;
```

The service() method takes two parameters:

- A ServletRequest object, which contains information about the service request and encapsulates information provided by the client
- A ServletResponse object, which contains the information returned to the client

You will not usually implement this method directly, unless you extend the GenericServlet abstract class. The most common implementation of the service() method is in the HttpServlet class. The HttpServlet class implements the Servlet interface by extending GenericServlet. Its service() method supports standard HTTP/1.1 requests by determining the request type and calling the appropriate method.

The destroy() Method

This method signifies the end of a servlet's life. When a Web application is shut down, the servlet's destroy() method is called. This is where all resources that were created in the init() method should be cleaned up. The following code snippet shows the signature of the destroy() method:

```
public void destroy();
```

Building a Servlet

Now that we have a basic understanding of what a servlet is and how it works, let's build a very simple servlet of our own. Its purpose will be to service a request and respond by outputting the address of the client. After we have examined the source for this servlet, we will take a look at the steps involved in compiling and installing it. Listing 2.1 contains the source code for this example.

```
package chapter2;

import javax.servlet.*;
import javax.servlet.http.*;
import java.io.*;
import java.util.*;

public class SimpleServlet extends HttpServlet {

  public void init(ServletConfig config)
    throws ServletException {

    // Always pass the ServletConfig object to the super class
    super.init(config);
  }

  //Process the HTTP Get request
  public void doGet(HttpServletRequest request,
    HttpServletResponse response)
    throws ServletException, IOException {

    doPost(request, response);
  }

  //Process the HTTP Post request
  public void doPost(HttpServletRequest request,
    HttpServletResponse response)
    throws ServletException, IOException {

    response.setContentType("text/html");
    PrintWriter out = response.getWriter();

    out.println("<html>");
    out.println("<head><title>Simple Servlet</title></head>");
    out.println("<body>");

    // Outputs the address of the calling client
    out.println("Your address is " + request.getRemoteAddr()
      + "\n");

    out.println("</body></html>");
    out.close();
  }
}
```

Listing 2.1 SimpleServlet.java.

Now that you have had a chance to look over the source of the SimpleServlet, let's take a closer look at each of its integral parts. We examine where the servlet fits into the Java Servlet Development Kit (JSDK) framework, the methods that the servlet implements, and the objects being used by the servlet. The following three methods are overridden in the SimpleServlet:

- init()
- doGet()
- doPost()

Let's take a look at each of these methods in more detail.

The init() Method

The SimpleServlet first defines a straightforward implementation of the init() method. It takes the ServletConfig object that it is passed and then passes it to its parent's init() method, which stores the object for later use. The code that performs this action is as follows:

```
super.init(config);
```

> **The SimpleServlet's parent that actually holds on to the ServletConfig object is the GenericServlet.**

You should also notice that this implementation of the init() method does not create any resources. This is why the SimpleServlet does not implement a destroy() method.

The doGet() and doPost() Methods

The SimpleServlet's doGet() and doPost() methods are where all of the business logic is truly performed, and in this case, the doGet() method simply calls the doPost() method. The only time that the doGet() method is executed is when a GET request is sent to the container. If a POST request is received, then the doPost() method services the request.

Both the doGet() and the doPost() methods receive HttpServletRequest and HttpServletResponse objects as parameters. The HttpServletRequest contains information sent from the client, and the HttpServletResponse contains the information that will be sent back to the client.

The first executed line of the doPost() method sets the content type of the response that will be sent back to the client. This is done using the following code snippet:

```
response.setContentType("text/html");
```

This method sets the content type for the response. You can set this response property only once, and it must be set prior to writing to a Writer or an OutputStream. In our example, we are setting the response type to text/html.

The next thing we do is get a PrintWriter. This is accomplished by calling the ServletResponse's getWriter() method. The PrintWriter will let us write to the stream that will be sent in the client response. Everything written to the PrintWriter will be displayed in the client browser. This step is completed in the following line of code:

```
PrintWriter out = response.getWriter();
```

Once we have a reference to an object that will allow us to write text back to the client, we use this object to write a message to the client. This message will include the HTML that will format this response for presentation in the client's browser. The next few lines of code show how this is done:

```
out.println("<html>");
out.println("<head><title>Simple Servlet</title></head>");
out.println("<body>");

// Outputs the address of the calling client
out.println("Your address is " + request.getRemoteAddr()
  + "\n");
```

The SimpleServlet uses a very clear-cut method of sending HTML to a client. It simply passes to the PrintWriter's println() method the HTML text we want included in the response and closes the stream. The only question you may have involves these few lines:

```
// Outputs the address of the calling client
out.println("Your address is " + request.getRemoteAddr()
  + "\n");
```

This section of code takes advantage of information sent by the client. It calls the HttpServletRequest's getRemoteAddr() method, which returns the IP address of the calling client. The HttpServletRequest object holds a great deal of HTTP protocol-specific information about the client. If you would like to learn more about the HttpServletRequest or HttpServletResponse objects, you can find additional information at the Sun Web site:

```
http://java.sun.com/products/servlet/
```

Building and Deploying a Servlet

To see the SimpleServlet in action, you need to first create a Web application that will host the servlet, and then you need to compile and deploy this servlet to the Web application. These steps are described below:

1. Create a Web application named ch02app, using the directory structure described in Chapter 1.
2. Add the servlet.jar file to your classpath. This file should be in the <CATALINA_HOME>/common/lib/ directory.
3. Compile the source for the SimpleServlet.
4. Copy the resulting class file to the <CATALINA_HOME>/webapps/ch02app/WEB-INF/classes/chapter2 directory.
5. Add the following Servlet definition to the web.xml file. This definition causes the SimpleServlet to be invoked when the requested URL contains the pattern simple.

```
<servlet>
  <servlet-name>SimpleServlet</servlet-name>
  <servlet-class>chapter2.SimpleServlet</servlet-class>
</servlet>
```

```
<servlet-mapping>
  <servlet-name>SimpleServlet</servlet-name>
  <url-pattern>simple</url-pattern>
</servlet-mapping>
```

Once you have completed these steps, you can execute the SimpleServlet and see the results. To do this, start Tomcat and open your browser to the following URL:

```
http://localhost:8080/ch02app/simple
```

You should see an image similar to Figure 2.3.

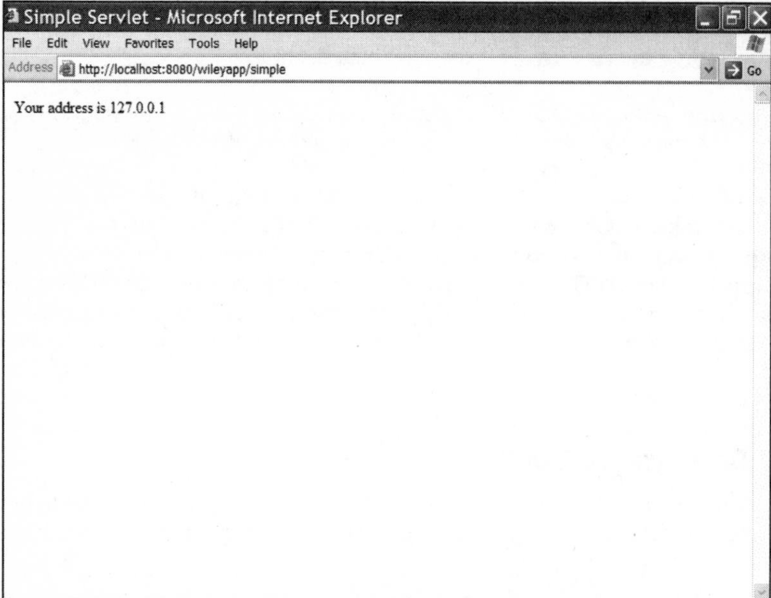

Figure 2.3 The output of the SimpleServlet.

The ServletContext

A *ServletContext* is an object that is defined in the javax.servlet package. It defines a set of methods that are used by server-side components of a Web application to communicate with the servlet container.

The ServletContext is most frequently used as a storage area for objects that need to be available to all of the server-side components in a Web application. You can think of the ServletContext as a shared memory segment for Web applications. When an object is placed in the ServletContext, it exists for the life of a Web application, unless it is explicitly removed or replaced. Four methods defined by the ServletContext are leveraged to provide this shared memory functionality. Table 2.1 describes each of these methods.

Table 2.1 The Shared Memory Methods of the ServletContext

Method	Description
setAttribute()	Binds an object to a given name and stores the object in the current ServletContext. If the name specified is already in use, this method removes the old object binding and binds the name to the new object.
getAttribute()	Returns the object referenced by the given name, or returns null if there is no attribute bind to the given key.
removeAttribute()	Removes the attribute with the given name from the ServletContext.
getAttributeNames()	Returns an enumeration of strings containing the object names stored in the current ServletContext.

The Relationship between a Web Application and the ServletContext

The ServletContext acts as the container for a given Web application. For every Web application, there can be only one instance of a ServletContext. This relationship is required by the Java Servlet Specification and is enforced by all servlet containers.

To see how this relationship affects Web components, let's use a servlet and a JSP. The first Web component we look at is a servlet that stores an object in the ServletContext, with the purpose of making this object available to all server-side components in this Web application. Listing 2.2 shows the source code for this servlet.

```
package chapter2;

import javax.servlet.*;
import javax.servlet.http.*;
import java.io.*;
import java.util.*;

public class ContextServlet extends HttpServlet {

  private static final String CONTENT_TYPE = "text/html";


  public void doGet(HttpServletRequest request,
    HttpServletResponse response)
    throws ServletException, IOException {

    doPost(request, response);
  }

  public void doPost(HttpServletRequest request,
    HttpServletResponse response)
    throws ServletException, IOException {

    // Get a reference to the ServletContext
    ServletContext context = getServletContext();
```

Code continued on following page

```
        // Get the userName attribute from the ServletContext
        String userName = (String)context.getAttribute("USERNAME");

        // If there was no attribute USERNAME, then create
        // one and add it to the ServletContext
        if ( userName == null ) {

          userName = new String("Bob Roberts");
          context.setAttribute("USERNAME", userName);
        }

        response.setContentType(CONTENT_TYPE);
        PrintWriter out = response.getWriter();
        out.println("<html>");
        out.println("<head><title>Context Servlet</title></head>");
        out.println("<body>");

        // Output the current value of the attribute USERNAME
        out.println("<p>The current User is : " + userName +
          ".</p>");
        out.println("</body></html>");
      }

      public void destroy() {
      }
    }
```

Listing 2.2 ContextServlet.java.

As you look over the ContextServlet, you notice that it performs the following steps:

1. It first gets a reference to the ServletContext, using the getServletContext() method:

   ```
   ServletContext context = getServletContext();
   ```

2. Once it has a reference to the ServletContext, it gets a reference to the object bound to the name USERNAME from the ServletContext, using the getAttribute() method:

   ```
   String userName =
     (String)context.getAttribute("USERNAME");
   ```

3. It then checks to see if the reference returned was valid. If getAttribute() returned null, then there was no object bound to the name USERNAME. If the attribute is not found, it is created and added to the ServletContext, bound to the name USERNAME, using the setAttribute() method:

   ```
   // If there was no attribute USERNAME, then create
   // one and add it to the ServletContext
   if ( userName == null ) {

     userName = new String("Bob Roberts");
     context.setAttribute("USERNAME", userName);
   }
   ```

4. The value of this reference is then printed to the output stream, using an instance of the PrintWriter.println() method:

```
// Output the current value of the attribute USERNAME
out.println("<p>The current User is : " +
  userName + ".</p>");
```

After you have looked over this servlet, complete these steps:

1. Compile the source for the SimpleServlet.
2. Copy the resulting class file to the <*CATALINA_HOME*>/webapps/ch02app/WEB-INF/classes/chapter2 directory.
3. Add the following Servlet definition to the web.xml file:

```
<servlet>
  <servlet-name>ContextServlet</servlet-name>
  <servlet-class>chapter2.ContextServlet </servlet-class>
</servlet>

<servlet-mapping>
  <servlet-name>ContextServlet</servlet-name>
  <url-pattern>context</url-pattern>
</servlet-mapping>
```

The JSP that we will be using is much like the servlet above; however, there are two differences:

- The code to access the ServletContext is in a JSP scriptlet, which we discuss later in this chapter.
- If the JSP cannot find a reference to the USERNAME attribute, then it does not add a new one.

Otherwise, the code performs essentially the same actions, but it does them in a JSP. You can see the source for the JSP in Listing 2.3.

```
<HTML>
<HEAD>
<TITLE>
Context
</TITLE>
</HEAD>
<BODY>
<%
  // Try to get the USERNAME attribute from the ServletContext
  String userName = (String)application.getAttribute("USERNAME");

  // If there was no attribute USERNAME, then create
  // one and add it to the ServletContext
  if ( userName == null ) {

    // Don't try to add it just, say that you can't find it
    out.println("<b>Attribute USERNAME not found");
  }
  else {

    out.println("<b>The current User is : " + userName +
```

Code continued on following page

```
            "</b>");
    }
%>
</BODY>
</HTML>
```

Listing 2.3 Context.jsp.

> **In Context.jsp, we are using two JSP implicit objects: the application object, which references the ServletContext, and the out object, which references an output stream to the client. We discuss each of these later in this chapter.**

Now, copy Context.jsp to the <*CATALINA_HOME*>/webapps/ch02app/ directory, restart Tomcat, and open your browser first to the following URL:

```
http://localhost:8080/ch02app/Context.jsp
```

You should see a page similar to Figure 2.4.

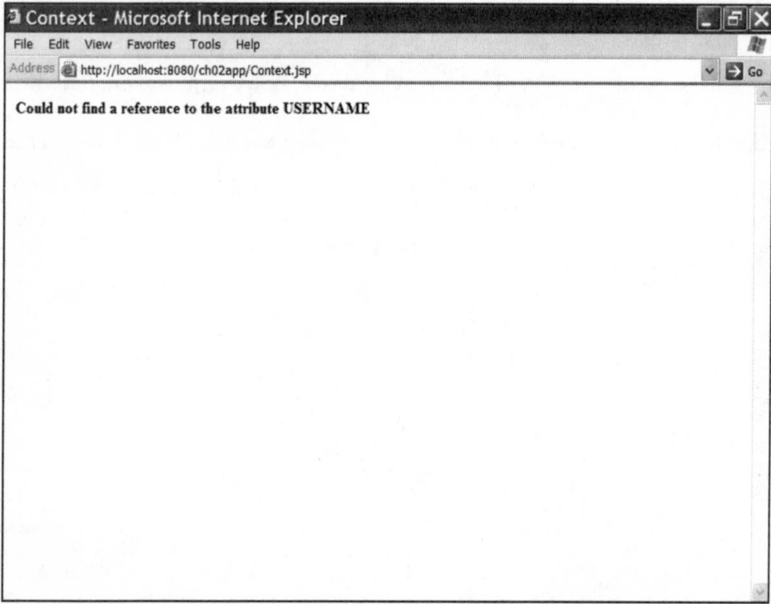

Figure 2.4 The output of the Context.jsp prior to the execution of the servlet ContextServlet.

As you can see, the Context.jsp cannot find a reference to the attribute USERNAME. It will not be able to find this reference until the reference is placed there by the ContextServlet. To do this, open your browser to the following URL:

```
http://localhost:8080/ch02app/context
```

You should see output similar to Figure 2.5.

Figure 2.5 The output of the ContextServlet.

After running this servlet, the ch02app Web application has an object bound to the name USERNAME stored in its ServletContext. To see how this affects another Web component in the ch02app Web application, open the previous URL that references the Context.jsp and look at the change in output. The JSP can now find the USERNAME, and it prints this value to the response.

> **To remove an object from the ServletContext, you can restart the JSP/servlet container or use the ServletContext.removeAttribute() method.**

Using Servlets to Retrieve HTTP Data

In this (our final) section on servlets, we are going to examine how servlets can be used to retrieve information from the client. Three methods can be used to retrieve request parameters: the ServletRequest's getParameter(), getParameterValues(), and getParameterNames() methods. Each method signature is listed here:

```
public String ServletRequest.getParameter(String name);
public String[] ServletRequest.getParameterValues(String name);
public Enumeration ServletRequest.getParameterNames ();
```

The first method in this list, getParameter(), returns a string containing the single value of the named parameter, or returns null if the parameter is not in the request. You should use this method only if you are sure the request contains only one value for the parameter. If the parameter has multiple values, you should use the getParameterValues() method.

The next method, getParameterValues(), returns the values of the specified parameter as an array of java.lang.Strings, or returns null if the named parameter is not in the request.

The last method, getParameterNames(), returns the parameter names contained in the request as an enumeration of strings, or an empty enumeration if there are no parameters. This method is used as a supporting method to both getParameter() and getParameterValues(). The enumerated list of parameter names returned from this method can be iterated over by calling getParameter() or getParameterValues() with each name in the list.

To see how you can use these methods to retrieve form data, let's look at a servlet that services POST requests: it retrieves the parameters sent to it and returns the parameters and their values back to the client. The servlet is shown in Listing 2.4.

```
package chapter2;

import javax.servlet.*;
import javax.servlet.http.*;
import java.io.*;
import java.util.*;

public class ParameterServlet extends HttpServlet {

  // Process the HTTP GET request
  public void doGet(HttpServletRequest request,
    HttpServletResponse response)
    throws ServletException, IOException {

    doPost(request, response);
  }

  // Process the HTTP POST request
  public void doPost(HttpServletRequest request,
    HttpServletResponse response)
    throws ServletException, IOException {

    response.setContentType("text/html");
    PrintWriter out = response.getWriter();

    out.println("<html>");
    out.println("<head>");
    out.println("<title>Parameter Servlet</title>");
    out.println("</head>");
    out.println("<body>");

    // Get an enumeration of the parameter names
    Enumeration parameters = request.getParameterNames();

    String param = null;

    // Iterate over the paramter names,
    // getting the parameters values
    while ( parameters.hasMoreElements() ) {
```

Code continued on following page

```
      param = (String)parameters.nextElement();
      out.println(param + " : " +
        request.getParameter(param) +
        "<BR>");
    }

    out.println("</body></html>");
    out.close();
  }
}
```

Listing 2.4 ParameterServlet.java.

The first notable action performed by this servlet is to get all of the parameter names passed in on the request. It does this using the getParameterNames() method. Once it has this list, it performs a while loop, retrieving and printing all of the parameter values associated with the matching parameter names, using the getParameter() method. You can invoke the ParameterServlet by encoding a URL string, with parameters and values, or simply by using the HTML form found in Listing 2.5.

```
<HTML>
<HEAD>
<TITLE>
Parameter Servlet Form
</TITLE>
</HEAD>
<BODY>

<form
 action="parameter"
 method=POST>
  <table width="400" border="0" cellspacing="0">
    <tr>
      <td>Name: </td>
      <td>
        <input type="text"
               name="name"
               size="20"
               maxlength="20">
      </td>
      <td>SSN:</td>
      <td>
        <input type="text" name="ssn" size="11" maxlength="11">
      </td>
    </tr>
    <tr>
      <td>Age:</td>
      <td>
        <input type="text" name="age" size="3" maxlength="3">
      </td>
      <td>email:</td>
      <td>
        <input type="text"
```

Code continued on following page

```
                name="email"
                size="30"
                maxlength="30">
        </td>
      </tr>
      <tr>
        <td> </td>
        <td>  </td>
        <td>  </td>
        <td>
          <input type="submit" name="Submit" value="Submit">
          <input type="reset" name="Reset" value="Reset">
        </td>
      </tr>
    </table>
  </FORM>

  </BODY>
  </HTML>
```

Listing 2.5 Form.html.

This HTML document contains a simple HTML form that can be used to pass data to the ParameterServlet. To see this example in action, complete the following steps:

1. Compile the source for the ParameterServlet.
2. Copy the resulting class file to the <*CATALINA_HOME*>/webapps/ch02app/WEB-INF/classes/chapter2 directory.
3. Add the following Servlet definition to the web.xml file:

```
<servlet>
  <servlet-name>ParameterServlet</servlet-name>
  <servlet-class>chapter2.ParameterServlet </servlet-class>
</servlet>

<servlet-mapping>
  <servlet-name>ParameterServlet</servlet-name>
  <url-pattern>parameter</url-pattern>
</servlet-mapping>
```

4. Copy the Form.html file to the <*CATALINA_HOME*>/webapps/ch02app/ directory.

   Now open your browser to the following URL:

```
http://localhost:8080/ch02app/Form.html
```

   Go ahead and populate the form (similar to what we've done in Figure 2.6), and then click the Submit button. The response you receive will, of course, depend on your entries, but it should resemble Figure 2.7.

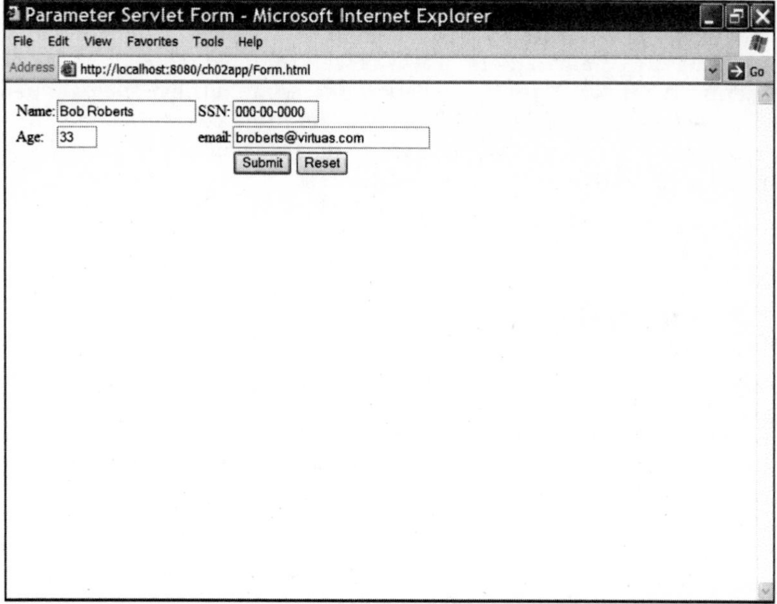

Figure 2.6 Output from Form.html.

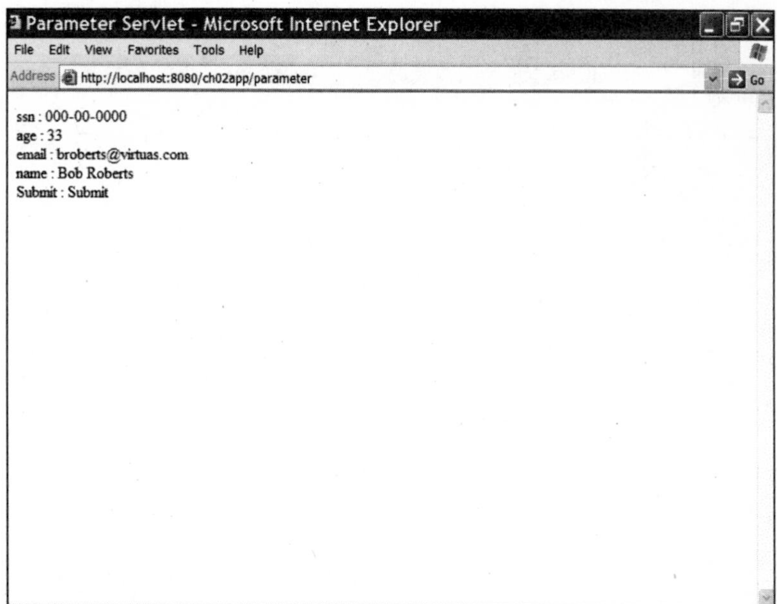

Figure 2.7 The response of the ParameterServlet.

This example shows just how easy it is to retrieve request parameters in a servlet. While the ParameterServlet works well for most requests, it does contain an error. When we chose to use getParameter() to retrieve the parameter values, we were counting on receiving only one value per request parameter. If we could not rely on this fact, then we should have used the getParameterValues() method discussed earlier.

What Are JavaServer Pages?

JavaServer Pages, or JSPs, are a simple but powerful technology used most often to generate dynamic HTML on the server side. JSPs are a direct extension of Java servlets designed to let the developer embed Java logic directly into a requested document. A JSP document must end with the extension .jsp. The following code snippet contains a simple example of a JSP file; its output is shown in Figure 2.8.

```
<HTML>
<BODY>

<% out.println("HELLO JSP READER"); %>

</BODY>
</HTML>
```

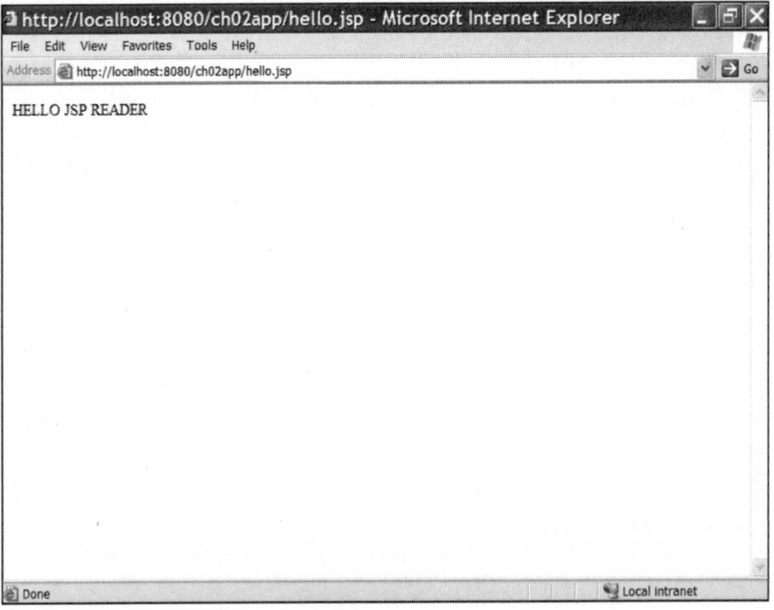

Figure 2.8 The output of the JSP example.

This document looks like any other HTML document, with some added tags containing Java code. The source code is stored in a file called hello.jsp and should be copied to the document directory of the Web application to which this JSP will be deployed. When a request is made for this document, the server recognizes the .jsp extension and realizes that special handling is required. The JSP is then passed to the JSP engine (which is just another servlet mapped to the extension .jsp) for processing.

The first time the file is requested, it is translated into a servlet and then compiled into an object that is loaded into resident memory. The generated servlet then services the request, and the output is sent back to the requesting client. On all subsequent requests, the server checks to see whether the original JSP source file has changed. If it has not changed, the server invokes the previously compiled servlet object. If the source has changed, the JSP engine re-parses the JSP source. Figure 2.9 shows these steps.

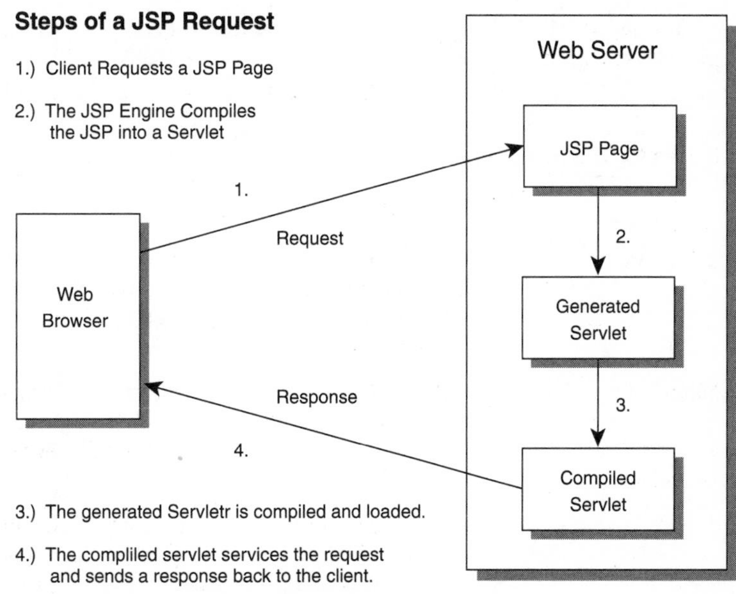

Figure 2.9 The steps of a JSP request.

> **It's essential to remember that JSPs are just servlets created from a combination of HTML and Java source. Therefore, they have the resources and functionality of a servlet.**

The Components of a JavaServer Page

This section discusses the components of a JSP, including directives, scripting, implicit objects, and standard actions.

JSP Directives

JSP directives are JSP elements that provide global information about a JSP page. An example is a directive that includes a list of Java classes to be imported into a JSP. The syntax of a JSP directive is:

```
<%@ directive {attribute="value"} %>
```

Three possible directives are currently defined by the JSP specification v1.2: page, include, and taglib. These directives are defined in the following sections.

The page Directive

The page directive defines information that will globally affect the JSP containing the directive. The syntax of a JSP page directive is:

```
<%@ page {attribute="value"} %>
```

Table 2.2 defines the attributes for the page directive.

> **Because all mandatory attributes are defaulted, you are not required to specify any page directives.**

Table 2.2 Attributes for the page Directive

Attribute	Definition
language="scriptingLanguage"	Tells the server which language will be used to compile the JSP file. Java is currently the only available JSP language, but we hope there will be other language support in the not-too-distant future.
extends="className"	Defines the parent class from which the JSP will extend. While you can extend JSP from other servlets, doing so limits the optimizations performed by the JSP/servlet engine and is therefore not recommended.
import="importList"	Defines the list of Java packages that will be imported into this JSP. It will be a comma-separated list of package names and fully qualified Java classes.
session="true | false"	Determines whether the session data will be available to this page. The default is true. If your JSP is not planning on using the session, then this attribute should be set to false for better performance.
buffer="none | size in kb"	Determines whether the output stream is buffered. The default value is 8KB.
autoFlush="true | false"	Determines whether the output buffer will be flushed automatically, or whether it will throw an exception when the buffer is full. The default is true.
isThreadSafe="true | false"	Tells the JSP engine that this page can service multiple requests at one time. By default, this value is true. If this attribute is set to false, the SingleThreadModel is used.

Table continued on following page

Attribute	Definition
info="text"	Represents information about the JSP page that can be accessed by invoking the page's Servlet.getServletInfo() method.
errorPage="error_url"	Represents the relative URL to a JSP that will handle JSP exceptions.
isErrorPage="true | false"	States whether the JSP is an errorPage. The default is false.
contentType="ctinfo"	Represents the MIME type and character set of the response sent to the client.

The following code snippet includes a page directive that imports the java.util package:

```
<%@ page import="java.util.*" %>
```

The include Directive

The include directive is used to insert text and/or code at JSP translation time. The syntax of the include directive is shown in the following code snippet:

```
<%@ include file="relativeURLspec" %>
```

The file attribute can reference a normal text HTML file or a JSP file, which is evaluated at translation time. This resource referenced by the file attribute must be local to the Web application that contains the include directive. Here's a sample include directive:

```
<%@ include file="header.jsp" %>
```

Because the include directive is evaluated at translation time, this included text is evaluated only once. Thus, if the included resource changes, these changes are not reflected until the JSP/servlet container is restarted or the modification date of the JSP that includes that file is changed.

The taglib Directive

The taglib directive states that the including page uses a custom tag library, uniquely identified by a URI and associated with a prefix that distinguishes each set of custom tags to be used in the page.

If you are not familiar with JSP custom tags, you can learn what they are and how they are used in my book *Mastering JSP Custom Tags and Tag Libraries*, published by Wiley.

The syntax of the taglib directive is as follows:

```
<%@ taglib uri="tagLibraryURI" prefix="tagPrefix" %>
```

The taglib attributes are described in Table 2.3.

Table 2.3 Attributes for the taglib Directive

Attribute	Definition
uri	A URI that uniquely names a custom tag library
prefix	The prefix string used to distinguish a custom tag instance

The following code snippet includes an example of how the taglib directive is used:

```
<%@ taglib
  uri="http://jakarta.apache.org/taglibs/random-1.0"
  prefix="rand" %>
```

JSP Scripting

Scripting is a JSP mechanism for directly embedding Java code fragments into an HTML page. Three scripting language components are involved in JSP scripting. Each component has its appropriate location in the generated servlet. This section examines these components.

Declarations

JSP declarations are used to define Java variables and methods in a JSP. A JSP declaration must be a complete declarative statement.

JSP declarations are initialized when the JSP page is first loaded. After the declarations have been initialized, they are available to other declarations, expressions, and scriptlets within the same JSP. The syntax for a JSP declaration is as follows:

```
<%! declaration %>
```

A sample variable declaration using this syntax is shown here:

```
<%! String name = new String("BOB"); %>
```

Here's a sample method declaration using the same syntax:

```
<%! public String getName() { return name; } %>
```

To get a better understanding of declarations, let's take the previous string declaration and embed it into a JSP document. The sample document would look similar to the following code snippet:

```
<HTML>
<BODY>

<%! String name = new String("BOB"); %>
```

```
</BODY>
</HTML>
```

When this document is initially loaded, the JSP code is converted to servlet code and the name declaration is placed in the declaration section of the generated servlet. It is now available to all other JSP components in the JSP.

> **It should be noted that all JSP declarations are defined at the class level, in the servlet generated from the JSP, and are therefore evaluated prior to all JSP expressions and scriptlet code.**

Expressions

JSP expressions are JSP components whose text, upon evaluation by the container, is replaced with the resulting value of the container evaluation. JSP expressions are evaluated at request time, and the result is inserted at the expression's referenced position in the JSP file. If the resulting expression cannot be converted to a string, then a translation-time error occurs. If the conversion to a string cannot be detected during translation, a ClassCastException is thrown at request time.

The syntax of a JSP expression is as follows:

```
<%= expression %>
```

A code snippet containing a JSP expression is shown here:

```
Hello <B><%= getName() %></B>
```

Here is a sample JSP document containing a JSP expression:

```
<HTML>
<BODY>

<%! public String getName() { return "Bob"; } %>

Hello <B><%= getName() %></B>

</BODY>
</HTML>
```

Scriptlets

Scriptlets are the JSP components that bring all the JSP elements together. They can contain almost any coding statements that are valid for the language referenced in the language directive. They are executed at request time, and they can make use of all the JSP components. The syntax for a scriptlet is as follows:

```
<% scriptlet source %>
```

When JSP scriptlet code is converted into servlet code, it is placed into the generated servlet's service() method. The following code snippet contains a simple JSP that uses a scripting element to print the text "Hello Bob" to the requesting client:

```
<HTML>
<BODY>

<% out.println("Hello Bob"); %>

</BODY>
</HTML>
```

You should note that while JSP scriplet code can be very powerful, composing all your JSP logic using scriptlet code can make your application difficult to manage. This problem led to the creation of custom tag libraries.

JSP Error Handling

Like all development methods, JSPs need a robust mechanism for handling errors. The JSP architecture provides an error-handling solution through the use of JSPs that are written exclusively to handle JSP errors.

The errors that occur most frequently are runtime errors that can arise either in the body of the JSP page or in some other object that is called from the body of the JSP page. Request-time errors that result in an exception being thrown can be caught and handled in the body of the calling JSP, which signals the end of the error. Exceptions that are not handled in the calling JSP result in the forwarding of the client request, including the uncaught exception, to an error page specified by the offending JSP.

Creating a JSP Error Page

Creating a JSP error page is a simple process: you create a basic JSP and then tell the JSP engine that the page is an error page. You do so by setting the JSP's page directive attribute, isErrorPage, to true. Listing 2.6 contains a sample error page.

```
<html>

<%@ page isErrorPage="true" %>

Error: <%= exception.getMessage() %> has been reported.

</body>
</html>
```

Listing 2.6 Creating a JSP error page: errorpage.jsp.

The first JSP-related line in this page tells the JSP compiler that this JSP is an error page. This code snippet is:

```
<%@ page isErrorPage="true" %>
```

The second JSP-related section uses the implicit exception object that is part of all JSP error pages to output the error message contained in the unhandled exception that was thrown in the offending JSP.

Using a JSP Error Page

To see how an error page works, let's create a simple JSP that throws an uncaught exception. The JSP shown in Listing 2.7 uses the error page created in the previous section.

```
<%@ page errorPage="errorpage.jsp" %>

<%

  if ( true ) {

    // Just throw an exception
    throw new Exception("An uncaught Exception");
  }

%>
```

Listing 2.7 Using a JSP error page: testerror.jsp.

Notice in this listing that the first line of code sets errorPage equal to errorpage.jsp, which is the name of the error page. To make a JSP aware of an error page, you simply need to add the errorPage attribute to the page directive and set its value equal to the location of your JSP error page. The rest of the example simply throws an exception that will not be caught. To see this example in action, copy both JSPs to the <*CATALINA_HOME*>/webapps/ch02app/ directory and open the testerror.jsp page in your browser. You will see a page similar to Figure 2.10.

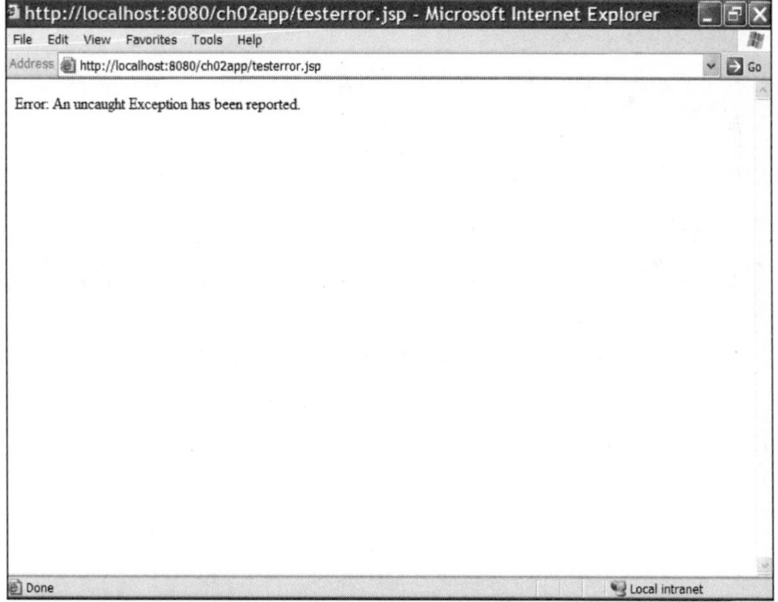

Figure 2.10 The output of the testerror.jsp example.

Implicit Objects

As a JSP author, you have implicit access to certain objects that are available for use in all JSP documents. These objects are parsed by the JSP engine and inserted into the generated servlet as if you defined them yourself.

out

The implicit out object represents a JspWriter (derived from a java.io.Writer) that provides a stream back to the requesting client. The most common method of this object is out.println(), which prints text that will be displayed in the client's browser. Listing 2.8 provides an example using the implicit out object.

```
<%@ page errorPage="errorpage.jsp" %>

<html>
  <head>
    <title>Use Out</title>
  </head>
  <body>
    <%
      // Print a simple message using the implicit out object.
      out.println("<center><b>Hello WROX" +
        " Reader!</b></center>");
    %>
  </body>
</html>
```

Listing 2.8 Using the out object: out.jsp.

To execute this example, copy this file to the *<CATALINA_HOME>*/webapps/ch02app/ directory and then open your browser to the following URL:

```
http://localhost:8080/ch02app/out.jsp
```

You should see a page similar to Figure 2.11.

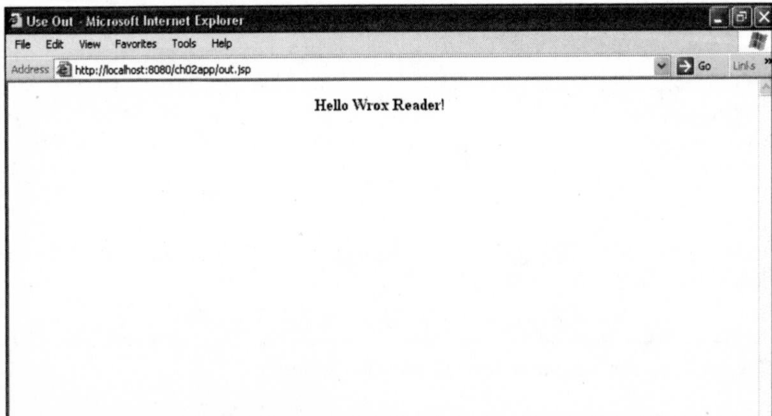

Figure 2.11 The output of out.jsp.

request

The implicit request object represents the javax.servlet.http.HttpServletRequest interface, discussed later in this chapter. The request object is associated with every HTTP request.

One of the more common uses for the request object is to access request parameters. You can do this by calling the request object's getParameter() method with the parameter name you are seeking. It returns a string with the value matching the named parameter. An example using the implicit request object appears in Listing 2.9.

```
<%@ page errorPage="errorpage.jsp" %>

<html>
  <head>
    <title>UseRequest</title>
  </head>
  <body>
    <%
      out.println("<b>Welcome: " +
        request.getParameter("user") + "</b>");
    %>
  </body>
</html>
```

Listing 2.9 Using the request object: request.jsp.

This JSP calls the request.getParameter() method, passing it the parameter *user*. This method looks for the key user in the parameter list and returns the value, if it is found. Enter the following URL in your browser to see the results from this page:

```
http://localhost:8080/ch02app/request.jsp?user=Robert
```

After loading this URL, you should see a page similar to Figure 2.12.

response

The implicit response object represents the javax.servlet.http.HttpServletResponse object. The response object is used to pass data back to the requesting client. This implicit object provides all the functionality of the HttpServletRequest, just as if you were executing in a servlet. One of the more common uses for the response object is writing HTML output back to the client browser; however, the JSP API already provides access to a stream back to the client using the implicit out object, as described earlier.

pageContext

The pageContext object provides access to the namespaces associated with a JSP page. It also provides accessors to several other JSP implicit objects. A common use for the pageContext is setting and retrieving objects using the setAttribute() and getAttribute() methods.

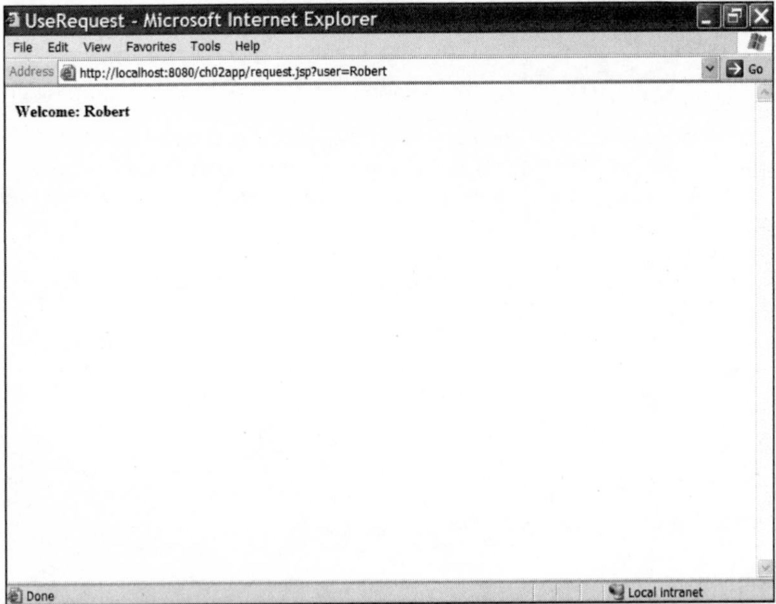

Figure 2.12 The output of request.jsp.

session

The implicit session object represents the javax.servlet.http.HttpSession object. It's used to store objects between client requests, thus providing an almost stateful HTTP interactivity.

An example of using the session object is shown in Listing 2.10.

```
<%@ page errorPage="errorpage.jsp" %>

<html>
  <head>
    <title>Session Example</title>
  </head>
  <body>
    <%
      // get a reference to the current count from the session
      Integer count = (Integer)session.getAttribute("COUNT");

      if ( count == null ) {

        // If the count was not found create one
        count = new Integer(1);
        // and add it to the HttpSession
        session.setAttribute("COUNT", count);
      }
      else {

        // Otherwise increment the value
```

Code continued on following page

```
            count = new Integer(count.intValue() + 1);
            session.setAttribute("COUNT", count);
          }
          out.println("<b>You have accessed this page: "
            + count + " times.</b>");
      %>
    </body>
</html>
```

Listing 2.10 Using the session object: session.jsp.

To use this example, copy the JSP to the <*CATALINA_HOME*>/ch02app/ directory and open your browser to the following URL:

```
http://localhost:8080/ch02app/session.jsp
```

Click the Refresh button a few times to see the count increment.

If everything went okay, you should see a page similar to Figure 2.13.

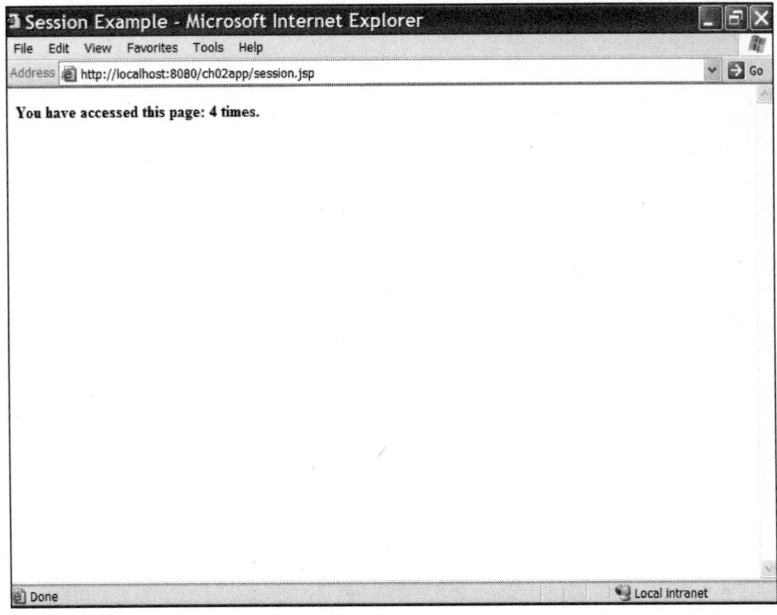

Figure 2.13 The output of session.jsp.

application

The application object represents the javax.servlet.ServletContext, discussed earlier in this chapter. The application object is most often used to access objects stored in the ServletContext to be shared between Web components in a global scope. It is a great place to share objects between JSPs and servlets. An example using the application object can be found earlier in this chapter, in the section "The ServletContext."

config

The implicit config object holds a reference to the ServletConfig, which contains configuration information about the JSP/servlet engine containing the Web application where this JSP resides.

page

The page object contains a reference to the current instance of the JSP being accessed. The page object is used just like this object, to reference the current instance of the generated servlet representing this JSP.

exception

The implicit exception object provides access to an uncaught exception thrown by a JSP. It is available only in JSPs that have a page with the attribute isErrorPage set to true.

Standard Actions

JSP standard actions are predefined custom tags that can be used to encapsulate common actions easily. There are two types of JSP standard actions: the first type is related to JavaBean functionality, and the second type consists of all other standard actions. We define and use each group in the following sections.

Three predefined standard actions relate to using JavaBeans in a JSP: <useBean>, <setProperty>, and <getProperty>. After we define these tags, we create a simple example that uses them.

<jsp:useBean>

The <jsp:useBean> JavaBean standard action creates or looks up an instance of a JavaBean with a given ID and scope. Table 2.4 contains the attributes of the <jsp:useBean> action, and Table 2.5 defines the scope values for that action. The <jsp:useBean> action is very flexible. When a <useBean> action is encountered, the action tries to find an existing object using the same ID and scope. If it cannot find an existing instance, it attempts to create the object and store it in the named scope associated with the given ID. The syntax of the <jsp:useBean> action is as follows:

```
<jsp:useBean id="name"
        scope="page|request|session|application"
        typeSpec>
        body
</jsp:useBean>

typeSpec ::=class="className" |
        class="className" type="typeName" |
        type="typeName" class="className" |
        beanName="beanName" type="typeName" |
        type="typeName" beanName="beanName" |
        type="typeName"
```

Table 2.4 Attributes for the <jsp:useBean> Standard Action

Attribute	Definition
id	The key associated with the instance of the object in the specified scope. This key is case sensitive. The id attribute is the same key as used in the page.getAttribute() method.
scope	The life of the referenced object. The scope options are page, request, session, and application. They are defined in Table 2.5.
class	The fully qualified class name that defines the implementation of the object. The class name is case sensitive.
beanName	The name of the JavaBean.
type	The type of scripting variable defined. If this attribute is unspecified, then the value is the same as the value of the class attribute.

The scope attribute listed in Table 2.4 can have four possible values, which are described in Table 2.5.

Table 2.5 Scope Values for the <jsp:useBean> Standard Action

Value	Definition
page	Beans with page scope are accessible only within the page where they were created. References to an object with page scope will be released when the current JSP has completed its evaluation.
request	Beans with request scope are accessible only within pages servicing the same request in which the object was instantiated, including forwarded requests. All references to the object are released once the request is complete.
session	Beans with session scope are accessible only within pages processing requests that are in the same session as the one in which the bean was created. All references to beans with session scope are released once their associated session expires.
application	Beans with application scope are accessible within pages processing requests that are in the same Web application. All references to beans are released when the JSP/servlet container is shut down.

<jsp:setProperty>

The <jsp:setProperty> standard action sets the value of a bean's property. Its name attribute represents an object that must already be defined and in scope. The syntax for the <jsp:setProperty> action is as follows:

```
<jsp:setProperty name="beanName" propexpr />
```

In the preceding syntax, the name attribute represents the name of the bean whose property you are setting, and propexpr can be represented by any of the following expressions:

```
property="*" |
property="propertyName" |
property="propertyName" param="parameterName" |
property="propertyName" value="propertyValue"
```

Table 2.6 contains the attributes and their descriptions for the <jsp:setProperty> action.

Table 2.6 Attributes for the <jsp:setProperty> Standard Action

Attribute	Definition
name	The name of the bean instance defined by a <jsp:useBean> action or some other action.
property	The bean property for which you want to set a value. If you set propertyName to an asterisk (*), then the action will iterate over the current ServletRequest parameters, matching parameter names and value types to property names and setter method types and setting each matched property to the value of the matching parameter. If a parameter has an empty string for a value, the corresponding property is left unmodified.
param	The name of the request parameter whose value you want to set the named property to. A <jsp:setProperty> action cannot have both param and value attributes referenced in the same action.
value	The value assigned to the named bean's property.

<jsp:getProperty>

The last standard action that relates to integrating JavaBeans into JSPs is <jsp:getProperty>. It takes the value of the referenced bean's instance property, converts it to a java.lang.String, and places it on the output stream. The referenced bean instance must be defined and in scope before this action can be used. The syntax for the <jsp:getProperty> action is as follows:

```
<jsp:getProperty name="name" property="propertyName" />
```

Table 2.7 contains the attributes and their descriptions for the <jsp:getProperty> action.

Table 2.7 Attributes for the <jsp:getProperty> Standard Action

Attribute	Definition
name	The name of the bean instance from which the property is obtained, defined by a <jsp:useBean> action or some other action.
property	The bean property for which you want to get a value.

A JavaBean Standard Action Example

To learn how to use the JavaBean standard actions, let's create an example. This example uses a simple JavaBean that acts as a counter. The Counter bean has a single int property, count, that holds the current number of times the bean's property has been accessed. It also contains the appropriate methods for getting and setting this property. Listing 2.11 contains the source code for the Counter bean.

```
package chapter2;

public class Counter {

  int count = 0;

  public Counter() {

  }

  public int getCount() {

    count++;

    return count;
  }

  public void setCount(int count) {

    this.count = count;
  }
}
```

Listing 2.11 Example of a Counter bean: Counter.java.

Let's look at integrating this sample JavaBean into a JSP, using the JavaBean standard actions. Listing 2.12 contains the JSP that leverages the Counter bean.

```
<!-- Set the scripting language to java -->
<%@ page language="java" %>

<HTML>
<HEAD>
<TITLE>Bean Example</TITLE>
</HEAD>

<BODY>

<!-- Instantiate the Counter bean with an id of "counter" -->
<jsp:useBean id="counter" scope="session"
  class="chapter2.Counter" />

<%

  // write the current value of the property count
  out.println("Count from scriptlet code : "
    + counter.getCount() + "<BR>");

%>
```

Code continued on following page

```
<!-- Get the the bean's count property, -->
<!-- using the jsp:getProperty action. -->
Count from jsp:getProperty :
  <jsp:getProperty name="counter" property="count" /><BR>

</BODY>
</HTML>
```

Listing 2.12 A JSP that uses the Counter bean: counter.jsp.

Counter.jsp has four JSP components. The first component tells the JSP container that the scripting language is Java:

```
<%@ page language="java" %>
```

The next step uses the standard action <jsp:useBean> to create an instance of the class Counter with a scope of session and ID of counter. Now you can reference this bean using the name counter throughout the rest of the JSP. The code snippet that creates the bean is as follows:

```
<jsp:useBean id="counter" scope="session"
  class="chapter2.Counter" />
```

The final two actions demonstrate how to get the current value of a bean's property. The first of these two actions uses a scriptlet to access the bean's property, using an explicit method call. It simply accesses the bean by its ID, counter, and calls the getCount() method. The scriptlet snippet is listed here:

```
<%

  // write the current value of the property count
  out.println("Count from scriptlet code : "
    + counter.getCount() + "<BR>");

%>
```

The second example uses the <jsp:getProperty> standard action, which requires the ID of the bean and the property to be accessed. The action takes the attribute, calls the appropriate accessor, and embeds the results directly into the resulting HTML document, as follows:

```
<!-- Get the bean's count property, -->
<!-- using the jsp:getProperty action. -->
Count from jsp:getProperty :
  <jsp:getProperty name="counter" property="count" /><BR>
```

When you execute the Counter.jsp, notice that the second reference to the count property results in a value that is one greater than the first reference. This is the case because both methods of accessing the count property result in a call to the getCount() method, which increments the value of count.

To see this JSP in action, compile the Counter class, move it to the *<CATALINA_HOME>*/ch02app/WEB-INF/classes/chapter2/ directory, and copy the Counter.jsp file to the *<CATALINA_HOME>*/ch02app/ directory. Then, open your browser to the following URL:

```
http://localhost:8080/ch02app/counter.jsp
```

Once the JSP is loaded, you should see an image similar to Figure 2.14.

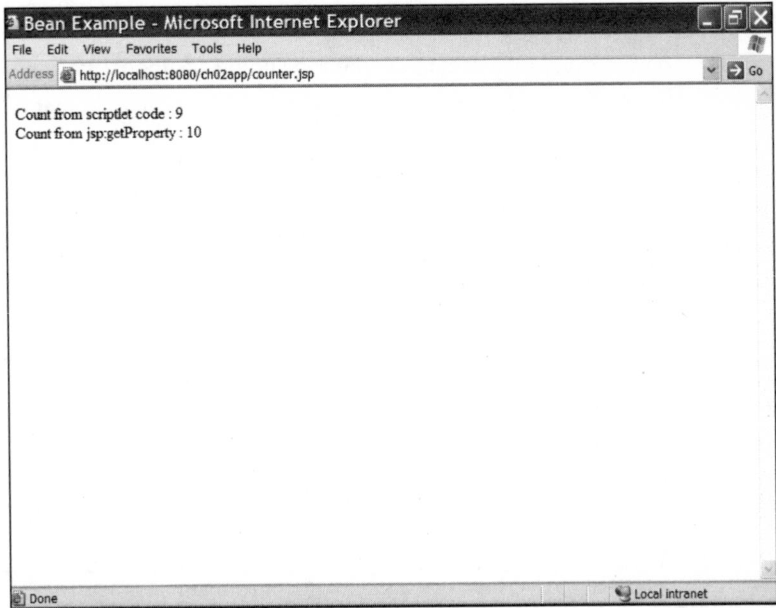

Figure 2.14 The results of counter.jsp.

The remaining standard actions are used for generic tasks, from basic parameter action to an object plug-in action. These actions are described in the following sections.

<jsp:param>

The <jsp:param> action provides parameters and values to the JSP standard actions <jsp:include>, <jsp:forward>, and <jsp:plugin>. The syntax of the <jsp:param> action is as follows:

```
<jsp:param name="name" value="value"/>
```

Table 2.8 contains the attributes and their descriptions for the <jsp:param> action.

Table 2.8 Attributes for the <jsp:param> Action	
Attribute	**Definition**
name	The name of the parameter being referenced
value	The value of the named parameter

<jsp:include>

The <jsp:include> standard action provides a method for including additional static and dynamic Web components in a JSP. The syntax for this action is as follows:

```
<jsp:include page="urlSpec" flush="true">
    <jsp:param ... />
</jsp:include>
```

Table 2.9 contains the attributes and their descriptions for the <jsp:include> action.

Table 2.9 Attributes for the <jsp:include> Action	
Attribute	**Definition**
page	The relative URL of the resource to be included
flush	A mandatory Boolean value stating whether the buffer should be flushed

It is important to note the difference between the include directive and the include standard action. The directive is evaluated only once, at translation time, whereas the standard action is evaluated with every request.

The syntax description shows a request-time inclusion of a URL that is passed an optional list of param subelements used to argument the request. You can see an example using the include standard action in Listing 2.13.

```
<html>
  <head>
    <title>Include Example</title>
  </head>
  <body>
    <table width="100%" cellspacing="0">
      <tr>
        <td align="left">
          <jsp:include page="header.jsp" flush="true">
            <jsp:param name="user"
              value='<%= request.getParameter("user") %>' />
          </jsp:include>
        </td>
```

```
      </tr>
    </table>
  </body>
</html>
```

Listing 2.13 Example of the include action: include.jsp.

This file contains a single include action that includes the results of evaluating the JSP header.jsp, shown in Listing 2.14.

```
<%
  out.println("<b>Welcome: </b>" +
    request.getParameter("user"));
%>
```

Listing 2.14 The JSP evaluated in include.jsp: header.jsp.

This JSP simply looks for a parameter named user and outputs a string containing a welcome message. To deploy this example, copy these two JSPs to the <*CATALINA_HOME*>/webapps/ch02app/ directory. Open your browser to the following URL:

```
http://localhost:8080/ch02app/include.jsp?user=Bob
```

The results should look similar to Figure 2.15.

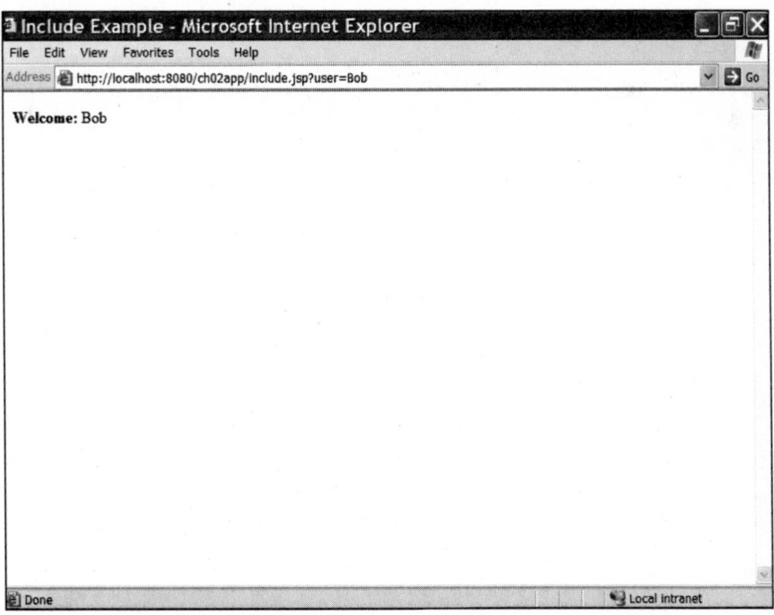

Figure 2.15 The results of include.jsp.

<jsp:forward>

The <jsp:forward> standard action enables the JSP engine to execute a runtime dispatch of the current request to another resource existing in the current Web application, including static resources, servlets, or JSPs. The appearance of <jsp:forward> effectively terminates the execution of the current JSP.

> **A <jsp:forward> action can contain <jsp:param> subattributes. These subattributes act as parameters that are forwarded to the targeted resource.**

The syntax of the <jsp:forward> action is as follows:

```
<jsp:forward page="relativeURL">
    <jsp:param .../>
</jsp:forward>
```

Table 2.10 contains the attribute and its description for the <jsp:forward> action.

Table 2.10 Attribute for the <jsp:forward> Action

Attribute	Definition
page	The relative URL of the target of the forward

The example in Listing 2.15 contains a JSP that uses the <jsp:forward> action. This example checks a request parameter and forwards the request to one of two JSPs based on the value of the parameter.

```
<html>
  <head>
    <title>JSP Forward Example</title>
  </head>
  <body>
    <%

      if ( (request.getParameter("role")).equals("manager") ) {

        %>
          <jsp:forward page="management.jsp" />
        <%
      }
      else {
        %>
          <jsp:forward page="welcome.jsp">
          <jsp:param name="user"
            value='<%=request.getParameter("user") %>' />
          </jsp:forward>
        <%
      }
    %>
  </body>
</html>
```

Listing 2.15 Example of the forward action: forward.jsp.

The forward.jsp simply checks the request for the parameter role and forwards the request, along with a set of request parameters, to the appropriate JSP based on this value. Listings 2.16 and 2.17 contain the source of the targeted resources.

```
<html>
<!-- Set the scripting language to java -->
<%@ page language="java" %>

<HTML>
<HEAD>
<TITLE>Welcome Home</TITLE>
</HEAD>

<BODY>
<table>
  <tr>
    <td>
      Welcome User: <%= request.getParameter("user") %>
    </td>
  </tr>
</table>
```

Listing 2.16 welcome.jsp.

```
<html>
<!-- Set the scripting language to java -->
<%@ page language="java" %>

<HTML>
<HEAD>
<TITLE>Management Console</TITLE>
</HEAD>

<BODY>
<table>
  <tr>
    <td>
      Welcome Manager: <%= request.getParameter("user") %>
    </td>
  </tr>
</table>
```

Listing 2.17 management.jsp.

To test this example, copy all three JSPs to the <*CATALINA_HOME*>/webapps/ch02app/ directory and open your browser to the following URL:

```
http://localhost:8080/ch02app/forward.jsp?role=user&user=Bob
```

You will see an image similar to Figure 2.16.

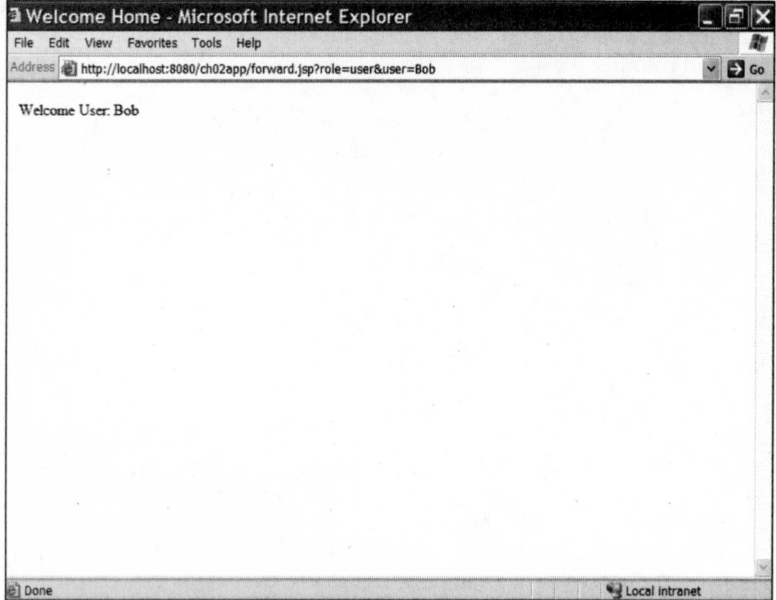

Figure 2.16 The output of forward.jsp.

You can also change the value of the role parameter to manager, to change the forwarded target.

<jsp:plugin>

The last standard action we discuss is <jsp:plugin>. This action enables a JSP author to generate the required HTML, using the appropriate client-browser independent constructs, to result in the download and subsequent execution of the specified applet or JavaBeans component.

The <jsp:plugin> tag, once evaluated, is replaced by either an <object> or <embed> tag, as appropriate for the requesting user agent. The attributes of the <jsp:plugin> action provide configuration data for the presentation of the embedded element. The syntax of the <jsp:plugin> action is as follows:

```
<jsp:plugin type="pluginType"
    code="classFile"
    codebase="relativeURLpath">

    <jsp:params>

    </jsp:params>
</jsp:plugin>
```

Table 2.11 contains the attributes and their descriptions for the <jsp:plugin> action.

Table 2.11 Attributes for the <jsp:plugin> Action

Attribute	Definition
type	The type of plug-in to include (an applet, for example)
code	The name of the class that will be executed by the plug-in
codebase	The base or relative path where the code attribute can be found

The <jsp:plugin> action also supports the use of the <jsp:params> tag to supply the plug-in with parameters, if necessary.

What's Next

In this chapter, we discussed the two technologies that the Struts Framework is based on—servlets and JSPs—and we examined both of their architectures and components. At this point, you should feel comfortable with the basic servlet and JSP technologies and how each of these technologies can be used to assemble a Web application. In the next chapter, we take our first real look at the Struts Framework.

Getting Started with Struts

In this chapter, we begin our Jakarta Struts coverage. First, we explain the steps that you must perform when installing and configuring a Struts application. Then, we create a sample application that displays the core components of a working Struts application. We conclude this chapter by walking through our sample application.

The goal of this chapter is to provide you with a quick introduction to the components of a Struts application. At the end of this chapter, you should have a pretty good understanding of the architecture of a basic Struts application.

Obtaining and Installing the Jakarta Struts Archive

Before you can get started with your Struts development, you need to prepare your environment. This begins with the acquisition of the latest release of the Struts project. For our examples, we will be using Struts 1.1, which you can find at http://jakarta.apache.org. You need to locate and download the binary distribution for your operating system.

Once you have the 1.1 Struts release, complete the following steps to prepare for the remainder of the text. You have to complete these steps for each Struts Web application that you intend to deploy.

1. Uncompress the Struts archive to your local disk.
2. Create a new Web application, using the directory structure described in Chapter 1, "Introducing the Jakarta-Struts Project and Its Supporting Components" (be sure to substitute the name of your Web application for the value *wroxapp*). In the case of this example, the name of our Web application is ch03app.

3. Copy the all of the JAR files, extracted from the lib directory, into the *<CATALINA_HOME>*/webapps/ch03app/WEB-INF/lib directory.

4. Create an empty web.xml file and copy it to the *<CATALINA_HOME>*/webapps/ch03app/WEB-INF/ directory. An example web.xml file is shown in the following code snippet.

```
<?xml version="1.0" encoding="ISO-8859-1"?>

<!DOCTYPE web-app
  PUBLIC "-//Sun Microsystems, Inc.//DTD Web Application
  2.3//EN"
  "http://java.sun.com/j2ee/dtds/web-app_2_3.dtd">

<web-app>

</web-app>
```

5. Create an empty strut-config.xml file and copy it to the *<CATALINA_HOME>*/webapps/ch03app/WEB-INF/ directory. The struts-config.xml file is the deployment descriptor for all Struts applications. It is the file that glues all of the MVC components together. Its normal location is in the *<CATALINA_HOME>*/webapps/*webappname*/WEB-INF/ directory. We use this file extensively throughout the remainder of this book. An empty struts-config.xml file is shown here:

```
<?xml version="1.0" encoding="ISO-8859-1" ?>

<!DOCTYPE struts-config
  PUBLIC "-//Apache Software Foundation//DTD Struts
  Configuration 1.1//EN"
  "http://jakarta.apache.org/struts/dtds/struts-
config_1_1.dtd">

<struts-config>

</struts-config>
```

At this point, you have all of the necessary components to build the simplest of Struts applications. As you begin the design and development of our example Struts application, you will need to install and configure further Struts components as necessary. The next section of this chapter takes you through the steps for developing our example application.

Creating Your First Struts Application

Now that you have Struts downloaded and installed, you can begin the development of your own sample Struts application. Our sample application consists of a simple set of JSP screens that queries a user for a stock symbol, performs a simple stock lookup, and returns the current price of the submitted stock. We use this example to describe the steps that must be performed when creating any Struts application.

Because Struts is modeled after the MVC design pattern, you can follow a standard development process for all of your Struts Web applications. This process begins with the identification of the application Views, the Controller objects that contain the application business logic, and the Model components being operated on. This process can be described using these steps:

1. Define and create all of the Views, in relation to their purpose, that will represent the user interface of your application.
2. Create and deploy all ActionForms used by the created Views. We discuss ActionForms later in this chapter.
3. Create the application's Controller components.
4. Define the relationships that exist between the Views and the Controllers (struts-config.xml).
5. Make the appropriate modifications to the web.xml file; describe the Struts components to the Web application.
6. Run the application.

These steps provide a high-level description of the Struts development process. In the sections that follow, we describe each of these steps in much greater detail.

Creating the Views

To begin the development of your application, you need to first describe the Views that will represent the presentation layer of your application. Two Views are associated with our sample application: index.jsp and quote.jsp. When creating Views in a Struts application, you are most often creating JSPs that are a combination of JSP/HTML syntax and some conglomeration of prepackaged Struts tag libraries.

As we discussed in Chapter 2, "An Overview of the Java Servlet and JavaServer Pages Architectures," the JSP/HTML syntax of a Struts View is similar to any other Web page and does not merit discussion, but the specialized Struts custom tag libraries do. We focus on the Struts tag libraries and more View details in Chapter 6, "Building the Presentation Layer," but for now we use simple JSP, without tags, to gain further insight into exactly how a Struts transaction works.

The Index View

The Index View, which is represented by the file index.jsp, is our starting View. It is the first page our application users will see, and its purpose is to query the user for a stock symbol and submit the inputted symbol to the appropriate action. The source for index.jsp is found in Listing 3.1.

```
<%@ page language="java" %>
<%@ taglib
  uri="/WEB-INF/struts-html.tld"
  prefix="html" %>

<html>
```

Code continued on following page

```
  <head>
    <title>Wrox Struts Application</title>
  </head>

  <body>
    <table width="500" border="0" cellspacing="0" cellpadding="0">
      <tr>
        <td> </td>
      </tr>
      <tr>
        <td height="68" width="48%">
          <div align="left">
            <img src="images/wxmainlogowhitespace.gif">
          </div>
        </td>
      </tr>
      <tr>
        <td> </td>
      </tr>
      <tr>
        <td> </td>
      </tr>
    </table>

    <html:form action="Lookup"
      name="lookupForm"
      type="ch03.LookupForm" >
      <table width="45%" border="0">
        <tr>
          <td>Symbol:</td>
          <td><html:text property="symbol" /></td>
        </tr>
        <tr>
          <td colspan="2" align="center"><html:submit /></td>
        </tr>
      </table>
    </html:form>

  </body>
</html>
```

Listing 3.1 index.jsp.

As you look over the source for the Index View, notice that it looks much like any other HTML page containing a form used to gather data, with the exception of the actual form and input tags. Instead of using the standard HTML Form tag, like most HTML pages, the index.jsp uses a Struts-specific Form tag: <html:form />. This tag, with its subordinate input tags, encapsulates Struts form processing. The form tag attributes used in this example are described in Table 3.1.

Table 3.1 Attributes of the Form Tag Used in Our Example

Attribute	Description
action	Represents the URL to which this form will be submitted. This attribute is also used to find the appropriate ActionMapping in the Struts configuration file, which we describe later in this section. The value used in our example is *Lookup*, which maps to an ActionMapping with a path attribute equal to Lookup.
name	Identifies the key that is used to look up the appropriate ActionForm that will represent the submitted form data. We use the value *LookupForm*. An ActionForm is an object that is used by Struts to represent the form data as a JavaBean. Its main purpose is to pass form data between View and Controller components. We discuss the LookupForm implementation later in this section.
type	Names the fully qualified classname of the form bean you want to use in this request. For this example, we use the value *wrox.LookupForm*, which is an ActionForm object containing data members matching the inputs of this form.

This instance of the <html:form /> tag is also the parent to two other HTML tags. The first of the tags is the <html:text> tag. This tag is synonymous with the HTML text input tag; the only difference is the property attribute, which names a unique data member found in the ActionForm bean class named by the form's type attribute. The named data member will be set to the text value of the corresponding input tag.

The second HTML tag that we use is the <html:submit> tag. This tag simply emulates an HTML submit button. The net effect of these two tags is:

1. Upon submission, the ActionForm object named by the <html:form /> tag is created and populated with the value of the <html:text /> tags.
2. Once the ActionForm object is populated with the appropriate values, the Action object referenced by the <html:form /> is invoked and passed a reference to the populated ActionForm. We look at this process in the "Creating the Controller Components" section of this chapter.

To use the previous two HTML tags, you must first add a taglib entry in the ch03app application's web.xml file that references the URI /WEB-INF/struts-html.tld. This TLD describes all of the tags in the HTML tag library. The following snippet shows the <taglib> element that must be added to the web.xml file:

```
<taglib>
  <taglib-uri>/WEB-INF/struts-html.tld</taglib-uri>
  <taglib-location>/WEB-INF/struts-html.tld</taglib-location>
</taglib>
```

Second, you must copy the struts-html.tld from the lib directory of the extracted Struts archive to the *<CATALINA_HOME>*/webapps/ch03app/WEB_INF/ directory.

> **In our sample application, we do use a single image. This image file, hp_logo_wrox.gif, can be found in the images directory of our sample application's source tree.**

The ActionForm

The ActionForm used in this example contains a single data member that maps directly to the symbol input parameter of the form defined in the Index View. As we stated in the previous section, when an <html:form /> is submitted, the Struts Framework populates the matching data members of the ActionForm with the values entered in the <html:input /> tags. The Struts Framework does this by using JavaBean introspection; therefore, the accessors of the ActionForm must follow the JavaBean standard naming convention.

In our example, ch03.LookupForm, we have a single data member symbol. To satisfy the JavaBean standard, the accessor used to set the symbol data member must be prefixed with *set* and *get* followed by the data member name, with its first letter being capitalized. Listing 3.2 contains the source for our ActionForm.

```
package ch03;

import javax.servlet.http.HttpServletRequest;
import org.apache.struts.action.ActionForm;
import org.apache.struts.action.ActionMapping;

public class LookupForm extends ActionForm {

  private String symbol = null;

  public String getSymbol() {

    return (symbol);
  }

  public void setSymbol(String symbol) {

    this.symbol = symbol;
  }

  public void reset(ActionMapping mapping,
    HttpServletRequest request) {

    this.symbol = null;
  }
}
```

Listing 3.2 The LookupForm implementation LookupForm.java.

There is really nothing special about this class. It is a simple JavaBean that extends org.apache.struts.action.ActionForm, as must all ActionForm objects, with a get and set accessor that match its single data member. It does have one method that is specific to an ActionForm bean: the reset() method. The reset() method is called by the Struts Framework with each request that uses the LookupForm. The purpose of this method is to reset all of the LookupForm's data members and allow the object to be pooled for reuse.

The reset() method is passed a reference to an ActionMapping class. At this point you can ignore this class; we fully describe it in Chapters 4 and 8.

To deploy the LookupForm to our Struts application, you need to compile this class, move it to the <*CATALINA_HOME*>/webapps/ch03app/WEB-INF/classes/ch03 directory, and add the following line to the <form-beans> section of the <*CATALINA_HOME*>/webapps/ch03app/WEB-INF/struts-config.xml file:

```
<form-beans>
    <form-bean name="lookupForm"
      type="ch03.LookupForm"/>
  </form-beans>
```

This entry makes the Struts application aware of the LookupForm and how it should be referenced.

The Quote View

The last of our Views is the quote.jsp. This View is presented to the user upon successful stock symbol lookup. It is a simple JSP with no Struts-specific functionality. Listing 3.3 contains its source.

```
<html>
  <head>
    <title>Wrox Struts Application</title>
  </head>
  <body>

    <table width="500"
      border="0" cellspacing="0" cellpadding="0">
      <tr>
        <td> </td>
      </tr>
      <tr>
        <td height="68" width="48%">
          <div align="left">
            <img src="images/wxmainlogowhitespace.gif">
          </div>
        </td>
      </tr>
      <tr>
        <td> </td>
      </tr>
      <tr>
        <td> </td>
      </tr>
      <tr>
        <td> </td>
      </tr>
      <tr>
        <td>
          Current Price : <%= request.getAttribute("PRICE") %>
```

Code continued on following page

```
            </td>
          </tr>
          <tr>
            <td> </td>
          </tr>
        </table>
      </body>
    </html>
```

Listing 3.3 quote.jsp.

As you look over this JSP, notice that it contains a single JSP functional line of code. This line of code retrieves the current price from the HttpServletRequest of the submitted stock symbol. This value is placed in the HttpServletRequest by the Action object that services this request, as shown in the next section.

Creating the Controller Components

In a Struts application, two main components make up the Controller: the org.apache.struts.action.ActionServlet and the org.apache.struts.action.Action classes. In most Struts applications, there is one org.apache.struts.action.ActionServlet implementation and many org.apache.struts.action.Action implementations.

> **Other components are associated with the Struts Controller—we discuss these components in Chapter 4, "Actions and the ActionServlet."**

The org.apache.struts.action.ActionServlet is the Controller component that handles client requests and determines which org.apache.struts.action.Action will process the received request. When assembling simple applications, such as the one we are building, the default ActionServlet satisfies your application needs, and therefore, you do not need to create a specialized Controller implementation. When the need arises, however, it is a simple process. For our example, let's stick with the ActionServlet as it is delivered in the Struts packages. We cover the process of extending the Controller in Chapter 4.

The second component of a Struts Controller is the org.apache.struts.action.Action class. As opposed to the ActionServlet, the Action class must be extended for each specialized function in your application. This class is where your application's specific logic begins.

For our example, we have only one process to perform: looking up the value of the submitted stock symbol. Therefore, we are going to create a single org.apache.struts.action.Action bean named LookupAction. The source for our Action is shown in Listing 3.4. As you examine this listing, be sure to pay close attention to the execute() method.

```
package ch03;

import java.io.IOException;
import javax.servlet.ServletException;
```

Code continued on following page

```
import javax.servlet.http.HttpServletRequest;
import javax.servlet.http.HttpServletResponse;
import org.apache.struts.action.Action;
import org.apache.struts.action.ActionForm;
import org.apache.struts.action.ActionForward;
import org.apache.struts.action.ActionMapping;

public class LookupAction extends Action {

  protected Double getQuote(String symbol) {

    if ( symbol.equalsIgnoreCase("SUNW") ) {

      return new Double(25.00);
    }
    return null;
  }

  public ActionForward execute(ActionMapping mapping,
    ActionForm form,
    HttpServletRequest request,
    HttpServletResponse response)
    throws IOException, ServletException {

    Double price = null;

    // Default target to success
    String target = new String("success");

    if ( form != null ) {

      // Use the LookupForm to get the request parameters
      LookupForm lookupForm = (LookupForm)form;

      String symbol = lookupForm.getSymbol();

      price = getQuote(symbol);
    }

    // Set the target to failure
    if ( price == null ) {

      target = new String("failure");
    }
    else {

      request.setAttribute("PRICE", price);
    }
    // Forward to the appropriate View
    return (mapping.findForward(target));
  }
}
```

Listing 3.4 The LookupAction bean.

Notice that this class extends the org.apache.struts.action.Action class and contains two methods: getQuote() and execute(). The getQuote() method is a simple method that returns a fixed price (if *SUNW* is the submitted symbol).

The second method is the execute() method, where the main functionality of the LookupAction is found. This is the method that must be defined by all HTTP Action class implementations. Before we can examine how the logic contained in the execute() method works, let's look at the four parameters passed to it (see Table 3.2).

Table 3.2 The Parameters of the Action.execute() Method

Component	Description
ActionMapping	The ActionMapping class contains all of the deployment information for a particular Action object. This class is used to determine where the results of the LookupAction will be sent once its processing is complete.
ActionForm	The ActionForm represents the form inputs containing the request parameters from the View referencing this Action bean. The reference being passed to our LookupAction points to an instance of our LookupForm.
HttpServletRequest	The HttpServletRequest attribute is a reference to the current HTTP request object.
HttpServletResponse	The HttpServletResponse is a reference to the current HTTP response object.

A second Action.execute() method is available for servicing non-HTTP requests. We take a look at this method in Chapter 4.

Now that we have described the parameters passed to the execute() method, we can move on to describing the actual method body. The first notable action taken by this method is to create a String object named *target* with a value of *success*. This object is used as a key to determine the View that will present successful results of this action.

The next step performed by this method is to get the request parameters contained in the LookupForm. When the form was submitted, the ActionServlet used Java's introspection mechanisms to set the values stored in this object. Note that the reference passed to the execute() method is an ActionForm that must be cast to the ActionForm implementation used by this action. The following code snippet contains the source used to access the request parameters:

```
// Use the LookupForm to get the request parameters
LookupForm lookupForm = (LookupForm)form;

String symbol = lookupForm.getSymbol();
```

Once we have references to the symbol parameters, we pass these values to the getQuote() method. This is a simple user-defined method that returns the Double value *25.00*. If the symbol *String* contains any values other than *SUNW*, then null is returned and we change the value of our target to *failure*. This has the effect of changing the targeted View. If the value is not null, then we add the returned value to the request with a key of PRICE.

At this point, the value of target equals either *success* or *failure*. This value is then passed to the ActionMapping.findForward() method, which returns an ActionForward object referencing the physical View that will actually present the results of this action. The final step of the execute() method is to return the ActionForward object to the invoking ActionServlet, which then forwards the request to the referenced View for presentation. This step is completed using the following line of code:

```
return (mapping.findForward(target));
```

To deploy the LookupAction to our Struts application, compile the LookupAction class, move the class file to the *<CATALINA_HOME>*/webapps/ch03app/WEB-INF/classes/ch03 directory, and add the following entry to the <action-mappings> section of the *<CATALINA_HOME>*/webapps/ch03app/WEB-INF/struts-config.xml file:

```
<action path="/Lookup"
  type="ch03.LookupAction"
  name="lookupForm">
  <forward name="success" path="/quote.jsp"/>
  <forward name="failure" path="/index.jsp"/>
</action>
```

This entry contains the data that will be stored in the ActionMapping object that is passed to the execute() method of the LookupAction. It contains all of the attributes required to use this instance of the LookupAction, including a collection of keyed <forward> sub-elements representing the possible Views that can present the results of the LookupAction.

Once you have made all of the previously listed additions, you should have a complete struts-config.xml file that looks similar to Listing 3.5.

```
<?xml version="1.0" encoding="ISO-8859-1" ?>

<!DOCTYPE struts-config
  PUBLIC "-//Apache Software Foundation//DTD Struts
  Configuration 1.1//EN"
  "http://jakarta.apache.org/struts/dtds/struts-
  config_1_1.dtd">

<struts-config>

  <form-beans>
    <form-bean name="lookupForm"
      type="ch03.LookupForm"/>
  </form-beans>

  <action-mappings>

    <action path="/Lookup"
```

Code continued on following page

```
        type="ch03.LookupAction"
        name="lookupForm" >
        <forward name="success" path="/quote.jsp"/>
        <forward name="failure" path="/index.jsp"/>
      </action>

    </action-mappings>

  </struts-config>
```

Listing 3.5 The complete struts-config.xml file.

Deploying Your Struts Application

At this point you have all of the necessary Struts components deployed and modified. You now need to tell the web application itself about your application components. To do this, you must make some simple changes to the web.xml file.

The first change is to tell the Web application about our ActionServlet. This is accomplished by adding the following servlet definition to the <CATALINA_HOME>/webapps/ch03app/WEB-INF/web.xml file:

```
<servlet>
  <servlet-name>action</servlet-name>
  <servlet-class>
    org.apache.struts.action.ActionServlet
  </servlet-class>
  <init-param>
    <param-name>config</param-name>
    <param-value>/WEB-INF/struts-config.xml</param-value>
  </init-param>
  <load-on-startup>1</load-on-startup>
</servlet>
```

This entry tells the Web application that we have a servlet named action that is implemented by the class org.apache.struts.action.ActionServlet, which as we stated earlier is the default ActionServlet provided with Struts.

It defines a servlet initialization parameter, config, which tells the ActionServlet where to find the struts-config.xml file.

And finally, it contains a <load-on-startup> sub-element that causes the ActionServlet to be loaded when the application is started. The ActionServlet must be loaded when the application starts. This guarantees the availability of the necessary Struts resources prior to the receipt of the first request.

Once you have told the container about the ActionServlet, you need to tell it when it should be executed. To do this, you add a <servlet-mapping> element to the <*CATALINA_HOME*>/webapps/ch03app/WEB-INF/web.xml file:

```
<servlet-mapping>
  <servlet-name>action</servlet-name>
  <url-pattern>*.do</url-pattern>
</servlet-mapping>
```

This mapping tells the Web application that whenever a request is received with .do appended to the URL, then the servlet named action should service the request.

Once you have made all of the previously listed additions, you should have a complete web.xml that looks similar to Listing 3.6.

```
<?xml version="1.0" encoding="ISO-8859-1"?>

<!DOCTYPE web-app
  PUBLIC "-//Sun Microsystems, Inc.//DTD Web Application
  2.3//EN"
  "http://java.sun.com/j2ee/dtds/web-app_2_3.dtd">

<web-app>

  <!-- Standard ActionServlet Configuration -->
  <servlet>
    <servlet-name>action</servlet-name>
    <servlet-class>
      org.apache.struts.action.ActionServlet
    </servlet-class>
    <init-param>
      <param-name>config</param-name>
      <param-value>/WEB-INF/struts-config.xml</param-value>
    </init-param>
    <load-on-startup>1</load-on-startup>
  </servlet>

  <!-- Standard ActionServlet Mapping -->
  <servlet-mapping>
    <servlet-name>action</servlet-name>
    <url-pattern>*.do</url-pattern>
  </servlet-mapping>

  <!-- Standard Welcome File List -->
  <welcome-file-list>
    <welcome-file>index.jsp</welcome-file>
  </welcome-file-list>

  <!-- Struts Tag Library Descriptors -->
  <taglib>
    <taglib-uri>
      /WEB-INF/struts-html.tld
    </taglib-uri>
    <taglib-location>
      /WEB-INF/struts-html.tld
    </taglib-location>
  </taglib>

</web-app>
```

Listing 3.6 The complete web.xml file.

Walking through the ch03app Web Application

At this point, you should have completed all of the steps described in the previous section and have a deployed ch03app Web application. In this section, we examine this sample application and discuss each of the steps performed by Struts along the way. The purpose is to provide you with a walkthrough that ties together all of the previously assembled components.

To begin using this application, restart Tomcat and open your Web browser to the following URL:

```
http://localhost:8080/ch03app/
```

If everything went according to plan, you should see a page similar to Figure 3.1.

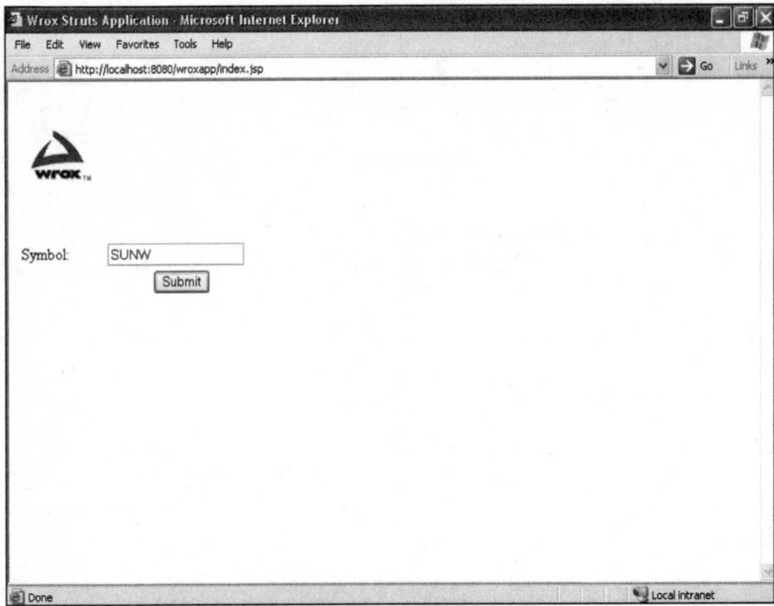

Figure 3.1 The ch03app Index View.

When this page loads, the following actions occur:

1. The <html:form> creates the necessary HTML used to represent a form and then checks for an instance of the wrox.LookupForm in session scope. If it finds an instance of the wrox.LookupForm, then the value stored in the ActionForm's symbol data member is mapped to the input element value on the form and the HTML form is written to the response. This is a helpful technique that can be used to handle errors in form data. (We see examples of handling form errors in Chapter 10, "Managing Errors.") The Index View is then presented to the user.

2. Before we move on, we must take a look at the HTML source generated when the Index View is evaluated. If you view the source generated by your browser, you should see that the action attribute of the <form /> tag has been modified:

```
<form name="lookupForm" method="post"
  action="/ch03app/Lookup.do">
```

```
    <table width="45%" border="0">
      <tr>
        <td>Symbol:</td>
        <td><input type="text" name="symbol" value=""></td>
      </tr>
      <tr>
        <td colspan="2" align="center">
          <input type="submit" value="Submit">
        </td>
      </tr>
    </table>
  </form>
```

If you remember the original action attribute, its value was simply *Lookup*. As you look over the modified action, notice that the new value has the string .do appended to it. This modification was performed by the Struts <html:form /> to connect this Struts request to the <servlet-mapping> associated with the ActionServlet. We see this process in action in the following steps.

3. To move on to the next step, enter the value *SUNW* into the Symbol text box and click the Submit button. This invokes the following functionality.

4. The Submit button causes the browser to invoke the URL named in the <html:form /> tag's action attribute, which in this case is *Lookup.do*. When the JSP/servlet container receives this request, it looks in the web.xml file for a <servlet-mapping> with a <url-pattern> that ends with .do. It finds the following entry, which tells the container to send the request to a servlet that has been deployed with the <servlet-name> of action:

```
<!-- Standard Action Servlet Mapping -->
<servlet-mapping>
  <servlet-name>action</servlet-name>
  <url-pattern>*.do</url-pattern>
</servlet-mapping>
```

5. The container finds the following <servlet> entry with a <servlet-name> of action that points to the ActionServlet, which acts as the Controller for our Struts application:

```
<servlet>
  <servlet-name>action</servlet-name>
  <servlet-class>
    org.apache.struts.action.ActionServlet
  </servlet-class>
</servlet>
```

6. The ActionServlet then takes over the servicing of this request by retrieving the previously created LookupForm, populating its symbol data member with the value passed on the request, and adding the LookupForm to the session with a key of lookupForm.

7. Next, the ActionServlet looks for an <ActionMapping> entry in the struts-config.xml file with a <path> element equal to Lookup. It finds the following entry:

```
<action path="/Lookup"
  type="ch03.LookupAction"
  name="lookupForm"
  input="/index.jsp">
  <forward name="success" path="/quote.jsp"/>
  <forward name="failure" path="/index.jsp"/>
</action>
```

8. It then creates an instance of the LookupAction class named by the type attribute. It also creates an ActionMapping class that contains all of the values in the <ActionMapping> element.

9. It then invokes LookupAction.execute() with the appropriate parameters. The LookupAction.execute() method performs its logic and calls the ActionMapping.findForward() method with a String value of either *success* or *failure*.

10. The ActionMapping.findForward() method looks for a <forward> sub-element with a name attribute matching the target value. It then returns an ActionForward object containing the results of its search, which is the value of the path attribute /quote.jsp (upon success) or /index.jsp (upon failure).

11. The LookupAction then returns the ActionForward object to the ActionServlet, which in turn forwards the request object to the targeted View for presentation. The results of a successful transaction are shown in Figure 3.2.

If you submit any value other than SUNW, you will be sent back to index.jsp, which is the failure path of the LookupAction. If this does happen, you will see that the input value on the index page is pre-populated with your originally submitted value. This is some of the handy error-handling techniques provided by the Struts application.

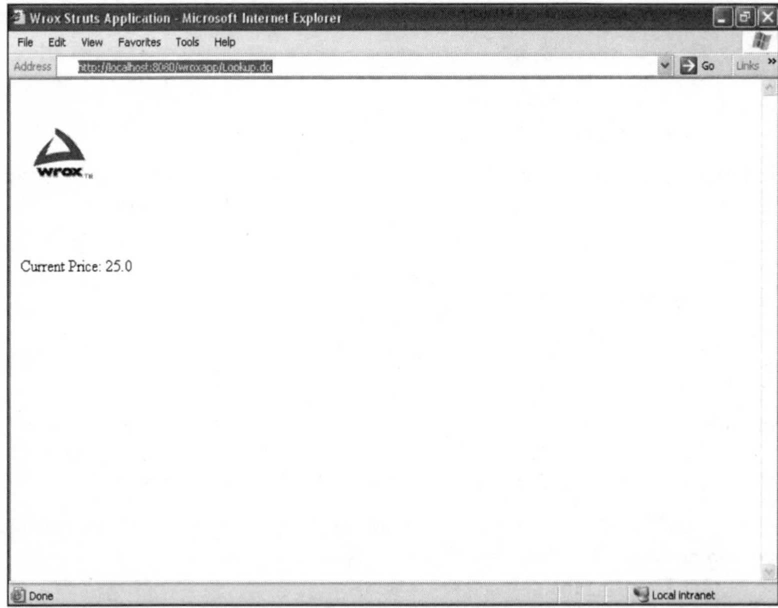

Figure 3.2 The ch03app Quote View.

What's Next

In this chapter, we began our Jakarta Struts coverage. We started by defining the Struts Framework, including the steps that you must perform when installing and configuring a Struts application. We created a sample application to display the components that exist in a working Struts application. We concluded the chapter by walking through our sample application and discussing each step performed by Struts as it processes a request.

In the next chapter, we continue our Struts conversations by digging further into the Controller components, including discussions of org.apache.struts.action.ActionServlet and other Struts Controller mechanisms.

Actions and ActionServlet

In this chapter, we dig further into the Controller components of the Struts Framework. We begin by looking at four distinct Struts Controller components: the ActionServlet class, the Action class, Plugins, and the RequestProcesser.

The goal of this chapter is to provide you with a solid understanding of the Struts Controller components and how they can be used and extended to create a robust and easily extended Web application.

The ActionServlet Class

The org.apache.struts.action.ActionServlet is the backbone of all Struts applications. It is the main Controller component that handles client requests and determines which org.apache.struts.action.Action will process each received request. It serves as an Action factory—creating specific Action classes based on the user's request.

While the ActionServlet sounds as if it might perform some extraordinary magic, it is a simple servlet. Just like any other HTTP servlet, it extends the class javax.servlet.http.HttpServlet and implements each of the HttpServlet's lifecycle methods, including the init(), doGet(), doPost(), and destroy() methods. The two main entry points into the ActionServlet are essentially the same as with any other servlet: doGet() and doPost(). The source for both of these methods is shown here:

```
public void doGet(HttpServletRequest request,
  HttpServletResponse response)
  throws IOException, ServletException {

  process(request, response);

}

public void doPost(HttpServletRequest request,
```

```
    HttpServletResponse response)
    throws IOException, ServletException {

    process(request, response);

}
```

Notice that the implementation of these two methods is exactly the same. They call a single method, named process(). The Struts-specific behavior begins with this method. The process() method handles all requests and has the following method signature:

```
protected void process(HttpServletRequest request,
  HttpServletResponse response);
```

When the ActionServlet receives a request, it completes the following steps:

1. The doPost() or doGet() methods receive a request and invoke the process() method.
2. The process() method gets the current RequestProcessor and invokes the RequestProcessor. process() method.

> **If you intend to extend the ActionServlet, the most logical place for customization is in the RequestProcessor object. It contains the logic that the Struts controller performs with each request. We discuss the RequestProcessor near the end of this chapter.**

3. The RequestProcessor.process() method is where the current request is actually serviced. This method retrieves, from the struts-config.xml file, the <action> element that matches the path submitted on the request. It does this by matching the path passed in the <html:form /> tag's action element to the <action> element with the same path value. Here's an example of this match:

```
<html:form action="/Lookup"
  name="lookupForm"
  type="ch04.LookupForm" >

<action path="/Lookup"
  type="ch04.LookupAction"
  name="lookupForm" >
  <forward name="success" path="/quote.jsp"/>
  <forward name="failure" path="/index.jsp"/>
</action>
```

4. When the RequestProcessor.process() method has a matching <action>, it looks for a <form-bean> entry that has a name attribute that matches the <action> element's name attribute. The following code snippet contains a sample match:

```
<form-beans>
  <form-bean name="lookupForm"
    type="ch04.LookupForm"/>
```

```
</form-beans>

<action path="/Lookup"
  type="ch04.LookupAction"
  name="lookupForm" >
  <forward name="success" path="/quote.jsp"/>
  <forward name="failure" path="/index.jsp"/>
</action>
```

5. When the RequestProcessor.process() method knows the fully qualified name of the FormBean, it creates or retrieves a pooled instance of the ActionForm named by the <form-bean> element's type attribute and populates its data members with the values submitted on the request.
6. After the ActionForm's data members are populated, the RequestProcessor.process() method calls the ActionForm.validate() method, which checks the validity of the submitted values.

There is more to the validate() method—you see how this method is configured and performs in Chapter 10, "Managing Errors."

7. At this point, the RequestProcessor.process() method knows all that it needs to know and it is time to actually service the request. It does this by retrieving the fully qualified name of the Action class from the <action> element's type attribute, creating or retrieving the named class, and calling the Action.execute() method. We look at this method in the section titled "The Action Class," later in this chapter.
8. When the Action class returns from its processing, its execute() method returns an ActionForward object that is used to determine the target of this transaction. The RequestProcessor.process() method resumes control, and the request is then forwarded to the determined target.
9. At this point, the ActionServlet instance has completed its processing for this request and is ready to service future requests.

Configuring the ActionServlet

Now that you have a solid understanding of how the ActionServlet performs its duties, let's take a look at how it is deployed and configured. The ActionServlet is like any other servlet and is configured using a web.xml <servlet> element.

You can take many approaches when setting up an ActionServlet. You can go with a bare-bones approach, as we did in Chapter 3, "Getting Started with Struts," or you can get more serious and include any combination of the available initialization parameters described in Table 4.1.

Table 4.1 The Initialization Parameters of the ActionServlet

Parameter	Description
config	Names the context-relative path to the struts-config.xml file. The default location is in the /WEB-INF/struts-config.xml directory. (Optional)
config/${module}	Names the context-relative path to the struts-config.xml file associated with a particular Struts Module. (Optional)
convertNull	A boolean parameter used to simulate Struts 1.0x functionality when populating an ActionForm. When this parameter is set to true, numeric objects (java.lang.Integer, etc.) are initialized to null. If it is set to false, these objects are set to 0.
debug	Determines the debugging level for the ActionServlet. The default value is 0, which turns debugging off. (Optional)
detail	Sets the debug level for the Digester object, which is used during ActionServlet initialization. The default value is 0. (Optional)
multipartClass	Names the fully qualified class of the MultipartRequestHandler implementation to be used when file uploads are being processed. The default value is *org.apache.struts.upload.DiskMultipartRequestHandler*. (Optional)
validating	If set to true, tells the ActionServlet that we want to validate the strut-config.xml file against its DTD. While this parameter is optional, it is highly recommended and therefore the default is set to true.

While none of these initialization parameters are required, a couple of the more common ones are the config and debug parameters. It is also common practice to use a <load-on-startup> element to ensure that the ActionServlet is started when the container starts the Web application. An example <serlvet> entry, describing an ActionServlet, is shown in the following code snippet:

```
<servlet>
  <servlet-name>action</servlet-name>
  <servlet-class>
    org.apache.struts.action.ActionServlet
  </servlet-class>
  <init-param>
    <param-name>config</param-name>
    <param-value>/WEB-INF/struts-config.xml</param-value>
  </init-param>
  <init-param>
    <param-name>debug</param-name>
    <param-value>4</param-value>
  </init-param>
  <load-on-startup>1</load-on-startup>
</servlet>
```

Using Struts Modules

Struts 1.1 introduced the Struts Modules, an often-overlooked, but sometimes extremely convenient, feature. Struts Modules allow teams of developers to logically segment their Struts applications.

One of the major problems with a Struts 1.0.x application is its dependence on a single struts-config.xml file. While a single configuration file can be handy for small applications, when you're developing a large application this type of monolithic configuration can be both cumbersome and contentious. Because everyone is fighting over this single file, you often step on one another's changes and may run into merge conflicts when checking your changes into version control.

Struts Modules were created with these conflicts in mind. Struts Modules allow a team to logically separate their segment of a single application into the equivalent of a "sub-Web" application, each with its own struts-config.xml file. Although this separation does not resolve all chances of conflict, it does reduce those chances significantly.

Configuring Struts Modules

It is extremely easy to configure a Struts Module. You can do it in a few simple steps. For this example, let's segment an Administrative piece of a Struts application:

1. Create a directory that describes your new Module. For this example, create a directory named admin/ that will be used as a logical slice containing the application's administrative functionality.
2. Copy all of the related JSP and View components into this directory.
3. Create a new struts-config.xml file that will describe the related Struts components of this new segment and copy it to the WEB-INF/ directory of your application. Let's name our sample admin/ module *struts-config-admin.xml*.

> **In step 3, we are copying the Module's struts-config-admin.xml file into the WEB-INF/ directory of the Web application, not the Module's WEB-INF/ directory. All Modules share the same WEB-INF/ directory, classpath, and web.xml file. They are different only in their subdirectory and their struts-config.xml files.**

4. In the newly created struts-config-*XXX*.file, add the prefix of your Module to all of your context-relative resources. An example of this is a <global-forward/>. If it referenced a JSP as userAdmin.jsp, you would need to change this reference to /admin/userAdmin.jsp.
5. Add a new Servlet <init-param> entry to the web.xml file that describes your new Module:

```
<init-param>
  <param-name>config/admin</param-name>
  <param-value>/WEB-INF/struts-config-admin.xml</param-value>
</init-param>
```

That's about it. The next time you start your Struts application, your new Module will be available and accessible when you insert the Module's name into the URL (following the Web application name and before the requested resource). This URL shows how you would reference our admin/ application's index.jsp:

```
http://locahost:8080/wroxapp/admin/index.jsp
```

We see more tips for using Struts Modules in Chapter 21, "Struts Cookbook."

The Action Class

The most common component of a Struts Controller is the org.apache.struts.action.Action class. As we stated in Chapter 3, the Action class must and will be extended for each specialized Struts function in your application. The collection of these Action classes is what defines your Web application.

To develop your own Action class, you must complete the following steps. These steps describe the minimum actions that you must take when creating a new Action and are the focus of this section:

1. Create a class that extends the org.apache.struts.action.Action class.
2. Implement the appropriate execute() method and add your specific business logic.
3. Compile the new Action and move it into the Web application's classpath. This would most often be your WEB-INF/classes directory.
4. Add an <action> element to the application's struts-config.xml file describing the new Action.

Extending the Action Class

Now that you have seen the steps required to create an Action class, let's take a look at how you can create your own Action class. Here's a skeleton Action class implementation:

```
package ch04;

import java.io.IOException;
import javax.servlet.ServletException;
import javax.servlet.http.HttpServletRequest;
import javax.servlet.http.HttpServletResponse;
import org.apache.struts.action.Action;
import org.apache.struts.action.ActionForm;
import org.apache.struts.action.ActionForward;
import org.apache.struts.action.ActionMapping;

public class SkeletonAction extends Action {

  // Add your Action class implementation
}
```

As you can see, there is really nothing special about this step--you simply create a Java object that extends the org.apache.struts.action.Action class. In the remainder of this book, we extend the Action class.

Implementing the execute() Method

The execute() method is where your application logic begins. It is the method that you need to override when defining your own Struts Actions. The execute() method has two functions:

- It performs the user-defined business logic associated with your application.
- It tells the Framework where it should next route the request.

The Struts Framework defines two execute() methods. The first execute() implementation is used when you are defining custom Actions that are not HTTP specific. This implementation of the execute() method is analogous to the javax.serlvet.GenericServlet class; its signature is:

```
public ActionForward execute(ActionMapping mapping,
                             ActionForm form,
                             ServletRequest request,
                             ServletResponse response)
        throws IOException, ServletException
```

Notice that this method receives, as its third and fourth parameter, a ServletRequest and a ServletResponse object, as opposed to the HTTP-specific equivalents HttpServletRequest and HttpServletResponse. This is the version of the Action.execute() method that you need to override when servicing requests that are not HTTP specific.

> **If you do receive a non-HTTP request to a Action that does not implement the previous execute() method, then the Framework will attempt to coerce the ServletRequest and ServletResponse objects into HttpServletRequest and HttpServletResponse objects, respectively, and then call the HTTP-specific perform() method. If you would like to see the source that performs this task, download the source, open the Action.java source file, and look at the execute() methods within it.**

The second execute() implementation is used when you are defining HTTP-specific custom Actions. This implementation of the method is analogous to the javax.servlet.http.HttpServlet class; its signature is:

```
public ActionForward execute(ActionMapping mapping,
                             ActionForm form,
                             HttpServletRequest request,
                             HttpServletResponse response)
        throws IOException, ServletException
```

Notice that this method (unlike the first one) receives, as its third and fourth parameter, an HttpServletRequest and an HttpServletResponse object. This implementation of the execute() method is the one that you will most often extend. Table 4.2 describes all of the parameters of the Action.execute() method.

Table 4.2 The Parameters of the Action.execute() Method

Component	Description
ActionMapping	Contains all of the deployment information for a particular Action bean. This class is to determine where the results of the LoginAction will be sent once its processing is complete.
ActionForm	Represents the Form inputs containing the request parameters from the View referencing this Action bean. The reference being passed to our LoginAction points to an instance of our LoginForm.
HttpServletRequest	A reference to the current HTTP request object.
HttpServletResponse	A reference to the current HTTP response object.

After examining the parameters passed to the execute() method, you should take a look at its return type, the ActionForward object. This object is used by the RequestProcessor to determine where the request will go next, whether it is a JSP or another Action. The following code snippet shows an example execute() method:

```
package ch04;

import java.io.IOException;
import javax.servlet.ServletException;
import javax.servlet.http.HttpServletRequest;
import javax.servlet.http.HttpServletResponse;
import org.apache.struts.action.Action;
import org.apache.struts.action.ActionForm;
import org.apache.struts.action.ActionForward;
import org.apache.struts.action.ActionMapping;

public class SkeletonAction extends Action {

  public ActionForward execute(ActionMapping mapping,
    ActionForm form,
    HttpServletRequest request,
    HttpServletResponse response)
    throws IOException, ServletException {

    if ( form != null ) {

      // 1. Get a reference to the ActionForm
      SkeletonForm actionForm = (SkeletonForm)form;

      // 2. Add Your Business Logic
    }
```

```
        // 3. return the appropriate ActionForward
        return (mapping.findForward("success"));
    }
}
```

As you build your own Action objects, you will notice that they almost all perform the same sequence of events.

1. Cast the ActionForm reference associated with this Action to your specific ActionForm implementation. In the previous example, we are casting the passed-in ActionForm object to a SkeletonForm. You see how ActionForms are associated with Actions in the next section of this chapter.
2. Add your specific business logic.
3. Use the ActionMapping.findForward() method to find the ActionForward object that matches the <forward> sub-element in the <action> definition. We look at the <forward> sub-element in the following section.
4. Return the retrieved ActionForward object. This object routes the request to the appropriate View.

Configuring the Action Class

Now that you have seen how an Action class is created, let's examine its configuration options. The Action class is a Struts-specific object and therefore must be configured using the struts-config.xml file.

The element that is used to describe a Struts action is an <action> element. The class that defines the <action> element's attributes is the org.apache.struts.action.ActionMappings class. In Chapter 8, "Working with Custom ActionMappings," you see how this class can be extended to define additional <action> attributes. Table 4.3 describes the attributes of an <action> element as they are defined by the default ActionMappings class.

When using an <action> element to describe an Action class, you are describing only one instance of the named Action class. There is nothing stopping you from using n-number of <action> elements that describe the same Action class. The only restriction is that the path attribute must be unique for each <action> element.

Table 4.3 Attributes of an <action> Element

Attribute	Description
attribute	Names a request or session scope attribute that is used to access an ActionForm bean, if it is other than the bean's specified "name".

Table continued on following page

Attribute	Description
className	Names the fully qualified class name of the ActionMapping implementation class you want to use in when invoking this Action class. If the className attribute is not included, the ActionMapping defined in the ActionServlet's mapping initialization parameter is used. We use the attribute when we create a new ActionMappings implementation in Chapter 8.
forward	Represents a Module-relative path of the servlet or JSP resource that will process this request. This attribute is used if you do not want an Action to service the request to this path. The forward attribute is valid only if no include or type attribute is specified.
include	Represents a Module-relative path of the servlet or JSP resource that will process this request. This attribute is used if you do not want an Action to service the request to this path. The include attribute is valid only if no forward or type attribute is specified.
input	Represents a Module-relative path of the input form to which control should be returned if a validation error is encountered. The input attribute is where control will be returned if ActionErrors are returned from the ActionForm or Action objects. (Optional)
name	Identifies the name of the form bean that is coupled with the Action being defined.
path	Represents the Module-relative path of the submitted request. The path must be unique and start with a / character.
parameter	A generic configuration parameter that is used to pass extra information to the Action object defined by this action mapping.
roles	A comma-delimited list of security roles that can access the defined <action /> object.
type	Names the fully qualified class name of the Action class being described by this ActionMapping. The type attribute is valid only if no include or forward attribute is specified.
scope	Names the scope of the form bean that is bound to the described Action. The possible values are request or session. The default value is session.
unknown	If set to true, this <action /> is used as the default action mapping when a request does not match another <action /> element. Only one ActionMapping can be marked as unknown per Module.
validate	If set to true, causes the ActionForm.validate() method to be called on the form bean associated to the Action being described. If the validate attribute is set to false, then the ActionForm.validate() method is not called. The default value is true.

A sample <action> sub-element using some of the previous attributes is shown here:

```
<action-mappings>

  <action path="/Lookup"
    type="ch04.LookupAction"
    name="lookupForm"
    input="/index.jsp">
    <forward name="success" path="/quote.jsp"/>
    <forward name="failure" path="/index.jsp"/>
  </action>

</action-mappings>
```

All <action> elements must be defined as sub-elements of <action-mappings />.

This <action> element tells the ActionServlet the following things about this Action instance:

- The Action class is implemented by the ch04.LookupAction class.
- This Action should be invoked when the URL ends with the path /Lookup.
- This Action class will use the <form-bean> with the name lookupForm.
- The originating resource that submitted the request to this Action is the JSP index.jsp.
- This Action class will forward the results of its processing to either quote.jsp or index.jsp depending on the returned ActionForward.

The previous <action> element uses only a subset of the possible <action> element attributes, but the attributes that it does use are some of the most common ones.

Struts Plugins

Struts Plugins are modular extensions to the Struts Controller. Introduced in Struts 1.1, they are defined by the org.apache.struts.action.Plugin interface. Struts Plugins are useful when you're allocating resources or preparing connections to databases or even JNDI resources. We look at an example of loading application properties on startup later in this section.

This interface, like the Java Servlet architecture, defines two methods that must be implemented by all used-defined Plugins: init() and destroy(). These are the lifecycle methods of a Struts Plugin.

The current Struts Project 1.1 is prepackaged with a couple of good Plugin examples: org.apache.struts.tiles.TilesPlugin, which is used to initialize the Tiles framework, and org.apache.struts.validator.ValidatorPlugin, which initializes the Commons Validator.

init()

The init() method of a Struts Plugin is called when the JSP/Servlet container starts the Struts Web application containing the Plugin. It has the following signature:

```
public void init(ActionServlet servlet,
  ApplicationConfig applicationConfig)
  throws javax.servlet.ServletException;
```

This method is used to load and initialize resources that are required by your Plugin. Notice that the init() method receives a reference to the ActionServlet and the ApplicationConfig when invoked. The ActionServlet reference allows you to reference any Controller information, and the ApplicationConfig object provides access to the configuration information describing a Struts application. The init() method marks the beginning of a Plugin's life.

destroy()

The destroy() method of a Struts Plugin is called whenever the JSP/Servlet container stops the Struts Web application containing the Plugin. It has the following signature:

```
public void destroy();
```

This method is convenient when you're reclaiming or closing resources that were allocated in the Plugin.init() method. This method marks the end of a Plugin's life.

Creating a Plugin

Now that we have discussed what a Plugin is, let's look at an example Plugin implementation. As we stated earlier, all Plugins must implement the two Plugin methods init() and destroy(). To develop your own Plugin, you must complete the following steps. These steps describe the minimum actions that you must complete when creating a new Plugin:

1. Create a class that implements the org.apache.struts.action.Plugin interface.
2. Add a default empty constructor to the Plugin implementation. You must have a default constructor to ensure that the ActionServlet properly creates your Plugin.
3. Implement both the init() and destroy() methods and your implementation.
4. Compile the new Plugin and move it into the Web application's classpath.
5. Add a <plug-in> element to the application's struts-config.xml file describing the new Plugin. We look at this step in the next section.

Listing 4.1 contains an example Plugin implementation.

```
package ch04;

import java.util.Properties;
import java.io.File;
import java.io.FileInputStream;
import java.io.FileNotFoundException;
```

Code continued on following page

```
import java.io.IOException;

import javax.servlet.ServletException;
import javax.servlet.ServletContext;

import org.apache.struts.action.PlugIn;
import org.apache.struts.config.ApplicationConfig;
import org.apache.struts.action.ActionServlet;

public class WroxPlugin implements PlugIn {

  public static final String PROPERTIES = "PROPERTIES";

  public WroxPlugin() {

  }

  public void init(ActionServlet servlet,
    ApplicationConfig applicationConfig)
    throws javax.servlet.ServletException {

    System.err.println("---->The Plugin is starting<----");
    Properties properties = new Properties();

    try {

      // Build a file object referening the properties file
      // to be loaded
      File file =
        new File("PATH TO PROPERTIES FILE");

      // Create an input stream
      FileInputStream fis =
        new FileInputStream(file);

      // load the properties
      properties.load(fis);

      // Get a reference to the ServletContext
      ServletContext context =
        servlet.getServletContext();

      // Add the loaded properties to the ServletContext
      // for retrieval throughout the rest of the Application
      context.setAttribute(PROPERTIES, properties);
    }
    catch (FileNotFoundException fnfe) {

      throw new ServletException(fnfe.getMessage());
    }
    catch (IOException ioe) {

      throw new ServletException(ioe.getMessage());
    }
```

Code continued on following page

```
    }

    public void destroy() {

    // We don't have anything to clean up, so
    // just log the fact that the Plugin is shutting down
    System.err.println("---->The Plugin is stopping<----");
    }
}
```

Listing 4.1 WroxPlugin.java.

As you look over Listing 4.1, you will see just how straightforward Plugin development can be. This example shows a simple Plugin that implements the init() method (which contains the property-loading logic) and the destroy() method (which cleans up after the init() method). The purpose of this Plugin is to make a set of properties available upon application startup. Next, let's see how you can make the ch04.WroxPlugin available to your Struts application.

Configuring a Plugin

In this section, we show you how to deploy and configure a Plugin. For this example, let's use our application from Chapter 3 as the host of our new Plugin. To deploy and configure our ch04.WroxPlugin, you must:

1. Compile and move the Plugin class file into your application's WEB-INF/classes/ch04/ directory.
2. Add a <plug-in> element to your struts-config.xml file. An example <plug-in> entry, describing the previously defined Plugin, is shown in the following code snippet:

    ```
    <plug-in className="ch04.WroxPlugin"/>
    ```

> **The <plug-in> element should be the last element in the struts-config.xml.**

3. Restart the Struts Web application.

> **You can find this complete application in the ch04/src/ directory of this text's source distribution.**

When this deployment is complete, this Plugin will begin its life when the hosting application restarts--you should be able to see its output in the console window of your Tomcat instance.

The RequestProcessor

The RequestProcessor is the class that you need to override when you want to customize the processing of the ActionServlet. It contains a predefined entry point that is invoked by the Struts Controller with each request. This entry point is the processPreprocess() method.

Creating Your Own RequestProcessor

If you want to add your own specialized processing to the Controller, implement the processPreprocess() method, adding your specific logic and returning true to continue normal processing. If you want to terminate normal processing, return false to tell the Controller that the current request is complete. The following code snippet shows the default processPreprocess() implementation:

```
protected boolean processPreprocess(HttpServletRequest request,
  HttpServletResponse response) {

  return (true);
}
```

To create your own RequestProcessor, follow these steps:

1. Create a class that extends the org.apache.struts.action.RequestProcessor class.
2. Add a default empty constructor to the RequestProcessor implementation.
3. Implement your processPreprocess() method.

To see how all of this works, take a look at our example RequestProcessor implementation in Listing 4.2.

```
package ch04;

import javax.servlet.http.HttpServletRequest;
import javax.servlet.http.HttpServletResponse;
import javax.servlet.http.HttpServlet;
import javax.servlet.ServletException;
import javax.servlet.http.Cookie;

import java.io.IOException;
import java.util.Enumeration;

import org.apache.struts.action.RequestProcessor;

public class WroxRequestProcessor extends RequestProcessor {

  public WroxRequestProcessor() {
  }

  public boolean processPreprocess(HttpServletRequest request,
    HttpServletResponse response) {

    log("----------processPreprocess Logging-------------");
    log("Request URI = " + request.getRequestURI());
```

Code continued on following page

```
    log("Context Path = " + request.getContextPath());

    Cookie cookies[] = request.getCookies();
    if (cookies != null) {

      for (int i = 0; i < cookies.length; i++) {

        log("Cookie = " + cookies[i].getName() + " = " +
        cookies[i].getValue());
      }
    }

    Enumeration headerNames = request.getHeaderNames();

    while (headerNames.hasMoreElements()) {

      String headerName =
        (String) headerNames.nextElement();

      Enumeration headerValues =
        request.getHeaders(headerName);

      while (headerValues.hasMoreElements()) {

        String headerValue =
          (String) headerValues.nextElement();

        log("Header = " + headerName + " = " + headerValue);
      }
    }
    log("Locale = " + request.getLocale());
    log("Method = " + request.getMethod());
    log("Path Info = " + request.getPathInfo());
    log("Protocol = " + request.getProtocol());
    log("Remote Address = " + request.getRemoteAddr());
    log("Remote Host = " + request.getRemoteHost());
    log("Remote User = " + request.getRemoteUser());
    log("Requested Session Id = "
      + request.getRequestedSessionId());
    log("Scheme = " + request.getScheme());
    log("Server Name = " + request.getServerName());
    log("Server Port = " + request.getServerPort());
    log("Servlet Path = " + request.getServletPath());
    log("Secure = " + request.isSecure());
    log("-------------------------------------------------");

    return true;
  }
}
```

Listing 4.2 WroxRequestProcessor.java.

In the processPreprocess() method we are retrieving the information stored in the request and logging it to the ServletContext log. Once the logging is complete, the processPreprocess() method returns the Boolean value true and normal processing continues. If the processPreprocess() method had returned false, then the Controller would have terminated normal processing and the Action would never have been performed.

Configuring an Extended RequestProcessor

To deploy and configure our ch04.WroxPlugin, you must:

1. Compile the new RequestProcessor and move it to the Web application's classpath. For our purposes, you should move the compiled class file to the WEB-INF/classes/ch04/ directory of your Web application.

> **Again, for this example we use our application from Chapter 3 as the host of our new Plugin. You can find this complete application in the ch04/src/ directory of this book's source distribution.**

2. Add a <controller> element to the application's struts-config.xml file. The <controller> is used to describe the new RequestProcessor. An example <controller> entry, describing our new RequestProcessor, is shown in the following code snippet:

```
<controller
  processorClass="ch04.WroxRequestProcessor" />
```

When you add the <controller> element, it must follow the <action-mappings> element and proceed the <message-resources /> elements in the struts-config.xml file. A full description of the <controller> element and its attributes is included in Chapter 16. If you followed along with the examples in this and the proceeding chapter, then you should have a struts-config.xml file that looks something like Listing 4.3.

Restart the Struts Web application.

When this deployment is complete, the new RequestProcessor will take effect. To see the results of these log statements, log in and open the *<CATALINA_HOME>*/logs/localhost_log.*todaysdate*.txt file. You will see the logged request at the bottom of the log file.

```
<?xml version="1.0" encoding="ISO-8859-1" ?>

<!DOCTYPE struts-config PUBLIC
"-//Apache Software Foundation//DTD Struts Configuration 1.1//EN"
"http://jakarta.apache.org/struts/dtds/struts-config_1_1.dtd">

<struts-config>

  <form-beans>
    <form-bean name="lookupForm"
```

Code continued on following page

```
        type="ch04.LookupForm"/>
    </form-beans>

    <action-mappings>

      <action path="/Lookup"
        type="ch04.LookupAction"
        name="lookupForm" >
        <forward name="success" path="/quote.jsp"/>
        <forward name="failure" path="/index.jsp"/>
      </action>

    </action-mappings>

    <controller
      processorClass="ch04.WROXRequestProcessor" />

    <plug-in className="ch04.WROXPlugin"/>

  </struts-config>
```

Listing 4.3 struts-config.xml.

What's Next

In the next chapter, we continue our Controller discussions with a look at some prepackaged Struts Action classes, including DispatchAction, ForwardAction, IncludeAction, LookupDispatchAction, and SwitchAction.

Advanced Action Classes

In this chapter, we dig further into the Controller components of the Struts framework by covering the built-in Action classes that come with Struts. Our goal is to provide you with a solid understanding of the Struts built-in actions and how they can be used to facilitate the design of your Struts applications.

The Struts Framework provides several built-in actions. A few of these are essential for any Struts application. Others are necessary to add cohesion to what would normally be a granular collection of related actions.

ForwardAction and Beyond

Generally speaking, it is a bad idea to place within your JSP pages any direct links to other JSP pages. For one reason, it is not a good design decision; the struts-config.xml file, which is part of the Controller, should contain the entire flow of your application.

In the Model-View-Controller (MVC) architecture, it is the role of the Controller to select the next View. The Controller consists of Struts configuration, the ActionServlet, and the actions. If you add a link directly to another JSP, you are violating the architectural boundaries of the Model 2 architecture. (Model 2 is the instantiation of the MVC architecture for Web applications.)

At times, however, all you really need is just a plain link; you don't want (or need) an action to execute first. Perhaps there are no objects from the domain that need to be mapped into scope in order for the View to display. Perhaps the page is very simple. In this case, a better approach is to use the ForwardAction.

The ForwardAction acts as a bridge from the current View (JSP) and the pages it links to. It uses the RequestDispatcher to forward to a specified Web resource. It is the glue that allows you to link to an action instead of directly to a JSP.

Later, if you need to, you can change the ActionMapping in the Struts configuration file so that every page that linked to that action will link to the new action. Also, you can change the action to a custom one that you write instead of using the ForwardAction that Struts provides.

To use the ForwardAction, follow these steps:

1. Using the html:link tag with the action attribute, add a link to the JSP page that points to the action.
2. Create an action mapping in the Struts configuration file that uses the ForwardAction with the parameter attribute to specify the JSP path.

Let's say you have a JSP page that has a direct link to another JSP page:

```
<html:link page="/index.jsp">Home</html:link>
```

You have recently converted to the MVC/Model 2 architecture religion and you want to change the html:link tag to link to an action. Because you already have a link, simply change it as follows:

```
<html:link action="home">Home</html:link>
```

All you do is remove the page attribute and add an action attribute that points to the home action. Now you have to create the home action mapping. (The link in the previous code snippet would be expanded to a URL, like http://localhost:8080/actions/home.do.)

To add an action mapping to the home action that you referenced in your html:link tag, use this code:

```
<action
    path="/home"
    type="org.apache.struts.actions.ForwardAction"
    parameter="/index.jsp"
    />
```

The ForwardAction uses the parameter attribute so that you can specify the path. Notice the parameter is set to /index.jsp, which was what the page attribute of the html:link tag was originally set to. Thus, the parameter attribute indicates to where you want the ForwardAction to forward.

Linking to JSP Directly: More than Just Bad Design

In addition to being a bad design decision, linking directly to JSP pages may result in errors. The Controller maps in the correct ModuleConfig based on the request. Having the correct module implies that the resource bundles for that module are loaded. If the JSP page uses the resource bundles to display messages (which is required for internationalized applications), then you need to link to the action directly because that is the only way the JSP page is guaranteed to work properly.

Linking to Global Forwards Instead of Actions

From a purely design perspective, there are other alternatives to using the ForwardAction. Rather than linking to an action or a page, you could link to a global forward:

```
<html:link forward="home">Home</html:link>
```

In order for this to work, you would need to add a home forward to the Struts configuration file as follows:

```
<global-forwards >
    <forward name="home" path="/index.jsp"/>
</global-forwards>
```

I find this approach more aesthetically pleasing (barring any other possible ramifications, as we mentioned earlier). Thus, the main problem with linking forwards is not the design per se but that the functionality is the same as when you link directly to a JSP page. The previous html:link tag would result in the generation of a URL like this:

```
http://localhost:8080/actions/index.jsp
```

which is identical to the version of the html:link tag that used the page attribute.

You just change the global forward to point to an action mapping as follows:

```
<forward name="home" path="/home.do"/>
```

This seems to be the best possible practice. It is much more natural to link to forwards than to actions. In addition, this approach gives you the functionality of linking to an action with the intuitiveness of linking to a forward. And just as before, the actions themselves can be simple ForwardAction actions, and later you can change them to full-blown custom actions that talk to the Model. With this approach, you have the best of both worlds.

Using the forward Attribute vs. ForwardAction

For better or for worse, ForwardActions get used quite a bit—so much so that the Struts configuration file includes support for them. Thus, rather than doing this:

```
<action
    path="/home"
    type="org.apache.struts.actions.ForwardAction"
    parameter="/index.jsp"
    />
```

you can do this:

```
<action
    path="/home"
    forward="/index.jsp"
    />
```

These two mappings are functionally equivalent. It is an easy decision to pick the one you should use (the shorter one, of course). The nice thing about this approach is that you have to specify only two attributes, and you don't have to type in the fully qualified ForwardAction path. The forward attribute specifies the Web resource (in this case a JSP) that will be acting as the action.

Thus, the best approach for our example is to add this in the JSP:

```
<html:link action="home">Home</html:link>
```

Then add this in the global forwards section of the Struts configuration file:

```
<forward name="home" path="/home.do"/>
```

And this in the action mappings section of the Struts configuration file:

```
<action path="/home" forward="/index.jsp" />
```

Concise, straightforward, and well designed. Exactly what we needed!

Don't Bleed Your V into Your C

If you find that you have a lot of links to JSP pages from other JSP pages, you may not understand MVC very well. Using ActionForward may mask the fact that your design is inherently messed up. JSPs linking to other JSPs, whether they use ForwardAction or not, works only for the simplest of Web applications in MVC. If it works for your application, you are probably doing something wrong.

Complex MVC Web applications typically need an action to execute first; it is the job of the action to map Model items into scope so that the View (typically JSP) can display them. If this is not the case for your nontrivial Web application, you are probably putting too much logic in the JSP pages (or in custom tags that JSP pages use)—which can be the source of huge maintenance issues.

The JSP pages and custom tags should contain only display logic, and this logic should be kept to a bare minimum. Thus, the JSP pages and custom tags should not talk directly to the Model—they only display different pieces of the Model. In essence, they should speak only to the Value object and Data Transfer objects. Again, the action talks directly to the Model and delegates the display of the Model objects to the View. The Model in turn implements the persistence and business rules for the application.

Adopting a strict MVC architecture is generally a good idea; it keeps your JSP smaller and more focused. JSP are harder to test than actions, so adopting MVC increases the liquidity and flexibility of your code base.

In short, if you overuse the ForwardAction, you need to evaluate your understanding of the MVC architecture.

Forwards for Legacy Access

A lot of folks wrote Web applications before Struts existed. A lot of other folks have had to integrate with commercial portal implementations and other frameworks that are built on top of servlets (legacy and otherwise). Using the ForwardAction (or the forward attribute) is a good way to encapsulate this legacy integration from your View components (JSP and custom tags). In this manner, the ForwardAction acts as "legacy glue" to other Web resources.

Let's say that you have a legacy Web resource that you want to use with the form validation of Struts. However, your legacy resources are part of an elaborate MVC-based Web application framework that you created before the dawn of the Struts Framework.

This legacy resource does all types of neat things that you have not ported to the Struts Framework yet. For some reason (time and money come to mind), you do not want to rewrite this legacy resource—at least not yet.

For the purposes of simplicity, our sample legacy Web resource will be a servlet. Essentially, you want the servlet's doGet method to be called only if the ActionForm validates. Here is our example servlet:

```
public class LegacyServlet extends HttpServlet {


    protected void doPost(
         HttpServletRequest request,
         HttpServletResponse response)
         throws ServletException, IOException {
              //Get the mapping
         ActionMapping mapping =(ActionMapping)
                    request.getAttribute(Globals.MAPPING_KEY);

           //Get the UserForm
         UserForm form = (UserForm)
                    request.getAttribute(mapping.getName());

             // Do some fly, super tricky, whiz
              // bang legacy stuff

              //Generate some output
         response.getWriter().println("User name "
                             + form.getFirstName());
    }
}
```

Notice how the servlet can access the context that the Struts Framework mapped into request scope. Now suppose this servlet was mapped into our Web application like so:

```
<servlet>
    <servlet-name>legacy</servlet-name>
    <servlet-class>legacy.LegacyServlet</servlet-class>
</servlet>

<servlet-mapping>
    <servlet-name>legacy</servlet-name>
    <url-pattern>/legacy/roar</url-pattern>
</servlet-mapping>
```

Thus, posts to /legacy/roar would cause this servlet's doPost method to be called. Now, to map this servlet as an action that acts as a form handler, you need to do this:

```
<action
    path="/legacy"
    forward="/legacy/roar"
    input="/form/userForm.jsp"
    name="userForm"
    parameter="/legacy/roar"
```

```
            validate="true"
            scope="request"
            />
```

Of course, the previous code assumes that you have a form bean:

```
<form-beans>
    <form-bean name="userForm" type="form.UserForm" />
</form-beans>
```

Your input JSP (/form/userForm.jsp) would look like this:

```
...
     <h1>Legacy: Struts Form for userForm s</h1>

     <html:form action="/legacy">
          email :
               <html:text property="email"/></br>
          first name :
               <html:text property="firstName"/></br>
          last name :
               <html:text property="lastName"/></br>
          password :
               <html:password property="password"/></br>
          password check :
                <html:password
                          property="passwordCheck"/></br>
          userName :
                <html:text property="userName"/></br>
               <html:submit/><html:cancel/>
     </html:form>
```

Notice that the html:form tag points to an action path, just as you expect. Because the RequestDispatcher forward method to the servlet is invoked only if the ForwardAction's execute method is invoked, the doPost method of the legacy servlet is called only if the ForwardsAction's execute method is called. We set the validate attribute to true in the action mapping for this servlet, so the execute method of the ForwardAction is called only if the ActionForm (UserForm) validates (returns no ActionError objects).

IncludeAction

To understand the IncludeAction, be sure to read about the ForwardAction in the previous section. The IncludeAction is similar to the ForwardAction but is not used as much. You could rewrite the last example using the include action as follows:

```
<action
    path="/legacy"
    type="org.apache.struts.actions.IncludeAction"
    parameter="/legacy/roar"
    input="/form/userForm2.jsp"
    name="userForm"
    validate="true"
```

```
        scope="request"
        />
```

This shorter form uses the include attribute:

```
<action
    path="/legacy"
    include="/legacy/roar"
    input="/form/userForm2.jsp"
    name="userForm"
    parameter="/legacy/roar"
    validate="true"
    scope="request"
    />
```

So what is the difference between the IncludeAction and the ForwardAction? The difference is that you need to use the IncludeAction only if the action is going to be included by another action or JSP.

Therefore, if you have code in your JSP that looks like this:

```
<jsp:include page="/someWebApp/someModule/someAction.do"/>
```

the action could not use a ForwardAction because it would forward control to the new action rather than including its output within the output of the JSP—or throw a nasty IllegalStateException if the output buffer was already committed.

This discussion also applies to using the Tiles framework. A Tile can be a Web resource, and an action can be a Web resource. Thus, you could define a Tile as an action. Refer to Chapters 13 and 17 for more details.

DispatchAction

Oftentimes actions seem to be too plentiful and too small. It would be nice to group related actions into one class.

For example, let's say that a group of related actions all work on the same set of objects in the user session (HttpServletSession)—a shopping cart, for example. Another example is a group of actions that are all involved in the same use case. Yet another example is a group of actions that all communicate with the same session facade. Another example, and one that I use often, is grouping all actions involved in CRUD operations on domain objects. (CRUD stands for create, read, update, and delete. Think of an add/edit/delete/listing of products for an online e-commerce store.)

If you can group related actions into one class, you can create helper methods that they all use, thus improving reuse (or at least facilitating it). Also, if these helper methods are only used by these related actions and these actions are in the same class, then the helper methods can be encapsulated (hidden) inside this one class.

The DispatchAction class is used to group related actions into one class. DispatchAction is an abstract class, so you must override it to use it. It extends the Action class.

Rather than having a single execute method, you have a method for each logical action. The DispatchAction dispatches to one of the logical actions represented by the methods. It picks a method to invoke based on an incoming request parameter. The value of the incoming request parameter is the name of the method that the DispatchAction will invoke.

To use the DispatchAction, follow these steps:

1. Create an action handler class that subclasses DispatchAction.
2. Create a method to represent each logical related action.
3. Create an action mapping for this action handler using the parameter attribute to specify the request parameter that carries the name of the method you want to invoke.
4. Pass the action a request parameter that refers to the method you want to invoke.

First, you create an action handler class that subclasses DispatchAction:

```
public class UserDispatchAction extends DispatchAction {
    ...

}
```

Then, you create a method to represent each logical related action:

```
public class UserDispatchAction extends DispatchAction {
     public ActionForward remove(
          ActionMapping mapping,
          ActionForm form,
          HttpServletRequest request,
          HttpServletResponse response)
          throws Exception {

               System.out.println("REMOVE USER");
               ...
               return mapping.findForward("success");
     }

     public ActionForward save(
          ActionMapping mapping,
          ActionForm form,
          HttpServletRequest request,
          HttpServletResponse response)
          throws Exception {

               System.out.println("SAVE USER");
                ...
               return mapping.findForward("success");
     }

}
```

Notice these methods have the same signature (other than the method name) of the standard Action.execute method.

The third step is to create an action mapping for this action handler using the parameter attribute to specify the request parameter that carries the name of the method you want to invoke:

```
<action
    path="/dispatchUserSubmit"
    type="action.UserDispatchAction"
    parameter="method"
    input="/form/userForm.jsp"
    name="userForm"
    scope="request"
    validate="false">
    <forward name="success" path="/success.jsp" />
</action>
```

Based on this code, the DispatchAction that we created uses the value of the request parameter named method to pick the appropriate method to invoke. The parameter attribute specifies the name of the request parameter that is inspected by the DispatchAction.

The final step is to pass the action a request parameter that refers to the method you want to invoke:

```
<%@ taglib uri="/WEB-INF/struts-bean.tld" prefix="bean"%>
<%@ taglib uri="/WEB-INF/struts-html.tld" prefix="html"%>
...

     <html:link action="home">Home</html:link>

     <html:form action="/dispatchUserSubmit">
               ...
          action:
           <html:select property="method" size="2">
             <html:option value="save">Save</html:option>
             <html:option value="remove">Remove</html:option>
          </html:select> <br/>

          <html:submit/><html:cancel/>
     </html:form>
...
```

This code is simple. If the user selects Remove from the list and clicks the Submit button, then the remove method is invoked. If the user selects Save from the list and clicks the Submit button, then the save method is invoked. Because the method name corresponds to a request parameter, it is submitted to the DispatchAction, which invokes the method with a name corresponding to the value of the method parameter.

A more likely implementation would send a hidden field parameter instead of a drop-down list. (Chapter 12 contains such an example; it performs validation for a wizard-style set of forms.)

If you were going to implement a CRUD operation, you might have methods called create, read, list, update, and delete. Essentially the action that was responsible for the read operation (the R in CRUD) would set a string in request scope (set to update) that could be written back out as the hidden parameter by the JSP. The action that was responsible for creating a new user would set that same string to create. The idea is that the action *before* the form display always sets up the hidden parameter for the form to submit back to the next action. If there were a listing of users, the listing would have two links that point to this action, with parameters set to delete users and to read/update (edit) users:

```
method=delete and method=read&userid=10
```

LookupDispatchAction

The LookupDispatchAction is a lot like the DispatchAction (which it subclasses). It does a reverse lookup against the resource bundle. You have to implement a special method that maps the message resource keys to the methods you want to invoke.

To use the LookupDispatchAction, perform the following steps:

1. Create an action handler class that subclasses LookupDispatchAction.
2. Create a method to represent each logical related action.
3. Implement the getKeyMethodMap method to map the resource keys to method names.
4. Create an action mapping for this action handler using the parameter attribute to specify the request parameter that carries the name of the method you want to invoke.
5. Set up the messages in the resource bundle for the labels and values of the buttons.
6. Use bean:message to display the labels of the button in the bean.

The first step is to create an action handler class that subclasses LookupDispatchAction:

```
public class UserLookupDispatchAction extends
                                       LookupDispatchAction {

}
```

Next, you create a method to represent each logical related action:

```
public class UserLookupDispatchAction extends
                                       LookupDispatchAction {


     ...
     public ActionForward remove(
          ActionMapping mapping,
          ActionForm form,
          HttpServletRequest request,
          HttpServletResponse response)
          throws Exception {

               System.out.println("REMOVE USER (LOOKUP)");

               return mapping.findForward("success");
     }

     public ActionForward save(
```

```
            ActionMapping mapping,
            ActionForm form,
            HttpServletRequest request,
            HttpServletResponse response)
            throws Exception {

                System.out.println("SAVE USER (LOOKUP)");
                return mapping.findForward("success");
        }

        ...
    }
```

Notice these methods have the same signature of the standard Action.execute method (except for the method name).

Third, you must implement the getKeyMethodMap method to map the resource keys to method names:

```
    public class UserLookupDispatchAction extends
                                    LookupDispatchAction {

        protected Map getKeyMethodMap() {
            Map map = new HashMap();
            map.put("userForm.remove", "remove");
            map.put("userForm.save", "save");
            return map;
        }
        ...


    }
```

Next, create an action mapping for this action handler using the parameter attribute to specify the request parameter that carries the name of the method you want to invoke:

```
          <action
             path="/lookupDispatchUserSubmit"
             type="action.UserLookupDispatchAction"
             input="/form/userForm.jsp"
             name="userForm"
             parameter="method"
             scope="request"
             validate="true">
             <forward name="success" path="/success.jsp" />
          </action>
```

The fifth step is to set up the messages in the resource bundle for the labels and values of the buttons. Inside your resource bundle (e.g., application.properties), add the following two entries:

```
    userForm.save=Save
    userForm.remove=Remove
```

Finally, use bean:message to display the labels of the button in the bean:

```
<%@ taglib uri="/WEB-INF/struts-bean.tld" prefix="bean"%>
<%@ taglib uri="/WEB-INF/struts-html.tld" prefix="html"%>
...

     <html:link action="home">Home </html:link>
          <html:form action="/lookupDispatchUserSubmit">
           ...

               <html:submit property="method">
               <bean:message key="userForm.remove"/>
               </html:submit>

               <html:submit property="method">
               <bean:message key="userForm.save"/>
               </html:submit>

               <html:cancel>
               </html:cancel>
          </html:form>
     <body>
</html>
```

When the user clicks the Remove button on the HTML form, the remove method is called on the action. When the user clicks the Save button, the save method is called on the action.

SwitchAction

The SwitchAction class is used to support switching from module to module. Let's say you have an action that wants to forward to an action in another module. You perform the following steps:

1. Map in a SwitchAction into your Struts configuration file.
2. Create a forward or link to the SwitchAction that passes the page parameter and the module prefix parameter.

Let's break this down. Say you have a Web application that uses Struts. Struts has two modules: the default and a module called admin, as follows:

```
<servlet>
    <servlet-name>action</servlet-name>
    <servlet-class>
       org.apache.struts.action.ActionServlet
    </servlet-class>
    <init-param>
        <param-name>config</param-name>
        <param-value>/WEB-INF/struts-config.xml
        </param-value>
    </init-param>
    <init-param>
```

```
            <param-name>config/admin</param-name>
            <param-value>/WEB-INF/struts-config-admin.xml
            </param-value>
        </init-param>
        <init-param>
            <param-name>debug</param-name>
            <param-value>3</param-value>
        </init-param>
        <init-param>
            <param-name>detail</param-name>
            <param-value>3</param-value>
        </init-param>
        <load-on-startup>1</load-on-startup>
    </servlet>
```

The init parameter config/admin defines the admin module. The config init parameter defines the default module.

Now let's say you have an action in the default module that edits users and you want to delegate the display of those users to an action in the admin module. First, map a SwitchAction into the default module as shown here:

```
        <action
            path="/switch"
            type="org.apache.struts.actions.SwitchAction"
            >
        </action>
```

Now you can set up a forward in the action that edits the users as follows:

```
      <action
            path="/userSubmit"
            attribute="userForm"
            input="/form/userForm.jsp"
            name="userForm"
            scope="request"
            type="action.UserAction">
        <forward name="success"
         path="/switch.do?page=/listUsers.do&amp;prefix=/admin"
            />

    </action>
```

Notice that this forward passes two request parameters. The page parameter specifies the module relative action. The second parameter specifies the prefix of the module—in this case admin. You don't have to use forwards to use the SwitchAction; any JSP can link to the SwitchAction to move to any module. The listUser.do action is not defined in the default module; it is defined in the admin. The forward in this example forwards to the action at the path /admin/listUsers.do. The listUser.do is defined in /WEB-INF/struts-config-admin.xml, and the userSubmit.do action is defined in /WEB-INF/struts-config.xml.

What's Next

Let's review the basics: Don't abuse ForwardActions, and limit your use of IncludeActions. As part of your Struts development, try to understand the goals of MVC architecture and Model 2. Limit the logic in your JSPs, and avoid mixing your View and Controller. DispatchActions and LookUpDispatchActions let you add cohesion to your actions and group related actions in one class. If you use modules, you will need SwitchAction to navigate from one module to another.

In the next chapter, we begin building the presentation layer by working with the View components of the Struts Framework. We show you how to apply tags from Struts tag libraries, use ActionForm and DynaActionForm beans, and wire Views into a Struts application.

Building the Presentation Layer

In this chapter, we examine the View components of the Struts Framework. We show you how to apply tags from Struts tag libraries, use ActionForm and DynaActionForm beans, and wire Views into a Struts application.

The goal of this chapter is to give you an understanding of the Struts View and the components that you can use to construct the View.

Building a Struts View

As we discussed in Chapter 1, "Introducing the Jakarta Struts Project and Its Supporting Components," the Struts View is represented by a combination of JSPs, custom tag libraries, and optional Form bean objects. In the sections that follow, we examine each of these components.

At this point, you should have a pretty good understanding of what JSPs are and how they can be used, which will allow us to now focus on how JSPs are leveraged in a Struts application.

JSPs in the Struts Framework serve two main functions. The first is to act as the presentation layer of a previously executed Controller Action. This is most often accomplished using a set of custom tags that are focused on iterating and retrieving data forwarded to the target JSP by the Controller Action.

The second of these Views is used to gather the data required to perform a particular Controller Action. This is done most often with a combination of tag libraries and Form objects. This is the type of View that we will focus on for the remainder of this chapter.

JSPs That Gather Data

Now that you know how JSPs are deployed in a Struts application, let's take a look at one of the two most common uses of a JSP in a Struts application: using JSPs to gather data.

> **Here, we're using the application from Chapter 4, "Actions and the ActionServlet," to demonstrate Struts forms.**

You can choose among several methods when gathering data using a JSP. The most common method entails using the HTML <form> element and any combination of <input> sub-elements. When gathering form data, Struts uses a set of Struts-specific JSP custom tags that emulate the HTML <form> and <input> elements. The following code snippet contains a JSP that uses the Struts tags to gather data:

```
<html:form action="Lookup">
  <table width="45%" border="0">
    <tr>
      <td>Symbol:</td>
      <td><html:text property="symbol" /></td>
    </tr>
    <tr>
      <td colspan="2" align="center"><html:submit /></td>
    </tr>
  </table>
</html:form>
```

If we break this JSP into logical sections, you see three Struts HTML tags: <html:form />, <html:text />, and <html:submit />. These tags include special Struts functionality that is used to gather HTML form data. We look at each of these tags in the sections that follow.

> **The Struts library that includes the HTML tags is named, appropriately enough, the HTML Tag Library. It includes tags that closely mimic the same functionality common to HTML form elements. In our example, we saw only a small fraction of the entire HTML tag library. The remaining tags are discussed in Chapter 16 "The HTML Tag Library."**

The <html:form /> Tag

The first of these tags is the <html:form /> tag. This tag serves as the container for all other Struts HTML input tags. It renders an HTML <form> element containing all of the child elements associated with this HTML form. This tag, with its children, encapsulates the presentation layer of Struts form processing.

The form tag, in our example, uses only one attribute action. The action attribute represents the URL to which this form will be submitted. This attribute is also used to find the appropriate ActionMapping in the Struts configuration file, which we describe later in this section. The value used in our example is */Lookup*, which maps to an ActionMapping with a path attribute equal to /Lookup:

```
<html:form action="Lookup">
```

The Input Tags

Once you get past the <html:form /> tag, you will see that it also acts as a parent to two other HTML tags. These tags are synonymous with the HTML input elements.

The <html:text /> Tag

The first of the HTML input tags is the <html:text /> tag. This tag is equivalent to the HTML text input tag, with the only difference being the property attribute, which names a unique data member found in the ActionForm bean class named by the form's type attribute. The following code snippet contains our <html:text /> tag:

```
<html:text property="symbol" />
```

As you can see, the property attribute of this instance is set to the value *symbol*; therefore, when the form is submitted the value of this input tag is stored in the LookupForm's symbol data member.

The <html:submit />Tag

The second HTML tag that we use is the <html:submit /> tag. This tag simply emulates an HTML Submit button by submitting the request to the targeted action:

```
<html:submit />
```

When a View containing the <html:submit /> tag is requested, it is evaluated and the resulting HTML looks similar to this:

```
<form name="lookupForm"
  method="post"
  action="/wroxapp/Lookup.do">

  <table width="45%" border="0">
    <tr>
      <td>Symbol:</td>
      <td><input type="text" name="symbol" value=""></td>
    </tr>
    <tr>
      <td colspan="2" align="center">
        <input type="submit" value="Submit">
      </td>
    </tr>
  </table>
</form>
```

As you examine the evaluated form, notice that the value of the <input> elements is an empty string. This will not always be the case. If the form has already been submitted, the values stored in its data members will be used to pre-populate the input values.

Deploying JSPs to a Struts Application

Before we can continue looking at the role of a JSP in the Struts Framework, we must take a look at how JSPs are deployed to the Framework. JSPs are most often the target of a previous request; whether they are gathering or presenting data usually makes no difference as to how they are deployed. All JSPs should be deployed to a Struts application by using a <forward> element. This element is used to define the targets of Struts Actions, as shown in the following code snippet:

```
<forward name="error" path="/errorpage.jsp"/>
```

In this example, the <forward> element defines a View named error with a path of /errorpage.jsp.

To make this <forward> element available to a Struts application, nest it within one of two possible Struts configuration elements. The first element, <global-forward>, makes a JSP available globally to the entire application. This type of JSP deployment is useful for error and login pages. You perform this type of deployment by adding a JSP <forward> to the <global-forwards> section of the struts-config.xml file. Here's an example:

```
<global-forwards>
  <forward name="error" path="/errorpage.jsp"/>
</global-forwards>
```

This <forward> element states that /errorpage.jsp will be the target of all Struts Actions that return an ActionForward instance with the name login, as shown here:

```
return (mapping.findForward("error"));
```

> **The only time that a global forward is not used is when an <action> element has a <forward> declaration with the same name. In this instance, the <action> element's <forward> takes precedence.**

The second type of <forward> declaration is defined as an Action <forward>. These types of <forward> elements are defined as sub-elements of an <action> definition and are accessible only from within that <action>. The following code snippet shows an example that deploys our index.jsp and quote.jsp to the Lookup action:

```
<action path="/Lookup"
  type="ch03.LookupAction"
  name="lookupForm" >
  <forward name="success" path="/quote.jsp"/>
  <forward name="failure" path="/index.jsp"/>
</action>
```

The first <forward> definition states that /quote.jsp will be the target of ch03.LookupAction when this Action returns an ActionForward instance with the name success, as shown here:

```
return (mapping.findForward("success"));
```

The second <forward> definition tells the Controller to forward the results of a failed Action to /index.jsp when this Action returns an ActionForward instance with the name failure, as shown here:

```
return (mapping.findForward("failure"));
```

ActionForm Beans

The next thing that we must discuss is the org.apache.struts.action.ActionForm object. ActionForms are JavaBeans that are used to encapsulate and validate the request data submitted by an HTTP request. Our sample ActionForm, named LookupForm, is shown in Listing 6.1.

```
package ch03;

import javax.servlet.http.HttpServletRequest;
import org.apache.struts.action.ActionForm;
import org.apache.struts.action.ActionMapping;

public class LookupForm extends ActionForm {

  private String symbol = null;

  public String getSymbol() {

    return (symbol);
  }

  public void setSymbol(String symbol) {

    this.symbol = symbol;
  }

  public void reset(ActionMapping mapping,
    HttpServletRequest request) {

    this.symbol = null;
  }
}
```

Listing 6.1 LookupForm.java.

As you look over this ActionForm, notice that it extends the org.apache.struts.action.ActionForm class; all ActionForm beans must extend this class. Also notice that the LookupForm definition itself contains one data member, username, as well as three methods.

The first two of these methods are simple setters and getters used to access and modify the symbol data member. Setter methods are called by the Struts Framework when a request is submitted with a parameter matching a data member's name. This is accomplished using JavaBean reflection; therefore, the accessors of an ActionForm must follow the JavaBean standard naming convention.

The last method of this ActionForm, probably the most important method of this implementation, is the reset() method. This method is called by the Struts Framework with each request that uses the defined ActionForm. The purpose of this method is to reset all of the ActionForm's data members prior to the new request values being set. You should implement this method to reset your form's data members to their original values; otherwise, the default implementation will do nothing and your ActionForm's data members could be left holding stale data.

> **The ActionForm contains another important method that we did not cover in this chapter--the validate() method, which is used to validate form data. We discuss this method and the Struts error-management process in much more detail in Chapter 10, "Managing Errors."**

Deploying ActionForms to a Struts Application

Now that you have actually seen what an ActionForm does, let's take a look at how they are deployed. An ActionForm is deployed much like any other Struts object, using a named element in the struts-config.xml file. The element used to describe an ActionForm is the <form-bean> element, and all <form-bean> elements must be nested within the <form-beans> element. Here's an example showing the definition of the ch03.LookupForm:

```
<form-beans>

  <form-bean name="lookupForm"
    type="ch03.LookupForm"/>

</form-beans>
```

As you can see, this definition has a single <form-bean> element surrounded by a <form-beans> element, which as we explained acts as the parent to all <form-bean> elements. The <form-bean> shown here contains two attributes: name and type. These two elements act as a key/pair with the name attribute representing the key used to index the ch03.LookupForm and the type attribute indicating the fully qualified path to our ActionForm object.

The Steps of a Struts Form Submission

Now that you have seen the HTML form and its matching ActionForm, let's see how they interact. The best way to do this is to examine the form-submission process. When a user enters the appropriate HTML form values and clicks the Submit button, the following actions take place:

1. The Controller creates or retrieves (if it already exists) an instance of the ch03.LookupForm object. It then stores the instance in the session, if necessary.
2. The Controller then calls the ch03.LookupForm.reset() method to set the form's data members back to their default values.
3. The Controller next populates the ch03.LookupForm's symbol data member with the value entered in the <html:text /> input box.
4. Once the data members of the Form have been set, the Controller invokes the ch03.LookupAction.execute() method.

5. When the LookupAction.execute() method finishes its processing, it returns an ActionForward and the request is forwarded to the next View, at which point the process begins all over again.

That's it!. There is almost no limit to the type of Views that can exist in a Struts application, but this type of View is most tightly bound to the Struts Framework. This is also the type of View that you will see evolve throughout the remainder of this text.

An Alternative ActionForm:DynaActionForm Bean

One thing that you will notice as you develop more and more Struts applications is its dependence on the ActionForm object. You will find yourself developing a new ActionForm object for just about every piece of business logic that you would like to perform. What you eventually end up with is an ActionForm for every Action object. This process can get extremely time-consuming as well as irritating—especially when you are capturing trivial (one or two elements) form data.

Creating a DynaActionForm

Struts solves this problem with the introduction of a dynamic ActionForm, called the *DynaActionForm*. This version of the ActionForm object (a direct extension of the ActionForm) gives the developer the ability to define a Form object using an XML entry in the struts-config.xml file. An example entry that would replace the ch03.LookupForm is shown in the following snippet:

```
<form-beans>

  <form-bean name="lookupForm"
    type="ch03.LookupForm"/>

  <form-bean name="dynamicLookupForm"
    type="org.apache.struts.action.DynaActionForm">
    <form-property name="symbol"
      type="java.lang.String"
      initial="MSFT"/>
  </form-bean>

</form-beans>
```

This looks much like any other <form-bean>, with two exceptions. First, the type attribute points to the org.apache.struts.action.DynaActionForm object. This object is the Struts component that encapsulates the logic required to process a dynamic form.

The second difference is the addition of the <form-property> sub-element. This sub-element defines the properties and respective data members of the dynamic form that is being created. The <form-property> that we use in this example defines three attributes, as described in Table 6.1.

Table 6.1 Attributes of an <action> Element

Attribute	Description
name	Defines the unique identifier of this form. This value will be used by the <action> element as an index into the collection defined in the <form-beans> element.

Table continued on following page

Attribute	Description
initial	The default value of the property.
type	Defines the Java type that this property will be mapped to. For our example, we are using a java.lang.String. The available types are: java.lang.BigDecimal java.lang.BigInteger boolean and java.lang.Boolean byte and java.lang.Byte char and java.lang.Character java.lang.Class double and java.lang.Double float and java.lang.Float int and java.lang.Integer long and java.lang.Long short and java.lang.Short java.lang.String java.sql.Date java.sql.Time java.sql.Timestamp

Using a DynaActionForm

Once you have defined your DynaActionForm, you need to modify your application to use it. To make things a bit easier to understand, we are going to mimic the functionality of our ch03.LookupForm and ch03.LookupAction examples.

Creating a New Action

The first thing that you need to do is create a new Action object that provides the same functionality as the previously defined ch03.LookupAction, with the only difference being the method in which it retrieves data from a form. Our new Action retrieves the data from a DynaActionForm as opposed to a user-defined ActionForm. Listing 6.2 contains the source for our new Action.

```
package ch06;

import java.io.IOException;
import javax.servlet.ServletException;
import javax.servlet.http.HttpServletRequest;
import javax.servlet.http.HttpServletResponse;
import org.apache.struts.action.Action;
```

Code continued on following page

```
import org.apache.struts.action.ActionForm;
import org.apache.struts.action.ActionForward;
import org.apache.struts.action.ActionMapping;
import org.apache.struts.action.DynaActionForm;

public class DynamicLookupAction extends Action {

  protected Double getQuote(String symbol) {

    if ( symbol.equalsIgnoreCase("SUNW") ) {

      return new Double(25.00);
    }
    return null;
  }

  public ActionForward execute(ActionMapping mapping,
    ActionForm form,
    HttpServletRequest request,
    HttpServletResponse response)
    throws IOException, ServletException {

    Double price = null;

    // Default target to success
    String target = new String("success");

    if ( form != null ) {

      // Use the LookupForm to get the request parameters
      DynaActionForm lookupForm = (DynaActionForm)form;

      String symbol = (String)lookupForm.get("symbol");

      price = getQuote(symbol);
    }

    // Set the target to failure
    if ( price == null ) {

      target = new String("failure");
    }
    else {

      request.setAttribute("PRICE", price);
    }
    // Forward to the appropriate View
    return (mapping.findForward(target));
  }
}
```

Listing 6.2 DynamicLookupAction.java.

Let's take a close look at two sections of DynamicLookupAction. First let's examine the additional import statement (this is the package that contains the class definition for the DynaActionForm):

```
import org.apache.struts.action.DynaActionForm;
```

The next section we should consider is the actual code that retrieves data from the form:

```
// Use the LookupForm to get the request parameters
DynaActionForm lookupForm = (DynaActionForm)form;

String symbol = (String)lookupForm.get("symbol");
```

This code first retrieves the ActionForm object passed to the execute() method and then casts this object to its real type, a DynaActionForm. Once it has a reference to the DynaActionForm, it calls the DynaActionForm.get() method, passing it the name of the property to look up. This code works just like a HashMap.

After the proper data has been retrieved, the execute() method performs exactly as it did in the ch03.LookupAction implementation.

Deploying the New Action

Now that you have an Action object that leverages the DynaActionForm, compile the new Action, move the class file into the WEB-INF/classes/ch06/ directory, and make the following changes (shown in bold) to the struts-config.xml file:

```
<action-mappings>

  <action path="/Lookup"
    type="ch03.LookupAction"
    name="lookupForm" >
    <forward name="success" path="/quote.jsp"/>
    <forward name="failure" path="/index.jsp"/>
  </action>

  <action path="/DynamicLookup"
    type="ch06.DynamicLookupAction"
    name="dynamicLookupForm" >
    <forward name="success" path="/quote.jsp"/>
    <forward name="failure" path="/dynamicindex.jsp"/>
  </action>

</action-mappings>
```

When you examine the <action> element, you see that the only thing worth noting is the type and name attributes—everything else is the same, and the values of the type and name attributes simply point to our new ch06.DynamicLookupAction and DynamicLookupForm, respectively.

Creating a New JSP

The final step is creating a JSP that references your new DynaActionForm. To do this, create a new JSP that references the previously defined <action-mapping>. There is really nothing to this—you just change the action attribute of the <html:form> tag to point to the DynamicLookup action. Listing 6.3 shows our new JSP.

```
<%@ page language="java" %>
<%@ taglib
  uri="/WEB-INF/struts-html.tld"
  prefix="html" %>

<html>
  <head>
    <title>Wrox Struts Application - Dynamic Index</title>
  </head>

  <body>
    <table width="500" border="0"
      cellspacing="0" cellpadding="0">
      <tr>
        <td> </td>
      </tr>
      <tr>
        <td height="68" width="48%">
          <div align="left">
            <img src="images/wxmainlogowhitespace.gif">
          </div>
        </td>
      </tr>
      </tr>
      <tr>
        <td> </td>
      </tr>
    </table>

    <html:form action="DynamicLookup">
      <table width="45%" border="0">
        <tr>
          <td>Symbol:</td>
          <td><html:text property="symbol" /></td>
        </tr>
        <tr>
          <td colspan="2" align="center"><html:submit /></td>
        </tr>
      </table>
    </html:form>

  </body>
</html>
```

Listing 6.3 Dynamicindex.jsp.

Now you can restart the server and your new Action and JSP will be deployed and running. To see your changes in action, open your browser to the following URL and enter the symbol SUNW just as you did before:

```
http://localhost:8080/wroxapp/dynamicindex.jsp
```

Everything should run as it did when you used a static ActionForm without having actually created an object to hold your data. As you can see, using DynaActionForms saves you a tremendous amount of time and effort.

What's Next

In this chapter, we discussed the View component of the Struts Framework. We talked about the objects associated with Views that gather data, including the ActionForm and DynaActionForm. We also added a DynaActionForm to our existing sample application. The next chapter focuses on several methods that enable you to quickly debug your Struts applications.

7

Debugging Struts Applications

This chapter looks at the steps involved in debugging a Struts applications. We step through both our source code and the Struts source code. We use two popular and extremely useful integrated development environments (IDEs): the open-source Eclipse IDE and JetBrains' IntelliJ IDEA. The goal of this chapter is to provide you with the knowledge you need to debug a Struts application—from the ActionServlet's process() method to your own Action implementations.

The steps in this chapter assume that you have the components shown in Table 7.1 installed.

Table 7.1 Required Components

Component	Location
Java Standard Edition 1.4x	http://java.sun.com/j2se/downloads.html
Tomcat 4.1.24	http://jakarta.apache.org/builds/jakarta-tomcat-4.0/release/v4.1.24/

Eclipse

In this section, we show you how to prepare the Eclipse IDE for debugging a Struts application. Once we have Eclipse configured, we move on to actually debugging a Struts application.

Installing the Tomcat Plugin

First, let's cover the installation process required when you're using the Sysdeo Tomcat Plugin:

1. Download Eclipse 2.1.1 from http://www.eclipse.org/downloads/index.php.
2. Extract Eclipse to a convenient location. I am using c:\eclipse for this example.
3. Download the Struts 1.1 source (in a zip format) from http://www.apache.org/dist/jakarta/struts/source/.
4. Place the Struts zip file into another convenient location. This example uses c:\StrutsSrc.

> **You do not need to unzip this file. Eclipse will read the source files in the compressed zip format.**

5. Download and extract the Sysdeo Tomcat Plugin version 2.1.1 from http://www.sysdeo.com/eclipse/tomcatPlugin.html to the <*ECLIPSE_HOME*>/plugins directory.

> **There are other Tomcat Plugins, but at the time of this writing the Sysdeo one is the most complete.**

6. Start the Eclipse application. You should see a screen similar to the one shown in Figure 7.1.

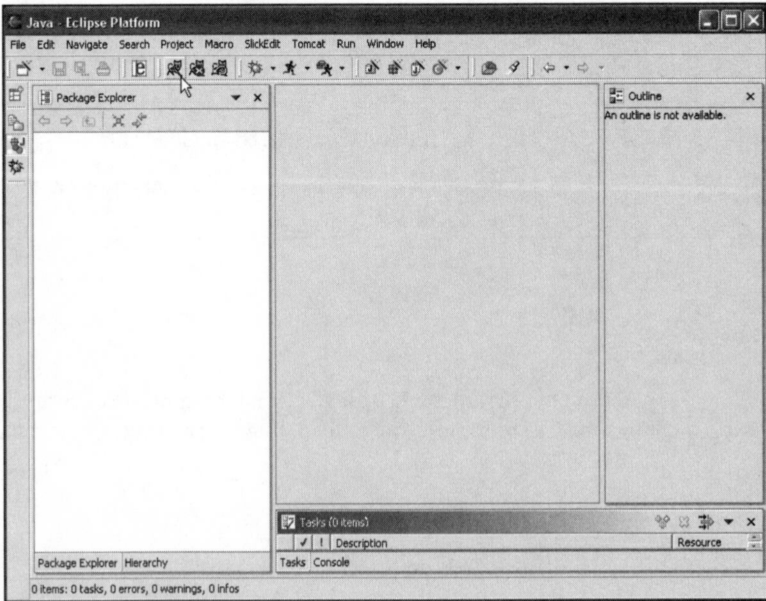

Figure 7.1 The Eclipse IDE.

As you look over Figure 7.1, notice that I have an extra menu: SlickEdit. This is a convenient tool (officially know as the Visual SlickEdit Plugin for WebSphere Studio & Eclipse) that I use to emulate a VI editor. This Plugin is something that I cannot get by without—it has nothing to do with debugging Struts applications.

7. You should now see a new toolbar that has three buttons on it. These buttons are used to start, stop, and restart Tomcat, respectively. If you do not see these buttons, select the Window > Customize Perspectives command, and in the resulting dialog box, choose Other Node and select the Tomcat checkbox. Your screen should resemble the one shown in Figure 7.2.

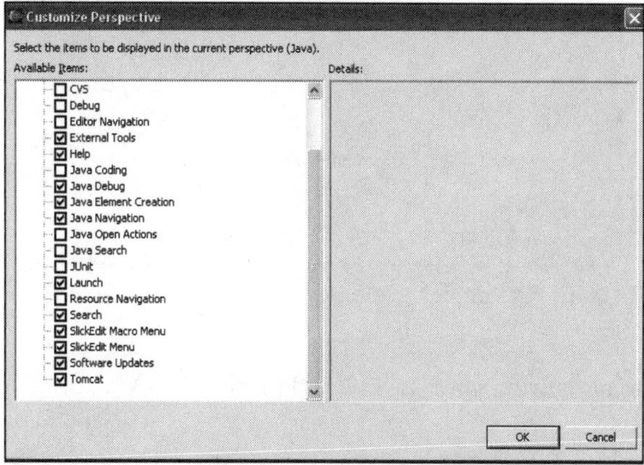

Figure 7.2 The Customize Perspectives dialog box.

8. Now you need to tell the Sysdeo Plugin the location of your Tomcat installation. You do this by first opening the Eclipse Preferences dialog box, shown in Figure 7.3.

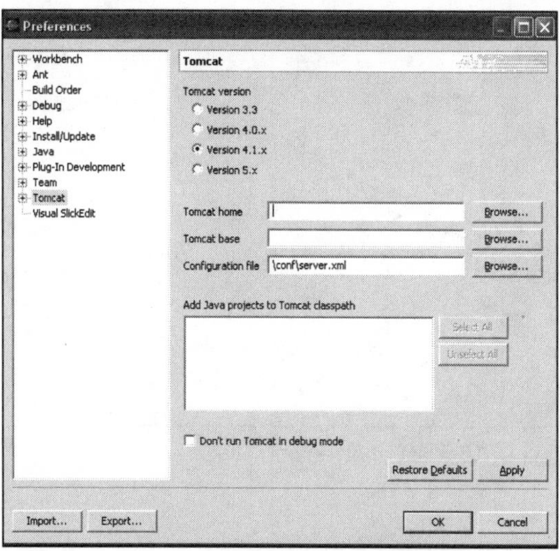

Figure 7.3 The Eclipse Preferences dialog box.

9. Go ahead and select Tomcat Version 4.1.*x*, enter the location of your Tomcat installation, and click the Apply button. Your settings should look like the ones shown in Figure 7.4.

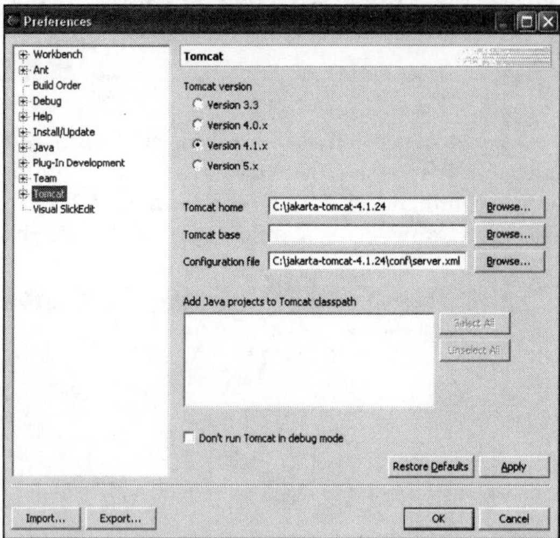

Figure 7.4 Tomcat settings.

10. The final step is configuring your Java Virtual Machine (JVM). You do this by going back to the Preferences menu.

11. Expand Java > Installed JREs and either make sure that you have an installed Java Runtime Environment (JRE) or browse to your installed JRE. Figure 7.5 shows a list of installed JREs.

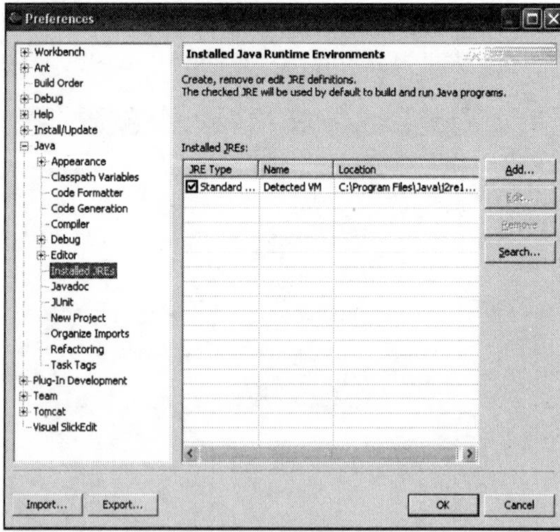

Figure 7.5 A list of installed JREs.

> **When using Sysdeo's Tomcat Plugin, have version 1.4*x* of the Java Development Kit (JDK) installed.**

Debugging Your Struts Application with Eclipse

Now let's begin debugging our wroxapp Web application, using our recently installed Sysdeo Plugin.

Complete the following steps:

1. Start the Eclipse application.
2. Select File > New Project. You should see a dialog box similar to the one shown in Figure 7.6.

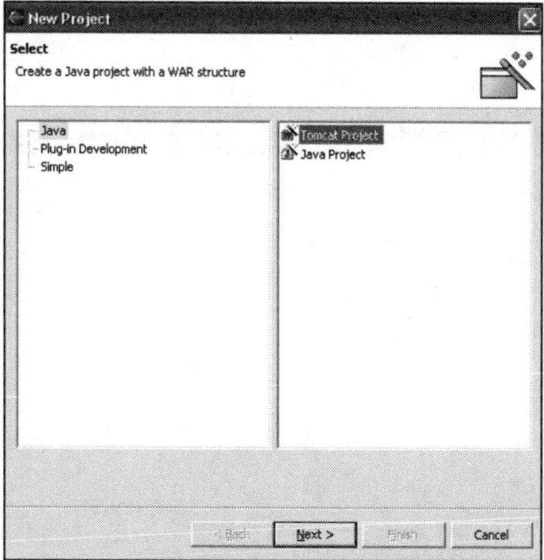

Figure 7.6 The New Project dialog box.

3. Click the Next button. In the New Tomcat Project dialog box, enter the value *wroxapp* as the name of the project, deselect the Use Default checkbox, browse to the directory containing the most recent version of the wroxapp Web application, and select the wroxapp directory. Your dialog box should now look like the one shown in Figure 7.7.
4. Now click the Next button, and you will be prompted to enter the Tomcat project settings. The settings on this screen should match the ones shown in Figure 7.8; if not, make the appropriate changes and then click the Finish button.

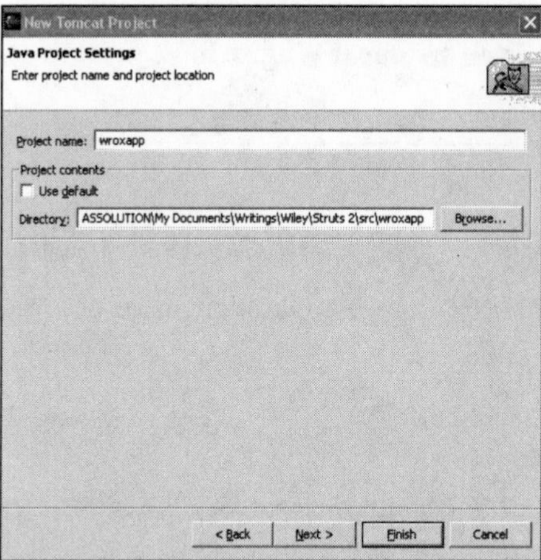

Figure 7.7 Our Java project settings.

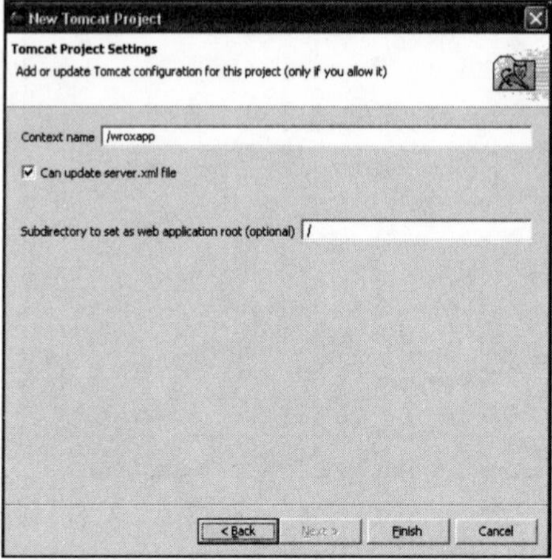

Figure 7.8 The Tomcat project settings.

5. You should now see the main Eclipse window with the wroxapp project, including its associated subcomponents, in the Package Explorer. Figure 7.9 shows the results of our efforts.

6. This next step seems to be a bit of a kludge and is necessary only if you have completed the examples from Chapter 9, "Internationalizing Your Struts Applications." (If you have not completed the examples in that chapter, you can skip ahead to Step 10.) As you may recall, we created two resource bundles containing Locale-dependent strings that we placed in the WEB-INF/classes directory. Eclipse does not by default treat the WEB-INF/classes directory as a source directory and therefore will remove any extraneous files prior to rebuilding the application. To change this behavior, complete the following three steps.

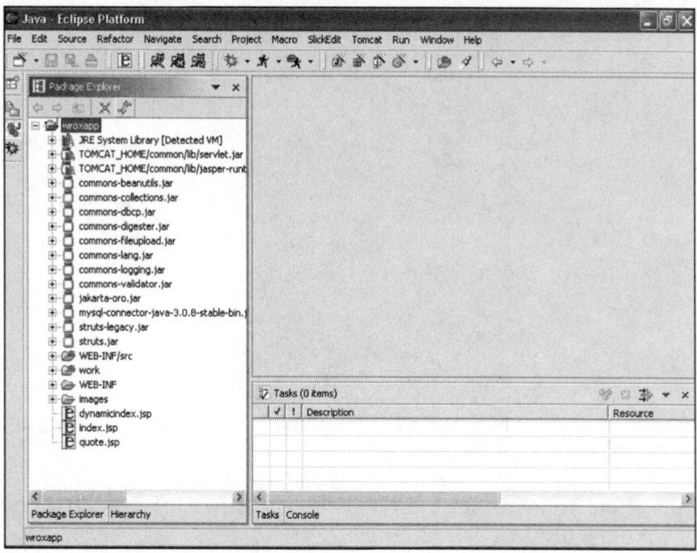

Figure 7.9 The main Eclipse window with the wroxapp project.

7. Select Project > Properties, expand the Java Build Path Node, and select the Source tab. You should see a dialog box similar to that shown in Figure 7.10.

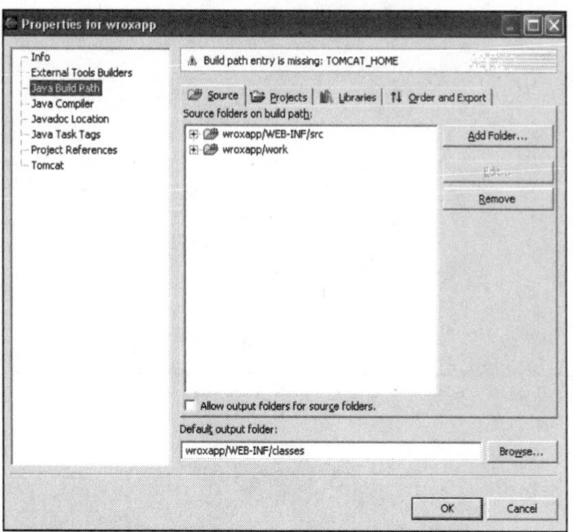

Figure 7.10 The Project Properties dialog box.

8. Now click the Add Folder button, expand the wroxapp node until you see the classes directory, and then select that directory, as shown in Figure 7.11.

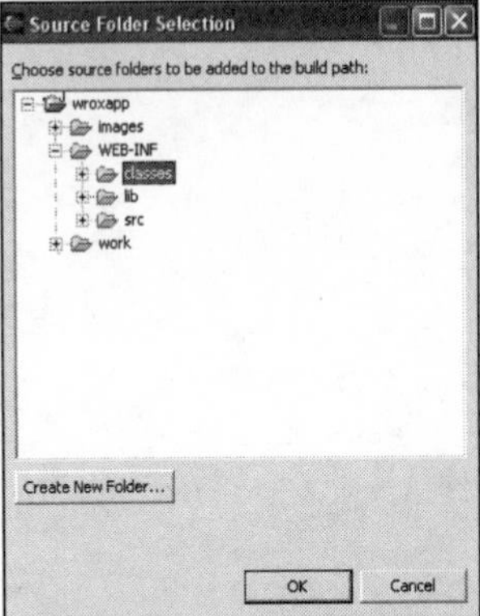

Figure 7.11 The Source Folder Selection dialog box.

9. Click OK. You should now see the WEB-INF/classes directory listed in the Source Folders Build Path, as shown in Figure 7.12.

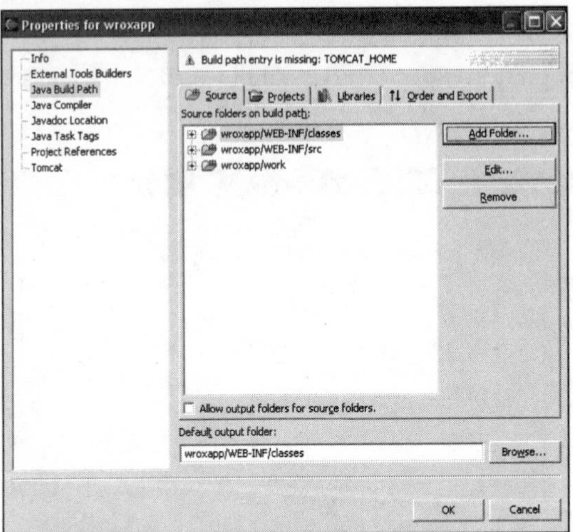

Figure 7.12 The Source Folders Build Path.

10. Now you need to rebuild the entire application. You can do this by selecting Project > Rebuild All.

At this point, you have everything you need to debug your Struts application—which is the focus of our next section.

Stepping Through Your Source

Now that you have everything configured to debug your application, let's get started. This is the easy part—there are only a few places that you will want to set breakpoints.

The first of these places is in the source of your ActionForm object. For this example, let's look at the ch03.LookupForm. To set a breakpoint in this ActionForm implementation, open the source file by double-clicking on it in the Package Explorer. Locate it in the WEB-INF/src/ch03/ directory. Once you have this file open, scroll down to the validate() method and double-click on the left side of the editor pane on the line containing the following snippet:

```
ActionErrors errors = new ActionErrors();
```

This sets a breakpoint on this line, which tells Eclipse that it should stop on this line whenever it encounters this piece of code while debugging. If you follow these steps correctly, your editor pane should have a breakpoint marker similar to the one in Figure 7.13.

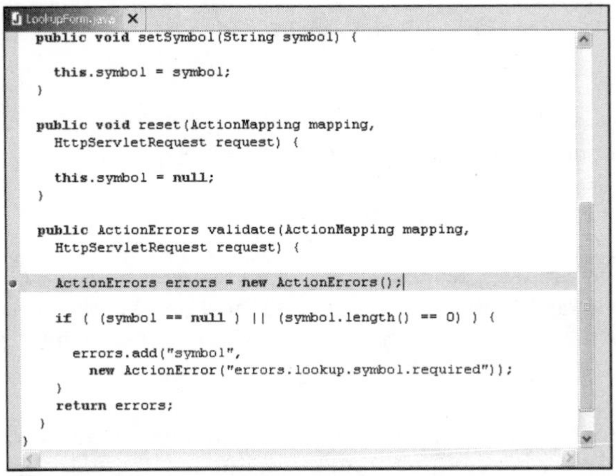

```
LookupForm.java
  public void setSymbol(String symbol) {

    this.symbol = symbol;
  }

  public void reset(ActionMapping mapping,
    HttpServletRequest request) {

    this.symbol = null;
  }

  public ActionErrors validate(ActionMapping mapping,
    HttpServletRequest request) {

    ActionErrors errors = new ActionErrors();

    if ( (symbol == null ) || (symbol.length() == 0) ) {

      errors.add("symbol",
        new ActionError("errors.lookup.symbol.required"));
    }
    return errors;
  }
}
```

Figure 7.13 A source breakpoint.

The next place that you want to test is the Action implementation, so find the ch03.LookupAction and open the source file by double-clicking on it in the Package Explorer. Locate it in the WEB-INF/src/ch03/ directory, and once you have the file open, scroll down to the execute() method. Double-click on the left side of the editor pane on the line containing this code snippet:

```
String target = new String("success");
```

Okay, now it is time to test your breakpoints. To begin this process, click the Start Tomcat button on the main toolbar. As the Tomcat Plugin starts, it prints quite a bit of information to the Eclipse console. The application is not ready for debugging until you see output similar to that shown in Figure 7.14. The line you are looking for is the Jk running line.

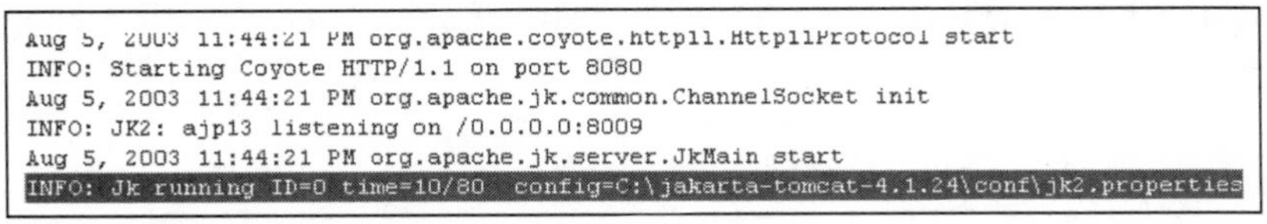

```
Aug 5, 2003 11:44:21 PM org.apache.coyote.http11.Http11Protocol start
INFO: Starting Coyote HTTP/1.1 on port 8080
Aug 5, 2003 11:44:21 PM org.apache.jk.common.ChannelSocket init
INFO: JK2: ajp13 listening on /0.0.0.0:8009
Aug 5, 2003 11:44:21 PM org.apache.jk.server.JkMain start
INFO: Jk running ID=0 time=10/80  config=C:\jakarta-tomcat-4.1.24\conf\jk2.properties
```

Figure 7.14 Starting the Tomcat Plugin.

You should also see a debug window. This window allows you to step through the actual application. It features a toolbar with nine buttons that you can use to perform various debug operations (only the appropriate buttons are enabled). Figure 7.15 shows the debug window for this application.

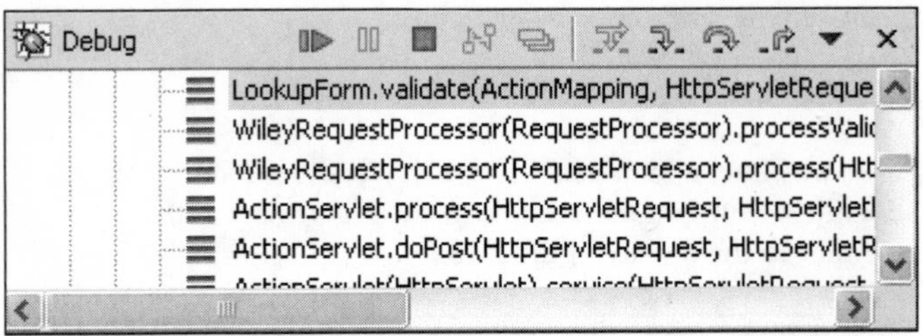

Figure 7.15 The Eclipse debug window.

Once this output is printed and you can see the active debug window, you can begin the debugging process. To get this process under way, open a browser to the following URL:

```
http://localhost:8080/wroxapp/index.jsp
```

Now enter the value *SUNW* into the text box and click the Submit button. This activates the Eclipse debugger and runs the wroxapp, until it reaches its first breakpoint in the LookupForm. To step through your source, select one of the buttons from the Debug toolbar—at this point, I recommend using the Step Over button.

As you are stepping through each line of code, keep an eye on the Variables window—you will see the values in this window change as your variables are manipulated. You can also expand this node when you want to view the data members local to the object you are currently debugging. Figure 7.16 shows the Variables window.

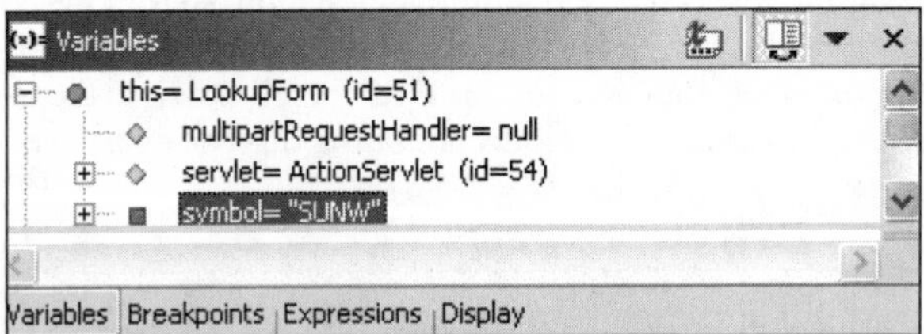

Figure 7.16 The Eclipse Variables window.

When you have stepped past the last line in the validate() method, the source code window displays a message stating that it cannot find the source for the RequestProcessor, as shown in Figure 7.17.

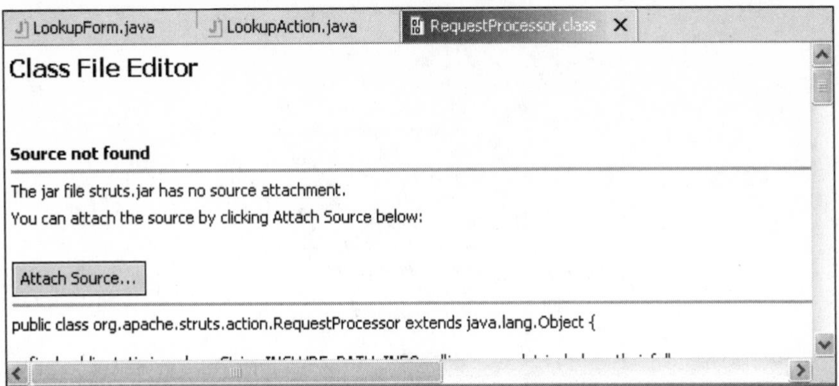

Figure 7.17 The missing source code message.

This message appears when you have not told the debugger about the Struts source code. We do this in the following section, but before we move on, go ahead and click the Resume button on the Debug menu. This resumes the current process, which continues until it reaches the next breakpoint (in this case, in the LookupAction.execute() method). This breakpoint allows you to step through your execute() method and monitor the processing of both the data passed to your Action and the logic encased in this Action.

As I am sure you are aware, there are many other places that can be debugged in a Struts application. The goal of this section was not to identify every debuggable entry point, but rather to give you a look at some of the more common places you can add breakpoints.

Stepping Through the Struts Source

In this section, we go one step further in our debugging efforts: we actually step through the Struts source. This exercise should give you a good handle on how Struts processes its requests.

To begin, make sure that you retrieved the Struts source (as described in Step 3 of the "Installing the Tomcat Plugin" section of this chapter). Also verify that you have version 1.1 of both the Struts source and JAR files. Once you have verified this, complete these steps:

1. Stop the Tomcat Plugin by selecting the Stop Tomcat button.
2. Select the struts.jar node from the Package Explorer (as shown in Figure 7.18).
3. Right-click on the struts.jar node and select Properties.
4. Select the Java Source Attachment node.
5. Click the External File button and browse to the location of your jakarta-struts-1.1-src.zip file. At this point, the Properties dialog box should look like the one in Figure 17.9.
6. Now click the OK button.

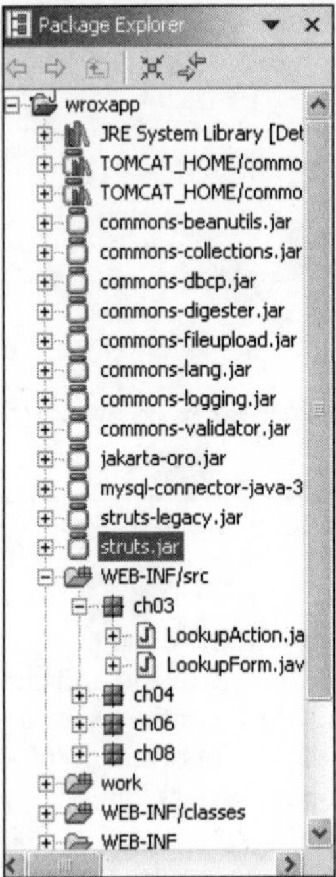

Figure 7.18 Selecting the struts.jar node from the Package Explorer.

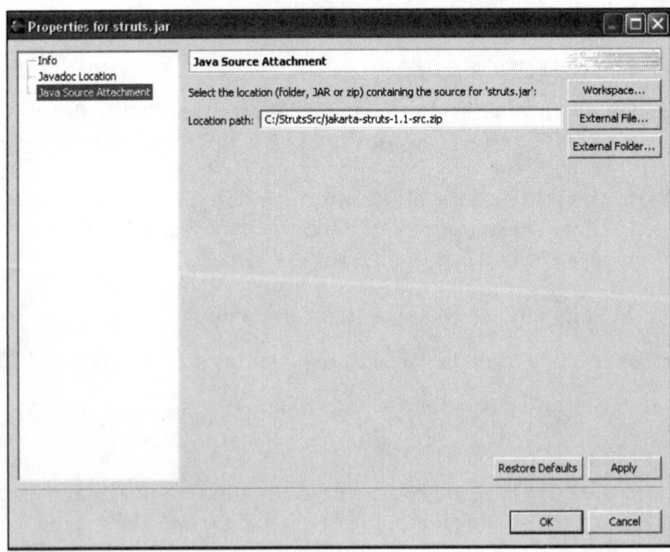

Figure 7.19 The Properties dialog box.

You are ready to step through the Struts source. Again, there are several places that you can set a breakpoint, but one of the best places to begin your debugging of a Struts application is in the ActionServlet—this is where everything begins in a Struts application. And the best place to begin within the ActionServlet is the process() method. If you remember from our previous discussions, the process() method is the first method called by the ActionServlet's doPost() and doGet() methods and is the entry point to all Struts requests.

To set a breakpoint in the process() method, complete the following steps:

1. Expand the struts.jar node (found in the Package Explorer).
2. Expand the org.apache.struts.action node.
3. Expand the ActionServlet node.
4. Scroll down until you find the process() method and double-click on it.
5. Find the following line and set a breakpoint:

```
RequestUtils.selectModule(request, getServletContext());
```

That's all there is to it. Now restart Tomcat and open your browser to the following wroxapp/index.jsp:

```
http://localhost:8080/wroxapp/index.jsp
```

Go ahead and enter *SUNW* again and click the Submit button. When Tomcat receives the request, it sends the request on to the ActionServlet, and its doPost() method calls the process() method—which is where you set your breakpoint. Now you can simply step through the application as if it was any other application.

When you are debugging the process() method, you must click the Step Into button if you want to follow the entire processing of the request.

IntelliJ

In this section, we explain the steps needed to prepare Idea's IntelliJ IDE for debugging a Struts application.

As you complete the following sections, notice that we include some text from the Eclipse sections of this chapter. This text is duplicated because it applies to both IDEs.

Configuring Tomcat

When debugging Web applications using Tomcat and IntelliJ, you have to make a few changes to the way Tomcat runs. This is because IntelliJ uses something called the Java Platform Debugger Architecture (JPDA).

> **If you are using a 4.0.*x* version of Tomcat, you may feel comfortable skipping this step. If so, you can move on to the next section, "Configuring IntelliJ."**

The JPDA is a multi-tiered debugging architecture that allows you to debug Java applications using a standard protocol. The implementation of this architecture supported by IntelliJ allows you to attach to a debug process using a special port you define during the configuration of Tomcat. To configure Tomcat for JPDA support, you must complete these steps:

1. Open catalina.bat or catalina.sh file (based on your operating system).
2. Find the environment variable JPDA_TRANSPORT and change its value from *dt_shmem* to *dt_socket*.
3. Find the environment variable JPDA_ADDRESS and change its value from *dt_jdbcon* to *dt_5050*.
4. Make sure that you have the wroxapp installed to Tomcat.
5. Start Tomcat (from the *<TOMCAT_HOME>*/bin directory) using the following command for Windows:

```
catalina.bat jpda start
```

and this command for UNIX:

```
catalina.sh jpda start
```

> **At this point, Tomcat should be properly configured. Let's move on to the following section, which focuses on setting up IntelliJ for Web application debugging.**

Configuring IntelliJ

This section covers the configuration process for IntelliJ's Tomcat Plugin. IntelliJ, much like many other IDEs, comes packaged with a Tomcat Plugin. To use it, follow these steps:

The following steps assume that you are using IntelliJ 3.0.4.

1. Acquire and install IntelliJ according to the documentation packaged with the IDE.
2. Start the IntelliJ application. You should see a figure similar to the image in Figure 7.20.
3. Select File >New Project.
4. Enter the name *wroxapp* into the Name text box.
5. Enter the location of your wroxapp. For our application this value is *<TOMCAT_HOME>*/webapps/wroxapp/wroxapp.ipr.

> **When working in a real development environment, you will want to locate your Web application outside Tomcat's webapps directory. If you choose to do this, be sure to add a <Context> entry to your Tomcat server.xml file that points to the location of your Web application.**

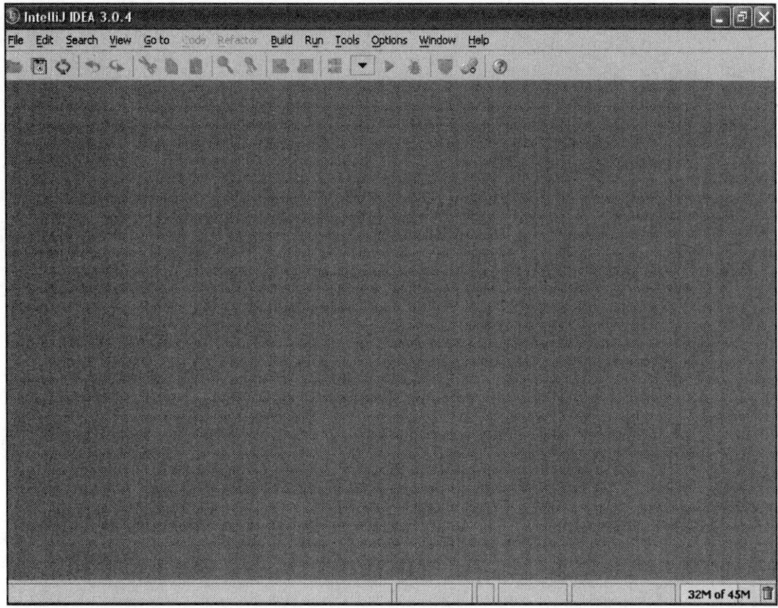

Figure 7.20 The IntelliJ IDE

6. Select the Target JDK. We are using 1.4.1_02.
7. Enter the location of your compiler output path. In this case, you will want it to point to the classes directory, which is directly under the WEB-INF directory. Figure 7.21 shows the completed dialog box.

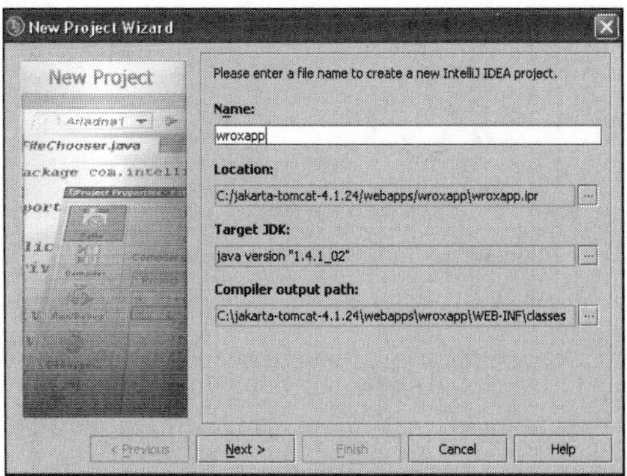

Figure 7.21 The New Project wizard.

8. Click the Next button twice. You can ignore the Project Path setting—the default will work fine.

9. Now add all of your source file locations. In this example, you should have the JDK 1.4 and <*TOMCAT_HOME*>/webapps/wroxapp/WEB-INF/src. Figure 7.22 shows the current values associated with the wroxapp project.

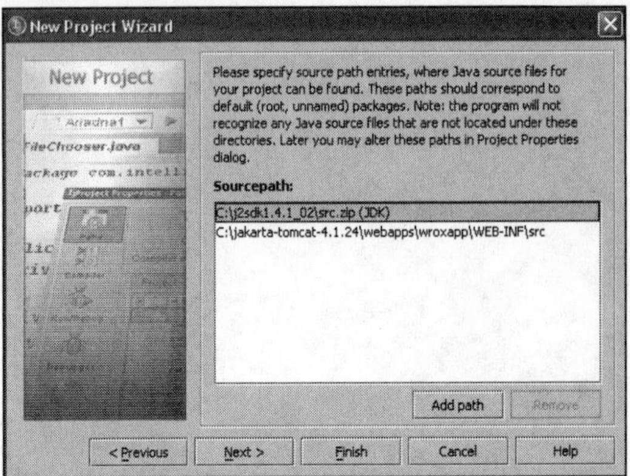

Figure 7.22 Our project's Source path settings.

10. Now click Finish. You should now see your new project in the Project window, as shown in Figure 7.23.

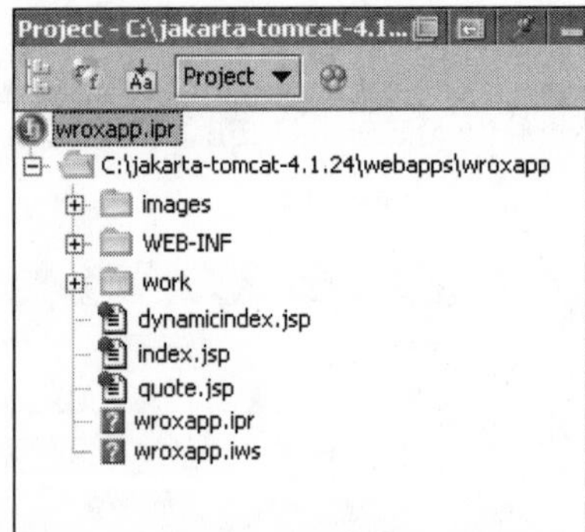

Figure 7.23 The wroxapp project.

11. At this point, you have a valid IntelliJ project, but you may notice that some of the objects listed in your source window are displayed in red. This is because the project is missing some JAR files from its classpath. To make the appropriate additions, right-click the project name in the Project window and select Project Properties.

12. Now select the Libraries tab. You should see the settings shown in Figure 7.24.

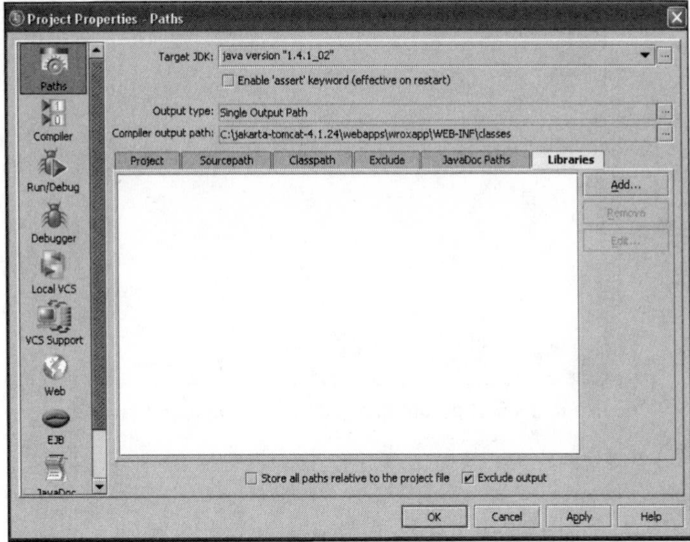

Figure 7.24 The Project Properties dialog box, Libraries tab.

13. Click the Add button. You should see the dialog box shown in Figure 7.25 (if you have not previously set up a library).

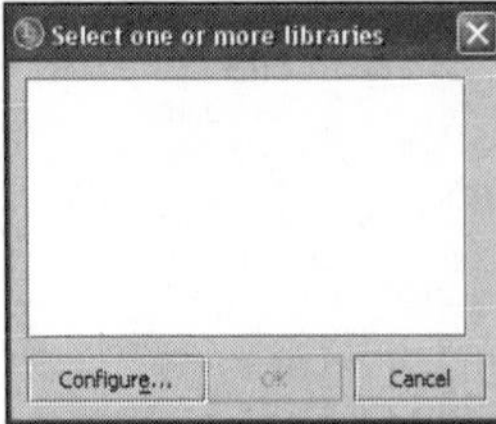

Figure 7.25 The Library Selection dialog box.

14. Click the Configure button.

15. The Configure Libraries dialog box opens (see Figure 7.26).

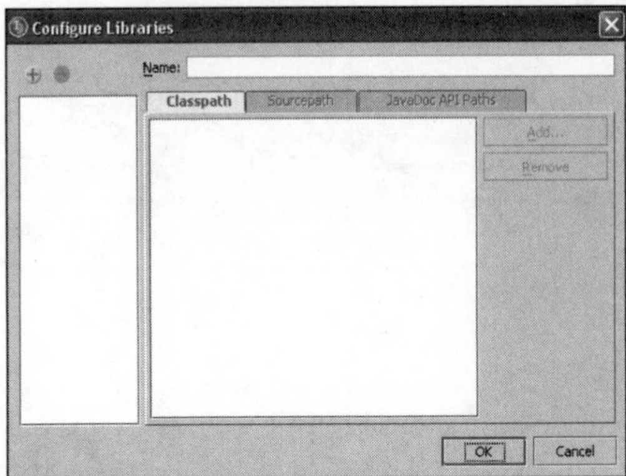

Figure 7.26 The Configure Libraries dialog box.

16. Select the Plus symbol and enter the name *Struts 1.1*.

17. Select the Classpath tab and click the Add button.

18. Browse to the location of your wroxapp/WEB-INF/lib directory and select all of the JAR files in this directory. You should see a dialog box similar to Figure 7.27.

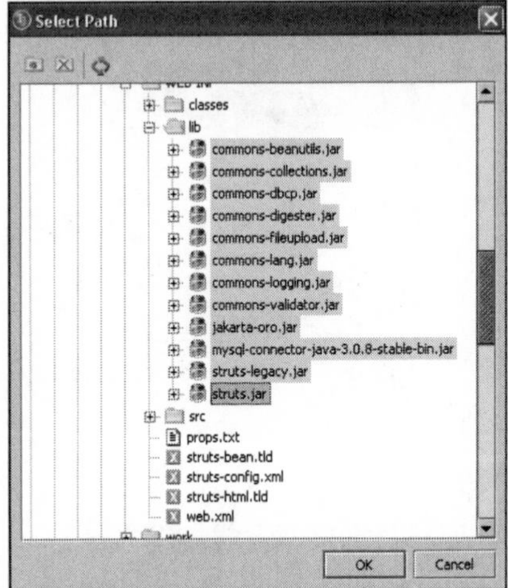

Figure 7.27 The Select Path dialog box.

19. Now click OK until you reach the Select Libraries dialog box.

20. Click the Configure button again and repeat the same process, except this time name the library *Servlets* and browse to the servlet.jar file within the *<TOMCAT_HOME>*/common/lib directory.

21. When you have defined both of these libraries, as shown in Figure 7.28, select them both and click OK until you are back at the main IDE window.

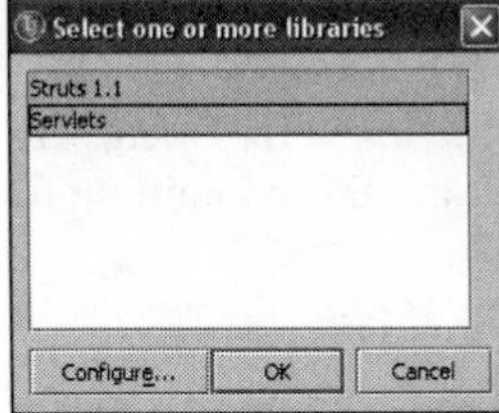

Figure 7.28 Select the Struts 1.1 and Servlets libraries.

22. Now you need to rebuild the entire application. You can do this by selecting the Build > Rebuild Project command.

At this point you have everything that you need to debug your Struts application—the focus of our next section.

Stepping Through Your Source

Now that you have everything configured to debug your application, let's get started. This is the easy part—there are only a few places that you will want to set breakpoints.

The first of these places is in the source of your ActionForm object. For this example, let's look at the ch03.LookupForm. To set a breakpoint in this ActionForm implementation, open the source file by double-clicking on it in the Package Explorer. You will find it in the WEB-INF/src/ch03/ directory. Once you have this file open, scroll down to the validate() method and double-click on the left side of the editor pane on the line containing the following snippet:

```
ActionErrors errors = new ActionErrors();
```

This sets a breakpoint on this line, which tells IntelliJ that it should stop on this line whenever it encounters this piece of code while debugging. If you follow these steps correctly, your editor pane should have a breakpoint marker similar to the one shown in Figure 7.29.

```
LookupAction.java    LookupForm.java

  public void reset(ActionMapping mapping,
    HttpServletRequest request) {

    this.symbol = null;
  }

  public ActionErrors validate(ActionMapping mapping,
    HttpServletRequest request) {

    ActionErrors errors = new ActionErrors();

    if ( (symbol == null ) || (symbol.length() == 0) ) {

      errors.add("symbol",
        new ActionError("errors.lookup.symbol.required"));
    }
    return errors;
  }
}
```

Figure 7.29 A source breakpoint.

The next place that you want to test is your Action implementation, so find the ch03.LookupAction and open the source file by double-clicking on it in the Package Explorer. Locate it in the WEB-INF/src/ch03/ directory, and once you have this file open, scroll down to the execute() method. Double-click on the left side of the editor pane on the line containing this code snippet:

```
String target = new String("success");
```

It is now time to test your breakpoints. To begin this process, click the Debug button on the main toolbar to display the Debug window. Select the WebApp tab and complete the following steps:

1. Select the Plus symbol.
2. Enter *wroxapp* in the Name text box.
3. Click the Configure button. You will see the Web dialog box.
4. Select the Enable Web Application Support checkbox.
5. Click the Add button and enter *wroxapp* for the name. Browse to the root directory of your wroxapp Web application. Once you enter these values, your dialog box should look the one shown in Figure 7.30.

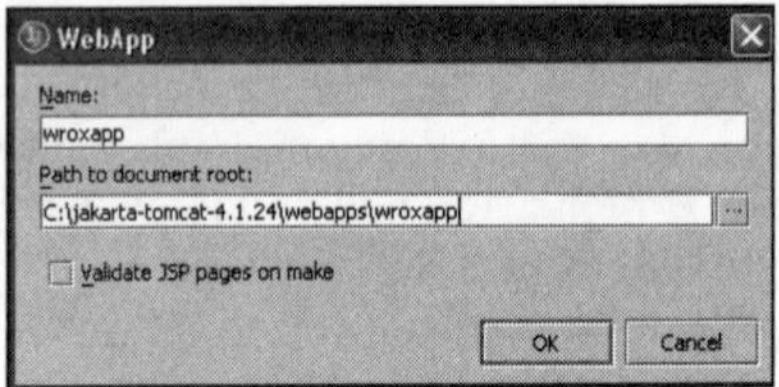

Figure 7.30 The WebApp dialog box.

6. Click OK until you return to the Debug dialog box.
7. Enter the location of your Tomcat installation in the Catalina Home text box. This should automatically populate the Path To Catalina Configs text box. When you have modified all these options, your dialog box should like the one shown in Figure 7.31.

> **If the Debug button in this dialog box is not active, try switching between tabs and check the availability of the Debug button once more. This seems to be a simple bug, and once the button is active, everything seems to work fine.**

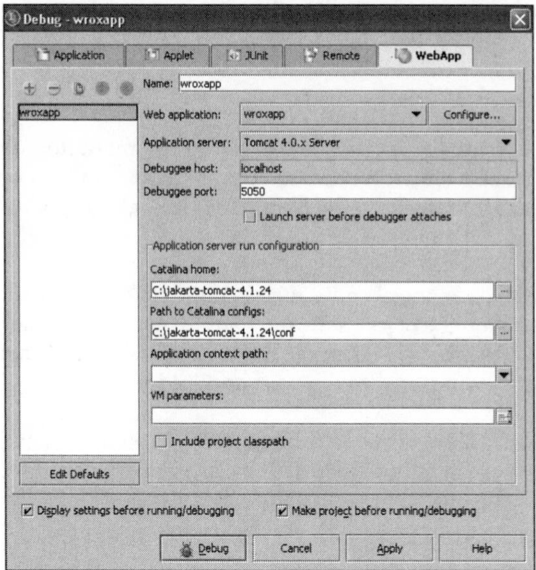

Figure 7.31 The Debug dialog box.

8. Make sure that Tomcat is running (as we described in the previous section) and click the Debug button. If everything went according to plan, you will see this message:

```
Connected to the target VM at 'localhost:5050' using socket
transport.
```

9. You should also see a debug window. This window allows you to step through the actual application. It features a toolbar with 13 buttons that you can use to perform various debug operations (only the appropriate buttons will be enabled). Figure 7.32 shows the debug window for this application.

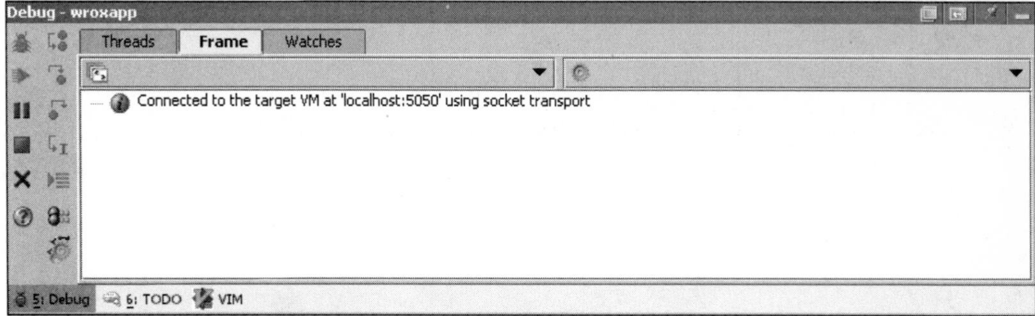

Figure 7.32 The IntelliJ debug window.

Once this output is printed and you can see the active debug window, you can begin the debugging process. To get this process under way, open a browser to the following URL:

```
http://localhost:8080/wroxapp/index.jsp
```

Now enter the value *SUNW* into the text box and click the Submit button. This activates the IntelliJ debugger and runs the wroxapp until it reaches its first breakpoint in the LookupForm. To step through your source, select one of the buttons from the Debug toolbar—at this point, I recommend using the Step Over button.

As you are stepping through each line of code, keep in mind that you can add objects to the Watch window by simply right-clicking on the object that you want to inspect and selecting Add To Watches from the pop-up menu. After doing this, you can select the Watches tab in the debug window and watch the value of the selected object as you step through your application.

After stepping through the LookupForm, the debugger moves on to the next breakpoint (which in this case is in the LookupAction.execute() method). This breakpoint allows you to step through your execute() method and monitor the processing of both the data passed to your Action and the logic encased in this Action.

As I am sure you are aware, there are many other places that can be debugged in a Struts application. The goal of this section was not to identify every debuggable entry point, but rather to give you a look at some of the more common places you can add breakpoints.

Stepping Through the Struts Source

This section goes one step further in our debugging efforts: we actually step through the Struts source. This exercise should give you a good handle on how Struts processes its requests.

To get this process started, complete the following steps:

1. If you have not done so already, download the Struts 1.1 source (in a zip format) from http://www.apache.org/dist/jakarta/struts/source/.
2. Extract the Struts source zip file into another convenient location. This example uses C:\StrutsSrc.
3. Right-click on wroxapp.ipr and select Project Properties.
4. Click the Libraries tab and select the Struts 1.1 library (Figure 7.33).

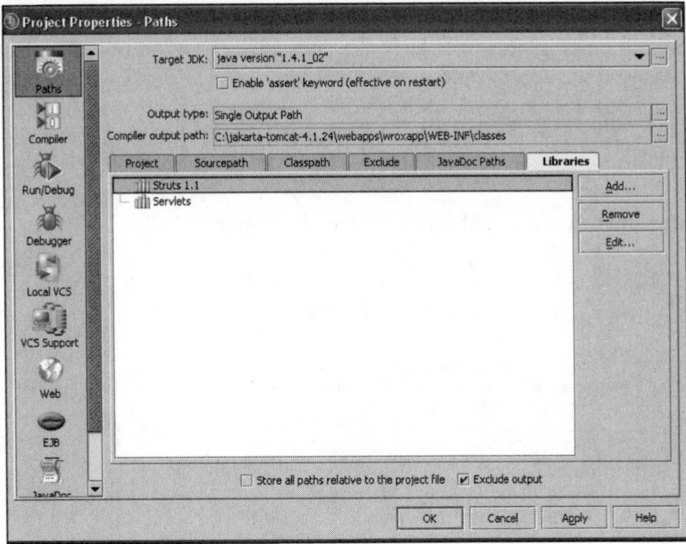

Figure 7.33 The Struts 1.1 library.

5. Click the Edit button and select the Sourcepath tab.
6. Click the Add button and browse to the /Jakarta-struts-1.1-src/src/share directory in the extracted source location. The fully qualified path in this example is C:\StrutsSrc\jakarta-struts-1.1-src\src\share. Once you have found this directory, select it and click OK. Your screen should look similar to Figure 7.34.

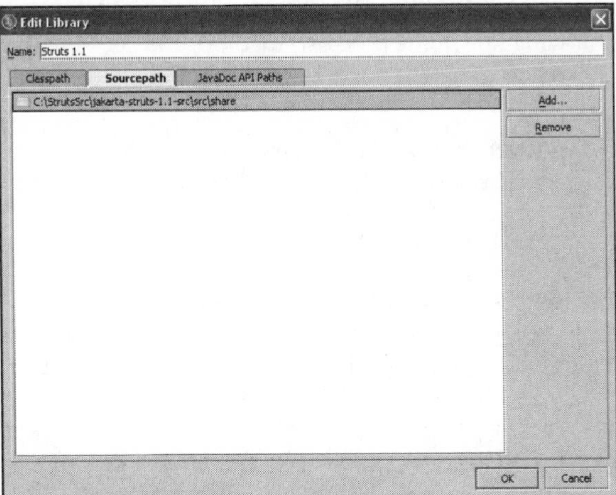

Figure 7.34 The Struts 1.1 source path.

7. Now click OK until you are back at the main IDE window.

You are now ready to step through the Struts source. Again, there are several places that you can set a breakpoint, but one of the best places to begin your debugging of a Struts application is in the ActionServlet—this is where everything begins in a Struts application. And the best place to begin within the ActionServlet is the process() method. If you remember from our previous discussions, the process() method is the first method called by the ActionServlet's doPost() and doGet() methods and is the entry point to all Struts requests.

To set a breakpoint in the process() method, complete these steps:

1. From the Project window, select the Sourcepath pull-down list to display all of the source paths associated with this project. Figure 7.35 shows the current set of project source paths.

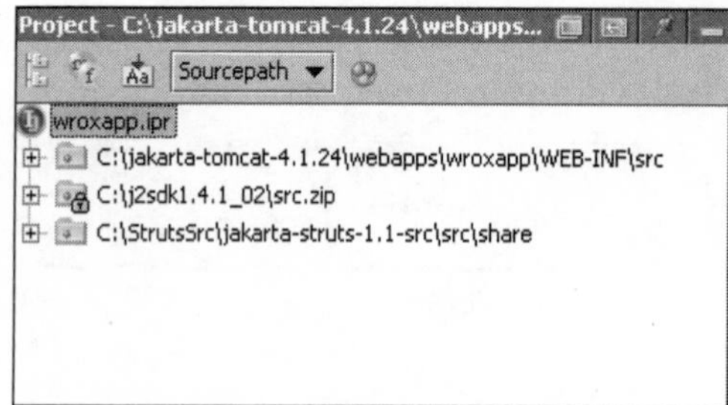

Figure 7.35 The project source paths.

2. Expand the C:\StrutsSrc\jakarta-struts-1.1-src\src\share node until you find the org.apache.struts.action.ActionServlet implementation.
3. Open this file and scroll down until you find the process() method.
4. Now find the following line in the process() method, and set a breakpoint on this line:

```
RequestUtils.selectModule(request, getServletContext());
```

That's all there is to it. Now restart Tomcat, if necessary, and start the IntelliJ debugger. Once the IntelliJ debugger has started, open your browser to the following wroxapp/index.jsp:

```
http://localhost:8080/wroxapp/index.jsp
```

Enter *SUNW* and click Submit. When Tomcat receives the request, it sends the request to the ActionServlet's doPost() method, which in turn calls the process() method containing our breakpoint. Now you can simply step through the application as if it was any other application.

> **When you are debugging the process() method, you must click the Step Into button if you want to follow the entire processing of the request.**

What's Next?

In this chapter, we focused on debugging Struts applications by stepping through both our source code and the source code packaged with this Struts project. In our debugging efforts, we also looked at two popular and extremely useful IDEs: the open-source Eclipse and JetBrains' IntelliJ IDEA. At this point, you should have the ability to step through an entire Struts request, from the ActionServlet's process() method to your own source.

In the next chapter, we look at the steps involved in working with Custom ActionMappings.

Working with Custom ActionMappings

In this chapter, we discuss the org.apache.struts.action.ActionMapping class and how you can extend it to provide specialized mapping information to the ActionServlet. We also present an example ActionMapping extension that will be leveraged in our wroxstruts application.

The goal of this chapter is to show you how custom ActionMappings are created and deployed. Our intention is also to demonstrate how useful an ActionMapping extension can be.

What Is an ActionMapping?

An ActionMapping object describes an Action instance to the ActionServlet. It represents the information that uniquely defines an instance of a particular action class. The values defined by an ActionMapping object are what make a particular <action> definition unique.

The ActionMapping object also provides useful information to the Action.execute() method, giving an Action object the ability to alter its behavior based on the values describing a particular ActionMapping instance. The following code snippet shows the method signature of the Action.execute() method:

```
public ActionForward execute(ActionMapping mapping,
  ActionForm form,
  HttpServletRequest request,
  HttpServletResponse response)
```

You have already used an ActionMapping in each one of our prior examples. It is defined by the <action> element in the struts-config.xml file. A sample <action> element is shown in this code snippet:

```
<action-mappings>

  <action path="/Lookup"
    type="ch03.LookupAction"
    name="lookupForm"
    validate="true"
    input="/index.jsp">
    <forward name="success" path="/quote.jsp"/>
    <forward name="failure" path="/index.jsp"/>
  </action>

</action-mappings>
```

As you may have noticed, we have been using this element throughout this text. The <action> element is how all Action objects are deployed. You should also notice that the <action> element is surrounded by an <action-mappings> element. All <action> elements must be nested within the <action-mappings> element.

The default attributes described by an ActionMapping are defined in Table 8.1.

Table 8.1 The Attributes of an ActionMapping Object

Attribute	Description
attribute	Represents the name under which the Action's ActionForm bean is bound, if it is other than the bean's specified name attribute. The attribute is often used when there is a need to use the same ActionForm bean instance at the same time. A better way to accomplish this is to create two unique <form-bean> definitions that reference the same ActionForm object.
className	Represents the fully qualified class name of the ActionMapping implementation class you want to use when invoking this Action class. If the className attribute is not included, then the ActionMapping defined in the ActionServlet's mapping initialization parameter is used.
exceptions	Specifies a collection of exception handlers that can be associated with a particular ActionMapping. We see this attribute used in Chapter 10, "Managing Errors."
forward	Represents the context-relative path of the servlet or JSP resource that will process this request using a forward. This attribute is used if you do not want an Action to service the request to this path. The forward attribute is valid only if no include or type attribute is specified.
type	Represents the fully qualified class name of the Action class being described by this ActionMapping. The type attribute is valid only if no include or forward attribute is specified.
include	Represents the context-relative path of the servlet or JSP resource that will process this request using an include. This attribute is used if you do not want an Action to service the request to this path. The include attribute is valid only if no forward or type attribute is specified.

Table continued on following page

Attribute	Description
input	Represents the context-relative path of the input form to which control should be returned if ActionErrors are returned from the ActionForm or Action objects.
name	Identifies the name of the ActionForm bean, if any, that is coupled with the Action being defined. This is not the classname of the ActionForm; it is the unique identifier used to look up the ActionForm object defined by a <form-bean> element.
path	Represents the context-relative path of the submitted request. The path must start with a / character.
parameter	Represents a generic configuration parameter that can be used to pass additional information to an Action instance.
roles	Identifies the collection of user roles that can successfully request this ActionMapping.
scope	Names the scope of the form bean that is bound to the described Action.
unknown	If set to true, this ActionMapping instance acts as the default <action-mapping> for the hosting application.
validate	If set to true, causes the ActionForm.validate() method to be called on the form bean associated to the Action being described. If the validate attribute is set to false, then the ActionForm.validate() method is not called.

Creating a Custom ActionMapping

In the previous section, we saw that the default ActionMapping defines quite a number of attributes. The combination of each of these attributes is used to uniquely describe an Action instance, and in most cases, these default attributes suffice. However, there are times when you need to further describe an Action.

The Struts Framework does provide a solution for this very problem by allowing you to define properties specific to your application needs. You can define these supplementary properties by simply extending the ActionMapping class and adding n-number of <action> subelements and <set-property> elements for each additional property.

> **The Struts Framework provides two extended ActionMapping classes for developer convenience. These two ActionMapping extensions—org.apache.struts.action.SessionActionMapping and org.apache.struts.action.RequestActionMapping—default the form bean scope to session and request, respectively, relieving the developer from specifically setting the ActionMapping scope attribute.**

Creating an ActionMapping Extension for the wroxapp Application

To see how a new ActionMapping is created, let's create our own ActionMapping extension that we can use to describe the Actions of our wroxapp application. The ActionMapping extension that we create will allow us to turn logging on or off in our ch03.LookupAction by using a single <set-property> element.

To create an ActionMapping extension, perform these steps:

1. Create a class that extends the org.apache.struts.action.ActionMapping class.
2. Define the additional properties that will be used to describe your Action objects.
3. Call the super() method, which calls the ActionMapping's default constructor, at the beginning of your ActionMapping's constructor.
4. Define matching setters and getters that can be used to modify and retrieve the values of the defined properties.

The source for our new WroxActionMapping is shown in Listing 8.1. As you look over this class, notice that it is a very simple class that satisfies the previous steps. It defines a single Boolean attribute, logResults, which we use in our ch03.LookupAction to determine whether or not it should log its results.

```
package ch08;

import org.apache.struts.action.ActionMapping;

// Step 1. Extend the ActionMapping class
public class WroxActionMapping extends ActionMapping {

  // Step 2. Add the new properties
  protected boolean logResults = false;

  public WroxActionMapping() {

    // Step 3. Call the ActionMapping's default Constructor
    super();
  }

  // Step 4. Add matching setter/getter methods
  public void setLogResults(boolean logResults) {

    this.logResults  = logResults;
  }

  public boolean getLogResults() {

    return logResults;
  }
}
```

Listing 8.1 WroxActionMapping.java.

Using the ch08.WroxActionMapping Extension in the wroxapp Application

To leverage our new ActionMapping, we need to make the appropriate modifications to our LookupAction. The changes that we want to make are both in the source file and the <action> element describing the LookupAction. The first change is to the actual LookupAction source code and is shown in Listing 8.2.

```
package ch03;

import java.io.IOException;
import javax.servlet.ServletException;
import javax.servlet.http.HttpServletRequest;
import javax.servlet.http.HttpServletResponse;
import org.apache.struts.action.Action;
import org.apache.struts.action.ActionForm;
import org.apache.struts.action.ActionForward;
import org.apache.struts.action.ActionMapping;

import ch08.WroxActionMapping;

public class LookupAction extends Action {

  protected Double getQuote(String symbol) {

    if ( symbol.equalsIgnoreCase("SUNW") ) {

      return new Double(25.00);
    }
    return null;
  }

  public ActionForward execute(ActionMapping mapping,
    ActionForm form,
    HttpServletRequest request,
    HttpServletResponse response)
    throws IOException, ServletException {

    WroxActionMapping WroxMapping =
     (WroxActionMapping)mapping;

    Double price = null;
    String symbol = null;

    // Default target to success
    String target = new String("success");

    if ( form != null ) {

      LookupForm lookupForm = (LookupForm)form;

      symbol = lookupForm.getSymbol();
```

Code continued on following page

```
            price = getQuote(symbol);
          }

          // if price is null, set the target to failure
          if ( price == null ) {

            target = new String("failure");
          }
          else {

            if ( wroxMapping.getLogResults() ) {

              System.err.println("SYMBOL:"
                + symbol + " PRICE:" + price);
            }

            request.setAttribute("PRICE", price);
          }
          // Forward to the appropriate View
          return (mapping.findForward(target));
        }
      }
```

Listing 8.2 The modified ch03.LookupAction.java.

We need to examine two sections of code from Listing 8.2. The first section takes the ActionMapping instance passed to the execute() method and casts it to a WroxActionMapping. We can do this because we know that this class is really an instance of the WroxActionMapping and we must do it to get access to the getLogResults() method. The casting that it performs is shown in the following snippet:

```
WroxActionMapping wroxMapping =
  (WroxActionMapping)mapping;
```

The second section of code uses the value retrieved from the getLogResults() method to determine whether it should log the results of its actions. If the value is true, the action logs its results, which in this case is simply a write to the System.err stream; otherwise, it skips over the System.err.println() statement. The following snippet shows this test:

```
if ( wroxMapping.getLogResults() ) {

  System.err.println("SYMBOL:"
    + symbol + " PRICE:" + price);
}
```

Deploying the ch08.WroxActionMapping Extension

Deploying an ActionMapping extension is also a simple process. The first thing that you need to do is compile the ActionMapping class and place it in the application classpath. For our example, compile the ch08.WroxActionMapping class and move it to the <*CATALINA_HOME*>/webapps/wroxapp/WEB-INF/classes/ch08/ directory.

You then need to tell the Controller about the new ActionMapping. You can accomplish this by using two different methods. The first method allows you to define an ActionMapping on the global level using the type attribute of the <action-mappings> element. An example of this method is shown in this code snippet:

```
<action-mappings type="ch08.WroxActionMapping">
```

When using this method, all actions in the hosting application will use the ch08.WroxActionMapping.

The second custom ActionMapping deployment method allows you to configure a custom ActionMapping on a more granular level—on an <action> by <action> basic. When using this deployment method, you use the className attribute of the <action> sub-element, as shown here:

```
<action className="ch08.WroxActionMapping">
```

This <action> by <action> deployment is the method that we will use in our example application. To see these changes working together, let's make one last modification. This modification is made to the actual <action> element that describes the ch03.LookupAction instance. The change itself includes:

- The addition of the className attribute to the <action> element
- The addition of the <set-property> element, with its property attribute set to the matching ch08.WroxActionMapping data member and its value attribute set to the value that you want the property set to.

  The following code snippet shows this modification:

  ```
  <action className="ch08.WroxActionMapping">
    path="/Lookup"
    type="ch03.LookupAction"
    name="lookupForm"
    input="/index.jsp">
    <set-property property="logResults" value="true"/>
    <forward name="success" path="/quote.jsp"/>
    <forward name="failure" path="/index.jsp"/>
  </action>
  ```

If you define an ActionMapping extension that includes more than one property, you must add a <set-property> element for each additional property.

The result of this entry is a WroxActionMapping instance with a logResults data member set to true.

Now you simply need to restart Tomcat and go through the normal process of looking up the SUNW stock symbol. If everything went according to plan, you should see the following output in the Tomcat console window:

```
SYMBOL:SUNW PRICE:25.0
```

What's Next

In this chapter, we discussed the org.apache.struts.action.ActionMapping class and how it can be extended to provide specialized mapping information to the ActionServlet. We then went on to create a sample ActionMapping extension that allows us to turn on and off debug logging on an Action-by-Action level.

At this point, you should feel comfortable with the process of creating and deploying custom ActionMappings. You should also have some insight into how useful an ActionMapping extension can be.

In the next chapter, we discuss internationalizing your Struts applications.

Internationalizing Your Struts Applications

In this chapter, we look at the internationalization (i18n) features of the Struts Framework. We begin by defining each Struts i18n component and how it is used and configured. We then examine the steps involved when internationalizing our existing stock lookup application.

The goal of this chapter is to cover all of the required components and processes involved when you're internationalizing a Struts application. At the end of this chapter, you should feel comfortable with internationalizing your own Struts applications.

> **In this chapter, notice that we use the terms i18n and internationalization interchangeably. While i18n looks like an acronym, we use it to represent "Internationalization," because 18 is the number of letters between the alphabetical characters i and n in the word internationalization—hence i18n.**

i18n Components of a Struts Application

Two main i18n components are packaged with the Struts Framework. The first of these components, which is managed by the application Controller, is a Message class that references a resource bundle containing Locale-dependent strings. The second i18n component is a JSP custom tag, <bean:message />, which is used in the View layer to present the actual strings managed by the Controller.

The Controller

The standard method used when internationalizing a Struts application begins with the creation of a set of simple Java properties files. Each file contains a key/value pair for each message that you expect your application to present, in the language appropriate for the requesting client.

Defining the Resource Bundles

A resource bundle is a file that contains the key/value pairs for the default language of your application. The naming format for this file is *ResourceBundleName_language_COUNTRY*.properties. An example of this default file, using English in the United States, would be:

```
ApplicationResources_en_US.properties
```

All resource requests from a client in the United States speaking the English language will use this file to retrieve its application-specific key/values pairs.

A sample entry in this file would be:

```
app.symbol=Symbol
```

This combination says that when a client, using the previous en_US Locale, requests the key app.symbol the value *Symbol* is substituted for every occurrence of the app.symbol key. You see how these keys are used when you get to the View section of this chapter.

When developing an i18n application, you must define a properties file for each language that your application will use. This file must follow the same naming convention as the previous properties file, except that it must include the Locale code of the language and country that it represents. An example of this naming convention for an Italian-speaking client in Italy would be:

```
ApplicationResources_it_IT.properties
```

And a sample entry in this file would be:

```
app.symbol=Simbolo
```

This file will be used by all clients in Italy using the Italian language. You can find all of Java supported Locales at http://java.sun.com/j2se/1.4.1/docs/guide/intl/locale.doc.html.

> **The ApplicationResources.properties files are loaded upon application startup. If you make changes to this file, you must reload the properties file, either by restarting the entire container or by restarting the Web application referencing the properties files.**

Deploying the Resource Bundles

Once you have defined all of the properties files for your application, you need to make Struts aware of them. This is accomplished using one of the ActionServlet's <init-parameter> tags. The parameter that is used is the application parameter. To make our instance of the ActionServlet aware of our properties files, we need to modify the ActionServlet's <servlet> definition (found in the web.xml file) to look like the following snippet:

```
<servlet>
  <servlet-name>action</servlet-name>
  <servlet-class>
    org.apache.struts.action.ActionServlet
```

```
      </servlet-class>
      <init-param>
        <param-name>config</param-name>
        <param-value>/WEB-INF/struts-config.xml</param-value>
      </init-param>
      <init-param>
        <param-name>application</param-name>
        <param-value>ApplicationResources</param-value>
      </init-param>
      <load-on-startup>1</load-on-startup>
    </servlet>
```

This <init-param> sub-element tells the Struts Controller that all of our properties files exist in the <*CATALINA_HOME*>/webapps/wroxapp/WEB-INF/classes/ directory and are named ApplicationResources_*xx*_*XX*.properties.

> **Notice that we are not using a package name in our <param-value> sub-element. This is because we are using the default package. If you were to place your properties files into a package structure, then you would need to prepend this structure just like any other class file.**

Now all you need to do is copy all of your resource bundles into the application classpath, which in this case is the <*CATALINA-HOME*>/webapps/wroxapp/WEB-INF/classes/ directory, and restart Tomcat.

The View

To actually leverage these new resource bundles, you must use Struts's second i18n component. The second i18n component defined by the Struts Framework is a JSP custom tag, <bean:message />, which is used to present the actual strings that have been loaded by the Controller. This section describes the <bean:message /> tag and how to configure it.

Deploying the bean Tag Library

Before you can use <bean:message />, you must first deploy the bean tag library. Deploying a Struts tag library is a simple process that requires only the addition of a new <taglib> entry in the web.xml file. Here is the entry that you should add:

```
<taglib>
  <taglib-uri>/WEB-INF/struts-bean.tld</taglib-uri>
  <taglib-location>/WEB-INF/struts-bean.tld</taglib-location>
</taglib>
```

This entry simply tells the JSP/servlet container that this Web application uses a tag library, which exists in the classpath and is described by the TLD located in the <*CATALINA_HOME*>/webapps/wroxapp/WEB-INF/struts-bean.tld file. To make this a true statement, you need to copy this TLD, struts-bean.tld, from the Struts archive to this directory and make sure the struts.jar file exists in the <*CATALINA_HOME*>/webapps/wroxapp/WEB-INF/lib directory.

Using the <bean:message /> Tag

The <bean:message /> tag is a useful tag that retrieves keyed values from a previously defined resource bundle and displays them in a JSP. The <bean:message /> tag defines nine attributes and has no body. Of these nine attributes, we are interested in only the first: key. The key attribute is the unique value used to retrieve a message from the previously defined resource bundle. The key attribute is a request-time attribute that is required.

To see the <bean:message /> tag in action, let's see how it is used. The following code snippet contains a simple example of using the <bean:message /> tag:

```
<%@ taglib uri="/WEB-INF/struts-bean.tld" prefix="bean" %>

<html>
  <head>
    <title><bean:message key="app.title"/></title>
  </head>
  <body>

  </body>
</html>
```

As you look over the previous snippet, you will see two lines in bold. We need to focus on these two areas. The first of these lines is a JSP taglib directive that must be included by all JSPs that will use the <bean:message /> tag.

> **The URI defined in the previous taglib directive should match the <taglib-uri> defined in the previously defined web.xml file.**

The second line that we need to look at is the actual <bean:message /> tag. The <bean:message /> instance that we use in this snippet contains the key attribute; it retrieves the value stored in the resource bundle that is referenced by the key app.title and substitutes it for the occurrence of the <bean:message /> tag. The result of this is a JSP that will have an HTML <title> that matches the Locale of the requesting client.

Internationalizing the wroxapp Application

Now that we have seen the components involved in internationalizing a Struts application, we can apply them to our wroxapp application. In this section, we take you through the step-by-step process for internationalizing a Struts Web application. Each of these steps is described below:

1. Create the resource bundles that will contain the key/value pairs used in your application. For our application, we have two properties files that contain our resource bundles. These properties files appear in Listings 9.1 and 9.2.

```
app.symbol=Simbolo
app.price=Prezzo Corrente
```

Listing 9.1 The Italian ApplicationResources_it_IT.properties file.

```
app.symbol=Symbol
app.price=Current Price
```

Listing 9.2 The English ApplicationResources_en_US.properties file.

2. Copy these properties files to the <*CATALINA_HOME*>/webapps/wroxapp/WEB-INF/classes/ directory.

3. Add an ActionServlet <init-param> sub-element, naming the ApplicationResources, to the web.xml file, as shown in the following snippet:

```
<init-param>
  <param-name>application</param-name>
  <param-value>ApplicationResources</param-value>
</init-param>
```

4. Add a <taglib> entry describing the bean tag library to the application's web.xml file, as shown in Listing 9.3.

```
<?xml version="1.0" encoding="ISO-8859-1"?>

<!DOCTYPE web-app
  PUBLIC "-//Sun Microsystems, Inc.//DTD Web Application 2.3//EN"
  "http://java.sun.com/j2ee/dtds/web-app_2_3.dtd">

<web-app>

  <!-- Standard ActionServlet Configuration -->
  <servlet>
    <servlet-name>action</servlet-name>
    <servlet-class>
      org.apache.struts.action.ActionServlet
    </servlet-class>
    <init-param>
      <param-name>config</param-name>
      <param-value>/WEB-INF/struts-config.xml</param-value>
    </init-param>
    <init-param>
      <param-name>application</param-name>
      <param-value>ApplicationResources</param-value>
    </init-param>
    <load-on-startup>1</load-on-startup>
  </servlet>


  <!-- Standard ActionServlet Mapping -->
  <servlet-mapping>
    <servlet-name>action</servlet-name>
    <url-pattern>*.do</url-pattern>
  </servlet-mapping>


  <!-- Standard Welcome File List -->
```

Code continued on following page

```
    <welcome-file-list>
      <welcome-file>index.jsp</welcome-file>
    </welcome-file-list>

    <!-- Struts Tag Library Descriptors -->
    <taglib>
      <taglib-uri>/WEB-INF/struts-html.tld</taglib-uri>
      <taglib-location>/WEB-INF/struts-html.tld</taglib-location>
    </taglib>

    <taglib>
      <taglib-uri>/WEB-INF/struts-bean.tld</taglib-uri>
      <taglib-location>/WEB-INF/struts-bean.tld</taglib-location>
    </taglib>

  </web-app>
```

Listing 9.3 The modified web.xml file.

> **Make sure that you are using the <load-on-startup> element when describing the ActionServlet. This ensures that all of the key/value pairs are loaded prior to any requests.**

5. Modify your JSP files to include a taglib directive referencing the bean tag library and replace all text strings presented to the user with matching <bean:message /> tags. Listings 9.4 and 9.5 show our modified JSPs. Notice that all of the former static strings have been placed in the properties files, listed earlier, and are now referenced using a <bean:message /> tag with the appropriate key.

```
<%@ taglib uri="/WEB-INF/struts-html.tld" prefix="html" %>
<%@ taglib uri="/WEB-INF/struts-bean.tld" prefix="bean" %>

<html>
  <head>
    <title>Wrox Struts Application</title>
  </head>

  <body>
    <table width="500"
      border="0" cellspacing="0" cellpadding="0">
      <tr>
        <td> </td>
      </tr>
      <tr>
        <td height="68" width="48%">
          <div align="left">
            <img src="images/wxmainlogowhitespace.gif">
          </div>
        </td>
      </tr>
      <tr>
```

Code continued on following page

```
          <td> </td>
        </tr>
      </table>

      <html:form action="Lookup">
        <table width="45%" border="0">
          <tr>
            <td><bean:message key="app.symbol" />:</td>
            <td><html:text property="symbol" /></td>
          </tr>
          <tr>
            <td colspan="2" align="center"><html:submit /></td>
          </tr>
        </table>
      </html:form>

    </body>
  </html>
```

Listing 9.4 The internationalized index.jsp.

```
<%@ taglib uri="/WEB-INF/struts-bean.tld" prefix="bean" %>

<html>
  <head>
    <title>Wrox Struts Application</title>
  </head>
  <body>

    <table width="500"
      border="0" cellspacing="0" cellpadding="0">
      <tr>
        <td> </td>
      </tr>
      <tr>
        <td height="68" width="48%">
          <div align="left">
            <img src="images/wxmainlogowhitespace.gif">
          </div>
        </td>
      </tr>
      <tr>
        <td> </td>
      </tr>
      <tr>
        <td> </td>
      </tr>
      <tr>
        <td> </td>
      </tr>
      <tr>
        <td>
          <bean:message key="app.price" />:
```

Code continued on following page

```
                <%= request.getAttribute("PRICE") %>
            </td>
          </tr>
          <tr>
            <td> </td>
          </tr>
        </table>
      </body>
    </html>
```

Listing 9.5 The internationalized quote.jsp.

That's all there is to it. To see these changes take effect, restart Tomcat and open the following URL:

```
http://localhost:8080/wroxapp/
```

You should see results that look exactly like your previous encounters with the wroxapp application, except that now all user-presented strings are retrieved from the ApplicationResources.properties file that matched the requesting client's Locale.

What's Next

In this chapter, we took a look at the internationalization (i18n) features of the Struts Framework. We began by defining each Struts i18n component and how it is used and configured. We then went through the steps involved when you're internationalizing an existing Struts application.

In the next chapter, we discuss how errors are managed by the Struts Framework. You will see how errors are both managed and presented to the user.

10

Managing Errors

In this chapter, we look at some of the methods available when you're managing errors in a Struts application. We begin by discussing the various error classes provided by the Struts Framework. We also examine how errors are managed in both the Controller and Views of a Struts application by adding error handling to our wroxapp stock quote application.

The goal of this chapter is to show you how errors can be managed in a Struts application. At the end of this chapter, you will know how and where the Struts error-management component can be leveraged.

Struts Error Management

The Struts Framework is packaged with two main classes that are intended for error management. The first of these classes is the ActionError class, which represents an encapsulation of a single error message. The second error management class is the ActionErrors class, which acts as a container for a collection of ActionError instances. These two classes are the focus of this chapter.

ActionError

The first of our error-management classes, the org.apache.struts.action.ActionError class, extends the org.apache.struts.action.ActionMessage class and represents a single error message. This message—most often created in either an Action or an ActionForm instance—is composed of a message key, which is used to look up a resource from the application resource bundle, and up to n-number of text replacement values, which can be used to dynamically modify an error message.

The ActionError class can be instantiated using one of six different constructors. The method signatures for each of these constructors are shown here:

```
public ActionError(java.lang.String key)

public ActionError(java.lang.String key,
                   java.lang.Object value0)

public ActionError(java.lang.String key,
                   java.lang.Object value0,
                   java.lang.Object value1)

public ActionError(java.lang.String key,
                   java.lang.Object value0,
                   java.lang.Object value1,
                   java.lang.Object value2)

public ActionError(java.lang.String key,
                   java.lang.Object value0,
                   java.lang.Object value1,
                   java.lang.Object value2,
                   java.lang.Object value3)

public ActionError(java.lang.String key,
                   java.lang.Object[] values)
```

The key attribute of the ActionError class is used to look up a resource from the application resource bundle, which we describe in Chapter 9, "Internationalizing Your Struts Applications." This allows you to provide error messages that are i18n enabled. We see examples of this when we add error management to our wroxapp application.

The value0..3 attributes allow you to pass up to four replacement objects that can be used to dynamically modify messages. This allows you to parameterize an internationalized message.

Here's an example of constructing an ActionError:

```
ActionError error = new ActionError("errors.lookup.unknown",
                                    symbol);
```

This ActionError instance looks up the resource bundle string with the key errors.lookup.unknown and substitutes the value of the symbol object as the retrieved resource's first parameter. If we were to assume our resource bundle contained the entry

```
errors.lookup.unknown=Unknown Symbol : {0}
```

and the symbol object was a String containing the value BOBCO, then the resulting message would look something like this:

```
Unknown Symbol : BOBCO
```

> **The placeholders used by the ActionError class are formatted according the standard JDK's java.text.MessageFormat, using the replacement symbols of {0}, {1}, {2}, and {3}.**

The final ActionError constructor allows you to pass an Object array of replace values—this allows you to substitute any number of string replacements in your error message.

ActionErrors

The second of our error-management classes, the org.apache.struts.action.ActionErrors class, extends the org.apache.struts.action.ActionMessages class and represents a collection of ActionError classes. The ActionErrors class is composed of two constructors and a single method that allows you to add an ActionError object to the current collection of ActionErrors.

In addition to the add() method, the ActionErrors class inherits eight extremely useful methods that are used to query and manipulate the contained ActionError instances. Table 10.1 describes the methods of the ActionErrors and ActionMessages classes.

Table 10.1 The Methods of the ActionErrors Class

Method	Description
ActionErrors.add()	Adds an ActionError instance, associated with a property, to the internal ActionErrors HashMap. Note that the internal HashMap contains an ArrayList of ActionErrors. This allows you to add multiple ActionError objects bound to the same property.
ActionMessages.clear()	Removes all of the ActionError instances currently stored in the ActionErrors object.
ActionMessages.isEmpty()	Returns true, if no ActionError objects are currently stored in the ActionErrors collection; otherwise, returns false.
ActionMessages.get()	Returns a Java Iterator referencing all of the current ActionError objects, without regard to the property they are bound to.
ActionMessages.get (java.lang.String)	Returns a Java Iterator referencing all of the current ActionError objects bound to the property represented by the String value passed to this method.
ActionMessages.properties()	Returns a Java Iterator referencing all of the current properties bound to ActionError objects.
ActionMessages.size()	Returns the number of ActionError objects, without regard to the property they are bound to.
ActionMessages.size (java.lang.String)	Returns the number of ActionError objects bound to the property represented by the String value passed to this method.

The get() methods listed in Table 10.1 actually return ActionMessage instances; therefore, you will need to downcast these objects to an ActionError object to get your original error objects back out.

The add() method is the method most often used when managing collections of errors. The following code snippet contains two add() methods and shows how ActionError objects can be added to the ActionErrors collection:

```
ActionErrors errors = new ActionErrors();

errors.add("propertyname",
           new ActionError("key");

errors.add(ActionErrors.GLOBAL_ERROR,
           new ActionError("key");
```

As you can see, the only difference between these two add()s is the first parameter. This parameter represents the property to which the ActionError being added should be bound.

The first add() example uses a String as the property value. This tells Struts that this error is bound to an input property from the HTML form that submitted this request. This method is most often used to report errors that have occurred when validating the form in the ActionForm.validate() method.

The second add() example uses a predefined static that tells the framework that this error message is not associated with a single form property but is instead related to the Action or application.

Adding Error Handling to the wroxapp Application

Now that you have seen the classes involved in Struts error management, let's see how they are actually used. We do this by adding the Struts error-management components to our wroxapp Web application in two areas: the ActionForm and the Action itself.

Before you can leverage the Struts error-management classes, make sure that the following two attributes have been added to the <action> element that describes the ch03.LookupAction. The following code snippet shows the changes to the struts-config.xml file:

```
<action className="ch08.WROXActionMapping"
  path="/Lookup"
  type="ch03.LookupAction"
  name="lookupForm"
  validate="true"
  input="/index.jsp">
  <set-property property="logResults" value="true"/>
  <forward name="success" path="/quote.jsp"/>
  <forward name="failure" path="/index.jsp"/>
</action>
```

The new attributes are the validate and input attributes. The first attribute, validate, when set to true tells the Struts Framework that validation should be performed. The second attribute tells the Struts Framework where the error originated and where the action should be redirected, if any errors have occurred. You must add these attributes to all <action> elements that will use the ActionForm.validate() mechanism described in the following section.

The ActionForm.validate() Method

The first area where we apply error-management techniques is in the ActionForm object. This is probably the best place to begin, because it is the first chance you will have to test the incoming request for errors. We are checking for validation errors that occur when the user submitting an HTML form enters incorrect data. The Struts Framework allows you to do this by simply overriding the ActionForm.validate() method. The signature of this method is as follows:

```
public ActionErrors validate(ActionMapping mapping,
  HttpServletRequest request)
```

The ActionForm.validate() method is called by the ActionServlet after the matching HTML input properties have been set. It provides you with the opportunity to test the values of the input properties before the targeted Action.execute() method is invoked. If the validate() method finds no errors in the submitted data, then it returns either an empty ActionErrors object or null and processing continues normally.

If the validate() method does encounter errors, then it should add an ActionError instance describing each encountered error to an ActionErrors collection and return the ActionErrors instance. When the ActionServlet receives the returned ActionErrors, it forwards the collection to the JSP that is referenced by the input attribute described earlier, which in our case is index.jsp. Later in this section you see what the index.jsp View will do with the ActionErrors collection. Listing 10.1 contains the changes we have made to our LookupForm to perform input validation.

```
package ch03;

import javax.servlet.http.HttpServletRequest;
import org.apache.struts.action.ActionForm;
import org.apache.struts.action.ActionMapping;
import org.apache.struts.action.ActionError;
import org.apache.struts.action.ActionErrors;

public class LookupForm extends ActionForm {

  private String symbol = null;

  public String getSymbol() {

    return (symbol);
  }

  public void setSymbol(String symbol) {

    this.symbol = symbol;
  }
```

Code continued on following page

```
    public void reset(ActionMapping mapping,
      HttpServletRequest request) {

      this.symbol = null;
    }

    public ActionErrors validate(ActionMapping mapping,
      HttpServletRequest request) {

      ActionErrors errors = new ActionErrors();

      if ( (symbol == null ) || (symbol.length() == 0) ) {

        errors.add("symbol",
          new ActionError("errors.lookup.symbol.required"));
      }
      return errors;
    }
  }
```

Listing 10.1 The modified LookupForm.java.

As you look over Listing 10.1, you will notice two areas of change. The first is the addition of two import statements. These statements include the ActionError and ActionErrors classes that we use to handle errors.

The second change is the addition of the validate() method. In this method, we test the symbol data member that was set by the HTML form tag. We test it for both a null and an empty String. If it returns true for either of these tests, then the input data is not valid, and it creates an ActionErrors instance and adds an ActionError object describing the error. It then returns the ActionErrors instance, which is forwarded to index.jsp for display.

You should take note of the values passed to the errors.add() method. The first value, *symbol,* binds this error to the symbol input property submitted by the HTML form. This tells the Struts Framework that the input value referenced by the symbol property failed validation.

The second parameter, *errors.lookup.symbol.required,* is a key to the resource bundle of this application. To make this a valid key, you need to add the following entries to both the ApplicationResources_en_US.properties and ApplicationResources_it_IT.properties files, respectively.

The following errors are surrounded by the HTML list item elements <li>. We do this to make the messages more readable when displayed in an HTML client. You learn the purpose of this in the following section.

```
errors.lookup.symbol.required=<li>A Symbol is Required</li>

errors.lookup.symbol.required=<li>Un simbolo richiesto</li>
```

<html:errors />

To see our new validate() method in action, let's modify the index.jsp to display any errors resulting from our validation. The easiest way to do this is with <html:errors />. The <html:errors /> tag is used to display the ActionError objects stored in an ActionErrors collection. It is extremely easy to use, and in most circumstances, you do not need to use any of its available attributes; however, you should define its header and footer.

The header and footer consist of HTML text that is placed before and after the list of ActionErrors. The text that describes the header and footer is stored in the application's resource bundles, allowing the text to be language independent. Like all other objects in a resource bundle, the header and footer values are identified using text keys. The two keys that describe the header and footer are errors.header and errors.footer, respectively. To use the header and footer values, add the following code snippet to the ApplicationResources-en_US.properties file:

```
errors.header=<h3>
  <font color="red">Error List</font></h3>
  <ul>
errors.footer=</ul><hr>
```

and this code snippet to the ApplicationResources_it_IT.properties file:

```
errors.header=<h3>
  <font color="red">Elenco degli errori</font></h3>
  <ul>
errors.footer=</ul><hr>
```

Both the header and the footer values are surrounded by HTML unnumbered list elements. This is for formatting purposes, as we mentioned earlier, and is not a required format. You can format your header and footer in just about any style that suits your needs.

Now that we have the header and footer of our error messages defined and in place, we simply need to add the <html:errors /> tag to our JSP. Listing 10.2 shows the index.jsp with the addition of the <html:errors /> tag.

```
<%@ taglib uri="/WEB-INF/struts-html.tld" prefix="html" %>
<%@ taglib uri="/WEB-INF/struts-bean.tld" prefix="bean" %>

<html>
  <head>
    <title>WROX Struts Application</title>
  </head>

  <body>
    <table width="500" border="0"
      cellspacing="0" cellpadding="0">
      <tr>
        <td> </td>
```

Code continued on following page

```
      </tr>
      <tr bgcolor="#36566E">
        <td height="68" width="48%">
          <div align="left">
            <img src="images/hp_logo_wrox.gif"
          width="220"
         height="74">
          </div>
        </td>
      </tr>
      <tr>
        <td> </td>
      </tr>
    </table>

    <html:errors />

    <html:form action="Lookup">
      <table width="45%" border="0">
        <tr>
          <td><bean:message key="app.symbol" />:</td>
          <td><html:text property="symbol" /></td>
        </tr>
        <tr>
          <td colspan="2" align="center"><html:submit /></td>
        </tr>
      </table>
    </html:form>

  </body>
</html>
```

Listing 10.2 The modified index.jsp.

As you can see, there is really nothing special about this change—you simply need to pick a location in your JSP that will not be missed by the user.

To see these changes take effect, recompile the ch03.LookupForm, copy the resulting class file to the <*CATALINA_HOME*>/webapps/wroxapp/WEB_INF/classes directory, restart Tomcat, and open your browser to the wroxapp application.

The first time the index.jsp is loaded, you will not see any differences. Recall that we have added code that ensures that the user enters a stock symbol, so to test this change, do not enter any value in the symbol input and click the Submit button. If everything went according to plan, you should see an error message similar to Figure 10.1. If you do not see the error message, check both the LookupForm.validate() method and the resource bundles for this application.

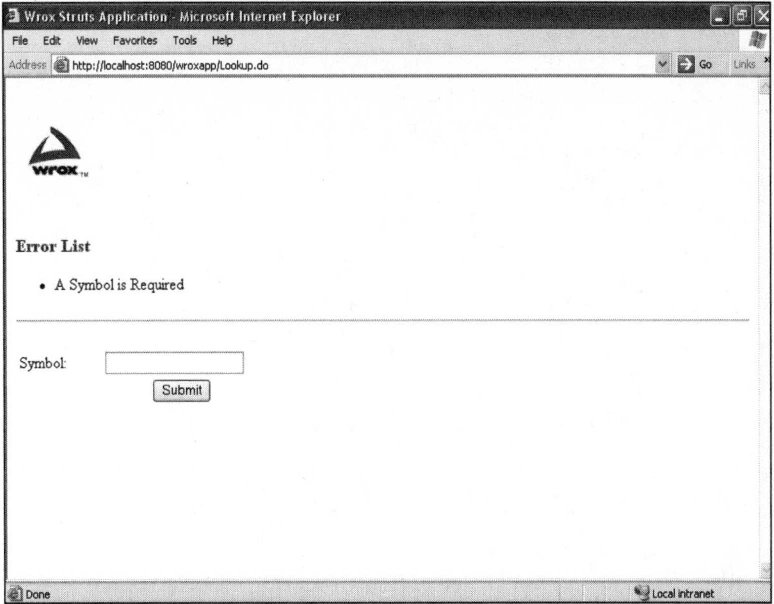

Figure 10.1 An error returned from the LookupForm.validate() method.

Error Management in the Action.execute() Method

The final area of Struts error management that we will look at addresses how you report errors that occur in the Action.execute() methods of your application. There is no defined place that errors can occur in an execute() method (as there is in a validate() method), but the important thing to consider is how an error is reported back to the user.

When reporting errors in the execute() method, the same two classes, ActionError and ActionErrors, are used. The only difference is how the collection of errors is sent back to the client. If you examine the code in Listing 10.3, you will see the changes that have been added to the ch03.LookupAction to report errors.

```
package ch03;

import java.io.IOException;
import javax.servlet.ServletException;
import javax.servlet.http.HttpServletRequest;
import javax.servlet.http.HttpServletResponse;
import org.apache.struts.action.Action;
import org.apache.struts.action.ActionForm;
import org.apache.struts.action.ActionForward;
import org.apache.struts.action.ActionMapping;
import org.apache.struts.action.ActionError;
import org.apache.struts.action.ActionErrors;


import ch08.WROXActionMapping;
```

Code continued on following page

```
public class LookupAction extends Action {

  protected Double getQuote(String symbol) {

    if ( symbol.equalsIgnoreCase("SUNW") ) {

      return new Double(25.00);
    }
    return null;
  }

  public ActionForward execute(ActionMapping mapping,
    ActionForm form,
    HttpServletRequest request,
    HttpServletResponse response)
    throws Exception{

    String theMapping = mapping.getClass().toString();

    WroxActionMapping wroxMapping =
      (WROXActionMapping)mapping;

    Double price = null;
    String symbol = null;

    // Default target to success
    String target = new String("success");

    if ( form != null ) {

      LookupForm lookupForm = (LookupForm)form;

      symbol = lookupForm.getSymbol();

      price = getQuote(symbol);
    }

 // if price is null, set the target to failure
    if ( price == null ) {

      target = new String("failure");

      ActionErrors errors = new ActionErrors();
      errors.add("symbol",
        new ActionError("errors.lookup.unknown",symbol));

      // Report any errors we have discovered
      if ( !errors.isEmpty() ) {

        saveErrors(request, errors);
      }
    }
    else {
```

Code continued on following page

```
            boolean logging = wroxMapping.getLogResults();
            if ( logging ) {

              System.err.println("SYMBOL:"
                + symbol + " PRICE:" + price);
            }

            request.setAttribute("PRICE", price);
          }
          // Forward to the appropriate View
          return (mapping.findForward(target));
        }
      }
```

Listing 10.3 The modified LookupAction.java.

You will see two changes in this file. The first change is just a couple of import statements that include the ActionError and ActionErrors classes.

The second change is the actual error-reporting section. In this section, we test the value of the price variable. If it is null—which it will be if any value other than SUNW was entered—then we need to report an error. This is accomplished by first setting the target to *failure*, then by creating an ActionErrors collection and adding an ActionError object to the collection.

The last thing to note about these changes is how the errors are reported back to the client. This is done using the Action.saveErrors() method, as shown here:

```
if (!errors.isEmpty()) {

  saveErrors(request, errors);
}
```

The saveErrors() method adds the ActionErrors collection to the HttpServletRequest object. The result of this action is a request containing the errors collection being forwarded to the index.jsp, which is the *failure* target that will display the errors using the <html:errors /> tag.

Notice the parameters passed to the errors.add() method. The first value that is passed to the add() method is the input property, *symbol*; this value indicates that this error is bound to the <html:text> tag with the property named *symbol*.

The second parameter acts no different than it did in the validate() method. It simply looks up a different key representing a different error. To add this error message to the wroxapp application, you need to modify both the ApplicationResources.properties and the ApplicationResources_it.properties files, as shown in Listings 10.4 and 10.5.

```
app.symbol=Symbol
app.price=Current Price
errors.lookup.symbol.required=<li>A Symbol is Required</li>
errors.lookup.unknown=<li>Unknown Symbol {0}</li>
```

Code continued on following page

```
errors.header=<h3><font color="red">Error List</font></h3><ul>
errors.footer=</ul><hr>
```

Listing 10.4 The modified ApplicationResources_en_US.properties file.

```
app.symbol=Simbolo
app.price=Prezzo Corrente
errors.lookup.symbol.required=<li>Un simbolo richiesto</li>
errors.lookup.unknown=<li>Simbolo Sconosciuto {0}</li>
errors.header=<h3><font color="red">Elenco degli errori</font></h3><ul>
errors.footer=</ul><hr>
```

Listing 10.5 The modified ApplicationResources_it_IT.properties file.

To see these changes take effect, compile the wrox.LookupAction, copy the resulting class file to the <*CATALINA_HOME*>/webapps/wroxapp/WEB_INF/classes directory, restart Tomcat, and open your browser to the wroxapp application. Now this time, instead of entering an empty stock symbol, enter any value other than SUNW and click the Submit button. You should see an error message similar to Figure 10.2. If you do not see this message, check both the LookupAction.execute() method and the application resource bundles.

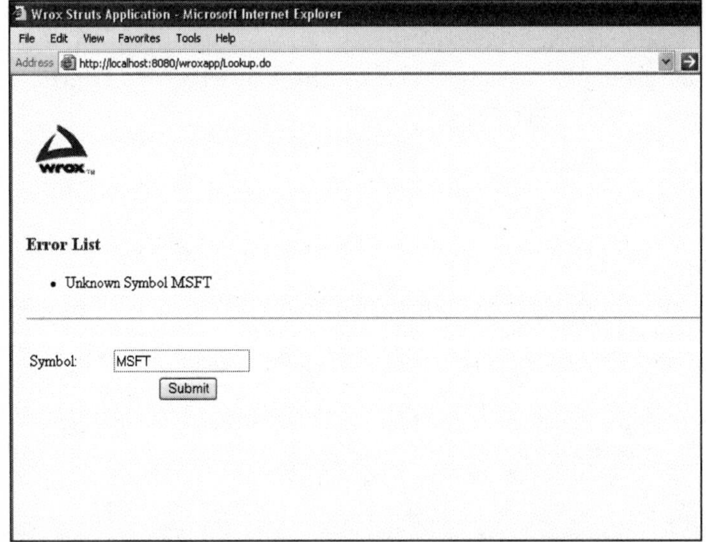

Figure 10.2 An error returned from the LookupAction.execute() method.

What's Next?

In the next chapter, we discuss connecting your Struts application to a database. This is as close to a discussion of a model in the MVC architecture as you'll find in this book. The tool that we use to connect to our database is the Jakarta Commons Database Connection Pool (DBCP).

11

Integrating the Jakarta Commons Database Connection Pool (DBCP)

In this chapter, we discuss connecting your Struts application to a database. The tool that we use to connect to our database is the Jakarta Commons Database Connection Pool (DBCP). This chapter is the closest to a Model discussion you'll find in this book.

What Is the Commons DBCP?

The Commons project is a Jakarta-managed project introduced to create and manage a collection of reusable Java objects. It currently encompasses about 30 sub-projects, ranging from logging to object validators.

The focus of this chapter is the Database Connection Pool sub-project. The goal of this sub-project is to provide a reusable JDBC DataSource that can help you manage all of your database connections. It is an extremely useful component that can be used either in a stand-alone fashion or as a DataSource integrated into other Jakarta projects, like Struts.

Integrating the DBCP into Your Struts Application

Integrating the DBCP project into a Struts application is an extremely easy task. It involves a few simple steps that we describe in this chapter. At the end of this section, you will have a Struts application that stores and retrieves its persistent data to and from a MySQL database using the DBCP project.

Creating a Sample Database

Before we can leverage the DBCP, we must have a database to connect to. The database we use in our Struts application is a MySQL database named *stocks* that contains a single table, also named *stocks*. This table contains a list of stock symbols and prices; its layout appears in Table 11.1. Table 11.2 shows the data that populates the stocks table.

Table 11.1 The stocks Table Structure

Column	Description
symbol	Contains a unique key identifying each stock. It is a varchar(15).
price	Contains the current price of the stock symbol being looked up. It is a double.

Table 11.2 The Contents of the stocks Table

Symbol	Price
SUNW	78.00
YHOO	24.45
MSFT	3.24

For our example, we use the MySQL database. To prepare, you must have an instance of the MySQL database server installed and running on your host machine. You can find the MySQL server at www.mysql.com. You should also download the latest JDBC driver for MySQL, which you can also find at this Web site.

Once you have MySQL installed, complete these steps to create and configure the MySQL database:

1. Start the MySQL client found in the <*MYSQL_HOME*>/bin/ directory by typing the following command:

```
mysql
```

2. Create the stocks database by executing this command:

```
create database stocks;
```

3. Make sure you are modifying the correct database by using this command:

```
use stocks;
```

4. Create the stocks table using the following command:

```
create table stocks
(
  symbol varchar(15) not null primary key,
  price double not null
);
```

5. Insert the user data into the stocks table by executing these commands:

```
insert into stocks values("SUNW", 78.00);
insert into stocks values("YHOO", 24.45);
insert into stocks values("MSFT", 3.24);
```

You now have a MySQL database of stocks. To test your installation, make sure you are still running the MySQL client and enter these two commands:

```
use stocks;
select * from stocks;
```

If everything was installed correctly, you should see results similar to the following:

```
+--------+-------+
| symbol | price |
+--------+-------+
| SUNW   |    78 |
| YHOO   | 24.45 |
| MSFT   |  3.24 |
+--------+-------+
3 rows in set (0.00 sec)
```

Using the DBCP in Your Struts Application

Now that we have a live database, let's work on the actual integration of the Commons DBCP into our Struts application. For our example, we revisit our wroxapp application, but this time let's use the previously defined database to look up the current stock price, as opposed to the hard-coded response that we are currently using.

The ways you can integrate the DBCP into a Struts application may be limitless, but one existing method leverages the functionality of the org.apache.struts.action.ActionServlet. For our example, let's take advantage of this built-in functionality.

To begin, add a new entry to the struts-config.xml file. This entry, <data-sources>, describes a collection of DataSource components that are managed by the ActionServlet. Table 11.3 describes the attributes of a <data-source> entry.

Table 11.3 The Attributes of a <data-source> Entry

Property	Description
type	The fully qualified class name of the DataSource object being used in this <data-source> definition. This class must extend javax.sql.DataSource and it must be completely configurable using <set-property> sub-elements (all configurable data members must satisfy the JavaBean specification).
className	The fully qualified class name of the configuration object for the instance of this DataSource. The implementation of this object must extend org.apache.struts.config.DataSourceConfig.

Table continued on following page

Property	Description
key	A unique key identifying a DataSource instance stored in the ServletContext. If this property is not used, the key defaults to Action.DATA_SOURCE_KEY. If you intend to use more than one DataSource in your application, you must include a key for each one.

To initialize the DBCP, you must add a new <data-source> element to the struts-config.xml file. Listing 11.1 contains our new <data-source> element, describing a DBCP DataSource.

The <data-sources> element, which acts as the parent to all <data-source> elements, must be added prior to the <form-beans> and <action-mappings> elements. The <data-sources> element must be the first element in a struts-config.xml file.

```
<?xml version="1.0" encoding="ISO-8859-1" ?>

<!DOCTYPE struts-config PUBLIC
"-//Apache Software Foundation//DTD Struts Configuration 1.1//EN"
"http://jakarta.apache.org/struts/dtds/struts-config_1_1.dtd">

<struts-config>

  <data-sources>
    <data-source
      type="org.apache.commons.dbcp.BasicDataSource">
      <set-property property="driverClassName"
        value="com.mysql.jdbc.Driver" />
      <set-property property="url"
        value="jdbc:mysql://localhost/stocks" />
      <set-property property="username"
        value="YOUR USERNAME" />
      <set-property property="password"
        value="YOUR PASSWORD" />
    </data-source>
  </data-sources>

  <form-beans>

    <form-bean name="lookupForm"
      type="ch03.LookupForm"/>

    <form-bean name="dynamicLookupForm"
      type="org.apache.struts.action.DynaActionForm">
      <form-property name="symbol"
        type="java.lang.String"
        initial="MSFT"/>
```

Code continued on following page

```
    </form-bean>

  </form-beans>

  <action-mappings>

    <action className="ch08.WROXActionMapping"
      path="/Lookup"
      type="ch03.LookupAction"
      name="lookupForm"
      validate="true"
      input="/index.jsp">
      <set-property property="logResults" value="true"/>
      <forward name="success" path="/quote.jsp"/>
      <forward name="failure" path="/index.jsp"/>
    </action>

    <action path="/DynamicLookup"
      type="ch06.DynamicLookupAction"
      name="dynamicLookupForm" >
      <forward name="success" path="/quote.jsp"/>
      <forward name="failure" path="/dynamicindex.jsp"/>
    </action>

  </action-mappings>

  <controller
    processorClass="ch04.WROXRequestProcessor" />

  <plug-in className="ch04.WROXPlugin"/>

</struts-config>
```

Listing 11.1 Code added to struts-config.xml to initialize the DataSource.

As you look over the previous addition, notice that our new <data-source> element uses only one of the previously described attributes and several <set-property> sub-elements. First we use the type attribute to define the DataSource implementation--we are describing the Commons DBCP org.apache.commons.dbcp.BasicDataSource in this instance.

Next, we define several <set-property> sub-elements. These elements are used to configure the data members of the Commons DBCP. This is why all DataSource implementations must implement their configurable properties using the JavaBean specification. Table 11.4 defines each of the properties that we are using.

Table 11.4 The <set-property> Sub-elements of a <data-source> Entry

Property	Description
driverClassName	The fully qualified class name of the JDBC driver that we are using to connect to our database.
url	The JDBC URL that identifies the instance of the database used by our application.
username	The username that the DataSource will use to connect to the database.
password	The password that the DataSource will use to connect to the database.

The <set-property> sub-elements used in this example are specific to the Commons DBCP. When configuring other DataSources, consult the appropriate documentation to determine the available property data.

Now that you have looked over the strut-config.xml changes, let's modify the ch03.LookupAction to use the new DataSource. First add the following import statements. These statements represent JDBC packages required to perform most DataSource operations:

```
import javax.sql.DataSource;
import java.sql.Connection;
import java.sql.Statement;
import java.sql.ResultSet;
import java.sql.SQLException;
```

The second change you must make is to the getQuote() method. This method must be modified to use the DBCP DataSource. These changes are shown in Listing 11.2.

```
protected Double getQuote(HttpServletRequest request,
  String symbol) {

  Double price = null;
  Connection conn = null;
  Statement stmt = null;
  ResultSet rs = null;
  DataSource dataSource = null;

  try {

    dataSource = getDataSource(request);
    conn = dataSource.getConnection();
    stmt = conn.createStatement();
    rs = stmt.executeQuery("select * from stocks where "
      + "symbol='" + symbol + "'");

    if ( rs.next() ) {
```

Code continued on following page

```
      double tmp = 0;
      tmp = rs.getDouble("price");

      price = new Double(tmp);

      System.err.println("price : "
        + price);
    }
    else {

      System.err.println("Symbol not found returning null");
    }
  }
  catch (SQLException e) {

    System.err.println(e.getMessage());
  }
  finally {

    if (rs != null) {

      try {

        rs.close();
      }
      catch (SQLException sqle) {

        System.err.println(sqle.getMessage());
      }
      rs = null;
    }
    if (stmt != null) {

      try {

        stmt.close();
      }
      catch (SQLException sqle) {

        System.err.println(sqle.getMessage());
      }
      stmt = null;
    }
    if (conn != null) {

      try {

        conn.close();
      }
      catch (SQLException sqle) {

        System.err.println(sqle.getMessage());
      }
      conn = null;
```

Code continued on following page

```
        }
    }
    return price;
}
```

Listing 11.2 Modifying the getQuote() method to use a DataSource object.

When reviewing the new getQuote() method, notice that the first thing we do is retrieve the DBCP DataSource using the getDataSource() method. This method is a convenience method that exists in the base org,apache.struts.action.Action class and is used to retrieve the defined DataSource from the ServletContext. The code snippet that retrieves the DataSource is shown here:

```
dataSource = getDataSource(request);
```

As you can see, retrieving the DataSource is a simple process: You pass the getDataSource() method a reference to the request and it pulls the DBCP DataSource out of the ServletContext.

> **If you have defined more than one DataSource, you must use the key property in the <data-source> element. If we had defined our DataSource using the key property, we would have to pass the same key as the second parameter of the getDataSource(HttpServletRequest request, String key) method.**

Once you have a reference to the DBCP DataSource, you can get a Connection object from it and continue with normal JDBC processing, as shown here:

```
conn = dataSource.getConnection();
stmt = conn.createStatement();
rs = stmt.executeQuery("select * from stocks where "
  + "symbol='" + symbol + "'");
```

There is nothing special about this code except for the retrieval of the Connection from the dataSource.getConnection() method. This method requests a Connection from the DBCP DataSource's pool of connections and returns the retrieved Connection to the calling action. While the returned Connection looks and acts just like any other JDBC Connection object, it is actually a wrapper object around a java.sql.Connection object. The purpose of this wrapped Connection is to allow the DataSource to manage the Connections stored in its pool.

After the getQuote() method has completed its inspection of the ResultSet, it goes through the normal process of resource cleanup and closes the ResultSet, Statement, and Connection. The only thing notable about this section involves the use of the Connection object. In the normal definition of the Connection class, this method would close the connection to the database and thus render it useless for later processes. Because this Connection object is an instance of a wrapper object, however, the Connection is returned to the pool for later use instead of being closed.

That's all there is to using the DataSource in a Struts application. You can now test your changes by completing these steps:

1. Download the Commons DBCP archive from:

```
http://jakarta.apache.org/builds/jakarta-
commons/release/commons-dbcp/v1.0/
```

2. Extract the archive to a convenient location and copy the resulting commons-dbcp.jar file to the <*CATALINA_HOME*>/webapps/wroxapp/WEB-INF/lib directory.
3. Copy the MySQL JDBC driver into the <*CATALINA_HOME*>/webapps/wroxapp/WEB-INF/lib directory.
4. Restart Tomcat.
5. Open your browser to the following URL and enter a stock symbol contained in the database:

```
http://localhost:8080/wroxapp/
```

If everything went according to plan, then you should see the quote.jsp with the price of the symbol that you entered.

> **As you may have noticed, we did not copy any of the Commons JAR files into our project. This is because the current version of Struts is prepackaged with several of the Commons libraries, including the DBCP. If you want to use a specific version of the DBCP, you need to identify that version and copy it to the <WEB-INF>/lib directory of your Web application.**

What's Next

In this chapter, you learned how to configure the DBCP DataSource for use in a Struts application. At this point, you should be able to easily set up almost any Struts application with Database support.

In the next chapter, we take a look at how you can debug your Struts applications using the open-source IDE Eclipse. We also look at some specific Struts source locations that will help you in your debugging efforts.

12

Working with the Validator

In this chapter, you learn how to use Struts to validate form fields. You will have to do the same validation in many forms—for example, a telephone number in both a user registration form and an order form. Instead of writing the phone validation twice (in each of the validate methods of the form beans corresponding to these forms), you can create a general validation mechanism for all phone numbers in the system.

The validation mechanism should have support for internationalization and be extensible. The goal of this chapter is to cover all of the required components needed to use the Validator Framework to validate your form fields. At the end of this chapter, you should feel comfortable with using the Validator Framework to validate form fields and with writing your own validation components to plug into the framework.

This chapter covers the following topics:

- Understanding how the Validator Framework integrates with Struts
- Using the Validator Framework with static ActionForms and with DynaActionForms
- Working with validation rules
- Building and using your own validation rules
- Using the Validator Framework and your own custom validation at the same time
- Employing JavaScript validation on the client side

Getting Started with the Validator Framework

The hardest part of the Validator Framework, as with many things, is just getting started. The validator.xml file can be especially intimidating, but after working with it on a few projects, I began to wonder how I had ever implemented validation without the framework. To reduce the learning curve, let's walk through using the Validator Framework step by step.

The easiest way to get started with the Validator Framework is to create a simple form. This example creates a user registration form. As part of this user registration, you want the end user to enter a username, which should consist of at least five characters.

The following ten steps are the same standard steps you would follow to create any form:

1. Create an ActionForm class (InputForm.java).
2. Create an Action (InputAction).
3. Set up a resource bundle for the application in the Struts configuration file.
4. For internationalization (I18N) purposes, add a label for the userName field to the resource bundle.
5. Create an input JSP (input.jsp).
6. Add a form to the input JSP.
7. Add a field to the form for the username.
8. Add a label to the field that references a string in the resource bundle.
9. Add the form bean declaration to the Struts configuration file.
10. Add the Action mapping for this form to the Struts configuration file.

To use the Validator Framework, follow these additional steps:

11. Add the Validator Plugin to the Struts configuration file.
12. Copy the validator-rules.xml and validator.xml files into WEB-INF (from the blank Struts Web application).
13. Change the ActionForm class (InputForm.java) to the subclass ValidatorForm (org.apache.struts.validator.ValidatorForm).
14. Add a form to the form set in the validator.xml file.
15. Add a field to the form declaration in the validator.xml file corresponding to the userName field.
16. Specify that the userName field correspond to the minlength rule.
17. Add the error message for the minlength rule to the resource bundle.
18. Specify that the username label be the first argument to the error message.

19. Configure the value of the minlength value to 5.
20. Specify that the value of the rules' minlength variable be the second argument to the error message.

Understanding the Standard Steps

Let's begin by examining the standard steps for creating a form; then in the following section we will discuss the steps specific to the Validator Framework.

Step 1 is to create an ActionForm that will hold the username as a property:

```
public class InputForm extends ActionForm {

     public String userName;

     public String getUserName() {
          return userName;
     }

     public void setUserName(String string) {
          userName = string;
     }

}
```

In step 2, you to create an Action (InputAction):

```
public class InputAction extends Action {

     public ActionForward execute(
          ActionMapping mapping,
          ActionForm form,
          HttpServletRequest request,
          HttpServletResponse response)
          throws Exception {
               InputForm inputForm = (InputForm) form;
               System.out.println(inputForm.getUserName());
               return mapping.findForward("success");
     }

}
```

The above code snippet shows a simple Action that prints out the value of userName from the InputForm to standard out.

Step 3 sets up a resource bundle for the application in the Struts configuration file. To internationalize the labels for our fields, you need to set up a resource bundle to contain the labels. Add the following entry to the Struts configuration file (struts-config.xml), just after the last Action mapping:

```
<message-resources parameter="ch12.application"/>
```

Step 4 involves adding a label for the userName field to the resource bundle. Based on the previous step, you find the resource bundle in WEB-INF/classes/ch12/application.properties. Add an entry to this file for the userName field:

```
inputForm.userName=User Name
```

If you had property files for a specific locale, you would have to create a properties file and make entries in that file for that locale—for example, WEB-INF/classes/ch12/application_fr.properties for the French language. Refer to Chapter 9, "Internationalizing Your Struts Applications," for more details.

It is a standard convention to use the form name, plus dot, plus the property name for the key of the message in the properties file.

Step 5 is to create an input JSP (input.jsp). Now that you have created the Action form, you create an input JSP that uses the Action form (input.jsp) as shown in Listing 12.1

```
<%@ taglib uri="struts-html"  prefix="html" %>
<%@ taglib uri="struts-bean"  prefix="bean" %>
<%@ taglib uri="struts-logic" prefix="logic" %>

<html>

<body>

<logic:messagesPresent>
There were errors
<ul>
<font color='red' >
<html:messages id="error">
  <li><%= error %></li>
</html:messages>
</font>
</ul>
</logic:messagesPresent>

<html:form action="inputSubmit">

 <bean:message key="inputForm.userName"/>
 <html:text property='userName'/> <br />

 <html:submit value="ok"/>
</html:form>

</body>
</html>
```

Listing 12.1 The input JSP that uses the Action form (input.jsp).

The above JSP page still has some static text strings. In order to implement i18n, you will need to replace all static text with bean:messages. Thus, you would have to replace the text "There were errors".

```
Adding a form to the input JSP is step 6:
<html:form action="inputSubmit">

...
</html:form>
```

Step 7 involves adding a field to the form for the username:

```
<html:form action="inputSubmit">

  <html:text property='userName'/> <br />
</html:form>
```

In step 8, you add a label to the field that references a string in the resource bundle:

```
<html:form action="inputSubmit">

 <bean:message key="inputForm.userName"/>
 <html:text property='userName'/> <br />

 </html:form>
```

Notice we use inputForm.userName as the key that defines the label. This pulls the string associated with this key out of the resource bundle you defined earlier. Keep this in mind; you use this same label later to refer to the field when you print an error message.

In step 9, you add the form bean declaration to the Struts configuration file:

```
<form-beans>

      <form-bean
          name="inputForm"
          type="ch12.InputForm"/>

</form-beans>
```

The name of the form bean is used in the validation.xml file to refer to this particular form (inputForm).

Finally, in step 10 you add the Action mapping for this form to the Struts configuration file:

```
<action-mappings>

      <action
          path="/inputSubmit"
          type="ch12.InputAction"
          name="inputForm"
          scope="request"
          validate="true"
          input="/input.jsp">
```

```
        <forward name="success" path="/success.jsp"    />
      </action>

  </action-mappings>
```

Note that this Action mapping uses the Action form that we defined earlier. Also note that validation is turned on so that the execute method will not be invoked until the Action form validates. Now we must examine how the sample application is structured so that we can set the context for configuring a validation rule for the userName property.

Understanding the Validator Framework

In this section, we add support for validation of the username with the Validator Framework.

Step 1 is to add the Validator Plugin to the Struts configuration file. The Validator Framework integrates with Struts via this Plugin, which is responsible for reading the configuration files for the Validator rules. To use the Validator Framework with Struts, you need to add this Plugin after any message resource elements in the Struts configuration file as follows:

```
<plug-in
    className="org.apache.struts.validator.ValidatorPlugIn">
  <set-property
      property="pathnames"
      value="/WEB-INF/validator-rules.xml,/WEB-INF/validation.xml"/>
</plug-in>
```

In step 2, you copy the validator-rules.xml and validator.xml files into WEB-INF (from the blank Struts web application). The validator-rules.xml file serves as the deployment descriptor for validation rule components. This example uses a preexisting validation rule component so that you do not have to modify the validator-rules.xml file. The validator.xml file enables you to set up the mappings from the Action form's property to the rules and any error message for the rules. Examples of both the validator-rules.xml file and the validator.xml file are in the blank starter Web application that ships with Struts.

Step 3 is to change the ActionForm class (InputForm.java) to the subclass ValidatorForm (org.apache.struts.validator.ValidatorForm). The Validator Framework includes its own custom ActionForm called ValidatorForm. The ValidatorForm overrides the validate method of the ActionForm and communicates with the framework to validate the fields of this form. Here are the changes you need to make to InputForm.java:

```
...
import org.apache.struts.validator.ValidatorForm;
...
public class InputForm extends ValidatorForm {

     public String userName;

     public String getUserName() {
          return userName;
     }

     public void setUserName(String string) {
```

```
            userName = string;
        }
    }
```

Step 4 is adding a form to the form set in the validator.xml file. You must add the mapping from the inputForm bean definition in the struts-config.xml file to the rules that should be invoked for the individual properties of the inputForm bean:

```
<formset>
      <form name="inputForm">
       ...
      </form>
</formset>
```

This code states that you are going to write rules for the properties of the form bean whose name is inputForm as defined in the struts-config.xml. The name has to match the name of the form bean you defined in the struts-config.xml file earlier.

In step 5, you add a field to the form declaration in the validator.xml file corresponding to the userName field. Now that you specified which form you want to associate with rules, you can start associating fields (also known as bean properties) with the predefined rules: The field sub-element maps inputForm's userName property to one or more rules.

```
<form name="inputForm">
     <field property="userName"
             depends="minlength">
             ...
     </field>
</form>
```

Step 6 is to specify that the userName field correspond to the minlength rule:

```
<form name="inputForm">
     <field property="userName"
             depends="minlength">
             ...
     </field>
</form>
```

The *depends* attribute of the field element takes a comma-delimited list of rules to associate with this property. Therefore, this code associates the userName property with the minlength rule. The minlength rule is one of the many rules built into the Validator Framework. This rule is associated with a minlength rule handler and an error message key. If you looked up the minlength rule in the validator-rules.xml file you would see the following:

```
<validator name="minlength"
      classname="org.apache.struts.validator.FieldChecks"
         method="validateMinLength"
         ...
        depends=""
            msg="errors.minlength">
...

</validator>
```

Notice that the validator element defines the minlength rule. It also uses the classname attribute to specify the rules handler. In our example, the handler for this rule is implemented in the class org.apache.struts.validator.FieldChecks by the validateMinLength method. The msg attribute specifies the key for the message that the framework will look up in the resource bundle to display an error message if the associated fields do not validate.

In step 7, you add the error message for the minlength rule to the resource bundle. Because you are using the minlength rule, you must import its associated message into the resource bundle for this Web application. The validator-rules.xml file has sample messages for all of the rules in a commented section. Find the message errors.minlength in the comments, and cut and paste it to the application.properties file as follows:

```
inputForm.userName=User Name
errors.minlength={0} can not be less than {1} characters.
```

You specify that the username label is the first argument to the error message in step 8. Notice that the errors.minlength message takes two arguments. The first argument is the name of the field as it appears to the end user. The second argument is the value of the minlength variable (we set this second argument later). To set up the first argument, use the arg0 element as follows:

```
<form-validation>
    <formset>
          <form name="inputForm">
               <field property="userName"
                      depends="minlength">
                    <arg0 key="inputForm.userName"/>
...
               </field>
          </form>
     </formset>
</form-validation>
```

The arg0 element passes the key of the message resource. Therefore, in this example the error message will display the inputForm.userName message, which you set to *User Name* in step 4 of setting up a standard form (see the previous section "Understanding the Standard Steps").

In step 9, you configure the value of the minlength value to 5. Rules take parameters. This particular rule takes a parameter that tells it what the numeric value of the minimum length is. To set a parameter you use the var element as follows:

```
     ...
          <field property="userName"
                      depends="minlength">
                     ...
                    <var>
                         <var-name>minlength</var-name>
                         <var-value>5</var-value>
                    </var>
          </field>
     ...
```

The var element has two sub-elements that specify the name of the parameter and the value of the parameter.

Finally, in step 10 you specify that the value of the rules' minlength variable is the second argument to the error message. As you recall, earlier you specified that the second argument to the error message be the value of the minlength parameter. Therefore, instead of getting the argument from the resource bundle, you want to get it from the variable that you just defined. To do this, you must specify another argument. This time, use the arg1 element:

```
<form name="inputForm">
     <field property="userName" ...

          <arg1 key="${var:minlength}"
                name="minlength"
                resource="false"/>
          <var>
               <var-name>minlength</var-name>
               <var-value>5</var-value>
          </var>
```

Notice that the code sets the resource attribute equal to false, which means that the second argument will not be looked up in the resource bundle. Instead, the second argument will use the minlength parameter defined in the previous step. To do this, the key attribute is set to ${var:minlength), which essentially states that the value of the second argument is equal to the value of the minlength parameter.

The name attribute states that this second argument is appropriate only for the minlength rule. Thus, the second argument will be the value of the minlength parameter if there is a validation problem with the minlength rule. Remember that the property can be associated with many rules because the depends attribute of the field element takes a comma-delimited list of rules to associate with the property. Therefore, the name attribute specifies which rule this argument is used with.

You may be thinking that you have to do a lot of work to use the Validator Framework. However, once you set up the framework, using additional rules is easy. Listing 12.2 shows the rules for our inputForm.

```
<form-validation>
   <formset>
         <form name="inputForm">
              <field property="userName"
                     depends="minlength">
                  <arg0 key="inputForm.userName"/>
                  <arg1 key="${var:minlength}"
                        name="minlength"
                        resource="false"/>
                  <var>
                       <var-name>minlength</var-name>
                       <var-value>5</var-value>
                  </var>
              </field>
         </form>
    </formset>
</form-validation>
```

Listing 12.2 Rules for the inputForm.

An Overview of the Standard Rules

Before you start writing your own rules, you should become familiar with Table 12.1, which describes the standard rules included with the framework. As you can see, you get a lot of functionality with very little work.

Table 12.1 Standard Rules

Rule Name	Description
Required	The field is required. It must be present for the form to be valid and takes no variables.
Mask	The field must match the specified regular expression (Perl 5 style). The Mask rule has a variable called *mask*. The mask variable is the regular expression.
maxlength	The field must have fewer characters than the specified maximum length. The *maxlength* rule has a variable called *maxlength*. The maxlength variable specifies the maximum number of characters allowed.
minlength	The field must have more characters than the specified minimum length. The *minlength* rule has a variable called *minlength*. The minlength variable specifies the minimum number of characters allowed.
intrange, floatrange	The field must equal a numeric value between the min and max variables.
byte, short, integer, long, float, double	The field must parse to one of these standard Java types (rules names equate to the expected Java type).
Date	The field must parse to a date. The optional variable datePattern specifies the date pattern (see java.text.SimpleDateFormat in the JavaDocs to learn how to create the date patterns). You can also pass a strict variable equal to false to allow a lenient interpretation of dates, i.e., 05/05/99 = 5/5/99. If you do not specify a date pattern, the short date form for the current locale is used, i.e., (DateFormat.SHORT).
creditCard	The field must be a possible credit card number.
Email	The field must be a possible e-mail address.

Let's cover using several combinations of the rules in Table 13.1 and see the ramifications of doing so. We don't cover all of the rules—just the most useful ones. Once you learn how to use the complex rules, using the simple ones is a straightforward process.

Using Two Rules on the Same Field (the maxfield Rule)

In the first example, we used one rule against one field in one form. You can apply many rules to the same field. In fact, it is common to apply more than one rule to the same field. Let's extend our validation rules for the username. Suppose you want to add the ability to limit the maximum characters in a username to 11. You would follow these steps:

1. Specify that the userName field correspond to the maxlength rule.
2. Add the error message for the maxlength rule to the resource bundle.
3. Configure the value of the maxlength variable to 11.
4. Specify that the value of the rules' maxlength variable be the second argument to the error message.

Note that you have to go through fewer steps because you are adding this new rule to the existing field. As we explained, the hardest part of the Validator Framework is getting started. Once you are using it, adding new rules to fields is easy.

Step 1 is to specify that the userName field correspond to the maxlength rule. You already set up that field, so now all you have to do is add maxlength to the depends attribute of the userName field as follows:

```
<field property="userName"
            depends="minlength,maxlength">
```

This code states that the userName field will not be valid unless both the minlength and the maxlength validation rules pass.

In step 2, you add the error message for the maxlength rule to the resource bundle. This is a simple matter of opening the application.properties file and adding this entry:

```
errors.maxlength={0} can not be greater than {1} characters.
```

Of course, you are free to change the wording of the message.

Remember that samples of the error messages for each rule can be found in the comments of the validation-rules.xml file. You may want to copy and paste all of the messages at once.

Remember that the {0} will be replaced with the first argument and that the {1} will be replaced with the second argument as with java.text.MessageFormat.

Configuring the value of the maxlength variable to 11 is the third step. To use the maxlength rule, you need to pass it the maxlength variable as follows:

```
<form name="inputForm">
     <field property="userName"
            depends="minlength,maxlength">
     ...
          <var>
               <var-name>maxlength</var-name>
               <var-value>11</var-value>
          </var>
```

The final step is to specify that the value of the rules' maxlength variable be the second argument to the error message. You do not have to specify the first argument to the field because you did this when you configured the minlength rule. However, you do have to specify an additional second argument (arg1). The second argument is activated only if the maxlength validation rule is not valid:

```
<form name="inputForm">
     <field property="userName"
            depends="minlength,maxlength">
          <arg0 key="inputForm.userName"/>
          <arg1 key="${var:minlength}"
                name="minlength" resource="false"/>
          <arg1 key="${var:maxlength}"
                name="maxlength" resource="false"/>
          ...
```

The new second argument (arg1) states that the maxlength variable will be passed as the second argument to the error message (errors.maxlength from the resource bundle).

That's it. Now the userName field is using both the minlength and the maxlength rule. Listing 12.3 shows the complete form for using both minlength and maxlength.

```
<form name="inputForm">
     <field property="userName"
            depends="minlength,maxlength">
          <arg0 key="inputForm.userName"/>
          <arg1 key="${var:minlength}"
                name="minlength" resource="false"/>
          <arg1 key="${var:maxlength}"
                name="maxlength" resource="false"/>
          <var>
               <var-name>minlength</var-name>
               <var-value>5</var-value>
          </var>
          <var>
               <var-name>maxlength</var-name>
               <var-value>11</var-value>
          </var>
     </field>
</form>
```

Listing 12.3 Form that uses minlength and maxlength.

Using the Mask Rule

The mask rule is fairly flexible and eliminates the need for writing a lot of custom validation rules. Because the mask rule uses Perl 5-style regular expressions, it is very powerful—assuming, of course, that you know regular expressions well. If you don't, now is a good time to learn. If you have used regular expressions with Perl, Python, or JavaScript, then you are in good shape. Also, if you have used the regular expression package that ships with JDK 1.4 and greater, you will do fine because most of the syntax works the same.

With the mask rule, you are essentially writing your own rule. When you use the mask rule, you are implementing the rule in regular expression syntax instead of Java. Since you are writing your own rule, starting with a blank slate if you will, the default message often does not make sense. Also, having a simple default message—like those with minlength, maxlength, and date—will probably not be useful. Thus, you need to specify your own custom message that the mask rule will use. The message should explain what the regular expression validation routine does so that the end user can understand how to fix the problem.

To demonstrate the mask rule, let's say that our username has to begin with a letter and that it can contain letters, numbers, and underscores.

The steps for using the mask rule and defining your own custom message are:

1. Specify that the userName field correspond to the mask rule.
2. Specify an error message key for the mask rule.
3. Add the error message for the mask rule to the resource bundle.
4. Configure the value of the mask variable to a pattern that implements your business rules.

```
<form name="inputForm">
      <field property="userName"
            depends="minlength,maxlength,mask">
          <msg name="mask"
               key="inputForm.userName.mask"/>
          <arg0 key="inputForm.userName"/>
          <arg1 key="${var:minlength}"
                name="minlength" resource="false"/>
          <arg1 key="${var:maxlength}"
                name="maxlength" resource="false"/>
          <var>
               <var-name>minlength</var-name>
               <var-value>5</var-value>
          </var>
          <var>
               <var-name>maxlength</var-name>
               <var-value>11</var-value>
          </var>
          <var>
               <var-name>mask</var-name>
               <var-value>^[a-zA-Z]{1}[a-zA-Z0-
9_]*$</var-value>
          </var>
      </field>
</form>
```

We will now examine these four steps in detail. Step 1 is to specify that the userName field correspond to the mask rule:

```
<form name="inputForm">
      <field property="userName"
             depends="minlength,maxlength,mask">
```

This step is similar to the one you performed in the previous example. Now the userName is associated with three rules: minlength, maxlength, and mask.

In step 2, you specify an error message key for the mask rule. Because a generic message for a mask rule would not make sense, you need to specify an error key for this rule using the msg element as follows:

```
<form name="inputForm">
     <field property="userName"
            depends="minlength,maxlength,mask">
          <msg name="mask"
               key="inputForm.userName.mask"/>
```

The msg element takes two attributes. The name attribute specifies which rule you want to associate the message key with. The key element specifies a key for the message in the resource bundler.

Now that you have specified the key, step 3 is to add the message to the resource bundle:

```
inputForm.userName.mask={0} must start with a letter and contain only
letters, numbers and underscores
```

Notice how specific this error message is. Essentially, you are describing what the regular expression does in plain English (or French, or whatever languages you plan on supporting). You can see how the message has to change each time you use the mask rule with other fields. For example, the message for a mask rule applied to a phone number is going to be very different from a message for a mask rule applied to a Zip code.

Finally, in step 4 you configure the value of the mask variable to a pattern that implements your business rules. The mask variable of the mask rule contains the regular expression that you want to apply to the field. If the field does not match this rule, then it will not validate. Here is the mask for our userName field:

```
<var>
     <var-name>mask</var-name>
     <var-value>^[a-zA-Z]{1}[a-zA-Z0-9_]*$</var-value>
</var>
```

Regular expressions are a necessary weapon in your developer arsenal. For the regular expression neophytes, the ^ specifies that we want to match the start of the line. Thus, ^[a-zA-Z]{1} means that we expect the first character to be an uppercase or lowercase letter. The {1} means we expect one of the items in the list. The expression [a-zA-Z0-9_]* specifies that we expect many (zero or more) letters (a-zA-Z), numbers (0-9), and underscores (_) after the first character. You could change the * to a {10}, which would mean that you expect 10 characters after the first character, and then you would not need the maxlength rule. However, the error messages are clearer if you can split them up among rules--for example, the error message for maxrule would be more specific than the error message for mask.

Our example code that uses regular expressions is shown in full in Listing 12.4.

```
<form name="inputForm">
     <field property="userName"
            depends="minlength,maxlength,mask">
          <msg name="mask"
               key="inputForm.userName.mask"/>
          <arg0 key="inputForm.userName"/>
          <arg1 key="${var:minlength}"
                name="minlength" resource="false"/>
          <arg1 key="${var:maxlength}"
                name="maxlength" resource="false"/>
          <var>
               <var-name>minlength</var-name>
               <var-value>5</var-value>
          </var>
          <var>
               <var-name>maxlength</var-name>
               <var-value>11</var-value>
          </var>
          <var>
               <var-name>mask</var-name>
<var-value>^[a-zA-Z]{1}[a-zA-Z0-9_]*$</var-value>
          </var>
     </field>
</form>
```

Listing 12.4 Sample code using regular expressions.

What if you want to use the same mask on more than one form? For example, the registration form and the login form will both have usernames on them. In the next section, we look at a way to globally define constants that you can reuse.

Constants

The Validator Framework allows you to define constants that can be used elsewhere in the file. If you have ever used Jakarta Ant, then using global constants is a lot like using Ant properties (but not exactly). First, you define the constant in the global area as follows:

```
<form-validation>
    <global>
        <constant>
            <constant-name>userNameMask</constant-name>
            <constant-value>
               ^[a-zA-Z]{1}[a-zA-Z0-9_]*$
            </constant-value>
        </constant>
    </global>
    ...
```

Then you refer to the constant using the ${} syntax, just as you would refer to an Ant property:

```
<var>
    <var-name>mask</var-name>
    <var-value>${userNameMask}</var-value>
</var>
```

You can use this constant again and again—for example, you can use it with the userName field on the LoginForm.

Note that you can also define constants inside form sets by using the same constant element structure. This is important because constants might be used only for one locale and form sets can be keyed to a certain local.

Working with Dates

Suppose that you want to track the birth dates of your users with the user registration form. To do this, you could use the date rule.

The date rule checks to see if the field is a valid date. The datePattern variable specifies the pattern used to parse the date; if it is not specified, the short form of the date is used. The datePattern format is specified in the JavaDocs for java.text.SimpleDateFormat because the underlying implementation uses java.text.SimpleDateFormat.

Instead of datePattern, you could specify a datePatternStrict variable. The datePatternStrict variable will ensure that 5/29/1970 works; when the pattern *MM-dd-yyyy* is being used, only 05-29-1970 works (notice the 0 before the 5).

The following ensures that users enter dates using the pattern *MM-dd-yyyy*:

```
<field property="birthDate"
            depends="date">
     <arg0 key="inputForm.birthDate" />
    <var>
       <var-name>datePattern</var-name>
       <var-value>MM-dd-yyyy</var-value>
    </var>
</field>
```

Thus, 05-29-1970 would be a valid date but 05-29-70 would be an invalid date. This code assumes that you have added a string property to your inputForm bean.

The user could decide to enter no date at all. If the birth date is a required field, this can be a real problem. Essentially, this rule determines the date only if it is present; otherwise, it is happy to validate a blank field.

Making Fields Required

To round out our example, let's add two fields to our form, namely, a first name and a last name field. Let's say that all you want is text in these fields; you don't care if it matches any pattern—just that it is present.

You have to add the bean properties to your Action form for firstName and lastName, and then add labels for these fields to your resource bundle. Once you have done that, you can make the fields required by adding them to rule associations in the form we have been working on:

```
<field property="firstName"
                depends="required">
        <arg0 key="inputForm.firstName" />
</field>

<field property="lastName"
                depends="required">
        <arg0 key="inputForm.lastName" />
</field>
```

Notice that the required rule takes no arguments. The required rule is likely the rule you will use the most.

> **It would be a good idea to restrict the fields lastName and firstName to letters only. You can do this by using the mask rule.**

To make the birth date field required, use this code:

```
<field property="birthDate"
                depends="required,date">
        <arg0 key="inputForm.birthDate" />
      <var>
         <var-name>datePattern</var-name>
         <var-value>MM-dd-yyyy</var-value>
      </var>
</field>
```

Simply add this code before the rules list (specified by the depends attribute of the field element). If the field is required, then you must use the required rule.

Working with E-Mail and Credit Cards

Working with e-mail and credit cards is quite easy because neither rule takes arguments. Both routines are converted from working routines that were used by JavaScript and Perl developers, respectively. Ted Husted translated these routines to Java and added them to the Validator Framework. Here's how you use them in the field declaration in validation.xml:

```
<field property="email"
               depends="required,email">
       <arg0 key="inputForm.email" />
</field>

<field property="creditCard"
               depends="creditCard">
       <arg0 key="inputForm.creditCard" />
</field>
```

This code maps the email rule to the email property and the creditCard rule to the creditCard field in our ActionForm. We added the creditCard and email properties in the Action and the corresponding labels in the resource bundle.

> **You can find the implementation for all the rules that ship with the Validator Framework in org.apache.struts.validator.FieldChecks and org.apache.commons.validator.GenericValidator.**

Extending Validate and Custom Validation in the Validate Method of an Action

There are two main types of form validation. The first type is per field—in other words, the validation takes into account only one field at a time. The Validator Framework excels with this type of form validation.

The other type of form validation is the relationship between two fields. For example, let's say that your product form has a price and a list price field. The rule is that the list price should never be less than the price. You can add this validation in the ActionForm's validate method, but you could argue that this type of validation is more of a business rule than true validation.

Another example comes to mind. Let's say that you need the end user to enter two passwords. One is the password itself, and the second is to ensure that users entered what they thought they did. To write this, you could choose to override the validate method of the ValidatorForm class.

The ValidatorForm is needed to integrate the Validator Framework to Struts. The ValidatorForm subclasses ActionForm and overrides the validate method to use the framework. You can take this a step further by overriding the validate method of ValidatorForm and extending the functionality of the ValidatorForm to provide your own custom validation by following these steps:

1. Override the validate method.
2. Call the superclass validate method.
3. Save a reference to the errors (if any) that the ValidatorForm superclass produces.
4. Perform additional error checking; add errors.
5. Return the errors.

To add password support to our ActionForm, add the following code:

```
import org.apache.struts.validator.ValidatorForm;

public class InputFormAll extends ValidatorForm {

    private String userName;
    private String birthDate;
    private String email;
    private String creditCard;
    private String firstName;
    private String lastName;
    private String middleName;
    private String website;
    private String password="";
    private String passwordCheck="";


    public ActionErrors validate(ActionMapping mapping,
                                 HttpServletRequest request){
        ActionErrors errors =
                super.validate(mapping, request);

        if (!(password.equals(passwordCheck))){
            errors.add(
               "password",
                new ActionError("errors.password.nomatch"));
        }
        return errors;
    }
```

You can use this approach anytime you want to add validation that the Validator Framework does not yet provide. Now this is one way to extend the Validator Framework without writing your own custom rules. However, you could just write your own validation rule; in the next section, we show you how.

Writing Your Own Rules

Let's begin with a simple rule for validating a phone number. To create a validation rule, you follow these steps:

1. Create a Java class.
2. Add a static method to the Java class that implements the validation routine.
3. Create an entry in the validator-rules.xml file that associates the static method with a rule.

The first step is to create a Java class. This class does not have to subclass any special class.

Step 2 is to add a static method to the Java class that implements the validation routine. The validation routine gets passed a bean, ValidatorAction, Field, and the servlet request as follows:

```
public class CustomValidatorRules {

      public static boolean validatePhone(
                                  Object bean,
                                  ValidatorAction va,
                                  Field field,
                                  ActionErrors errors,
                              HttpServletRequest request) {
```

The ValidatorAction contains information for dynamically instantiating and running the validation method. The ValidatorAction is the rule. This is the object representation of the XML validator element that we will define in step 3.

The Field contains the list of rules (pluggable validators; for example, ValidatorAction), the associated form property, message arguments, messages, and variables used to perform the validations and generate error messages. This is the object representation of the field element we've been using all along.

Inside the validator method, you need to get the string value of the current field. Then you must see if that String value is a valid phone number. If the field is not a valid phone number, you need to add an error to the ActionErrors as shown in Listing 12.5:

```
      public static boolean validatePhone(
                                 Object bean,
                                 ValidatorAction va,
                                 Field field,
                                 ActionErrors errors,
                                 HttpServletRequest request){

            //Get the string value of the current field
          String phone = ValidatorUtil.
                getValueAsString(bean, field.getProperty());

            //Check to see if the value is a valid phone
          char [] chars = phone.toCharArray();
          int numberCount=0;

          for (int index=0; index < chars.length; index++){
               char c = chars[index];
               if (Character.isDigit(c)){
                    numberCount++;
               }else if (Character.isWhitespace(c)){
                  //White space okay
               } else if (c == '(' || c ==')' || c =='-'){
                    // ()- okay too
               }
               else {
                    return false;
               }
          }
```

Code continued on following page

```
            //If not 10 digits then not a valid phone
        if (numberCount != 10){

            errors.add(field.getKey(),
                         Resources.getActionError(request,
                           va,
                         field));
            return false;
        } else {
            return true;
        }
    }
```

Listing 12.5 Validating a US phone number.

This code checks to see if the string value of the field contains only white space; the characters (,), and -; and digits; for instance, (520) 555-1212, which is the common way to express a phone number in the United States. Then, it checks to see if there were exactly 10 digits, as in 520 555 1212.

Step 3 involves creating an entry in the validator-rules.xml file that associates the static method to a rule. The validator-rules.xml file serves as a deployment descriptor for validation rules. This is the entry you need to add:

```
<form-validation>

   <global>

      <validator name="phone"
                 classname="ch12.CustomValidatorRules"
                 method="validatePhone"
                 methodParams="java.lang.Object,
                  org.apache.commons.validator.ValidatorAction,
                  org.apache.commons.validator.Field,
                  org.apache.struts.action.ActionErrors,
                  javax.servlet.http.HttpServletRequest"
                 msg="errors.phone">
      </validator>
      ...
```

The validator element defines the rule. The name attribute specifies the name of the new rule. The classname specifies the name of the new class you just created that contains the static method validatePhone. The method attribute defines the method that will be called. The methodParams specifies the arguments that will be passed to the validatePhone method. Lastly, the msg attribute specifies the resource key of the message that will be used from the resource bundle if a validation failure occurs.

That's it. Now, to actually use the validator rule you need to do the following:

1. Create a field entry in the inputForm in the validator.xml file that associates the phone property of the inputForm with the new validator rule.
2. Add the errors.phone message to the resource bundle.

First, add another field attribute that maps this new rule to the phone property of our ActionForm:

```
<field property="phone"
    depends="required,phone">
    <arg0 key="inputForm.phone" />
</field>
```

Then add the error message that corresponds to this rule to the application.properties file:

```
errors.phone={0} must be a valid phone number.
```

What if you wanted to create a more complicated rule—for example, one that you pass a variable to. Let's add the ability to work with 7-digit local phone numbers or 10-digit national phone numbers by using
a variable. In order to do this, you need to get the variable by using the field method getVarValue as follows:

```
public static boolean validatePhoneExt(
                            Object bean,
                            ValidatorAction va,
                            Field field,
                            ActionErrors errors,
                            HttpServletRequest request){

        String sAllowLocal =
                field.getVarValue("allowLocal");
        boolean allowLocal =
           sAllowLocal!=null && sAllowLocal.equals("true");

        String phone = ValidatorUtil.
                getValueAsString(bean, field.getProperty());

        char [] chars = phone.toCharArray();
        int numberCount=0;

        for (int index=0; index < chars.length; index++){
             char c = chars[index];
             if (Character.isDigit(c)){
                  numberCount++;
             }else if (Character.isWhitespace(c)){
                //White space okay
             } else if (c == '(' || c ==')' || c =='-'){
                  // ()- okay too
             }
             else {
                  return false;
             }
        }

        if (allowLocal == false && numberCount == 10){
             return true;
        } else if (allowLocal == true &&
                  (numberCount == 10 || numberCount==7)){
            return true;
```

```
            }
            else{
                 errors.add(field.getKey(),
                           Resources.getActionError(request, va,
                           field));

              return false;
            }


        }
```

Now that you have defined the variable allowLocal, use it by configuring a variable in the validation.xml file as follows:

```
<field property="phone"
              depends="required,phoneext">
       <arg0 key="inputForm.phone" />
      <var>
         <var-name>allowLocal</var-name>
         <var-value>true</var-value>
      </var>
</field>
```

Why use strings and not other primitive types? You should use Strings for form property types when you are doing any type of validation with any type of text field. The problem with using other types is that Struts does conversion. Therefore, if you have an integer property, Struts will convert the incoming request parameter into an integer. If the incoming type is invalid, Struts will convert it to a 0, and it is likely that your validation rule will either not run or not run correctly, and the users will just see the field as a 0 instead of the text that they typed in the text field.

Working with DynaActionForms

Working with DynaActionForms is quite easy. When you set up the dynamic form in the Struts configuration file, use the DynaValidatorForm class instead of the DynaActionForm class as follows:

```
<form-bean
name="inputForm"
type="org.apache.struts.validator.DynaValidatorForm">

    <form-property name="userName"
    type="java.lang.String"
    initial=""/>
```

The validate method of the DynaValidatorForm provides the necessary hooks into the Validator Framework to tie the validation rules you define in validation.xml to the fields you define in your DynaForm. The Validator Framework and the DynaForms have a special relationship. DynaForms typically rely on the Validator Framework to perform validation. All of the rules we configured and wrote would work the same with the DynaValidatorForm—we simply have to configure the form-property for each field.

Working with Client-Side JavaScript

It's very useful to validate some fields on the client with JavaScript: it saves the user a round trip to the server. The Validator Framework provides a mechanism to generate JavaScript code. The validator-rules.xml file can have JavaScript associated with each validator. The JavaScript is the client-side equivalent of the validator rule if applicable. To use the JavaScript validator routines, you need to do the following:

1. Add the html:javascript tag to your input JSP page.
2. Add the onsubmit attribute to the html:form tag.

First you must add the html:javascript tag to your input JSP page as follows:

```
<head>
<title>Input Form</title>
<html:javascript formName="inputForm"/>
</head>
```

Notice that you need to specify the formName. The formName will be used by the tag to generate the JavaScript validation routine dynamically. If your form name is inputForm (setup in the struts configuration file), the html:javascript will generate a JavaScript function called validateInputForm. The validateInputForm will validate the form and return *true* if the validation succeeded; otherwise it will return *false*.

Much of the JavaScript code generated by html:javascript is static. You can optimize what gets sent to the browser by setting the staticJavaScript attribute to false and including a js file that contains all of the static JavaScript. This allows the browser to cache the JavaScript routines instead of downloading them for each form in your Web application. The JavaScript routines are quite large. In your input JSP, create an HTML script tag and add a src attribute that points to the js file that contains all of the validation routines. You can even generate these routines with the html:javascript tag.

In order to tie the validateInputFormAll to the form submission, we need to add a JavaScript event handler to the form using the onsubmit attribute:

```
<html:form action="inputSubmit"
           onsubmit="return validateInputForm (this)">
```

If validateInputForm returns false, then the form submission will not occur. The validateInputForm function will display a validation error message and cause the form not to be submitted. Thus, the end user will need to handle all of the validation errors before they can submit the form to the server.

Some validator rules are too complex to easily express in JavaScript. It is up to the rules validator developer to write the JavaScript equivalent. If there is no JavaScript equivalent or if the end user has JavaScript disabled, the Java validator will run on the server instead.

A common mistake is to forget to use the return statement in the onsubmit. If you forget the return statement then both of the validators, JavaScript and Java, would execute, and you will not save the roundtrip to the server.

Canceling JavaScript validate

Adding a cancel to your form can cause problems if not handled correctly. The end user clicks on the cancel button, but instead of canceling the operation as expected, it runs the JavaScript validation routines. The generated validate[FormName] function checks to see the bCancel variable was set. If it was set, it does not perform the JavaScript validation routine as follows:

```
var bCancel = false;

function validateInputFormAll(form) {
    if (bCancel)
       return true;
    else
       return validateMaxLength(form) && validateRequired(form) ...
}
```

Thus you need to set the bCancel variable when the cancel button is clicked as follows:

```
<html:cancel onclick="bCancel=true"/>
```

When the cancel button is clicked, the request parameter org.apache.struts.action.CANCEL is sent (Globals.CANCEL_KEY). You can check to see if the form has been cancelled using the Action's isCancelled method in the Action's execute method as follows:

```
if (this.isCancelled(request)){
    System.out.println("this has been cancelled");
    return mapping.findForward("home");
}
```

Using a Workflow Form

At times you will want to develop a wizard-style workflow. You can do this with the Validator Framework by using the page attribute of the field element. To make the page attribute work, the ValidatorForm includes a page property. You must include the current page in your HTML form (your JSP input page) with a hidden field that corresponds to the page property. The field described with the fields element will only be evaluated if the field element's "page" attribute is less than or equal to the page property of the ActionForm.

Let's consider the steps to convert our sample registration form into a two step process.

1. Change the Action to subclass DispatchAction
2. Create two ActionMappings entries into the struts-config file, one for each step
3. In the Action, create two methods with the same signature as the execute method
4. Add the method field to the ActionForm
5. Create two input JSP pages, one page for each step
6. Ensure each input JSP page passes the page property
7. Ensure the first JSP page also passes which method to invoke on the second
8. Modify the validation.xml file, add the page attribute for the fields in the form

The first step is to change the Action to subclass DispatchAction. The old action was built to handle just one form submission. This version of the action is a two-step process. Thus we want to create a method for each step. To accomplish this, we will use the DispatchAction as follows:

```
import org.apache.struts.actions.DispatchAction;

public class InputWorkflowAction extends DispatchAction {
      ...
```

Step 2: Create two ActionMappings entries into the struts-config file, one for each step. You need to define different forwards and inputs for each action. If there is a problem with form validation, you don't want the user to be forwarded to the first form in the wizard; instead, you want the user to be forwarded to the correct, current form. In order to accomplish this, you need to add two action mapping entries as follows:

```
 <action
     path="/inputSubmitStep1"
     type="ch12.InputWorkflowAction"
     name="inputFormTwoStep"
     scope="session"
     validate="true"
     parameter="method"
     input="/step1.jsp">
  <forward name="success" path="/step2.jsp"   />
</action>

 <action
     path="/inputSubmitStep2"
     type="ch12.InputWorkflowAction"
     name="inputFormTwoStep"
     scope="session"
     validate="true"
     parameter="method"
     input="/step2.jsp">
  <forward name="success" path="/success.jsp"   />
</action>
```

Notice that we specify the action element's parameter attribute. Since our action is now subclassing the DispatchAction, the parameter attribute refers to the request parameter name that will hold the method to invoke on our action. Thus, if the request parameter named *method* is set to *step1* then the step1 method will be invoked on our action. Notice that both mappings map to the action class, namely, ch12.InputWorkflowAction.

> **Notice that we put the entire form into session by setting the scope attribute of the action mapping to session. This is desirable because we are dealing with a multi-step process. You could use request scope, but then you would have to pass all of the form fields that were not currently being entered as hidden fields in the input.jsp. You would not want to pass the password as a hidden field.**

Step 3: In the Action, create two methods with the same signature as the execute method. You need to add a method per step as follows:

```
public ActionForward step1(
    ActionMapping mapping,
    ActionForm form,
    HttpServletRequest request,
    HttpServletResponse response)
    throws Exception {

    InputWorkflowForm inputForm =
                (InputWorkflowForm) form;
    inputForm.setPage(1);
    System.out.println("Step1 "
                + inputForm.getUserName());
    inputForm.setMethod("step2");
    return mapping.findForward("success");

}

public ActionForward step2(
    ActionMapping mapping,
    ActionForm form,
    HttpServletRequest request,
    HttpServletResponse response)
    throws Exception {

    InputWorkflowForm inputForm =
                (InputWorkflowForm) form;
    System.out.println("Step2: "
                + inputForm.getUserName());
          //remove the form from Session scope
       request.getSession()
          .removeAttribute(mapping.getAttribute());

    inputForm.setPage(2);
    inputForm.reset(mapping, request);
```

```
        return mapping.findForward("success");
    }
```

Notice that the step1 method sets the page property of the input form to 1. Then it sets the method property to *step2*. Setting the page property will limit which fields get validated by the Validator framework. Setting the method property to *step2* will cause the step2 method to be invoked the next time the form is submitted.

Step 4: Add the method field to the ActionForm. The page property is part of the Validator framework. The method property is something we added to use with the DispatchAction class. Thus, we need to add this property to our ActionForm as follows:

```
public class InputWorkflowForm extends ValidatorForm {
    ...
    private String method="step1";
    /**
     * @return
     */
    public String getMethod() {
        return method;
    }


    /**
     * @param string
     */
    public void setMethod(String string) {
        method = string;
    }

    public void reset(ActionMapping mapping,
                      HttpServletRequest request) {

        super.reset(mapping, request);
        System.out.println("RESET");
        if(this.getPage()==2){
            this.setMethod("step1");
            this.setBirthDate("");
            this.setEmail("");
            this.setFirstName("");
            this.setLastName("");
            this.setMiddleName("");
            this.setUserName("");
            this.setPassword("");
            this.setPasswordCheck("");
            this.setPhone("");
            this.setWebsite("");
        }
    }
     ...
```

Notice that we do not want the fields reset until we are done with them. The reset method is called before every submission.

Step 5: Create two input JSP pages, one page for each step. Now that we have the action setup its time to create the two forms. A close examination of the action mappings reveal that we need to input forms: step1.jsp, and step2.jsp. Listing 12.6 shows step1.jsp; Listing 12.7 shows step2.jsp.

```
<%@ taglib uri="struts-html"  prefix="html" %>
<%@ taglib uri="struts-bean"  prefix="bean" %>
<%@ taglib uri="struts-logic" prefix="logic" %>

<html>

<head>
<title>Input Step 1</title>
</head>

<body>
<h1>Step 1</h1>
<logic:messagesPresent>
There were errors
<ul>
<font color='red' >
<html:messages id="error">
  <li><%= error %></li>
</html:messages>
</font>
</ul>
</logic:messagesPresent>


<html:form action="inputSubmitStep1">

 <bean:message key="inputForm.userName"/>
 <html:text property='userName'/> <br />

 <bean:message key="inputForm.password"/>
 <html:password property='password'/> <br />

 <bean:message key="inputForm.passwordCheck"/>
 <html:password property='passwordCheck'/> <br />

 <bean:message key="inputForm.firstName"/>
 <html:text property='firstName'/> <br />

 <bean:message key="inputForm.middleName"/>
 <html:text property='middleName'/> <br />

 <bean:message key="inputForm.lastName"/>
 <html:text property='lastName'/> <br />

 <html:hidden property='method'/>
 <html:hidden property='page'/>

 <html:submit value="ok"/>
</html:form>
```

Code continued on following page

```
</body>
</html>
```

Listing 12.6 Step1.jsp.

```
<%@ taglib uri="struts-html"  prefix="html" %>
<%@ taglib uri="struts-bean"  prefix="bean" %>
<%@ taglib uri="struts-logic" prefix="logic" %>

<html>

<head>
<title>Step 2</title>
</head>

<body>
<h1>Step 2</h1>
<logic:messagesPresent>
There were errors
<ul>
<font color='red' >
<html:messages id="error">
  <li><%= error %></li>
</html:messages>
</font>
</ul>
</logic:messagesPresent>

<html:form action="inputSubmitStep2">

 <bean:message key="inputForm.website"/>
 <html:text property='website'/> <br />

 <bean:message key="inputForm.birthDate"/>
 <html:text property='birthDate'/> <br />

 <bean:message key="inputForm.email"/>
 <html:text property='email'/> <br />

 <bean:message key="inputForm.phone"/>
 <html:text property='phone'/> <br />

 <html:hidden property='method'/>
 <html:hidden property='page'/>


 <html:submit value="ok"/>
</html:form>

</body>
</html>
```

Listing 12.7 Step2.jsp.

The first form (step1.jsp) now only has the userName, passwords, firstName, lastName, and middleName properties on it. The second form (step2.jsp) has website, birthdate, phone, and email properties on it. We only want the userName, passwords, firstName, lastName, and middleName validated when the first form submits; and we want both the sets of properties validated when the second form submits. Remember that we will only validate the properties we are interested in validating on each step (e.g., we never validate a middle name).

Step 6: Ensure each input JSP page passes the page property. The page property is what gets used by the Validator framework to determine if the other properties should be validated or not. Initially, the page property is set to 0 by the ValidatorForm. After the first form from step1.jsp is submitted, the page property is set to 1 by the step1 method of the action. Then the step 1 method forwards to the step2.jsp (its success forward). The step2.jsp uses the html:hidden parameter to submit the new page number when the user submits the form.

Step 7: Ensure the first JSP page also passes which method to invoke on the second. In addition to the step1 method setting the page, it also sets the method property to step2. Then the step2.jsp uses the html:hidden parameter to submit the method as *step2*, causing the step2 method to be invoked when the form is submitted.

Step 8: Modify the validation.xml file, and add the page attribute for the fields in the form. Now that we have the page properties being submitted via the form, let's set up the validation.xml file to use them. You need to add page attributes to each of the fields that correlate to the inputFormTwoStep. For fields that you want to be validated on step1.jsp submission, add page='0'. For fields that you want to be validated on step2.jsp submission, add page='1'. The entry for this new workflow user registration (validation.xml) is shown in Listing 12.8.

```
<form name="inputFormTwoStep">

    <field property="userName"
        depends="required,minlength,maxlength"
        page='0'>
        <arg0 key="inputForm.userName"/>

        <arg1 key="${var:minlength}"
            name="minlength" resource="false"/>
        <arg1 key="${var:maxlength}"
            name="maxlength" resource="false"/>

        <var>
            <var-name>minlength</var-name>
            <var-value>5</var-value>
        </var>
        <var>
            <var-name>maxlength</var-name>
            <var-value>11</var-value>
        </var>
    </field>

    <field property="firstName"
        depends="required"
        page='0'>
        <arg0 key="inputForm.firstName" />
```

Code continued on following page

```
            </field>

            <field property="lastName"
                 depends="required"
                 page='0'>
                 arg0 key="inputForm.lastName" />
             </field>

            <field property="website"
                 depends="required"
                 page='1'>
                 <arg0 key="inputForm.website" />
            </field>

            <field property="birthDate"
                 depends="required,date"
                 page='1'>
                 <arg0 key="inputForm.birthDate" />
                 <var>
                     <var-name>datePattern</var-name>
                     <var-value>MM-dd-yyyy</var-value>
                 </var>
             </field>

             <field property="email"
                 depends="required,email"
                 page='1'>
                 <arg0 key="inputForm.email" />
             </field>

             <field property="phone"
                 depends="required,phoneext"
                 page='1'>
                 <arg0 key="inputForm.phone" />
                 <var>
                     <var-name>allowLocal</var-name>
                     <var-value>true</var-value>
                 </var>
             </field>

    </form>
```

Listing 12.8 Example validation.xml using workflow.

Notice how the page attribute for the fields userName, firstName, and lastName are set to 0, and the page attribute for fields email, phone, webstie, and birthdate are set to 1. This means that userName, firstName and lastName will be validated when step1.jsp is submitted. When step2.jsp is submitted the validator framework will validate email, phone, website, and birthdate as well as userName, firstName, and lastName.

i18n for Validation

Validation requirements often vary quite a bit based on locale. For example, if we had a Web site that designed for users from France and the US, the forms these users fill out might have unique validation needs. In this case you need to create formset per language. If you do not specify a locale, it becomes the default locale. You specify the locale with the language attribute of the formset as follows:

```
      <formset language="fr">
         <form    name=" inputFormTwoStep">
   ...
```

Summary

This chapter discussed the core functionality of the Validator Framework and provided step-by-step examples on for using the framework. The more useful validator rules were covered, as well as advanced topics like how to create and validate a wizard-style application. You also learned how to create your own validator rule in Java, and how to perform validation in both the validate method of an ActionForm and with the Validator Framework.

In the next chapter we use Tiles to create reusable presentation components.

13

Using Tiles

In this chapter, we look at using Tiles to create reusable presentation components. The Tiles framework was originally called *Components*. The name was nixed because it was too common—it means too many things to too many people. But the spirit of the name remains. With Tiles, you can compartmentalize your presentation tier to achieve greater reuse of layouts, HTML, and other visual components. You build these visual components in JSPs using custom tags and Java scriptlets.

In this chapter, we use the term *Tile* and *page* interchangeably. This is because any Web resource can be a Tile. A Tile layout is a special type of Tile that you can use to hold other Tiles. A Tile layout can be used as a Tile in another Tile layout.

The goals of this chapter are to:

- Define the Tiles framework and architecture.
- Cover the Tile architecture and how it integrates with Struts.
- Clarify key concepts in Tiles.
- Demonstrate how to build and use a Tile layout as a site template.
- Show how to use Tile definitions both in XML and JSP.
- Define Tile scope and show how to move objects in and out of scope.
- Work with lists of attributes.
- Demonstrate how to nest Tiles.
- Show how to build and use a Tile layout as small visual components.

- Examine how to subclass a definition.
- Create a Controller for a Tile.
- Demonstrate using a Tile as an ActionForward.

The Tiles Framework

The Tiles framework turns the concept of jsp:includes inside out. Developers can build pages by assembling reusable Tiles. You can think of Tiles as visual components.

A Tile and a Tile layout can be reused on more than one page. Essentially Tiles are other JSP pages or any Web resource. Tile layouts dictate how the Tiles will be laid out on the page.

In many respects, the Tile layout is similar to a template layout. In fact, if you have used Struts templates before, you will note that the Tile framework is backward compatible with the template custom tag library.

The Tile layout is like a display function in some respects. First you pass the Tile layout the parameters you want to use. The parameters are other JSP pages (called *Tiles*) or Web resources that can be inserted at predefined locations in the layout. The predefined locations are called *regions*. The parameters also consist of strings that can be inserted into the Tile layout. In fact, you can pass many types of parameters that are used by the Tile. The parameters are attributes in *Tile scope*.

Tile scope is similar to page scope and is less general than request scope. Tile scope allows users of the Tile to pass arguments (called *attributes*) to the Tile. The scope lets you pass variables that are available only to that Tile layout or Tile. The parameters become attributes in Tile scope. Custom tags allow you to copy attributes from Tile scope to page, request, session, or application scope, or display the attribute as an included Web resource.

Some programming languages, like C++, Visual Basic, Python, and Ruby allow you to pass default arguments to functions and methods. To further extend the display function metaphor, the Tiles framework also allows you to pass default arguments to a Tile layout. To do this, you must create a *Tile definition*. Definitions allow you to define default parameters for Tiles. You can create definitions in either JSP or XML.

Definitions can extend other definitions, similar to how one class can extend another class. By using definitions and Tile layouts, you create reusable display components.

Although Tiles can be used in a stand-alone fashion, they also work well with Struts. Struts ships with a Tiles tag library. In addition, the Tiles framework includes its own RequestProcessor for handling Tile layouts as ActionForwards. This means that you can forward to a Tile definition instead of a JSP.

Clarification of Terms

You may find all of these terms a bit overwhelming. Before we get into the details of the Tiles framework, let's review some of the terms (Table 13.1).

Table 13.1 Tiles Framework Terms

Term	Definition
Tiles	The template framework for Struts that you use to create reusable presentation components.
Page	A Web resource that is included by a Tile layout.
Tile	The same as a page.
Region	An area in a Tile layout that inserts another Tile. Regions have logical names, like header, footer, etc.
Tile layout	A JSP that describes where other pages should be positioned. It is a template; it defines regions where other Tiles are inserted. A Tile layout can be a Tile to another Tile layout.
Definition	Defines parameters for calling a Tile layout.

A typical Tile layout may define rectangular regions for the header, footer, menu, and body, as shown in Figure 13.1.

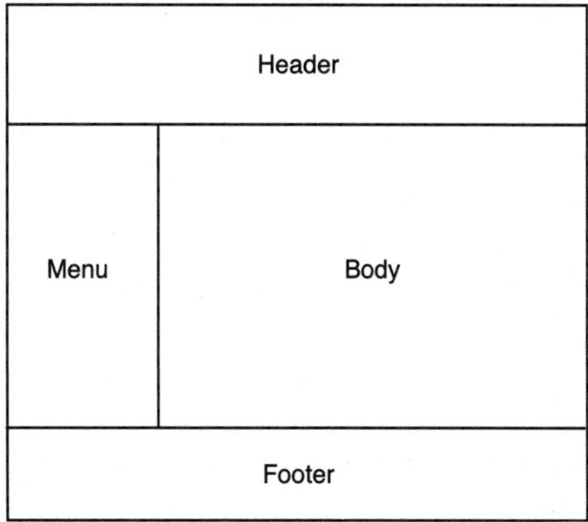

Figure 13.1 A typical Tile layout.

The regions in Figure 13.1 may map to a Web site that looks like the one shown in Figure 13.2.

Notice that we can easily redefine reusable pieces of this application just by passing the correct parameters. For example, the employee listing might use the same header and footer but a different menu and body, and yet still have full use of the general layout defined by the Tile layout. This approach allows you to reuse the same Tile layout with different contents. Instead of including the HTML markup, you include the content in the markup.

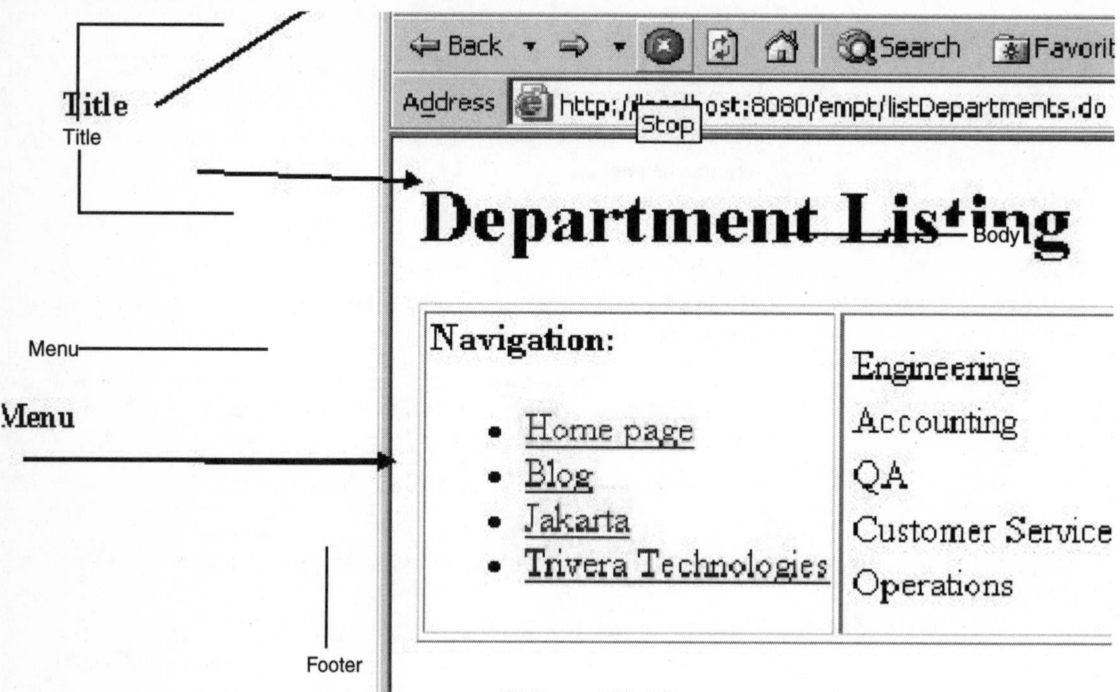

Figure 13.2 The resulting Web site.

Building and Using Your First Tile Layout

If you remember from our earlier example of the Stock Quote application, we repeat HTML code in both the quote.jsp and the index.jsp. The look and feel of the quote.jsp and index.jsp files are very similar. It would be nice to reuse the same layout (implemented with an HTML table) and images in both without duplicating the same HTML code.

For an example of the Tiles framework, let's refactor quote.jsp and index.jsp to utilize a Tile layout. By the end of this chapter, you will have changed the site to feature the layout shown in Figure 13.3.

Follow these steps:

1. Find the similarities between the two pages.
2. Create a new layout page.
3. Create two new content pages that contain just the differences—that is, the parts of quote.jsp and index.jsp that are not the same
4. Insert the Tile layout in the page—in other words, have index.jsp and quote.jsp insert the Tile layout into their page, passing the content as a parameter and any other parameters that are needed (such as Title).

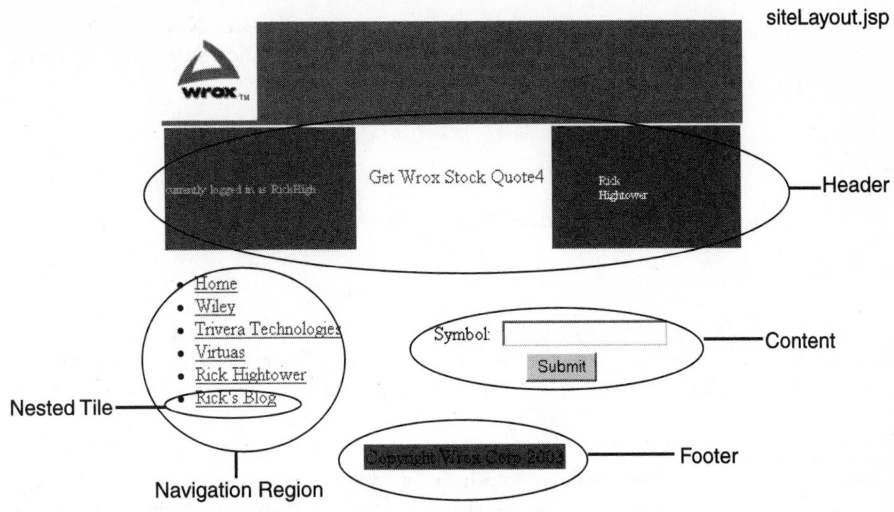

Figure 13.3 The new Web site layout.

Finding similarities between the two pages requires skill in HTML layout and Web site usability. It is more of an art than a science. However, this section's focus is on Struts and not on these particular HTML skills. Let's cover steps 2 through 3 in detail.

Creating a Tile Layout

Once you find the similarities, you can create the new layout page. Identifying the similarities is the difficult part; using Tiles is easy. To create a Tile layout, you must do the following:

1. Import the Tiles taglib into the JSP (along with any other taglibs you need) by using the taglib directive.
2. Use string parameters to display such elements as the title of the page using the tiles:getAsString tag.
3. Insert the Tiles in the correct regions of the layout using the tiles:insert tag.
4. Pass any needed parameters to the internal Tiles using the sub-tag of tiles:insert called tiles:put.

First, you import the Tiles taglib (and any other taglibs you need) into the JSP (siteLayout.jsp) as follows. Remember that before you can use the Tiles taglib, you must declare it in your web.xml file.

```
<%@ taglib uri="/WEB-INF/struts-html.tld" prefix="html" %>
<%@ taglib uri="/WEB-INF/struts-bean.tld" prefix="bean" %>
<%@ taglib uri="/WEB-INF/struts-tiles.tld" prefix="tiles" %>
  <taglib>
    <taglib-uri>/WEB-INF/struts-tiles.tld</taglib-uri>
    <taglib-location>/WEB-INF/struts-tiles.tld
    </taglib-location>
  </taglib>
```

Next, you use string parameters to display elements such as the page title. Not only do you want to change the content of the page, you also want to change the title that shows up in the browser. To do that, you need to pass in a title that will be used by the Tile layout:

```
<html>
  <head>
    <title>
        <tiles:getAsString name="title" ignore="true"/>
    </title>
  </head>
```

Notice that we use the tiles:getAsString tag to display string parameters. In addition to passing string parameters, we can pass other pages that we want to insert into this page. This assumes that the calling JSP passes a title to this Tile layout; otherwise, the title will be blank.

If true, the ignore attribute tells the code to ignore the parameter if it is missing. If ignore is false, the Tiles framework throws an exception and the page will not display if the parameter is not passed (false is the default).

To insert the content JSP, use the tiles:insert tag. The tiles:insert tag inserts any page or Web resource that the framework refers to as a Tile. It effectively defines a region in the Tile layout. Here is an example of inserting a Tile into the layout:

```
<tiles:insert attribute="content"/>
```

Anytime you insert a Tile, you have the option of passing it parameters. The parameters you pass the Tile are put into that Tile's Tile scope and are referred to as Tile attributes. For example, suppose that in addition to having the title displayed in the browser's title bar you would like it to appear in the header region of the page. You have a header.jsp file that you are using to accomplish this. Even though the title variable is in the Tile layout page scope, it would not be in the scope of the Tiles that the Tile layout inserts. Each Tile and Tile layout has its own context—that is, its own Tile scope. Thus, you need to pass the title variable to the header Tile as follows:

```
<tiles:insert attribute="header" ignore="true">
      <tiles:put name="title"
                  beanName="title" beanScope="tile"/>
</tiles:insert>
```

The tiles:put tag puts the title parameter in this Tile layout scope into the header Tile's scope. That way, the header Tile can use the parameter just as the Tile layout did using the tiles:getAsString tag. The parameter name is the name of the attribute in the header's Tile scope. The bean parameter is the name of the bean in the current scope (i.e., siteLayout.jsp). The beanScope is the scope where you want to look for this attribute (the possible values are *page*, *tile*, *request*, *session*, and *application*). You can pass beans from any scope to the Tile.

Listing 13.1 contains the complete new layout page (siteLayout.jsp) that quote.jsp and index.jsp will use. Please take a few moments to study this listing. Notice how we are inserting Tiles into various regions (header, footer, content) and how we are using an HTML layout to define the regions for Tiles, thus defining the complete layout for our application.

```
<%@ taglib uri="/WEB-INF/struts-html.tld" prefix="html" %>
<%@ taglib uri="/WEB-INF/struts-bean.tld" prefix="bean" %>
<%@ taglib uri="/WEB-INF/struts-tiles.tld" prefix="tiles" %>

<html>
  <head>
    <title>
        <tiles:getAsString name="title" ignore="true"/>
    </title>
  </head>

  <body>
    <table width="500" border="0" cellspacing="0" cellpadding="0">

      <tr bgcolor="#36566E">
        <td height="68" width="48%">
          <div align="left">
            <img src="images/hp_logo_wrox.gif"
                 width="220" height="74">
          </div>
        </td>
      </tr>

      <tr>
        <td height="68" width="2000">
            <tiles:insert attribute="header" ignore="true">
               <tiles:put name="title"
                          beanName="title" beanScope="tile"/>
            </tiles:insert>
         </td>
      </tr>
      <tr>
        <td>
            <div align="center">
            <tiles:insert attribute="content"/>
            </div>
        </td>
      </tr>
      <tr>
        <td>
            <tiles:insert attribute="footer" ignore="true"/>
        </td>
      </tr>

    </table>

  </body>
</html>
```

Listing 13.1 siteLayout.jsp.

Using a Tile Layout

Now that you have defined a Tile layout that uses Tiles, you need to take advantage of that layout. Both index.jsp and quote.jsp will use the same layout. This seems like a lot of work for just two pages. However, for a real Web application, you might use the same layout for 20 pages or more. You will not have to repeat this HTML in different 20 locations or include several JSP fragments in 20 different pages.

> **Including JSP fragments in the right location is a fragile way of reusing HTML. Imagine having 20 pages including the same 5 JSP fragments. You would have to repeat yourself 100 times.**

To use a Tile, you need to perform the following steps:

1. Import the Tiles taglib with the taglib directive.
2. Use tiles:insert to insert the Tile layout into the current page.
3. Use tiles:put to pass string parameters.
4. Use tiles:put to pass parameter Tiles.

By using a Tile layout, you can externalize the entire HTML needed for the layout of the site in one location and then just insert it in each page. Here is an example of inserting the Tile layout into index.jsp:

```
<%@ taglib uri="/WEB-INF/struts-tiles.tld" prefix="tiles" %>

<tiles:insert page="/siteLayout.jsp" flush="true">
    <tiles:put name="title" type="string"
                    value="Get WROX Stock Quote" />
    <tiles:put name="header" value="/header.jsp" />
    <tiles:put name="footer" value="/footer.jsp" />
    <tiles:put name="content" value="/indexContent.jsp"/>
</tiles:insert>
```

Now when you want to do the same thing in quote.jsp, all you have to do is change the content and the header.

You need to call the Tile layout (the display function) by using the insert tag. Here we use the tiles:insert tag to insert the Tile layout into the current page:

```
<tiles:insert page="/siteLayout.jsp" flush="true">
```

The page attribute is used to specify the Tile layout that you defined earlier. If the flush attribute is set to true, this Tile (and the page up to this point) will be written to the browser before the rest of the page (or the buffer fills and forces a flush).

One of the things you need to change between quote.jsp and header.jsp is the page title. To do this, use the sub-tag tiles:put:

```
    <tiles:put name="title" type="string"
                    value="Get WROX Stock Quote" />
```

In this code snippet, we use tiles:put to pass string parameters to the Tile layout. The name attribute of the tiles:put tag specifies the name of the parameter. The type attribute specifies the type of the parameter. Finally, the value parameter passes the value of the title attribute. This allows you to pass simple strings as parameters when the Tile layout (the display function) is called with the tiles:insert tag. The parameters become attributes of the Tile layout—that is, they are inserted in the Tile scope of the Tile layout.

In our example, we pass three Tiles as parameters—header, footer, and content (header.jsp, footer.jsp, and indexCotent.jsp)—as follows:

```
<tiles:put name="header" value="/header.jsp" />
<tiles:put name="footer" value="/footer.jsp" />
<tiles:put name="content" value="/indexContent.jsp"/>
```

The header.jsp page will be inserted in the header region of the Tile layout; footer.jsp will be inserted into the footer region, and indexContent.jsp will be inserted into the content region. If you want to insert a different content and title, all you have to do is change the value of the content parameter.

Notice that the form for index.jsp is no longer in index.jsp. The form has been moved to indexContent.jsp:

```
<%@ taglib uri="/WEB-INF/struts-html.tld" prefix="html" %>
<%@ taglib uri="/WEB-INF/struts-bean.tld" prefix="bean" %>

<html:form action="Lookup">
  <table width="45%" border="0">
    <tr>
      <td><bean:message key="app.symbol" />:</td>
      <td><html:text property="symbol" /></td>
    </tr>
    <tr>
      <td colspan="2" align="center"><html:submit /></td>
    </tr>
  </table>
</html:form>
```

In addition to specifying Tiles as JSP pages, you can pass in text in the body of the tiles:put tag as the tile. The quote.jsp page does just this:

```
<%@ taglib uri="/WEB-INF/struts-bean.tld" prefix="bean" %>
<%@ taglib uri="/WEB-INF/struts-tiles.tld" prefix="tiles" %>

<tiles:insert page="/siteLayout.jsp" flush="true">
    <tiles:put name="title" type="string"
                    value="WROX Stock Quote" />
    <tiles:put name="header" value="/header.jsp" />
    <tiles:put name="footer" value="/footer.jsp" />
    <tiles:put name="content" type="string">
          <bean:message key="app.price"/>
          <%= request.getAttribute("PRICE") %>
    </tiles:put>
</tiles:insert>
```

Notice that the body of the tiles:put tag contains the contents of quote.jsp. Everything else is defined by the layout and by the same Tiles we used in the previous example.

The advantage of this approach is that it reduces the number of JSP pages in the system. I've seen long debates about which approach is best, and I've concluded that the answer depends on how much code will be in the body of the put.

Do you see a problem here? We have broken the "don't repeat yourself" (DRY) rule. Let's take a look.

Creating a Definition

The problem with quote.jsp and index.jsp is that they break the DRY rule: They repeat the header and footer parameter definitions. They use the same parameter values, so it would be nice if we did not have to repeat those parameters for both pages.

If this were a real application, the Tile layout would likely have a lot more regions (say, eight regions) and a lot more pages. It would be a real pain to repeat every one of these parameters every time you wanted to use a Tile layout. Because most pages will use the same header and footer, our goal is to define them in one place instead of in each page.

As you'll recall, earlier we compared the Tile layout to a display function. You invoke the Tile layout using tiles:insert. You pass in parameters using tiles:put. The parameters are other JSP pages and strings that can be inserted into regions of the Tile layout.

What you need now is the ability to define default parameters that correspond to the header and footer regions. The Tiles framework also allows you to pass default arguments to a Tile layout using definitions.

In this section, we show you how to create and use definitions. Definitions specify default parameters for Tile layouts. You can create definitions in JSP or XML. By the end of this section, you will be able to do both.

Creating and Using a JSP Definition

The simplest way to create a definition is with the JSPs. This approach requires the least amount of configuration.

Creating a JSP Tile Definition

To create a JSP definition, follow these steps:

1. Import the Tiles tag library using the taglib directive.
2. Ensure that the definition is created only once using the logic:notPresent tag.
3. Define the definition with the tiles:definition tag and pass the JSP that defines the Tile layout and the scope of the newly created definition.
4. Define the default parameters with the tiles:put tag.

The siteLayoutDefinition.jsp page (Listing 13.2) creates a definition that uses the siteLayout.jsp page as the Tile layout and specifies default values for the header and footer parameters (as well as other parameters).

```
<%@ taglib uri="/WEB-INF/struts-logic.tld" prefix="logic" %>
<%@ taglib uri="/WEB-INF/struts-tiles.tld" prefix="tiles" %>

<logic:notPresent name="siteLayoutDef" scope="application">
  <tiles:definition id="siteLayoutDef"
                    page="/siteLayout.jsp"
                    scope="application">
    <tiles:put name="title" type="string"
                     value="WROX Stock Quote System" />
    <tiles:put name="header" value="/header.jsp" />
    <tiles:put name="footer" value="/footer.jsp" />
    <tiles:put name="content" type="string">
       Content goes here
    </tiles:put>
  </tiles:definition>
</logic:notPresent>
```

Listing 13.2 siteLayoutDefinition.jsp.

The tiles:definition tag defines a JavaBean of type ComponentDefinition (org.apache.struts.tiles.ComponentDefinition). ComponentDefinition has getter and setters for all of the attributes that you can pass it. The logic:notPresent tag ensures that the ComponentDefinition is created only once per application by checking to see if it is already in scope before defining it.

> **Notice that we define default parameters for the content and title as well. This is considered bad practice. Why? If someone forgets to use the title, he or she will get the default. Because the title should change for every page, we should not define a default for it. This way, if someone forgets to pass the title the Tile layout will fail. In order for it to fail, you need to do two things. First, don't define a default in the definition. Second, don't set ignore equal to true when defining the region in the Tile layout with the tiles:insert tag.**

Using a JSP Tile Definition

Using a Tile definition is not much different than using a Tile layout directly. The only differences are that you will specify the definition instead of the Tile layout JSP page and that you will pass in fewer parameters with tiles:put.

To use a Tile definition, follow these steps:

1. Import the Tiles taglib with the taglib directive.
2. Include the JSP page that creates the definition by using jsp:include.

3. Use the tiles:insert tag, but specify the definition bean name and scope instead of the Tile layout page.
4. Use the tiles:put attribute to specify the title and content but not header and footer parameters.

Here is an example of using a Tiles definition (index2.jsp):

```
    <%@ taglib uri="/WEB-INF/struts-tiles.tld" prefix="tiles" %>
    <jsp:include page="siteLayoutDefinition.jsp"/>

    <tiles:insert beanName="siteLayoutDef" beanScope="application">
        <tiles:put name="title" type="string"
                   value="Get WROX Stock Quote 2" />
        <tiles:put name="content" value="indexContent2.jsp"/>
</tiles:insert>
```

Notice that in this example we specify the definition that we created in the previous section with the beanName attribute (siteLayoutDef). The beanName attribute value corresponds to the id attribute value of the bean definition in the previous section. Also note that here we specify two parameters with tiles:put instead of four. This means less typing—and less code to maintain. The joys of DRY. . .

Do you see a problem here? We have a lot of JSP pages to create: one for the definition (siteLayoutDefinition.jsp), one for the content (indexContent.jsp), one for the index.jsp itself, one for the layout (siteLayout.jsp), one for the header, and one for the footer. Whew! Sum it up and you get six JSP pages instead of one (and this is a simple example). Granted, you are getting a lot of reusability, but it appears that you get this advantage at the expense of simplicity.

Another thing you should note about this example is the definition itself. JSP pages are meant to express visual things in a document-centric fashion. There is nothing inherently visual about the definition. In fact, it is mostly just configuration data. A layout may have several sets of definitions; it would be a hassle to have a JSP page for each. Wouldn't it be nice to have all of this configuration data in one location?

> **If you have worked with Tiles, you may have seen examples that use the include directive (@page include) instead of the dynamic include action (jsp:include). I prefer jsp:include. The problem I have found with the include directive is that it takes place at translation time and unless the page that includes it changes, the new JSP definition will not be redefined. Save yourself some development hassles and use the jsp:include action instead. The performance difference is negligible (the directive is slightly faster), but the pain of dated JSP definitions is mind-boggling.**

Creating and Using an XML Definition

XML definitions are the answer to problems related to the explosion of nonvisual JSPs. Instead of creating one definition per JSP, you can build all of your definitions in one configuration file. Before you can start using XML definitions, you need to install the corresponding Tiles Plugin for Struts. Add the following to your Struts configuration file:

```
<plug-in className="org.apache.struts.tiles.TilesPlugin" >
  <set-property property="definitions-config"
               value="/WEB-INF/tiles-defs.xml" />
  <set-property property="moduleAware" value="true" />
  <set-property property="definitions-parser-validate" value="true" />
</plug-in>
```

The definition-config property specifies the XML file that will contain the XML-based definitions. The code also specifies that the Tiles engine is module aware and that it validates the XML file.

Creating an XML Tile Definition

Creating an XML definition is easy using the Plugin. All you have to do is add another entry in the Tiles definition file (tiles-def.xml, for our example) as follows:

```
<tiles-definitions>

  <definition name="siteLayoutDef" path="/siteLayout.jsp">
    <put name="title" value="WROX Stock Quote System" />
    <put name="header" value="/header.jsp" />
    <put name="footer" value="/footer.jsp" />
    <put name="content" type="string">
       Content goes here
    </put>
  </definition>
...
```

The root element is tiles-definitions; all of the Tile definitions for this module will be defined inside this element.

The definition element specifies a Tile definition. The definition we created here is functionally equivalent to the JSP version we defined earlier. Notice that the attributes of the definition are a little different; you use name instead of id and path instead of page. If you know how to define a JSP-based definition, then defining an XML-based one is child's play because they are nearly identical in form and function.

Using an XML Tile Definition

Now that you have defined your XML definition, you need to change quote.jsp and index.jsp to use it. Using the definition is not much different than before, as shown here (index3.jsp). The only difference is the attributes you pass the tiles:insert tag:

```
<%@ taglib uri="/WEB-INF/struts-tiles.tld" prefix="tiles" %>
<tiles:insert definition="siteLayoutDef">
    <tiles:put name="title" type="string"
              value="Get WROX Stock Quote 3" />
```

```
    <tiles:put name="content" value="indexContent3.jsp"/>
</tiles:insert>
```

You now use the definition attribute to specify the name of the definition created in the Tiles definition file (tiles-def.xml) instead of using beanName and beanScope. You do not have to use jsp:include or logic:notPresent in the definition JSP.

Once you start using XML definitions instead of JSP definitions, life with Tiles gets a little easier. You have to write less code and you won't have as many tiny, nonvisual JSP pages to maintain.

Understanding Tile Scope

The Tiles framework defines an additional scope called Tile scope. Like page scope, Tile scope is more private than request scope. It allows the user of the Tile to pass arguments (called parameters) to the Tile. Like a display function, it makes the page callable.

Remember, jsp:include allows you to call a page and pass it request parameters (jsp:param); tiles:insert is similar but is more powerful. The tiles:insert directive allows you to call a page and pass it sub-pages (called Tiles) and attributes. Tile scope lets you pass variables that are available only to that Tile layout.

It becomes easier to understand Tile scope if you know how it is implemented. In my travels, I created a debug utility called listTileScope (Listing 13.3) that allows me to print out variables that are in Tile scope. This code should help you understand how Tile scope is implemented.

```
import org.apache.struts.taglib.tiles.ComponentConstants;
import org.apache.struts.tiles.ComponentContext;

public static void listTileScope(PageContext context)
                 throws JspException, IOException {

    JspWriter out = context.getOut();
    ComponentContext compContext =
            (ComponentContext)context.getAttribute(
                        ComponentConstants.COMPONENT_CONTEXT,
                        PageContext.REQUEST_SCOPE);

    out.println("--- TILE Attributes --- <br />");


    if (compContext!=null){

        Iterator iter = compContext.getAttributeNames();
        while(iter.hasNext()){
            String name = (String)iter.next();
            Object value = compContext.getAttribute(name);
            printNameValueType(name, value, out);
        }
    }else{
        out.println("---TILE Attributes NOT FOUND---<br />");
    }
```

Code continued on following page

```
    out.println("--------------------------- <br />");

}

private static void printNameValueType(
                        String name,
                        Object value,
                        JspWriter out)
                                throws IOException{

    if (value !=null){

        out.println(
        name + " = " +  value +
        " type (" +
            value.getClass().getName()+ ") " +
        "<br /><br />");

    }else{
        out.println(name + " = " +  value +
        "<br /><br />");

    }
}
```

Listing 13.3 listTileScope.

Notice that the class ComponentContext implements Tile scope. The ComponentContext class is located in request scope under the key ComponentConstants.COMPONENT_CONTEXT. The Tiles system ensures that each Tile gets its own component context.

Nested Tiles do not share the same Tile scope as their parent (I learned this one the hard way). The Tile scope of the current Tile is saved before the nested Tile is displayed; after the nested Tile finishes, the parent's Tile scope is restored to the request. This magic is done in the InsertTag (org.apache.struts.taglib.tiles.InsertTag) class's nested class InsertHandler.

So far, you have passed attributes to the Tile layout that corresponds to sub-Tiles or simple strings. You can pass in *any* bean type as attributes to the Tile layout and then use those attributes inside the Tile layout.

Let's say you have an action in your application that puts a User object into session scope, perhaps after the user logs into the system:

```
public ActionForward execute(ActionMapping mapping,
  ActionForm form,
  HttpServletRequest request,
  HttpServletResponse response)
  throws IOException, ServletException {
```

```
        // Default target to success
        String target = new String("success");

        //if login successful.
        UserDomainObject user = new UserDomainObject();
        ...
        request.getSession().setAttribute("user", user);
        return (mapping.findForward(target));
    }
```

Now you want to pass that user to a Tile you are inserting. In this example, use the Tile you used inside your Tile layout (siteLayout2.jsp):

```
<tiles:insert attribute="header" ignore="true">
    <tiles:put name="title" beanName="title" beanScope="tile"/>
    <tiles:put name="user" beanName="user"
                                              beanScope="session"/>
</tiles:insert>
```

The Tile layout passes the user bean to the header Tile by specifying a scope of session and a bean name of user. You can pass any bean from any JSP scope into the Tile or Tile layout using this technique; thus, the Tile scope becomes just another scope. This is not much different than before.

To use this user bean in header.jsp, you have to copy it from Tile scope into a scope that other beans understand. You can do this by using the tiles:useAttribute tag. This tag is analogous to the jsp:useBean action, except that it works only with Tile scope:

```
<tiles:useAttribute id="user"
                    name="user"
                    classname="ch13.UserDomainObject"
                    />
```

This code defines a user in page scope of the header.jsp JSP. Once the bean is defined, you can start using it as you would any bean defined in page scope:

```
   <bean:write name="user" property="userName"/>
```

Listing 13.4 contains the new header2.jsp file.

```
<%@ taglib uri="/WEB-INF/struts-tiles.tld" prefix="tiles" %>
<%@ taglib uri="/WEB-INF/struts-bean.tld" prefix="bean" %>
<center>
<table>
<tr>


<tiles:useAttribute id="user"
                    name="user"
                    classname="ch13.UserDomainObject"
                    />
```

Code continued on following page

```
        <td width="33%" bgcolor="#36566E">
           
           <div align='left'>
           <font size="1" color="orange">

                  currently logged in as
                  <bean:write name="user" property="userName"/>

           </font>
           </div>
            
        </td>


        <td width="33%">
             
            <font color="#36566E">
                <tiles:getAsString name="title" ignore="true"/>
            </font>
             
        </td>

        <td width="33%" bgcolor="#36566E">
             
            <div align='left'>
            <font size="1" color="white">
                <blockquote>
                   <bean:write name="user" property="firstName"/>
                <br />
                   <bean:write name="user" property="lastName"/>
                <br />
                   </blockquote>
            </font>
            </div>
             
        </td>
</tr>
</table>
</center>
```

Listing 13.4 header2.jsp.

As you can see, the header now displays information about the current user logged into the site. This is a powerful feature. You can create Tiles that specialize in displaying domain objects and then reuse those Tiles in many parts of your application—you can in effect create display components. Unlike custom tags (pre–JSP 2.0), these components are all created in JSP pages.

Understanding Lists

In many cases, you want to pass more than one parameter. For example, you may want to pass a list of parameters to display links in the navigation region of the Tile layout.

Going back to our employee listing example, suppose you have a Web application that displays a company's divisions, departments, and employees. When you are in the employee listing view, employeeListing.jsp is in the *content* region of the Tile layout and the department links of the current division appear in the *navigation* region. When you click on a department link, a new listing of the employees in that department appears. In the department view, the deptListing.jsp displays in the content region of the Tile layout and the list of division links of the company appears in the navigation region. When you click on a division link, a new listing of departments appears. Thus, each page (employeeListing.jsp and deptListing.jsp) passes in a new list of links.

Using putList in XML

Tiles allow users to pass in links using the putList sub-element, which can be used in XML and JSP definitions or in calls to a definition or Tile layout from a JSP.

Suppose you want to have a standard set of navigational links for your site layout. You can specify these links with the putList sub-element in your Tiles configuration file (tiles-def.xml), shown in Listing 13.5.

```
<definition name="siteLayoutDef3" path="/siteLayout3.jsp">
  <put name="title" value="WROX Stock Quote System" />
  <put name="header" value="/header2.jsp" />
  <put name="footer" value="/footer.jsp" />
  <put name="content" type="string">
     Content goes here
  </put>

  <putList name="items" >
    <item value="Home"
          link="/index.html"  />
    <item value="WROX"
          link="http://www.wrox.com"  />
    <item value="Trivera Technologies"
          link="http://www.triveratech.com/"  />
    <item value="Virtuas"
          link="http://www.virtuas.com/"  />
    <item value="Rick Hightower"
          link="http://www.rickhightower.com"  />
    <item value="Rick's Blog"
          link="http://rickhightower.blogspot.com/"  />
  </putList>
</definition>
```

Listing 13.5 tiles-def.xml.

The putList element lets you specify a list of items associated with links. In Listing 13.5, putList defines six links. The list (java.util.List) put into Tile scope consists of items specified with the putList element's name attribute.

The item element defines a link by putting an instance of org.apache.struts.tiles.beans.MenuItem in the list. The value attribute corresponds to the label on the link, and the link element refers to the link's URL.

The item element also has elements for specifying the tool tip and the icon for the link. You can learn more about the item element and putList by looking at tiles-config_1_1.dtd, which can be found in the Struts source.

Using the List in the Tile Layout

To use the list of links, you need to modify your Tile layout (siteLayout3.jsp) as shown in Listing 13.6. The changes appear in bold.

```
<%@ taglib uri="/WEB-INF/struts-html.tld" prefix="html" %>
<%@ taglib uri="/WEB-INF/struts-bean.tld" prefix="bean" %>
<%@ taglib uri="/WEB-INF/struts-tiles.tld" prefix="tiles" %>
<%@ taglib uri="/WEB-INF/struts-logic.tld" prefix="logic" %>

<tiles:importAttribute />

<html>
  <head>
    <logic:present name="title">
        <title>
        <tiles:getAsString name="title" ignore="true"/>
        </title>
    </logic:present>
  </head>

  <body>
    <table width="500" border="0" cellspacing="0" cellpadding="0">

      <tr bgcolor="#36566E">
        <td height="68" width="70%">
          <div align="left">
   <img src="images/hp_logo_wrox.gif" width="220" height="74">
          </div>
        </td>
      </tr>

      <tr>
        <td height="68" width="2000">
            <tiles:insert attribute="header" ignore="true">
                <tiles:put name="title"
                              beanName="title" beanScope="tile"/>
                <tiles:put name="user"
```

Code continued on following page

```
                        beanName="user" beanScope="session"/>
                </tiles:insert>
              </td>
            </tr>

            <table>
            <tr>
              <td width="50%">
              <ul>
              <logic:iterate id="item" name="items"
                      type="org.apache.struts.tiles.beans.MenuItem" >
                 <li>

                 <bean:define id="link" name="item" property="link"
                              type="java.lang.String"/>

                 <logic:match name="link"
                              location="start" value="/" >
                           <html:link page="<%=link%>" >
                               <bean:write name="item"
                                         property="value"/>
                           </html:link>
                       </logic:match>
                 <logic:notMatch name="link"
                                 location="start" value="/" >
                           <html:link href="<%=link%>">
                               <bean:write name="item"
                                         property="value"/>
                           </html:link>
                       </logic:notMatch>

                 </li>
                    </logic:iterate>
              </ul>
              </td>
              <td width="50%">
                  <div align="center">
                  <tiles:insert attribute="content"/>
                  </div>
              </td>
            </tr>
            </table>

            <tr>
              <td>
                  <tiles:insert attribute="footer" ignore="true"/>
              </td>
            </tr>

          </table>

        </body>
      </html>
```

Listing 13.6 siteLayout3.jsp.

The tiles:importAttribute tag

The tiles:importAttribute tag imports all of the attributes in Tile scope into page scope. It is similar to the tiles:useAttribute tag—but much more like a shotgun than a scalpel. It is lazy, dirty and cheap; I use it all the time. This effectively copies the items list from Tile scope into page scope.

> **By default, tiles:importAttribute copies all of the attributes into page scope. You can copy the attributes into other scopes as well by using the scope attribute.**

Once the items list is in page scope, you can access it with the standard Struts tags:

```
<logic:iterate id="item" name="items"
   type="org.apache.struts.tiles.beans.MenuItem" >

  ...
</logic:iterate>
```

Notice the logic this code implements with the logic tag to display the link. First, the code checks to see if the link begins with a slash (/) to determine if the link is relative. If the link is relative, the code uses the page attribute of the html:link tag; otherwise, it uses the href attribute of the html:link tag (if the link refers to an absolute URL):

```
<bean:define id="link" name="item" property="link"
             type="java.lang.String"/>

<logic:match name="link"
             location="start" value="/" >
          <html:link page="<%=link%>" >
              <bean:write name="item"
                          property="value"/>
         </html:link>
   </logic:match>
<logic:notMatch name="link"
                location="start" value="/" >
          <html:link href="<%=link%>">
              <bean:write name="item"
                          property="value"/>
          </html:link>
   </logic:notMatch>
```

You may want to use this bit of display logic to display menu items in more than one location—in others words, you may want to reuse it outside the scope of this page. In the section "Nesting Tiles," we show you how to do this by nesting one Tile layout into another.

Using putList in JSP

In addition to adding items to the list in the Tile definition, you can add items to the list in the JSP using the tiles:putList element and its tiles:add sub-element, as shown in Listing 13.7 (index6.jsp).

```
<%@ taglib uri="/WEB-INF/struts-tiles.tld" prefix="tiles" %>

<%@ page import="org.apache.struts.tiles.beans.SimpleMenuItem" %>
<tiles:insert definition="siteLayoutDef4">
    <tiles:put name="title" type="string"
               value="Get WROX Stock Quote6" />
    <tiles:put name="content" value="indexContent5.jsp"/>

    <tiles:putList name="items" >
        <jsp:useBean id="item1" class="SimpleMenuItem"/>
        <jsp:setProperty name="item1" property="link"
                         value="/index.html"/>
        <jsp:setProperty name="item1" property="value"
                         value="Home" />
        <tiles:add beanName="item1"/>
    </tiles:putList>
</tiles:insert>
```

Listing 13.7 index6.jsp.

Listing 13.7 uses jsp:useBean to create an instance of SimpleMenuItem. Then it uses jsp:setProperty to set the link and value properties of the SimpleMenuItem bean. Finally, it uses tiles:add to add this bean to the list.

In this example, we added a SimpleMenuItem, which subclasses the MenuItem that our Tile layout uses. However, you can add any bean type.

To add any bean type in the Tiles XML definition, you can use the putList's subelement bean. The bean element takes an id and a classtype attribute. For simple types, you can use putList's subelement add as well. See the Tiles configuration DTD (tiles-config_1_1.dtd) for more information.

Extending Definitions

It is often the case that several JSP pages use the same default parameters. Yet other pages use the same Tile layout but use different Tile parameters. Instead of creating a completely different definition, you can extend one definition to another definition by using the extends attribute. Here's an example:

```
<definition name="siteLayoutDef3" path="/siteLayout3.jsp">
  <put name="title" value="WROX Stock Quote System" />
  <put name="header" value="/header2.jsp" />
  <put name="footer" value="/footer.jsp" />
  <put name="content" type="string">
     Content goes here
  </put>

  <putList name="items" >
    <item value="Home"
```

```
            link="/index.html"  />
      <item value="WROX"
            link="http://www.wrox.com"  />
      <item value="Trivera Technologies"
            link="http://www.triveratech.com/"  />
      <item value="Virtuas"
            link="http://www.virtuas.com/"  />
      <item value="Rick Hightower"
            link="http://www.rickhightower.com"  />
      <item value="Rick's Blog"
            link="http://rickhightower.blogspot.com/"  />
    </putList>
  </definition>

  <definition name="siteLayoutDef4" extends="siteLayoutDef3">
    <put name="title" value="WROX Quote Sub System" />
    <putList name="items" >
      <item value="Home"
            link="/index.html"  />
      <item value="WROX"
            link="http://www.wrox.com"  />
      <item value="Trivera Technologies"
            link="http://www.triveratech.com/"  />
      <item value="Virtuas"
            link="http://www.virtuas.com/"  />
    </putList>
  </definition>

  <definition name="siteLayoutDef5"  extends="siteLayoutDef4">
    <putList name="items" >
    </putList>
  </definition>

  <definition name="siteLayoutDef6" path="/siteLayout4.jsp"
              extends="siteLayoutDef4">
  </definition>
```

Note that siteLayoutDef4 extends siteLayoutDef3, overrides the title values, and defines a shorter navigation list. It inherits all the other parameters from siteLayoutDef3 that it did override—header, footer, and content. Also note that siteLayoutDef5 extends siteLayout4, except it blanks out the list of items. A definition inherits all of the attributes of its super definition and all of its super definition's super definitions ad infinitum.

In addition to overriding attributes, you can change the Tile layout JSP. Look at siteLayoutDef6; it extends siteLayoutDef5 and specifies a new Tile layout (siteLayout4.jsp).

Nesting Tiles

One Tile layout can insert another Tile layout, and so on. In fact, you can create Tile layouts that are so small they are not really templates per se. Instead, they become small visual components more similar to custom tags than page templates.

Remember the logic we implemented for displaying a link. We check to see if the link begins with / to determine whether the link is relative and then display it correctly. What if you want to use that same routine in several places in your application? You can create a visual component to do this.

Creating a Visual Component

A visual component is just another Tile layout. Whether a Tile layout is a visual component or a template is really just a point of view. The Tile layout in Listing 13.8 defines a visual component for displaying a link.

```
<%@ taglib uri="/WEB-INF/struts-html.tld" prefix="html" %>
<%@ taglib uri="/WEB-INF/struts-bean.tld" prefix="bean" %>
<%@ taglib uri="/WEB-INF/struts-tiles.tld" prefix="tiles" %>
<%@ taglib uri="/WEB-INF/struts-logic.tld" prefix="logic" %>

   <tiles:useAttribute id="item"
          name="item"
          classname="org.apache.struts.tiles.beans.MenuItem"
                   />
   <bean:define id="link" name="item" property="link"
                type="java.lang.String"/>

   <logic:match name="link" location="start" value="/" >
       <html:link page="<%=link%>" >
           <bean:write name="item" property="value"/>
             </html:link>
   </logic:match>
   <logic:notMatch name="link" location="start" value="/" >
       <html:link href="<%=link%>">
           <bean:write name="item" property="value"/>
             </html:link>
   </logic:notMatch>
```

Listing 13.8 linkLayout.jsp.

The nice thing about using this approach rather than JSP custom tags is that you can use other custom tags. Also, this is document-centric JSP versus a Java class (like a custom tag).

> **Many of the advantages of using Tile layouts in this manner can now be achieved with JSP tag files, which are available in JSP 2.0 and later. If you are using an older version of JSP that does not support tag files, you can start using this technique now.**

Using the Visual Component

Once you have defined the visual component, you need to create a definition for it:

```
<definition name="linkLayoutDef" path="/linkLayout.jsp">
</definition>
```

At this point, you can use your visual component on any page by using the tiles:insert tag. You even use this visual component inside another Tile. The following code uses this visual component inside the Tile layout we defined earlier:

```
...
    <td width="50%">
          <ul>
          <logic:iterate id="item" name="items"
                 type="org.apache.struts.tiles.beans.MenuItem" >
             <li>

                       <tiles:insert definition="linkLayoutDef">
                      <tiles:put name="item"
                                 beanName="item"
                                 beanScope="page"/>
                       </tiles:insert>

             </li>
                </logic:iterate>
          </ul>
          </td>
...
```

This code iterates over the list of items, then calls tiles:insert and passes the current item to the visual component (linkLayoutDef) to display. The visual component knows how to display a domain object (a menu item). Any time you catch yourself repeating the same lines of JSP code over and over again, consider writing a visual component using a Tile layout.

Using a Tile as a Parameter to Another Tile

The previous example explicitly called the visual component that we defined. What if the Tile layout you use varies based on several factors (whether the user is logged in, whether the user is in a certain role, which part of the site you are looking at)? Wouldn't it be nice to be able to pass the Tile as a parameter? You can do just that by using the put element, as shown in this code (tiles-def.xml):

```
<definition name="link.layout.def" path="/linkLayout.jsp">
</definition>

<definition name="siteLayoutDef7" path="/siteLayout5.jsp"
                  extends="siteLayoutDef4">
  <put name="title" value="WROX Quote System 9" />
  <putList name="items" >
  </putList>
  <put name="linkDisplay" value="link.layout.def"/>
</definition>
```

Notice that siteLayoutDef7 has an attribute called linkDisplay. The value of linkDisplay is equal to link.layout.def. Now inside the Tile layout (siteLayout5.jsp) you can specify the attribute linkDisplay instead of calling a particular Tile layout definition:

```
<ul>
<logic:iterate id="item" name="items"
       type="org.apache.struts.tiles.beans.MenuItem">
   <li>

    <tiles:insert attribute="linkDisplay">
          <tiles:put name="item"
                     beanName="item"
                     beanScope="page"/>

    </tiles:insert>

   </li>
      </logic:iterate>
</ul>
```

In this example, the site layout does not know which visual component it is using. You can programmatically switch how pieces of the layout are displayed by switching which visual component the site layout uses.

Tile Controllers

If you feel you are putting too much Java code into your Tile layout, or you have to put the same Java code into every Action that forwards to a page that uses a particular Tile layout, then you should use a Tile Controller. You can specify a Controller class that is called before a Tile is inserted by using the controllerClass attribute:

```
<%@ taglib uri="/WEB-INF/struts-tiles.tld" prefix="tiles" %>

<tiles:insert definition="siteLayoutDef5"
              controllerClass="ch13.SimpleController">
    <tiles:put name="content" value="indexContent5.jsp" />
</tiles:insert>
```

The Controller class is similar to an Action. You can map model objects into scope so that the Tile can display the items.

To write a Tile Controller, follow these steps:

1. Create a class that implements org.apache.struts.tiles.Controller.
2. Implement the perform method.
3. In the perform method, do something with the model and map the results into scope so the Tile can use it.

Listing 13.9 contains an example of implementing a Controller.

```
package ch13;

import java.io.IOException;

import javax.servlet.ServletContext;
import javax.servlet.ServletException;
import javax.servlet.http.HttpServletRequest;
import javax.servlet.http.HttpServletResponse;

import org.apache.struts.tiles.ComponentContext;
import org.apache.struts.tiles.Controller;

import org.apache.struts.tiles.beans.MenuItem;
import org.apache.struts.tiles.beans.SimpleMenuItem;

import java.util.ArrayList;
import java.util.List;


/**
 * @author rhightower
 */
public class SimpleController implements Controller{

    private MenuItem createMenuItem(String label, String link){
              SimpleMenuItem item = new SimpleMenuItem();
              item.setLink(link);
              item.setValue(label);
              return item;
    }

    private List getLinks(){
              List list = new ArrayList();

              list.add(createMenuItem("Home",
                     "/index.html"));

              list.add(createMenuItem("Rick's",
            "http://www.rickhightower.com"));

              list.add(createMenuItem("Trivera",
                     "http://www.triveratech.com"));

              return list;

    }
       /* (non-Javadoc)
        *
      */
       public void perform(ComponentContext context,
                          HttpServletRequest request,
                          HttpServletResponse response,
```

Code continued on following page

```
                                    ServletContext servletContext)
                                  throws ServletException, IOException {
                 List items = (List)getLinks();
                 context.putAttribute("items",items);
        }

}
```

Listing 13.9 ch13.SimpleController.

Notice that the perform method is passed the component context. The component context holds all of the attributes of Tile scope. Putting things in the component context places them in Tile scope. In this simple example, we call getLinks, which returns a simple list of MenuItems that we map into Tile scope. A real-world example would likely talk to the model—perhaps a facade that communicates with a database to look up links specific to the type of user logged into the system.

> **You can instead use an Action as the Controller for the Tile. To do this, you have to specify the path of the Action with the controllerUrl attribute.**

Using a Tile as an ActionForward

You probably did not realize this, but when you installed the Tiles Plugin you installed a custom request processor. This custom request processor extends the way Struts handles ActionForward. This means that you can forward to a Tile definition instead of a JSP page.

Let's say you have this definition:

```
<definition name="main.index" extends="siteLayoutDef7">
  <put name="content" value="/indexContent.jsp"/>
</definition>
```

In your Struts configuration file, you can define a forward that forwards to the main.index definition instead of specifying a JSP page:

```
<action
                path="/Lookup"
                type="ch13.SimpleLookupAction"
                name="lookupForm"
                input="/index.jsp">

        <forward name="success" path="/quote.jsp"/>
        <!-- forward name="failure" path="/index.jsp"/ -->
        <forward name="failure" path="main.index" />
</action>
```

What's Next

If you are using Struts and you are not using Tiles, then you are not getting the full benefit of Struts and are probably repeating yourself a lot. As you learned in this chapter, the Tiles framework makes it possible for you to create reusable site layouts and visual components.

In the next chapter, we use all the information presented so far in this book to build a complete Struts application from the ground up.

14

Developing a Complete Struts Application

In this chapter we develop a complete Struts application. We begin by defining each component of the application and then continue with the actual development and implementation of the application. The goal of this chapter is to tie the majority of our previous discussions together through the use of an example that leverages the components most often used in a Struts application. We also use MySQL as our preferred database for the application.

The Employees Application Definition

Our example application, named *employees*, acts as an employee directory service that will allow a user to list, add, edit, and delete employees stored in the company database. In this section we will define all of the components of our employees application including the Models, the Views, and the Controller.

Preparing the employees Application

Before we can begin developing our example, we must perform the basic steps of preparing the application. These steps are the minimum number of steps that must be completed when defining any Struts application.

1. Create a new Web application, named *employees*, using the directory structure described in Chapter 1, "Introducing the Jakarta-Struts Project and its Supporting Components."
2. Copy the Jar files, extracted from the Jakarta Struts archive, to the <*CATALINA_HOME*>/webapps/employees/WEB-INF/lib directory.
3. Copy the MySql JDBC driver file, used in Chapter 11, to the <*CATALINA_HOME*>/webapps/employees/WEB-INF/lib directory.

4. Copy the Commons DBCP Jar files, also used in Chapter 11, to the *<CATALINA_HOME>*/webapps/employees/WEB-INF/lib directory.

5. Create an empty struts-config.xml file and copy it to the *<CATALINA_HOME>*/webapps/employees/WEB-INF/ directory. Listing 14.1 contains an example of an empty struts-config.xml file:

```
<?xml version="1.0" encoding="ISO-8859-1" ?>

<!DOCTYPE struts-config
  PUBLIC
  "-//Apache Software Foundation//DTD Struts Configuration 1.0//EN"
  "http://jakarta.apache.org/struts/dtds/struts-config_1_1.dtd">

<struts-config>

</struts-config>
```

Listing 14.1 An Empty struts-config.xml File.

6. Create a web.xml file with a Servlet definition for the ActionServlet, and copy this file to the *<CATALINA_HOME>*/webapps/employees/WEB-INF/ directory. Listing 14.2 contains our initial web.xml file. This file will evolve as we add additional components to our employees application.

```
<?xml version="1.0" encoding="ISO-8859-1"?>

<!DOCTYPE web-app
  PUBLIC "-//Sun Microsystems, Inc.//DTD Web Application 2.3//EN"
  "http://java.sun.com/dtd/web-app_2_3.dtd">

<web-app>

  <servlet>
    <servlet-name>action</servlet-name>
    <servlet-class>
      org.apache.struts.action.ActionServlet
    </servlet-class>
    <init-param>
      <param-name>debug</param-name>
      <param-value>5</param-value>
    </init-param>
    <init-param>
      <param-name>config</param-name>
      <param-value>/WEB-INF/struts-config.xml</param-value>
    </init-param>
    <load-on-startup>1</load-on-startup>
  </servlet>

  <servlet-mapping>
    <servlet-name>action</servlet-name>
    <url-pattern>*.do</url-pattern>
```

Code continued on following page

```
  </servlet-mapping>

</web-app>
```

Listing 14.2 Default web.xml File.

7. Create an English application resource bundle and copy it to the <*CATALINA_HOME*>/webapps/employees/WEB-INF/classes directory. In our examples we will have resource bundles for the English language only. Listing 14.3 contains the resource bundle for our application.

```
app.title=Wrox Employee Database
app.username=User Name
app.password=Password
app.name=Name
app.phone=Phone
app.email=Email
app.role=Role
app.department=Department
app.administration=Administration
app.network=Network
app.sales=Sales
app.engineering=Engineering
app.manager=Manager
app.employee=Employee

errors.login.unknown=<li>Unknown User : {0}</li>
errors.login.required=<li>You must login before proceeding</li>
errors.username.required=<li>A Username is Required</li>
errors.password.required=<li>A Password is Required</li>
errors.name.required=<li>A Name is Required</li>
errors.phone.required=<li>A Phone is Required</li>
errors.email.required=<li>An Email Address is Required</li>
errors.roleid.required=<li>A Role is Required</li>
errors.depid.required=<li>A Department is Required</li>
errors.database.error=<li>A Database error occurred : {0}</li>

errors.header=<h3><font color="red">Error List</font></h3><ul>
errors.footer=</ul><hr>
```

Listing 14.3 The English Resource Bundle ApplicationResources.properties.

8. Add this resource bundle to the employees application. The modification requires inserting an additional <init-param> to the previously defined <servlet> element. Source 14.4a contains the application's new web.xml, with this modification.

> **We discussed creating new resource bundles in Chapter 9, "Internationalizing Your Struts Applications."**

```
<?xml version="1.0" encoding="ISO-8859-1"?>

<!DOCTYPE web-app
  PUBLIC "-//Sun Microsystems, Inc.//DTD Web Application 2.3//EN"
  "http://java.sun.com/dtd/web-app_2_3.dtd">

<web-app>

  <servlet>
    <servlet-name>action</servlet-name>
    <servlet-class>
      org.apache.struts.action.ActionServlet
    </servlet-class>
    <init-param>
      <param-name>debug</param-name>
      <param-value>5</param-value>
    </init-param>
    <init-param>
      <param-name>config</param-name>
      <param-value>/WEB-INF/struts-config.xml</param-value>
    </init-param>
    <init-param>
      <param-name>application</param-name>
      <param-value>ApplicationResources</param-value>
    </init-param>
    <load-on-startup>1</load-on-startup>
  </servlet>

  <servlet-mapping>
    <servlet-name>action</servlet-name>
    <url-pattern>*.do</url-pattern>
  </servlet-mapping>

</web-app>
```

Listing 14.4a The web.xml File after Adding the Application Resource Bundle.

9. We next need to add the tag libraries that we intend to leverage in our application development. This step is an optional step and is only required when your application leverages one or more custom tag libraries. The libraries that we will be using are the HTML, Logic, and Bean libraries. To add these libraries, you must add a <taglib> entry describing each library to the <*CATALINA_HOME*>/webapps/employees/WEB-INF/web.xml file. Listing 14.4b contains the application's modified web.xml, with the addition of these libraries.

> **See chapters 16, 18, and 20 for more detailed explanations of the HTML, Logic, and Bean tag libraries.**

```
<?xml version="1.0" encoding="ISO-8859-1"?>

<!DOCTYPE web-app
  PUBLIC "-//Sun Microsystems, Inc.//DTD Web Application 2.3//EN"
  "http://java.sun.com/dtd/web-app_2_3.dtd">

<web-app>

  <servlet>
    <servlet-name>action</servlet-name>
    <servlet-class>
      org.apache.struts.action.ActionServlet
    </servlet-class>
    <init-param>
      <param-name>debug</param-name>
      <param-value>5</param-value>
    </init-param>
    <init-param>
      <param-name>config</param-name>
      <param-value>/WEB-INF/struts-config.xml</param-value>
    </init-param>
    <init-param>
      <param-name>application</param-name>
      <param-value>ApplicationResources</param-value>
    </init-param>
    <load-on-startup>1</load-on-startup>
  </servlet>

  <servlet-mapping>
    <servlet-name>action</servlet-name>
    <url-pattern>*.do</url-pattern>
  </servlet-mapping>

  <taglib>
    <taglib-uri>/WEB-INF/struts-html.tld</taglib-uri>
    <taglib-location>/WEB-INF/struts-html.tld</taglib-location>
  </taglib>

  <taglib>
    <taglib-uri>/WEB-INF/struts-logic.tld</taglib-uri>
    <taglib-location>
      /WEB-INF/struts-logic.tld
    </taglib-location>
  </taglib>

  <taglib>
    <taglib-uri>/WEB-INF/struts-bean.tld</taglib-uri>
    <taglib-location>/WEB-INF/struts-bean.tld</taglib-location>
  </taglib>

</web-app>
```

Listing 14.4b The web.xml File after Adding the HTML, Logic, and Bean Tag Libraries.

10. Now add the TLDs associated with the previously added tag libraries. You will want to copy the struts-bean.tld, struts-html.tld, and struts-logic.tld to the WEB-INF directory.

That is it. We now have our application defined at the Web level. It is now time to define the remainder of the application, which is completed in the following sections.

Creating the employees Model

In this section we are defining the data layer of the employees application. This layer is defined as the Model and is represented by a relational database, an EmployeeData object, and a business object Employee.

The employees application's persistent data will be stored in three database tables employees, roles, and departments. Each of these tables and their contents are defined in the following sections.

The Employees Table

The employees table holds the actual list of people (the employees) found in the application. It is the main table of our application. The structure of this table is described in Table 14.1. The data that populates this table can be found in Table 14.2.

Table 14.1 The employees Table Structure

Column	Description
username	The username is a unique key identifying the employee. It is a varchar(10).
password	The password acts as the security credentials of the employee. It is a varchar(10).
name	The name is the string represents the employee's name. It is a varchar(30).
roleid	The roleid is used to identify the Role that the employee belongs to. It is an integer.
phone	The phone is the string representation of the employee's phone number. It is a varchar(30).
email	The email is the string representation of the employee's email address. It is a varchar(30).
depid	The depid is used to identify the Department that the employee belongs to. It is an integer.

Table 14.2 The Contents of the employees Table

username	password	name	roleid	phone	email	depid
abrickey	$word	Art Brickey	1	(303) 555-1214	abrickey@where.com	2
tharris	ralph	Todd Harris	1	(206) 555-9482	tharris@where.com	2
sriley	$mindy$	Sean Riley	2	(206) 555-3412	sriley@where.com	4
jgoodwill	$pass$	James Goodwill	1	(303) 555-1214	jgoodwill@where.com	3
tgray	password	Tim Gray	2	(303) 555-9876	tgray@anywhere.com	1

The Roles Table

The roles table holds the list of roles that a user may be assigned. It is the table that we will be using to determine the rights of the current user. The structure of this table is described in Table 14.3. The data that populates this table can be found in Table 14.4.

Table 14.3 The roles Table Structure

Column	Description
roleid	The roleid is used to uniquely identify the roles of the application. It is an integer.
rolename	The rolename is the string representation of the role. It is a varchar(30).

Table 14.4 The Contents of the roles Table

roleid	rolename
1	manager
2	employee

The Departments Table

The departments table holds the list of departments that an employee may be assigned to. The structure of this table is described in Table 14.5. The data that populates this table can be found in Table 14.6.

Table 14.5 The departments Table Structure

Column	Description
depid	The depid is used to uniquely identify the departments of the application. It is an integer.
depname	The depname is the string representation of the department. It is a varchar(30).

Table 14.6 The Contents of the departments Table

depid	depname
1	Administration
2	Network
3	Sales
4	Engineering

Creating the employees Database

Now that you have seen the employees database structure and its contents, it is time to actually create this database.

Make sure you have MySQL installed and running on your host machine and then complete the following steps:

1. Start the mysql client found in the <MYSQL_HOME>/bin/ directory by typing the following command:

```
mysql
```

2. Create the employees database by executing the following command:

```
create database employees;
```

3. Make sure you are modifying the appropriate database by executing the following command:

```
use employees;
```

4. Create and populate the employees table by executing the following commands:

```
create table employees
(
  username varchar(15) not null primary key,
  password varchar(15) not null,
  roleid integer not null,
  name varchar(30) not null,
  phone varchar(15) not null,
  email varchar(30) not null,
  depid integer not null
);

insert into employees values("abrickey", "$word", 1,
  "Art Brickey", "(303) 555-1214",
  "abrickey@where.com", 2);

insert into employees values("tharris", "ralph", 1,
  "Todd Harris", "(303) 555-9482",
  "tharris@where.com", 2);

insert into employees values("sriley", "$mindy$", 2,
  "Sean Riley", "(303) 555-3412",
  "sriley@where.com", 4);

insert into employees values("jgoodwill", "$pass$", 1,
  "James Goodwill", "(303) 555-1214",
  "jgoodwill@where.com", 3);

insert into employees values("tgray", "password", 2,
  "Tim Gray", "(303) 555-9876",
  "tgray@where.com", 1);
```

5. Create and populate the roles table by executing the following commands:

```
create table roles
(
  roleid integer not null primary key,
  rolename varchar(30) not null
```

```
);

insert into roles values(1, "manager");
insert into roles values(2, "employee");
```

6. Create and populate the departments table by executing the following commands:

```
create table departments
(
  depid integer not null primary key,
  depname varchar(30) not null
);

insert into departments values(1, "Administration");
insert into departments values(2, "Network");
insert into departments values(3, "Sales");
insert into departments values(4, "Engineering");
```

The Employee Object

Now that we have defined the database that will house our employee data, it is time to create the Java object that will model this data. The object that we will use is the com.wrox.Employee object. This object is a very simple JavaBean that is used only to hold the values of an individual employee. The source for the Employee object is shown in Listing 14.5.

We could have modeled each table in the employees database, but to keep things simple, we have chosen only to model the Employee object, which has both a role and a department.

```
package com.wrox;

public class Employee {

  protected String username;
  protected String password;
  protected String name;
  protected String department;
  protected String rolename;
  protected String phone;
  protected String email;
  protected Integer depid;
  protected Integer roleid;

  public void setUsername(String username) {

    this.username = username;
  }

  public String getUsername() {

    return username;
  }

  public String getPassword() {

    return password;
```

Code continued on following page

```
    }

    public void setPassword(String password) {

      this.password = password;
    }

    public void setName(String name) {

      this.name = name;
    }

    public String getName() {

      return name;
    }

    public void setDepartment(String department) {

      this.department = department;
    }

    public String getDepartment() {

      return this.department;
    }

    public void setRolename(String rolename) {

      this.rolename = rolename;
    }

    public String getRolename() {

      return rolename;
    }

    public void setPhone(String phone) {

      this.phone = phone;
    }

    public String getPhone() {

      return phone;
    }

    public void setEmail(String email) {

      this.email = email;
    }

    public String getEmail() {

      return email;
```

Code continued on following page

```
    }

    public void setDepid(Integer depid) {

      this.depid = depid;
    }

    public Integer getDepid() {

      return depid;
    }

    public void setRoleid(Integer roleid) {

      this.roleid = roleid;
    }

    public Integer getRoleid() {

      return roleid;
    }
  }
```

Listing 14.5 The Employee Object.

After you have had a chance to look over the Employee object, go ahead and compile it and move the resulting class file to the <*CATALINA_HOME*>/webapps/employees/WEB-INF/classes/com/wrox directory.

The EmployeeData Object

Now we have business object to represent our data, let's create an object that will handle the transferring of data to this object. The object that we will use is the com.wrox.EmployeeData object, which is a static object that encapsulates the JDBC layer of the application. Table 14.7 describes each of the methods in the EmployeeData object. The source for the EmployeeData object is shown in Listing 14.6.

Table 14.7 The Methods of the EmployeeData Object

Method	Description
getEmployee()	Takes a username and a DataSource reference, and returns an Employee object matching the passed in username.
getEmployees()	Takes a DataSource and returns an ArrayList containing all of the current Employees.
removeEmpoyee()	Takes a username and a DataSource reference, and removes the Employee object matching the passed in username.
addEmployee()	Takes an Employee and a DataSource reference and inserts the Employee into the Database.
updateEmployee()	Takes an Employee and a DataSource reference and updates the matching Employee row in the Database.

```
package com.wrox;

import javax.sql.DataSource;
import java.util.ArrayList;
import java.sql.Connection;
import java.sql.Statement;
import java.sql.ResultSet;
import java.sql.SQLException;

public class EmployeeData {

  public static Employee getEmployee(String username,
    DataSource dataSource)
    throws Exception {

    Connection conn = null;
    Statement stmt = null;
    ResultSet rs = null;
    Employee employee = null;
    try {

      conn = dataSource.getConnection();
      stmt = conn.createStatement();
      rs =
        stmt.executeQuery("select * from employees where"
        + "username=\'" +username + "'");

      if ( rs.next() ) {

        employee = new Employee();

        employee.setUsername(rs.getString("username"));
        employee.setPassword(rs.getString("password"));
        employee.setDepid(new Integer(rs.getInt("depid")));
        employee.setRoleid(
          new Integer(rs.getString("roleid")));
        String name = rs.getString("name");
        employee.setName(name);
        employee.setPhone(rs.getString("phone"));
        employee.setEmail(rs.getString("email"));
      }
      else {

        throw new Exception(username + " not found!");
      }
    }
    finally {

      if ( rs != null ) {

        rs.close();
      }
      if ( stmt != null ) {
```

Code continued on following page

```
        stmt.close();
      }
      if ( conn != null ) {

        conn.close();
      }
    }
    return employee;
  }

  public static ArrayList getEmployees(DataSource dataSource) {

    Employee employee = null;
    ArrayList employees = new ArrayList();
    Connection conn = null;
    Statement stmt = null;
    ResultSet rs = null;

    try {

      conn = dataSource.getConnection();
      stmt = conn.createStatement();
      rs =
        stmt.executeQuery("select * from employees, roles, "
        + "departments where employees.roleid=roles.roleid "
        + "and employees.depid=departments.depid");

      while (rs.next()) {

        employee = new Employee();

        employee.setUsername(rs.getString("username"));
        employee.setName(rs.getString("name"));
        employee.setRolename(rs.getString("rolename"));
        employee.setPhone(rs.getString("phone"));
        employee.setEmail(rs.getString("email"));
        employee.setRoleid(new Integer(rs.getInt("roleid")));
        employee.setDepid(new Integer(rs.getInt("depid")));
        employee.setDepartment(rs.getString("depname"));

        employees.add(employee);

        System.err.println("Username : "
          + employee.getUsername()
          + " Department : " + rs.getString("depname"));
      }
    }
    catch ( SQLException e ) {

      System.err.println(e.getMessage());
    }
    finally {

      if ( rs != null ) {
```

Code continued on following page

```
        try {

          rs.close();
        }
        catch ( SQLException sqle ) {

          System.err.println(sqle.getMessage());
        }
        rs = null;
      }
      if ( stmt != null ) {

        try {

          stmt.close();
        }
        catch ( SQLException sqle ) {

          System.err.println(sqle.getMessage());
        }
        stmt = null;
      }
      if ( conn != null ) {

        try {

          conn.close();
        }
        catch ( SQLException sqle ) {

          System.err.println(sqle.getMessage());
        }
        conn = null;
      }
    }
    return employees;
  }

  public static void removeEmployee(String username,
    DataSource dataSource)
    throws Exception {

    Connection conn = null;
    Statement stmt = null;
    ResultSet rs = null;

    try {

      conn = dataSource.getConnection();
      stmt = conn.createStatement();

      StringBuffer sqlString =
        new StringBuffer("delete from employees ");
```

Code continued on following page

```
      sqlString.append("where username='" + username + "'");

      stmt.execute(sqlString.toString());
    }
    finally {

      if ( rs != null ) {

        rs.close();
      }
      if ( stmt != null ) {

        stmt.close();
      }
      if ( conn != null ) {

        conn.close();
      }
    }
  }

  public static void addEmployee(Employee employee,
    DataSource dataSource)
    throws Exception {

    Connection conn = null;
    Statement stmt = null;
    ResultSet rs = null;

    try {

      conn = dataSource.getConnection();
      stmt = conn.createStatement();

      StringBuffer sqlString =
        new StringBuffer("insert into employees ");

      sqlString.append("values (\""
        + employee.getUsername() + "\", ");
      sqlString.append("\"" +
        employee.getPassword() + "\", ");
      sqlString.append("\""
        + employee.getRoleid() + "\", ");
      sqlString.append("\""
        + employee.getName() + "\", ");
      sqlString.append("\""
        + employee.getPhone() + "\", ");
      sqlString.append("\""
        + employee.getEmail() + "\", ");
      sqlString.append("\""
        + employee.getDepid() + "\")");

      stmt.execute(sqlString.toString());
    }
```

Code continued on following page

```
      finally {

        if ( rs != null ) {

          rs.close();
        }
        if ( stmt != null ) {

          stmt.close();
        }
        if ( conn != null ) {

          conn.close();
        }
      }
    }

  public static void updateEmployee(Employee employee,
    DataSource dataSource)
    throws Exception {

      Connection conn = null;
      Statement stmt = null;
      ResultSet rs = null;

      try {

        conn = dataSource.getConnection();
        stmt = conn.createStatement();

        StringBuffer sqlString =
          new StringBuffer("update employees ");

        sqlString.append("set password='"
          + employee.getPassword() + "', ");
        sqlString.append("roleid="
          + employee.getRoleid() + ", ");
        sqlString.append("name='"
          + employee.getName() + "', ");
        sqlString.append("phone='"
          + employee.getPhone() + "', ");
        sqlString.append("email='"
          + employee.getEmail() + "', ");
        sqlString.append("depid="
          + employee.getDepid());
        sqlString.append(" where username='"
          + employee.getUsername() + "'");

        stmt.execute(sqlString.toString());
      }
      finally {

        if ( rs != null ) {

          rs.close();
```

Code continued on following page

```
        }
        if ( stmt != null ) {

          stmt.close();
        }
        if ( conn != null ) {

          conn.close();
        }
      }
    }
  }
```

Listing 14.6 The EmployeeData Object.

After you have had a chance to look over the EmployeeData object, go ahead and compile it and move the resulting class file to the <*CATALINA_HOME*>/webapps/employees/WEB-INF/classes/com/wrox directory.

Data Source Configuration

The final step that we must complete to make our data layer available to the remainder of the employees application is to add a DataSource definition to the employees Struts configuration file. To do this we are going to add a <data-source> entry into the <*CATALINA_HOME*>/webapps/employees/WEB-INF/struts-config.xml file. The following snippet contains our new DataSource.

```
<data-sources>
  <data-source type="org.apache.commons.dbcp.BasicDataSource">
    <set-property property="driverClassName"
      value="com.mysql.jdbc.Driver" />
    <set-property property="url"
      value="jdbc:mysql://localhost/employees" />
    <set-property property="username"
      value="YOUR USERNAME"/>
    <set-property property="password"
      value="YOUR PASSWORD"/>
  </data-source>
</data-sources>
```

> **Before continuing with this example, make sure that you have copied the MySQL JDBC driver to the <*CATALINA_HOME*>/webapps/employees/WEB-INF/lib directory. We discussed how to set up data sources in Chapter 11, "Integrating the Jakarta Commons Database Connection Pool (DBCP)."**

Building the Employees Application

As we discussed earlier, the employees application is intended to be used as an employee directory service that allows a user to list, add, edit, and delete employees stored in the company database. To accomplish these tasks we need to define the Views and Actions that will allow the user to perform each of these functions. The following sections describe each of these functions from the input View through the Action ending with the target View.

> **In this section we will be using the word *transaction* to describe an entire application function, which consists of the Views and Actions associated with one application requirement, such as the add transaction or the edit transaction.**

The Welcome Page

The Welcome page is the first page that a user will see. It is a simple JSP, index.jsp, that will have only one function and that is to forward the current request to the EmployeeListAction. The source for the login.jsp is shown in Listing 14.7.

```
<%@ page language="java" %>
<jsp:forward page="/EmployeeList.do" />
```

Listing 14.7 index.jsp.

As stated earlier, the index.jsp acts as the entry point to our application; therefore, we need to add it to the application's web.xml file as one of the welcome files. Listing 14.8 contains the application's current web.xml, including this addition.

```
<?xml version="1.0" encoding="ISO-8859-1"?>

<!DOCTYPE web-app PUBLIC
  "-//Sun Microsystems, Inc.//DTD Web Application 2.3//EN"
  "http://java.sun.com/dtd/web-app_2_3.dtd">

<web-app>

  <servlet>
    <servlet-name>action</servlet-name>
    <servlet-class>
      org.apache.struts.action.ActionServlet
    </servlet-class>
    <init-param>
      <param-name>debug</param-name>
      <param-value>5</param-value>
    </init-param>
    <init-param>
      <param-name>config</param-name>
      <param-value>/WEB-INF/struts-config.xml</param-value>
    </init-param>
    <init-param>
      <param-name>application</param-name>
      <param-value>ApplicationResources</param-value>
    </init-param>

    <load-on-startup>1</load-on-startup>
  </servlet>

  <servlet-mapping>
```

Code continued on following page

```
    <servlet-name>action</servlet-name>
    <url-pattern>*.do</url-pattern>
  </servlet-mapping>

  <welcome-file-list>
    <welcome-file>/index.jsp</welcome-file>
  </welcome-file-list>

  <taglib>
    <taglib-uri>/WEB-INF/struts-html.tld</taglib-uri>
    <taglib-location>/WEB-INF/struts-html.tld</taglib-location>
  </taglib>

  <taglib>
    <taglib-uri>/WEB-INF/struts-logic.tld</taglib-uri>
    <taglib-location>
      /WEB-INF/struts-logic.tld
    </taglib-location>
  </taglib>

  <taglib>
    <taglib-uri>/WEB-INF/struts-bean.tld</taglib-uri>
    <taglib-location>/WEB-INF/struts-bean.tld</taglib-location>
  </taglib>

</web-app>
```

Listing 14.8 The web.xml file after adding the index.jsp welcome file.

The EmployeeListAction

Once the EmployeeListAction receives control, then the EmployeeListAction.perform() method is invoked. The EmployeeListAction is used to retrieve all of the employees currently contained in the employees database.

If the employees are successfully retrieved from the employees database, then an Employee object, which was described in the data layer of this chapter, is created and populated with the contents of each returned row, and each one of these Employee objects is added to an ArrayList. The ArrayList is then added to the request and the request is forwarded to the success target, which in this case is the employeelist.jsp. The source for the EmployeeListAction can be found in Listing 14.9.

```
package com.wrox;

import java.io.IOException;
import javax.servlet.ServletException;
import javax.servlet.http.HttpServletRequest;
import javax.servlet.http.HttpServletResponse;

import org.apache.struts.action.Action;
import org.apache.struts.action.ActionForm;
import org.apache.struts.action.ActionForward;
import org.apache.struts.action.ActionMapping;
```

Code continued on following page

```
import java.util.ArrayList;

public class EmployeeListAction extends Action {

  public ActionForward execute(ActionMapping mapping,
    ActionForm form,
    HttpServletRequest request,
    HttpServletResponse response)
    throws IOException, ServletException {

    // Default target to success
    String target = new String("success");

    ArrayList employees = null;

    employees =
      EmployeeData.getEmployees(getDataSource(request));

    request.setAttribute("employees", employees);

    // Forward to the appropriate View
    return (mapping.findForward(target));
  }
}
```

Listing 14.9 EmployeeListAction.java.

The Employee List JSP

The Employee List JSP is used to display all of the employees stored in the employees database. The Employees List View is a simple JSP that takes an ArrayList of Employee objects, forwarded by the EmployeeListAction which we described previously, and iterates over them printing the contents of each Employee object to the output stream. This View also presents the user with the ability to initiate an edit or delete of an employee. The source for the employeelist.jsp is listed in Listing 14.10.

```
<%@ taglib uri="/WEB-INF/struts-bean.tld" prefix="bean" %>
<%@ taglib uri="/WEB-INF/struts-logic.tld" prefix="logic" %>
<%@ taglib uri="/WEB-INF/struts-html.tld" prefix="html" %>

<html>
  <head>
    <title><bean:message key="app.title" /></title>
  </head>
  <body>

    <table width="650"
      border="0" cellspacing="0" cellpadding="0">
      <tr>
        <td colspan="7"> </td>
      </tr>
      <tr>
```

Code continued on following page

```
<td height="68" width="48%">
        <div align="left">
          <img src="images/wxmainlogowhitespace.gif">
        </div>
      </td>
    </tr>
    <tr>
      <td colspan="7"> </td>
    </tr>
  </table>

  <html:errors />

  <table width="700"
    border="0" cellspacing="0" cellpadding="0">
    <tr align="left">
      <th><bean:message key="app.username" /></th>
      <th><bean:message key="app.name" /></th>
      <th><bean:message key="app.phone" /></th>
      <th><bean:message key="app.email" /></th>
      <th><bean:message key="app.department" /></th>
      <th><bean:message key="app.role" /></th>
    </tr>
    <!-- iterate over the results of the query -->
    <logic:iterate id="employee" name="employees">
  <tr align="left">
    <td>
          <bean:write name="employee" property="username" />
    </td>
    <td>
          <bean:write name="employee" property="name" />
    </td>
    <td>
          <bean:write name="employee" property="phone" />
    </td>
    <td>
          <bean:write name="employee" property="email" />
    </td>
    <td>
          <bean:write name="employee" property="department" />
    </td>
    <td>
          <bean:write name="employee" property="rolename" />
    </td>
    <td>
         <a href="Edit.do?username=<bean:write name="employee"
      property="username" />">Edit</a>
     <a href="Delete.do?username=<bean:write
           name="employee" property="username" />">Delete</a>
    </td>
  </tr>
     </logic:iterate>
     <tr>
       <td colspan="7">
```

Code continued on following page

```
    <hr>
  </td>
      </tr>
    </table>
    <font size="-1" face="arial">
      <a href="addemployee.jsp">Add New Employee</a>
    </font>

  </body>
</html>
```

Listing 14.10 The employeelist.jsp.

As you look over the source for the Employee List View, pay particular attention to the bolded text. This section includes the occurrences of the <logic:iterate /> tag, which is used to iterate over the ArrayList that is passed to the employeelist.jsp by the EmployeeListAction.jsp.

Deploying the Components of the Employee List Transaction

Now that we have all of the components of the Employee List transaction defined, we need to deploy them to our employees application. The code shown in Listing 14.11, contains the struts-config.xml file, including the changes necessary to deploy the previously described Employee List components.

```
<?xml version="1.0" encoding="ISO-8859-1" ?>

<!DOCTYPE struts-config PUBLIC
  "-//Apache Software Foundation//DTD Struts Configuration 1.0//EN"
  "http://jakarta.apache.org/struts/dtds/struts-config_1_1.dtd">

<struts-config>

  <data-sources>
    <data-source
      type="org.apache.commons.dbcp.BasicDataSource">
      <set-property property="driverClassName"
        value="com.mysql.jdbc.Driver" />
      <set-property property="url"
        value="jdbc:mysql://localhost/employees" />
      <set-property property="username"
        value="jim"/>
      <set-property property="password"
        value="password"/>
    </data-source>
  </data-sources>

  <global-forwards>
    <forward name="employeelist" path="/EmployeeList"/>
  </global-forwards>

  <action-mappings>

    <action path="/EmployeeList"
```

Code continued on following page

```
        type="com.wrox.EmployeeListAction"
        scope="request" >
        <forward name="success" path="/employeelist.jsp"/>
      </action>

    </action-mappings>

  </struts-config>
```

Listing 14.11 The web.xml file after adding the Employee List components.

Once you have looked over the new struts-config.xml file, you should have noticed that it looks very similar to any other struts-config.xml file, except for the two lines of code.

The Add Employee Transaction

The Add Employee transaction is used to add employees to the employees database. It is initiated when a user selects the Add New Employee link from the employeelist.jsp. When this link is selected, the Add Employee transaction presents its components in the following order:

1. Add Employee JSP
2. EmployeeForm
3. AddEmployeeAction
4. EmployeeListAction
5. Employee List JSP

The Add Employee JSP

The Add Employee View, represented by the JSP addemployee.jsp, is used to retrieve the values of the new employee being added to the employees database. The source for the addemployee.jsp is shown in Listing 14.12.

```
<%@ page language="java" %>
<%@ taglib uri="/WEB-INF/struts-html.tld" prefix="html" %>
<%@ taglib uri="/WEB-INF/struts-bean.tld" prefix="bean" %>

<html>
  <head>
    <title><bean:message key="app.title" /></title>
  </head>

  <body>
    <table width="500"
      border="0" cellspacing="0" cellpadding="0">
      <tr>
        <td> </td>
      </tr>
      <tr>
        <td height="68" width="48%">
```

Code continued on following page

```
      <div align="left">
        <img src="images/wxmainlogowhitespace.gif">
      </div>
    </td>
  </tr>
  <tr>
    <td> </td>
  </tr>
</table>

<html:errors />

<html:form action="/Add"
  name="employeeForm"
  type="com.wrox.EmployeeForm" >
  <table width="500" border="0">
    <tr>
      <td><bean:message key="app.username" />:</td>
      <td><html:text property="username" /></td>
      <td><bean:message key="app.password" />:</td>
      <td><html:text property="password" /></td>
    </tr>
    <tr>
      <td><bean:message key="app.name" />:</td>
      <td><html:text property="name" /></td>
      <td><bean:message key="app.phone" />:</td>
      <td><html:text property="phone" /></td>
    </tr>
    <tr>
      <td><bean:message key="app.email" />:</td>
      <td><html:text property="email" /></td>
      <td><bean:message key="app.department" />:</td>
      <td>

        <html:select property="depid" size="1">
          <html:option value="1">
            <bean:message key="app.administration" />
          </html:option>
          <html:option value="2">
            <bean:message key="app.network" />
   </html:option>
          <html:option value="3">
    <bean:message key="app.sales" />
   </html:option>
          <html:option value="4">
    <bean:message key="app.engineering" />
   </html:option>
        </html:select>

      </td>
    </tr>
    <tr>
      <td><bean:message key="app.role" />:</td>
      <td>
```

Code continued on following page

```
            <html:select property="roleid" size="1">
              <html:option value="1">
                <bean:message key="app.manager" />
              </html:option>
              <html:option value="2">
                <bean:message key="app.employee" />
              </html:option>
            </html:select>

          </td>
          <td colspan="2" align="center">
            <html:submit /><html:cancel /><html:reset />
          </td>
        </tr>
      </table>
    </html:form>

  </body>
</html>
```

Listing 14.12 The Add Employee View.

The EmployeeForm

Now that you have seen the JSP that will be submitting the new employee values, we need to create an ActionForm that will validate and encapsulate these new employee values. The source for EmployeeForm is shown in Listing 14.13.

> **The EmployeeForm is used by both the Add and Edit employee transactions.**

```
package com.wrox;

import javax.servlet.http.HttpServletRequest;

import org.apache.struts.action.ActionForm;
import org.apache.struts.action.ActionMapping;
import org.apache.struts.action.ActionErrors;
import org.apache.struts.action.ActionError;

public class EmployeeForm extends ActionForm {

  protected String username;
  protected String password;
  protected String name;
  protected String phone;
  protected String email;
  protected String depid;
  protected String roleid;

  public void setUsername(String username) {
```

Code continued on following page

```
    this.username = username;
  }

  public String getUsername() {

    return username;
  }

  public void setPassword(String password) {

    this.password = password;
  }

  public String getPassword() {

    return password;
  }

  public void setName(String name) {

    this.name = name;
  }

  public String getName() {

    return name;
  }

  public void setPhone(String phone) {

    this.phone = phone;
  }

  public String getPhone() {

    return phone;
  }

  public void setEmail(String email) {

    this.email = email;
  }

  public String getEmail() {

    return email;
  }

  public void setDepid(String depid) {

    this.depid = depid;
  }
```

Code continued on following page

```
public String getDepid() {

  return depid;
}

public void setRoleid(String roleid) {

  this.roleid = roleid;
}

public String getRoleid() {

  return roleid;
}

// This method is called with every request. It resets the
// Form attribute prior to setting the values in the new
// request.
public void reset(ActionMapping mapping,
  HttpServletRequest request) {

  this.username = "";
  this.password = "";
  this.name = "";
  this.phone = "";
  this.email = "";
  this.depid = "1";
  this.roleid = "1";
}

public ActionErrors validate(ActionMapping mapping,
  HttpServletRequest request) {

  ActionErrors errors = new ActionErrors();

  if ( (roleid == null) || (roleid.length() == 0) ) {

    errors.add("roleid",
      new ActionError("errors.roleid.required"));
  }
  if ( (depid == null) || (depid.length() == 0) ) {

    errors.add("depid",
      new ActionError("errors.depid.required"));
  }
  if ( (email == null) || (email.length() == 0) ) {

    errors.add("email",
      new ActionError("errors.email.required"));
  }
  if ( (phone == null) || (phone.length() == 0) ) {

    errors.add("phone",
      new ActionError("errors.phone.required"));
```

Code continued on following page

```
        }
        if ( (name == null) || (name.length() == 0) ) {

          errors.add("name",
            new ActionError("errors.name.required"));
        }
        if ( (password == null) || (password.length() == 0) ) {

          errors.add("password",
            new ActionError("errors.password.required"));
        }
        if ( (username == null) || (username.length() == 0) ) {

          errors.add("username",
            new ActionError("errors.username.required"));
        }
        return errors;
      }
    }
```

Listing 14.13 The EmployeeForm.java.

As you look over the EmployeeForm.java, you will notice that there is nothing out of the ordinary about it. It provides accessors to data members that map to the values submitted by the Add Employee View, and it performs some simple validation of those values. If the values pass the validation, then the transaction continues; otherwise ActionErrors are created and the request is forwarded back to the addemployee.jsp, which is named by the input attribute of the AddEmployeeAction definition.

The Add Employee Action

The AddEmployeeAction is a simple Struts Action that takes the values submitted in the EmployeeForm object and inserts them into the employees database as a new employee record.

If the insert is successful, then the request is forwarded to the EmployeeListAction, which will retrieve all of the employees from the database (including the newly inserted record) and forward the results to the employeelist.jsp for display. The source for the AddEmployeeAction can be found in Listing 14.14.

```
package com.wrox;

import java.io.IOException;
import javax.servlet.ServletException;
import javax.servlet.http.HttpServletRequest;
import javax.servlet.http.HttpServletResponse;

import org.apache.struts.action.Action;
import org.apache.struts.action.ActionForm;
import org.apache.struts.action.ActionForward;
import org.apache.struts.action.ActionMapping;
import org.apache.struts.action.ActionErrors;
import org.apache.struts.action.ActionError;

public class AddEmployeeAction extends Action {
```

Code continued on following page

```
    public ActionForward execute(ActionMapping mapping,
      ActionForm form,
      HttpServletRequest request,
      HttpServletResponse response)
      throws IOException, ServletException {

      // Default target to success
      String target = new String("success");

      if ( isCancelled(request) ) {

        // Cancel pressed back to employee list
        return (mapping.findForward("success"));
      }

      try {

        Employee employee = new Employee();
        EmployeeForm employeeForm = (EmployeeForm) form;

        employee.setUsername(employeeForm.getUsername());
        employee.setPassword(employeeForm.getPassword());
        employee.setRoleid(
          new Integer(employeeForm.getRoleid()));
        employee.setName(employeeForm.getName());
        employee.setPhone(employeeForm.getPhone());
        employee.setEmail(employeeForm.getEmail());
        employee.setDepid(new Integer(employeeForm.getDepid()));

        EmployeeData.addEmployee(employee,
          getDataSource(request));
      }
      catch ( Exception e ) {

        System.err.println("Setting target to error");
        target = new String("error");
        ActionErrors errors = new ActionErrors();

        errors.add(ActionErrors.GLOBAL_ERROR,
          new ActionError("errors.database.error",
          e.getMessage()));

        // Report any errors
        if ( !errors.isEmpty() ) {

          saveErrors(request, errors);
        }
      }
      // Forward to the appropriate View
      return (mapping.findForward(target));
    }
  }
```

Listing 14.14 The AddEmployeeAction.java.

Deploying the Components of the Add Employee Transaction

Now that we have the components of the Add Employee transaction defined, we can deploy them to our employees application. The code shown in Listing 14.15 contains the struts-config.xml file, including the changes necessary to deploy the Add Employee components.

```
<?xml version="1.0" encoding="ISO-8859-1" ?>

<!DOCTYPE struts-config PUBLIC
  "-//Apache Software Foundation//DTD Struts Configuration 1.0//EN"
  "http://jakarta.apache.org/struts/dtds/struts-config_1_1.dtd">

<struts-config>

  <data-sources>
    <data-source
      type="org.apache.commons.dbcp.BasicDataSource">
      <set-property property="driverClassName"
        value="com.mysql.jdbc.Driver" />
      <set-property property="url"
        value="jdbc:mysql://localhost/employees" />
      <set-property property="username"
        value="jim"/>
      <set-property property="password"
        value="password"/>
    </data-source>
  </data-sources>

  <form-beans>
    <form-bean name="employeeForm"
      type="com.wrox.EmployeeForm" />
  </form-beans>

  <global-forwards>
    <forward name="employeelist" path="/EmployeeList"/>
  </global-forwards>

  <action-mappings>

    <action path="/EmployeeList"
      type="com.wrox.EmployeeListAction"
      scope="request" >
      <forward name="success" path="/employeelist.jsp"/>
    </action>

    <action path="/Add"
      type="com.wrox.AddEmployeeAction"
      name="employeeForm"
      scope="request"
      input="/addemployee.jsp"
      validate="true" >
      <forward name="success" path="/EmployeeList.do"/>
      <forward name="error" path="/addemployee.jsp"/>
    </action>
```

Code continued on following page

```
    </action-mappings>

  </struts-config>
```

Listing 14.15 The web.xml file after adding the Add Employee components.

Once you have looked over the new struts-config.xml file, you should have noticed that we added two new elements. The first element is a new <form-bean> sub-element named employeeForm, which references the com.wrox.EmployeeForm object. This just tells the application that we want to use the EmployeeForm when performing an AddEmployeeAction.

The second sub-element added to the struts-config.xml file actually defines the AddEmployeeAction. The only thing to note about this entry is that the success target, like the LoginAction, is the EmployeeList.do, which will cause the updated list of employees to be displayed.

The Edit Employee Transaction

The Edit Employee transaction is used to modify employees that currently exist in the employees database. It is initiated when a user selects the Edit link, next to the employee to be edited, from the employeelist.jsp. When this link is selected the Edit Employee transaction presents its components in the following order:

1. GetEmployeeAction
2. Edit Employee JSP
3. EmployeeForm
4. EditEmployeeAction
5. EmployeeListAction
6. Employee List JSP

The Get Employee Action

The GetEmployeeAction is the first Action that is invoked in the Edit Employee transaction. It is invoked from the employeelist.jsp using the following code snippet:

```
<a href="Edit.do?username=<bean:write name="employee"
  property="username" />">Edit</a>
```

As you will notice, this link executes a get request to the Edit.do path with the request parameter *username* set to the username to be edited. The purpose of the GetEmployeeAction is to retrieve the selected employee from the database and then populate an EmployeeForm with the retrieved values. This allows the editemployee.jsp, which is the successful target of the GetEmployeeAction, to pre-populate the input elements of the <html:form /> with the values of the created EmployeeForm object. The source for the GetEmployeeAction object is shown in Listing 14.16.

```
package com.wrox;

import java.io.IOException;
import javax.servlet.ServletException;
import javax.servlet.http.HttpServletRequest;
import javax.servlet.http.HttpServletResponse;
import javax.servlet.http.HttpSession;

import org.apache.struts.action.Action;
import org.apache.struts.action.ActionForm;
import org.apache.struts.action.ActionForward;
import org.apache.struts.action.ActionMapping;
import org.apache.struts.action.ActionErrors;
import org.apache.struts.action.ActionError;

public class GetEmployeeAction extends Action {

  protected ActionForm buildEmployeeForm(String username,
    HttpServletRequest request)
    throws Exception {

    EmployeeForm form = null;

    Employee employee =
      EmployeeData.getEmployee(username,
      getDataSource(request));

    if ( employee != null ) {

      form = new EmployeeForm();

      form.setUsername(employee.getUsername());
      form.setPassword(employee.getPassword());
      form.setDepid((employee.getDepid()).toString());
      form.setRoleid(employee.getRoleid().toString());
      form.setName(employee.getName());
      form.setPhone(employee.getPhone());
      form.setEmail(employee.getEmail());
    }
    else {

      throw new Exception(username + " not found!");
    }
    return form;
  }

  public ActionForward execute(ActionMapping mapping,
    ActionForm form,
    HttpServletRequest request,
    HttpServletResponse response)
    throws IOException, ServletException {

    // Default target to success
    String target = new String("success");
```

```
        if ( isCancelled(request) ) {

          // Cancel pressed back to employee list
          return (mapping.findForward(target));
        }

        try {

          form =
            buildEmployeeForm(request.getParameter("username"),
              request);

          if ( "request".equals(mapping.getScope()) ) {

            request.setAttribute(mapping.getAttribute(), form);
          }
          else {

            HttpSession session = request.getSession();
            session.setAttribute(mapping.getAttribute(), form);
          }
        }
        catch ( Exception e ) {

          System.err.println("Setting target to error");
          System.err.println("---->" + e.getMessage() + "<----");
          target = new String("error");
          ActionErrors errors = new ActionErrors();

          errors.add(ActionErrors.GLOBAL_ERROR,
            new ActionError("errors.database.error",
              e.getMessage()));

          // Report any errors
          if ( !errors.isEmpty() ) {

            saveErrors(request, errors);
          }
        }
        // Forward to the appropriate View
        return (mapping.findForward(target));
      }
    }
```

Listing 14.16 The GetEmployeeAction.java.

The GetEmployeeAction begins its processing, just like any other Action class, with the perform() method. It first makes sure that the user is logged in; it then makes sure that the Action was not cancelled.

At this point the GetEmployeeAction is ready to perform its specific logic. It begins by invoking the buildEmployeeForm() method, which retrieves the employee with the passed in username, creates and populates an EmployeeForm object, and returns the newly created form to the perform() method.

The perform() then determines where the EmployeeForm object should be stored, using the ActionMapping.getScope() method. Once the Action knows where the EmployeeForm should be stored, it then retrieves the name attribute of the <action> element and adds the EmployeeForm—bound to the retrieved name—to the appropriate scope. This logic is performed using the following code snippet:

```
form =
  buildEmployeeForm(request.getParameter("username"),
    request);

if ( "request".equals(mapping.getScope()) ) {

  request.setAttribute(mapping.getAttribute(), form);
}
else {

  HttpSession session = request.getSession();
  session.setAttribute(mapping.getAttribute(), form);
}
```

Once the EmployeeForm is added to the appropriate object (either the request or session), then the perform() method forwards the request to the success target, which in this case will be the editemployee.jsp. At this point there should be an EmployeeForm instance stored in either the request or session, with the values retrieved from the employees database.

The Edit Employee JSP

The Edit Employee View, represented by the JSP editemployee.jsp, is used to modify the values of the selected employee. The editemployee.jsp presents the user with an HTML form that should be pre-populated by the GetEmployeeAction described previously. When the user has completed their modifications, they select the Submit button and the modified values, stored in an EmployeeForm instance, are submitted to the EditEmployeeAction. The source for the editemployee.jsp is shown in Listing 14.17.

```
<%@ page language="java" %>
<%@ taglib uri="/WEB-INF/struts-html.tld" prefix="html" %>
<%@ taglib uri="/WEB-INF/struts-bean.tld" prefix="bean" %>

<html>
  <head>
    <title><bean:message key="app.title" /></title>
  </head>

  <body>
    <table width="500"
      border="0" cellspacing="0" cellpadding="0">
      <tr>
        <td> </td>
      </tr>
      <tr>
```

Code continued on following page

```
      <td height="68" width="48%">
        <div align="left">
          <img src="images/wxmainlogowhitespace.gif">
        </div>
      </td>
    </tr>
    <tr>
      <td> </td>
    </tr>
  </table>

  <html:errors />

  <html:form action="/EditEmployee"
    name="employeeForm"
    type="com.wrox.EmployeeForm"
    scope="request" >
    <table width="500" border="0">
      <tr>
        <td><bean:message key="app.username" />:</td>
        <td><html:text property="username" /></td>
        <td><bean:message key="app.password" />:</td>
        <td><html:password property="password" /></td>
      </tr>
      <tr>
        <td><bean:message key="app.name" />:</td>
        <td><html:text property="name" /></td>
        <td><bean:message key="app.phone" />:</td>
        <td><html:text property="phone" /></td>
      </tr>
      <tr>
        <td><bean:message key="app.email" />:</td>
        <td><html:text property="email" /></td>
        <td><bean:message key="app.department" />:</td>
        <td>
          <html:select property="depid" size="1">
            <html:option value="1">
              <bean:message key="app.administration" />
            </html:option>
            <html:option value="2">
              <bean:message key="app.network" />
            </html:option>
            <html:option value="3">
              <bean:message key="app.sales" />
            </html:option>
            <html:option value="4">
              <bean:message key="app.engineering" />
            </html:option>
          </html:select>

        </td>
      </tr>
      <tr>
        <td><bean:message key="app.role" />:</td>
```

Code continued on following page

```
    <td>

      <html:select property="roleid" size="1">
               <html:option value="1">
          <bean:message key="app.manager" />
        </html:option>
               <html:option value="2">
          <bean:message key="app.employee" />
        </html:option>
             </html:select>

           </td>
           <td colspan="2" align="center">
      <html:submit />
      <html:cancel />
      <html:reset />
    </td>
         </tr>
       </table>
     </html:form>

   </body>
</html>
```

Listing 14.17 The Edit Employee view.

The EmployeeForm

The EmployeeForm object used in the Edit Employee Transaction is the same EmployeeForm used by the Add Employee Transaction.

The Edit Employee Action

The EditEmployeeAction is a very basic Struts Action that takes the submitted employee values, from the editemployee.jsp View, and performs a SQL update on the record with the matching username. The source for the EditEmployeeAction object is shown in Listing 14.18.

```
package com.wrox;

import java.io.IOException;
import javax.servlet.ServletException;
import javax.servlet.http.HttpServletRequest;
import javax.servlet.http.HttpServletResponse;

import org.apache.struts.action.Action;
import org.apache.struts.action.ActionForm;
import org.apache.struts.action.ActionForward;
import org.apache.struts.action.ActionMapping;
import org.apache.struts.action.ActionErrors;
import org.apache.struts.action.ActionError;

public class EditEmployeeAction extends Action {
```

Code continued on following page

```
protected void editEmployee(EmployeeForm form,
  HttpServletRequest request)
  throws Exception {

  Employee employee = new Employee();

  employee.setPassword(form.getPassword());
  employee.setRoleid(new Integer(form.getRoleid()));
  employee.setName(form.getName());
  employee.setPhone(form.getPhone());
  employee.setEmail(form.getEmail());
  employee.setDepid(new Integer(form.getDepid()));
  employee.setUsername(form.getUsername());

  EmployeeData.updateEmployee(employee,
    getDataSource(request));
}

public ActionForward execute(ActionMapping mapping,
  ActionForm form,
  HttpServletRequest request,
  HttpServletResponse response)
  throws IOException, ServletException {

  // Default target to success
  String target = new String("success");

  if ( isCancelled(request) ) {

    // Cancel pressed back to employee list
    return (mapping.findForward("success"));
  }

  try {

    editEmployee((EmployeeForm) form, request);
  }
  catch ( Exception e ) {

    System.err.println("Setting target to error");
    target = new String("error");
    ActionErrors errors = new ActionErrors();

    errors.add(ActionErrors.GLOBAL_ERROR,
      new ActionError("errors.database.error",
        e.getMessage()));

    // Report any errors
    if ( !errors.isEmpty() ) {

      saveErrors(request, errors);
    }
  }
```

Code continued on following page

```
        // Forward to the appropriate View
        return (mapping.findForward(target));
    }
}
```

Listing 14.18 The EditEmployeeAction.

The EditEmployeeAction begins by first making sure the user is logged in and the Action was not cancelled. Once these conditions are satisfied, then the EditEmployeeAction.perform() method is ready to perform it specific logic, which is simply to invoke the editEmployee() method with the submitted EmployeeForm.

The editEmployee() method then calls the EmployeeData.updateEmployee() method, which in turn performs a SQL update using the employee record referenced by the username contained in the EmployeeForm instance. Assuming that no Exceptions were thrown, then the request is forwarded to the success target, which is the previously described employeelist.jsp.

If the editEmployee() method does throw an Exception, then an ActionError is created and the request is forwarded to the failure target, which in this case is back to the editemployee.jsp.

Deploying the Components of the Edit Employee Transaction

At this point we have the components of the Edit Employee transaction are defined and we can now deploy them to our employees application. Listing 14.19 contains the struts-config.xml file, including the changes necessary to deploy the Edit Employee components.

```
<?xml version="1.0" encoding="ISO-8859-1" ?>

<!DOCTYPE struts-config PUBLIC
  "-//Apache Software Foundation//DTD Struts Configuration 1.0//EN"
  "http://jakarta.apache.org/struts/dtds/struts-config_1_1.dtd">

<struts-config>

  <data-sources>
    <data-source
      type="org.apache.commons.dbcp.BasicDataSource">
      <set-property property="driverClassName"
        value="com.mysql.jdbc.Driver" />
      <set-property property="url"
        value="jdbc:mysql://localhost/employees" />
      <set-property property="username"
        value="jim"/>
      <set-property property="password"
        value="password"/>
    </data-source>
  </data-sources>

  <form-beans>
    <form-bean name="employeeForm"
      type="com.wrox.EmployeeForm" />
```

Code continued on following page

```
    </form-beans>

    <global-forwards>
      <forward name="employeelist" path="/EmployeeList"/>
    </global-forwards>

    <action-mappings>

      <action path="/EmployeeList"
        type="com.wrox.EmployeeListAction"
        scope="request" >
        <forward name="success" path="/employeelist.jsp"/>
      </action>

      <action path="/Add"
        type="com.wrox.AddEmployeeAction"
        name="employeeForm"
        scope="request"
        input="/addemployee.jsp"
        validate="true" >
        <forward name="success" path="/EmployeeList.do"/>
        <forward name="error" path="/addemployee.jsp"/>
      </action>

      <action path="/Edit"
        type="com.wrox.GetEmployeeAction"
        name="employeeForm"
        scope="request"
        validate="false" >
        <forward name="success" path="/editemployee.jsp"/>
        <forward name="error" path="/EmployeeList.do"/>
      </action>

      <action path="/EditEmployee"
        type="com.wrox.EditEmployeeAction"
        name="employeeForm"
        scope="request"
        input="/editemployee.jsp"
        validate="true" >
        <forward name="success" path="/EmployeeList.do"/>
        <forward name="error" path="/editemployee.jsp"/>
      </action>

    </action-mappings>

  </struts-config>
```

Listing 14.19 The struts-config.xml file after adding the Edit Employee components.

As you examine the new struts-config.xml file, you will notice that we added two new <action> elements. These two elements are used to describe the GetEmployeeAction and EditEmployeeAction, respectively.

The only thing that should be noted about these <action> elements is that we have set the validate attribute of the GetEmployeeAction to false. This is because the instance of the EmployeeForm will be empty when first submitted to the GetEmployeeAction.

> **In the <action> element defining the GetEmployeeAction, we are setting the name attribute to point to employeeForm. This would not be necessary if we were not retrieving the name attribute in the GetEmployeeAction.perform() method, but because we are using the name as the key to bind our EmployeeForm instance, we must specify the name attribute.**

The Delete Employee Transaction

The Delete Employee transaction is used to remove a selected employee from the employees database. It is initiated when a user selects the Delete link, next to the employee to be removed, from the employeelist.jsp. When this link is selected, the Delete Employee transaction presents its components in the following order:

1. DeleteEmployeeAction
2. EmployeeListAction
3. Employee List JSP

The Delete Employee Action

The final transaction that we will be adding to our employees application is also the simplest. It is invoked from the employeelist.jsp using the following code snippet:

```
<a href="Delete.do?username=<bean:write name="employee"
  property="username" />">Delete</a>
```

As you will notice, this link executes a get request to the Delete.do path with the request parameter username, which will contain the username of the employee to be deleted. The source for the DeleteEmployeeAction object is shown in Listing 14.20.

```
package com.wrox;

import java.io.IOException;
import javax.servlet.ServletException;
import javax.servlet.http.HttpServletRequest;
import javax.servlet.http.HttpServletResponse;

import org.apache.struts.action.Action;
import org.apache.struts.action.ActionForm;
import org.apache.struts.action.ActionForward;
import org.apache.struts.action.ActionMapping;
import org.apache.struts.action.ActionErrors;
import org.apache.struts.action.ActionError;

public class DeleteEmployeeAction extends Action {
```

Code continued on following page

```
    public ActionForward execute(ActionMapping mapping,
      ActionForm form,
      HttpServletRequest request,
      HttpServletResponse response)
      throws IOException, ServletException {

      // Default target to success
      String target = new String("success");

      try {

        EmployeeData.removeEmployee(
          request.getParameter("username"),
          getDataSource(request));
      }
      catch ( Exception e ) {

        System.err.println("Setting target to error");
        target = new String("error");
        ActionErrors errors = new ActionErrors();

        errors.add(ActionErrors.GLOBAL_ERROR,
          new ActionError("errors.database.error",
            e.getMessage()));

        // Report any errors
        if ( !errors.isEmpty() ) {

          saveErrors(request, errors);
        }
      }
      // Forward to the appropriate View
      return (mapping.findForward(target));
    }
  }
```

Listing 14.20 The DeleteEmployeeAction.

The DeleteEmployeeAction begins by first making sure the user is logged in and the Action was not cancelled. Once these conditions are satisfied, then the DeleteEmployeeAction.perform() method is ready to perform it specific business logic, which is simply to invoke the EmployeeData.removeEmployee() method with the submitted username.

The EmployeeData.removeEmployee() method then performs a SQL delete, removing the employee record referenced by the username and returns control back to the perform() method. Assuming that no Exceptions were thrown by the EmployeeData.removeEmployee() method, then the request is forwarded to the success target, which was previously described EmployeeListAction.

If the EmployeeData.removeEmployee() method does throw Exceptions, then an ActionError is created and the request is forwarded to the failure target (which in this case is the same as the success target).

Deploying the Delete Employee Transaction

The Delete Employee Transaction has only a single component, the DeleteEmployeeAction. To deploy this action, we simply need a single <action> element describing it. The code shown in Listing 14.21, contains the struts-config.xml file, including the changes necessary to deploy the DeleteEmployeeAction.

```
<?xml version="1.0" encoding="ISO-8859-1" ?>

<!DOCTYPE struts-config PUBLIC
  "-//Apache Software Foundation//DTD Struts Configuration 1.0//EN"
  "http://jakarta.apache.org/struts/dtds/struts-config_1_1.dtd">

<struts-config>

  <data-sources>
    <data-source
      type="org.apache.commons.dbcp.BasicDataSource">
      <set-property property="driverClassName"
        value="com.mysql.jdbc.Driver" />
      <set-property property="url"
        value="jdbc:mysql://localhost/employees" />
      <set-property property="username"
        value="jim"/>
      <set-property property="password"
        value="password"/>
    </data-source>
  </data-sources>

  <form-beans>
    <form-bean name="employeeForm"
      type="com.wrox.EmployeeForm" />
  </form-beans>

  <global-forwards>
    <forward name="employeelist" path="/EmployeeList"/>
  </global-forwards>

  <action-mappings>

    <action path="/EmployeeList"
      type="com.wrox.EmployeeListAction"
      scope="request" >
      <forward name="success" path="/employeelist.jsp"/>
    </action>

    <action path="/Add"
      type="com.wrox.AddEmployeeAction"
      name="employeeForm"
      scope="request"
      input="/addemployee.jsp"
      validate="true" >
      <forward name="success" path="/EmployeeList.do"/>
      <forward name="error" path="/addemployee.jsp"/>
```

Code continued on following page

```
    </action>

    <action path="/Edit"
      type="com.wrox.GetEmployeeAction"
      name="employeeForm"
      scope="request"
      validate="false" >
      <forward name="success" path="/editemployee.jsp"/>
      <forward name="error" path="/EmployeeList.do"/>
    </action>

    <action path="/EditEmployee"
      type="com.wrox.EditEmployeeAction"
      name="employeeForm"
      scope="request"
      input="/editemployee.jsp"
      validate="true" >
      <forward name="success" path="/EmployeeList.do"/>
      <forward name="error" path="/editemployee.jsp"/>
    </action>

    <action path="/Delete"
      type="com.wrox.DeleteEmployeeAction"
      scope="request"
      validate="false" >
      <forward name="success" path="/EmployeeList.do"/>
    </action>

  </action-mappings>

</struts-config>
```

Listing 14.21 The struts-config.xml file after adding the DeleteEmployee components.

As you examine the new struts-config.xml file, you will notice that we added a single <action> element that describes the DeleteEmployeeAction with a very basic definition.

Walkthrough

We have now described and deployed all of the components of our employees application. To see this application in action, you need make sure that you have completed the following:

1. Move all of your JSPs to the <*CATALINA_HOME*>/webapps/employees directory.
2. Compile all of the Java classes and move them to the <*CATALINA_HOME*>/webapps/employees/classes/com/wrox directory.
3. Start MySQL, if it is not already running.
4. Start Tomcat, if it is not already running.
5. Open your browser to the following URL:

   ```
   http://localhost:8080/employees/
   ```

If you logged in correctly, you should see a page similar to Figure 14.1, the Employee List view.

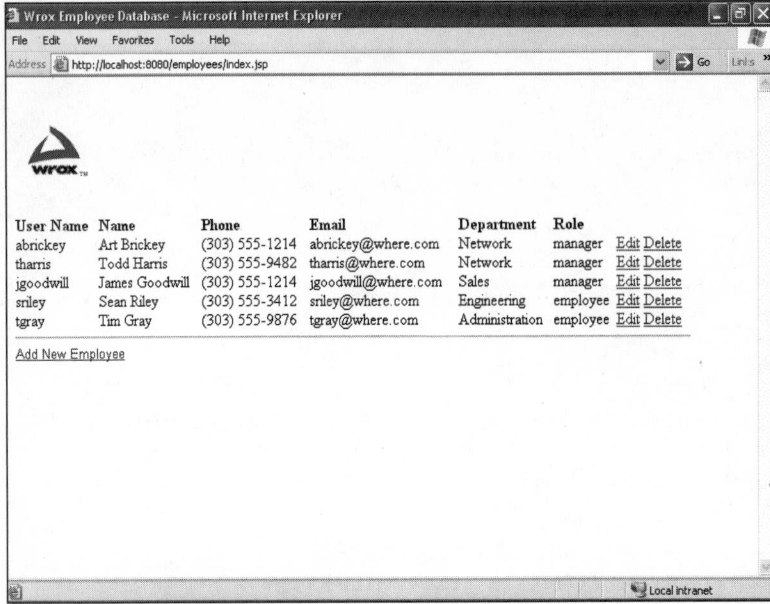

Figure 14.1 The Employee List view.

Now select the Edit link next to a user that you want to edit. In this example we selected the user tharris. You should now see the Edit Employee view, which should look similar to Figure 14.2.

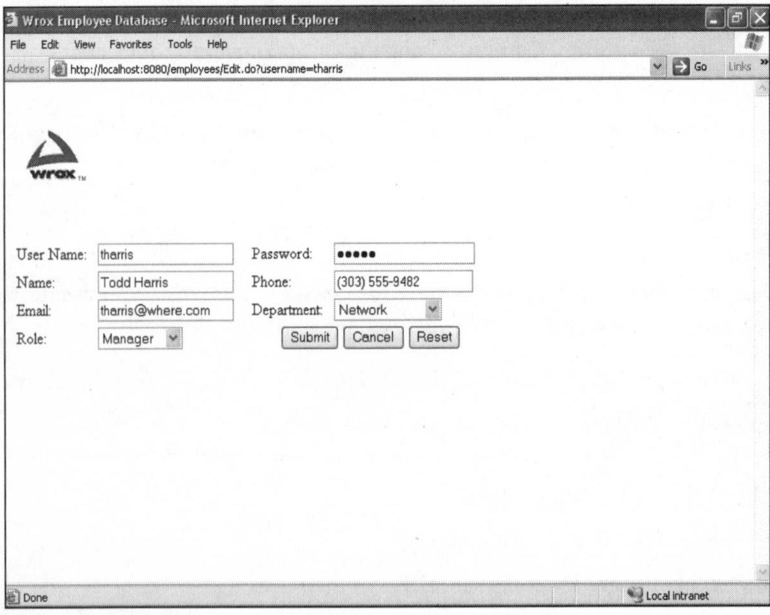

Figure 14.2 The Edit Employee View.

Go ahead and change one of the attributes of the employee and press the Submit button. You should now see the Employee List View with the changes you made being displayed.

Now select the Add New Employee Link. You should see an empty HTML form similar to Figure 14.3, which represents the possible attributes of an Employee.

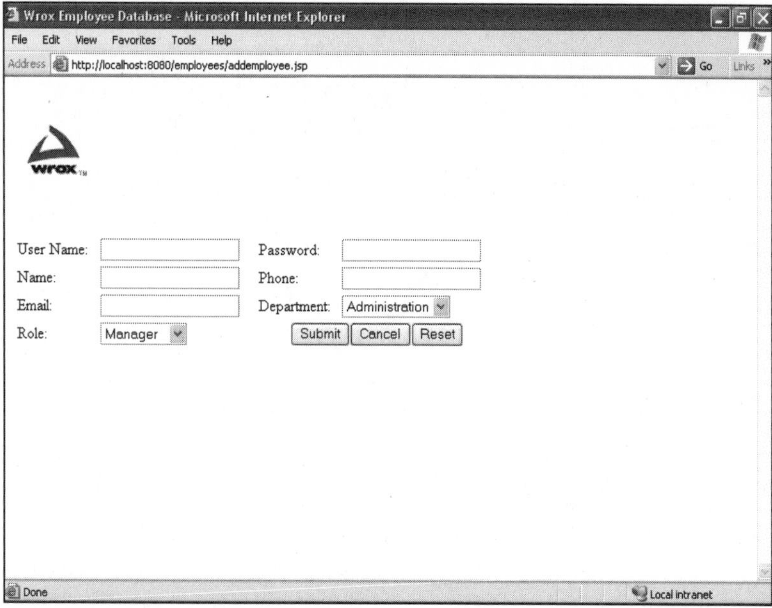

Figure 14.3 The Add Employee View.

Go ahead and enter a new employee and press the submit button. If everything went according to plan, you should see the Employee List View with the new Employee displayed.

What's Next?

In the next chapter we are going discuss the struts-config.xml file. In particular we are going to cover how you deploy all of the major Struts components, including DataSources, FormBeans, Global Forwards, and ActionMappings. We will also describe each of the subordinate components available as sub-elements of the four major Struts components.

The struts-config.xml File

In this chapter, we discuss the file that is at the heart of the Jakarta Struts Project: the struts-config.xml file. You describe all of your Struts components within this file.

This chapter examines the configuration of the top-level Struts components, including DataSources, FormBeans, Global Exception, Global Forwards, ActionMappings, the Controller, message resources, and Plugins. We also describe each of the subordinate components available as sub-elements of the top-level Struts components.

Listing 15.1 shows a stripped-down version of the struts-config.xml file. This example shows all of the top-level components of a Struts configuration file.

```
<?xml version="1.0" encoding="ISO-8859-1" ?>

<!DOCTYPE struts-config PUBLIC
"-//Apache Software Foundation//DTD Struts Configuration 1.1//EN"
"http://jakarta.apache.org/struts/dtds/struts-config_1_1.dtd">

<struts-config>

  <data-sources>
    <data-source
      type="org.apache.commons.dbcp.BasicDataSource">
      <set-property property="driverClassName"
        value="com.mysql.jdbc.Driver" />
      <set-property property="url"
        value="jdbc:mysql://localhost/stocks" />
      <set-property property="username"
        value="YOUR USERNAME" />
      <set-property property="password"
        value="YOUR PASSWORD" />
    </data-source>
  </data-sources>
```

Code continued on following page

```
    <form-beans>
      <form-bean name="registrationForm"
        type="com.wrox.RegistrationForm"/>
    </form-beans>

    <global-exceptions>
      <exception
        key="com.wrox.error"
        type="java.io.Exception"
        handler="com.wrox.ExceptionHandler">
    </global-exceptions>

    <global-forwards>
      <forward name="registration" path="/registration.jsp"/>
    </global-forwards>

    <action-mappings>
      <action path="/saveRegistration"
        type="com.wrox.SaveRegistrationAction"
        name="registrationForm"
        scope="request"
        input="registration"/>
    </action-mappings>


    <controller>
      <set-property property="inputForward" value="true"/>
    </controller>

    <message-resources
      parameter="com.wrox.ApplicationResources"/>

    <plug-in className="com.wrox.plugins.ModuleConfigVerifier"/>

  </struts-config>
```

Listing 15.1 The struts-config.xml file.

> **It is important to note the order of each of the elements in Listing 15.1. This is the order in which they must appear in the struts-config.xml file. If the order deviates from that shown in the listing, Struts throws an exception upon startup.**

The Struts Sub-Elements

In this section, we discuss the sub-elements available to the top-level Struts components. Not all of these elements are used by each top-level component, but they are available to further describe each of them.

The <icon /> Sub-Element

The <icon> sub-element contains <small-icon> and <large-icon> sub-elements that can be used to graphically represent its parent element in a Struts development tool. The syntax of the <icon> sub-element is:

```
<icon>
  <small-icon>
    path to somegraphicsfile (16x16 pixels)
  </small-icon>
  <large-icon>
    somelargergraphicsfile (32x32 pixels)
  </large-icon>
</icon>
```

Table 15.1 describes the properties of an <icon> element.

Table 15.1 The Attributes of an <icon> Element

Property	Description
<small-icon>	The <small-icon> sub-element contains a path, relative to the location of the Struts configuration file, naming a graphics file that contains a 16x16-pixel iconic image.
<large-icon>	The <large-icon> sub-element contains a path, relative the location of the Struts configuration file, naming a graphics file that contains a 32x32-pixel iconic image.

The following code snippets uses these <icon> sub-elements:

```
<icon>
  <small-icon>
    /images/smalllogo.gif
  </small-icon>
  <large-icon>
    /images/largelogo.gif
  </large-icon>
</icon>
```

Note that the images referenced in these sub-elements are made strictly for Struts development and configuration tools. They are not intended for client-side display.

The <display-name /> Sub-Element

The <display-name> sub-element contains a short text description of its parent element for use in a Struts development tool. The syntax of the <display-name> sub-element is:

```
<display-name>
  short text discription of its parent element
</display-name>
```

The <description /> Sub-Element

The <description> sub-element contains a full-length text description of its parent element for use in a Struts development tool. The syntax of the <description> sub-element is:

```
<description>
  full-length text discription of its parent element
</description>
```

The <set-property /> Sub-Element

You can use the <set-property> sub-element to set the value of additional JavaBean properties of objects described by the <set-property> sub-element's parent. The <set-property> sub-element is commonly used to set GenericDataSource properties, extended ActionMappings, and extended global forwards. The syntax of the <set-property> sub-element is:

```
<set-property
  property="name of bean property"
  value="value of bean property" />
```

Table 15.2 describes the attributes of a <set-property> element.

Table 15.2 The Attributes of a <set-property> Element

Property	Description
property	The property of the JavaBeans property whose setter method will be called. (required)
value	The large-icon String representation of the value to which this property will be set after suitable type conversion. (required)

Here's an example that uses the <set-property> sub-element:

```
<set-property
  property="driverClass"
  value="org.gjt.mm.mysql.Driver" />
```

> **The <set-property> sub-element contains no body. It is configured using only its two attributes.**

Adding a DataSource

The first component that we configure is a DataSource. As we discussed in Chapter 11, "Integrating the Jakarta Commons Database Connection Pool (DBCP)," there are two methods for configuring a DataSource. With the first method, which is not applicable to this discussion, you directly manipulating a DataSource instance using one of your own components. The second method, which we demonstrate in this section, involves modifying the struts-config.xml file. This method leaves management of the DataSource in the capable hands of the Controller, allowing you, the developer, to focus on project-specific efforts.

When describing DataSource instances, you must use the <data-sources> element. This element contains n-number of <data-source> sub-elements, which describe each DataSource instance. The syntax of the <data-sources> element, containing a single <data-source> sub-element, is shown in the following code snippet:

```
<data-sources>
  <data-source
    type="org.apache.commons.dbcp.BasicDataSource">
    <set-property property="driverClassName"
      value="com.mysql.jdbc.Driver" />
    <set-property property="url"
      value="jdbc:mysql://localhost/stocks" />
    <set-property property="username"
      value="YOUR USERNAME" />
    <set-property property="password"
      value="YOUR PASSWORD" />
  </data-source>
</data-sources>
```

As you can see, the <data-source> sub-element is described completely using <set-property> sub-elements. Each one of the properties listed in the <set-property> elements maps to a single <data-source> attribute. Table 15.3 describes the attributes of a <data-source> entry.

As we stated earlier, the actual attributes used by a specific DataSource are dependent on that DataSource's implementation. Therefore, the contents of your particular <set-property> sub-elements also depend on your specific implementation.

Table 15.3 The Attributes of a <data-source> Entry

Attribute	Description
type	The fully qualified class name of the DataSource object being used in this <data-source> definition. This class must extend javax.sql.DataSource, and it must be completely configurable using <set-property> sub-elements (all configurable data members must satisfy the JavaBean specification). (optional)

Table continued on following page

Attribute	Description
className	The fully qualified classname of the configuration object for the instance of this DataSource. The implementation of this object must extend org.apache.struts.config.DataSourceConfig. (optional)
key	A unique key identifying a DataSource instance stored in the ServletContext. If this property is not used, then the key is defaulted to Action.DATA_SOURCE_KEY. If you intend to use more than one DataSource in your application, you must include a key for each one. (optional)

This code snippet shows an example that uses the <data-source> sub-element:

```
<data-sources>
  <data-source
    type="org.apache.commons.dbcp.BasicDataSource">
    <set-property property="driverClassName"
      value="com.mysql.jdbc.Driver" />
    <set-property property="url"
      value="jdbc:mysql://localhost/stocks" />
    <set-property property="username"
      value="YOUR USERNAME" />
    <set-property property="password"
      value="YOUR PASSWORD" />
  </data-source>
</data-sources>
```

Adding FormBean Definitions

The <form-bean> sub-element is used to describe an instance of a FormBean that is later bound to an Action. The syntax of the <form-bean> sub-element is:

```
<form-beans>
  <form-bean name="name used to uniquely identify a FormBean"
    type="fully qualified class name of FormBean" />
</form-beans>
```

All <form-bean> sub-elements must be nested within a single <form-beans> element. The <form-beans> element is used only as a container for <form-bean> sub-elements.

Table 15.4 describes the attributes of a <form-bean> sub-element.

Table 15.4 The Attributes of a <form-bean> Sub-Element

Attribute	Description
name	Contains the unique identifier that identifies this bean. This value is used in an action mappings element to bind a FormBean to an Action. (required)
type	Specifies the fully qualified class name of the FormBean class. (required)

This code snippet uses the <form-bean> sub-element:

```
<form-beans>
  <form-bean name="lookupForm"
    type="wrox.LookupForm" />
</form-beans>
```

The <form-bean> sub-element contains no body. It is configured using only its two attributes.

Adding Global Exceptions

The <global-exceptions> sub-element is used to define n-number of <exception> sub-elements that are throwable by any Action in a Struts application. This sub-element acts as a container for all public <exception> sub-elements.

The <exception> sub-element is used to associate a global exception with an ExceptionHandler. The sub-element is the core piece of the <global-exceptions> definition. The syntax of the <global-exceptions> sub-element, including an example nested <exception> element, is shown here:

```
<global-exceptions>
  <exception key="Key" type="Exception Type"
    handler="Exception Handler">
</global-exceptions>
```

Table 15.5 describes the attributes of an <exception> sub-element.

Table 15.5 The Attributes of an <exception> Sub-Element

Attribute	Description
bundle	A ServletContext attribute that names the resource bundle associated with the ExceptionHandler handling the defined <exception> elements. The default attribute is defined by the Globals.MESSAGES_KEY (org.apache.struts.Globals.MESSAGES_KEY). (optional)

Table continued on following page

Attribute	Description
className	The fully qualified class name of the configuration bean associated with the defined handler. The default class is org.apache.struts.config.ExceptionConfig.
handler	The fully qualified class name of the ExceptionHandler that will process the contained <exception> sub-elements. The default class is org.apache.struts.action.ExceptionHandler.
key	Used to retrieve the message template associated with this exception. (required)
path	The module-relative path that will act as the target of the ExceptionHandler associated with this exception. (optional)
scope	The scope of the ActionError object coupled with this exception. (optional)
type	The fully qualified class name of the exception defined by this <exception> sub-element. (required)

An example of using the <global-exceptions> sub-element is shown in the following code snippet:

```
<global-exceptions>
  <exception
    key="wrox"
    type="ch15.WroxException"
    handler="ch15.WroxExceptionHandler">
</global-exceptions>
```

Adding Global Forwards

The <global-forwards> sub-element is used to define n-number of <forward> sub-elements that are available to any Action in the Struts application. It acts as a container for public <forward> sub-elements.

You can use the <forward> sub-element to describe a mapping of a logical name to a context-relative URI path. A forward is used to identify the target of an Action class when it returns its results. This target is most often used to present the results of the Action that names it. The syntax of the <global-forwards> sub-element, including an example nested <forward> element, is:

```
<global-forwards>
  <forward name="unique target identifier"
    path="context-relative path to targetted resource "/>
</global-forwards>
```

All <forward> sub-elements that are to be made available to the entire application must be nested within a single <global-forwards> element.

Table 15.6 describes the attributes of a <forward> sub-element.

Table 15.6 The Attributes of a <forward> Sub-Element

Attribute	Description
name	Contains the unique identifier identifying this target. This attribute is used by an Action class to identify its targeted resource. (required)
path	Specifies the context-relative path of the targeted resource. (required)
redirect	If set to true, causes the ActionServlet to use the HttpServletResponse.sendRedirect() method, as opposed to the RequestDispatcher.forward() method, when sending the Action results to the targeted resource. The default value is false. (optional)

If the redirect attribute is set to true, causing the HttpServletResponse. sendRedirect() method to be used, then the values stored in the original HttpServletRequest will be lost.

An example of using the <global-forwards> sub-element appears in the following code snippet:

```
<global-forwards>
  <forward name="success" path="/welcome.jsp"/>
  <forward name="failure" path="/index.jsp"/>
</global-forwards>
```

The <forward> sub-element contains no body. It is configured using only its two attributes.

Adding Actions

The <action-mappings> sub-element is used to define n-number of <action> sub-elements. It acts as a container for <action> sub-elements; therefore, this section focuses on the actual configuration of individual <action> sub-elements.

The <action> sub-element is used to describe an Action instance to the ActionServlet. It represents the information that uniquely defines an instance of a particular Action class. The syntax of the <action-mappings> sub-element, including an example <action> sub-element, is:

```
<action-mappings>

  <action
    path="context-relative path mapping action to a request"
    type="fully qualified class name of the Action class"
    name="the name of the form bean bound to this Action">
```

```
        <forward name="forwardname1" path="context-relative path"/>
        <forward name="forwardname2" path="context-relative path"/>
    </action>

  </action-mappings>
```

Notice that the <action> element in the previous code snippet contains two <forward> sub-elements. These sub-elements are defined as the <forward> elements nested inside a <global-forwards> element, except that they are local to the defined <action> sub-element. These <forward> sub-elements can be referenced only by their parent <action>.

Table 15.7 describes the attributes of an <action> sub-element.

Table 15.7 The Attributes of an <action> Sub-Element

Attribute	Description
path	Represents the context-relative path of the submitted request. The path must start with a / character. (required)
type	Specifies the fully qualified class name of the Action class being described by this ActionMapping. The type attribute is valid only if no include or forward attribute is specified. (optional)
name	Identifies the name of the form bean, if any, that is coupled with the Action being defined. (optional)
scope	Specifies the scope of the form bean that is bound to the described Action. The default value is session. (optional)
input	Represents the context-relative path of the input form to which control should be returned if a validation error is encountered. Control is returned to the input attribute if ActionErrors are returned from the ActionForm or Action objects. (optional)
className	Specifies the fully qualified class name of the ActionMapping implementation class you want to use in when invoking this Action class. If the className attribute is not included, then the ActionMapping defined in the ActionServlet's mapping initialization parameter is used. (optional)
forward	Represents the context-relative path of the servlet or JSP resource that will process this request. This attribute is used if you do not want an Action to service the request to this path. The forward attribute is valid only if no include or type attribute is specified. (optional)
include	Represents the context-relative path of the servlet or JSP resource that will process this request. This attribute is used if you do not want an Action to service the request to this path. The include attribute is valid only if no forward or type attribute is specified. (optional)

Table continued on following page

Attribute	Description
validate	If set to true, causes the ActionForm.validate() method to be called on the form bean associated to the Action being described. If the validate attribute is set to false, then the ActionForm.validate() method is not called. The default value is true. (optional)

The following code snippet contains an example using the <action-mappings> sub-element:

```
<action-mappings>

  <action path="/lookupAction"
    type="wrox.LookupAction"
    name="LookupForm"
    scope="request"
    validate="true"
    input="/index.jsp">
    <forward name="success" path="/quote.jsp"/>
    <forward name="faliue" path="/index.jsp"/>
  </action>

</action-mappings>
```

Adding Controller Elements

The <controller> element is used to define a ControllerConfig bean (org.apache.struts.config.ControllerConfig) that represents an application's runtime module configuration. The syntax of the <controller> element is:

```
<global-forwards>
  <forward name="unique target identifier"
    path="context-relative path to targeted resource "/>
</global-forwards>
```

Table 15.8 describes the attributes of a <controller> sub-element.

Table 15.8 The Attributes of a <controller> Sub-Element

Attribute	Description
bufferSize	Defines the size of the available input buffer when uploading files. (optional)
className	Specifies the fully qualified class name of the configuration class that is defined by this <controller> element. This class must be derived from org.apache.struts.config.ControllerConfig, which is also the default value. (optional)
contentType	Indicates the content type of each response. The default value is text/html. (optional)

Table continued on following page

Attribute	Description
inputForward	If set to true, the input attribute of all <action> elements will be used as the name of a defined forward. If this attribute is set to false, then the input name will be used as a module-relative path. The default value is false. (optional)
locale	If set to true, then the user's Locale will be placed in his or her HttpSession. If the Locale is already in the HttpSession, then it will be ignored. The default value is true. (optional)
maxFileSize	Represents the maximum file size (in bytes) of a single file upload. The value can be expressed as K (kilobytes), M (megabytes), or G (gigabytes). The default value is 250M. (optional)
memFileSize	Represents the maximum file size (in bytes) of a single file whose contents remain in memory after a file upload. The value can be expressed in as K (kilobytes), M (megabytes), or G (gigabytes). The default value is 256K. (optional)
multipartClass	Identifies the fully qualified class name of a multipart request handler class to be used when uploading files. The default value is org.apache.struts.upload.CommonsMultipartRequestHandler. (optional)
nocache	If this attribute is set to true, the controller adds HTTP headers for defeating HTTP caching to every response. The default value is false. (optional)
processorClass	Specifies the fully qualified class name of the RequestProcessor subclass that will be used when processing each request associated with the containing module. The default value is org.apache.struts.action.RequestProcessor. (optional)
tempDir	A temporary working directory that is used to hold files when processing uploads. The default value is named by the JSP/servlet container. (optional)

The following code snippet uses the <controller> sub-element:

```
<controller
  processorClass="ch04.WroxRequestProcessor"
  nocache="true" />
```

This example changes the default RequestProcessor to the ch04.WroxRequestProcess, which was used in Chapter 4, "Actions and the ActionServlet," and ensures that all responses from this module will not be cached.

Adding Message Resources

The <message-resources> element is used to describe a MessageResources object for the containing application. The syntax of the <message-resources> element is:

```
<message-resources
  parameter="configuration parameter"
  key="main" />
```

Table 15.9 describes the attributes of a <message-resources> element.

Table 15.9 The Attributes of a <message-resources> Element

Attribute	Description
className	Specifies the fully qualified class name for the message resources configuration object. The default value is org.apache.struts.config.MessageResourcesConfig. (optional)
factory	Represents the fully qualified class name for the message resources factory. The default value is org.apache.struts.util.PropertyMessageResourcesFactory. (optional)
key	Binds to the ServletContext attribute representing the Message Resource bundle. The default value is Globals.MESSAGES_KEY. (optional)
null	If this attribute is set to true, null is returned when you are searching for a missing key. The default value is false. (optional)
parameter	Represents a configuration parameter that is passed to the named factory's createResources() method. (required)

An example of using the <message-resources> element is:

```
<message-resources
  parameter="ch15.MainResources"
  key="main" />
```

Adding Plugins

The <plug-in> element is used to add Plugins to the Struts Controller. As we discussed in Chapter 4, "Actions and the ActionServlet," Struts Plugins are useful when allocating resources or preparing connections to databases or even JNDI resources. The <plug-in> element has a single attribute, className, which is used to define the fully qualified Plugin class.

The syntax of the <plug-in> element is:

```
<plug-in className="Fully qualified Plugin class name"/>
```

This example uses the <plug-in> element:

```
<plug-in className="ch04.WroxPlugin"/>
```

What's Next

In the next chapter, we discuss the Jakarta Struts HTML tag library. This taglib contains tags used to create Struts input forms, as well as other tags you will find helpful when creating HTML-based user interfaces.

16

The HTML Tag Library

In this chapter, we discuss the Jakarta Struts HTML tag library. This taglib contains tags used to create Struts input forms, as well as other tags you will find helpful when creating HTML-based user interfaces.

Installing the HTML Tags

To use the HTML tag library in a Web application, you must complete the following steps. Be sure to replace the value *webappname* with the name of the Web application that will be using this library.

1. Copy the TLD file packaged with this tag library (struts-html.tld) to the *<CATALINA_HOME>*/webapps/*webappname*/WEB-INF directory.
2. Make sure that the struts.jar file is in the *<CATALINA_HOME>*/webapps/*webappname*/WEB-INF/lib directory.
3. Add the following <taglib> sub-element to the web.xml file of the Web application:

```
<taglib>
  <taglib-uri>/WEB-INF/struts-html.tld</taglib-uri>
  <taglib-location>/WEB-INF/struts-html.tld</
taglib-location>
</taglib>
```

You must add the following taglib directive to each JSP that will leverage the HTML tag library:

```
<%@ taglib uri="/WEB-INF/struts-html.tld" prefix="html" %>
```

This directive identifies the URI defined in the previously listed <taglib> element and states that all HTML tags should be prefixed with the string html.

<html:base />

The <html:base /> tag is used to insert an HTML <base> element, including an href pointing to the absolute location of the hosting JSP page. This tag allows you to use relative URL references, rather than a URL that is relative to the most recent requested resource. The <html:base /> tag has no body and supports two attributes, described in Table 16.1.

Table 16.1 <html:base /> Tag Attributes

Attribute	Description
target	Represents the target attribute of the HTML <base> tag (optional)
server	Identifies a server name to use in the href as opposed to the results of a call to request.getServerName() (optional)

The <html:base /> tag must be nested inside the body of an HTML <head> element.

<html:button />

The <html:button /> tag is used to render an HTML <input> element with an input type of button. The <html:button /> tag has a body type of JSP and supports the attributes described in Table 16.2.

The <html:button /> tag must be nested inside the body of an <html:form /> tag.

Table 16.2 <html:button /> Tag Attributes

Attribute	Description
property	Identifies the name of the input field being processed. (required)
accessKey	Identifies a keyboard character to be used to immediately move focus to the HTML element defined by this tag. (optional)
alt	Defines an alternate text string for this element. (optional)
altKey	Defines a resources key (to be retrieved from a resource bundle) that references an alternate text string for this element. (optional)
disabled	If set to true, causes this HTML input element to be disabled. The default value is false. (optional)
indexed	If set to true, then the name of the HTML tag is rendered as propertyName[indexnumber]. The [] characters surrounding the index are generated for every iteration and taken from its ancestor, the <logic:iterate /> tag. The indexed attribute is valid only when the tag using it is nested with a <logic:iterate /> tag. The default value is false. (optional)

Table continued on following page

Attribute	Description
onblur	Specifies a JavaScript function that is executed when the containing element loses its focus. (optional)
onchange	Specifies a JavaScript function that is executed when this element loses input focus and its value has changed. (optional)
onclick	Specifies a JavaScript function that is executed when this element receives a mouse click. (optional)
ondblclick	Specifies a JavaScript function that is executed when this element receives a mouse double-click. (optional)
onfocus	Specifies a JavaScript function that is executed when this element receives input focus. (optional)
onkeydown	Specifies a JavaScript function that is executed when this element has focus and a key is pressed. (optional)
onkeypress	Specifies a JavaScript function that is executed when this element has focus and a key is pressed and released. (optional)
onkeyup	Specifies a JavaScript function that is executed when this element has focus and a key is released. (optional)
onmousedown	Specifies a JavaScript function that is executed when this element is under the mouse pointer and a mouse button is pressed. (optional)
onmousemove	Specifies a JavaScript function that is executed when this element is under the mouse pointer and the pointer is moved. (optional)
onmouseout	Specifies a JavaScript function that is executed when this input object is under the mouse pointer but the pointer is then moved outside the element. (optional)
onmouseover	Specifies a JavaScript function that is executed when this input object is not under the mouse pointer but the pointer is then moved inside the input object. (optional)
onmouseup	Specifies a JavaScript function that is executed when this input object is under the mouse pointer and a mouse button is released. (optional)
style	Specifies a Cascading Style Sheet style to apply to this HTML element. (optional)
styleClass	Specifies a Cascading Style Sheet class to apply to this HTML input component. (optional)
styleId	Specifies an HTML identifier to be associated with this HTML input component. (optional)
tabindex	Identifies the tab order of this input component in relation to the other elements of the containing Form. (optional)
title	Specifies the advisory title for this HTML input component. (required)
titleKey	Specifies a resources key (to be retrieved from a resource bundle) that references a title string for this input component. (optional)
value	Specifies the label to be placed on this button. The body of this tag can also be used for the button label. (optional)

<html:cancel />

The <html:cancel /> tag is used to render an HTML <input> element with an input type of cancel. The<html:cancel /> has a body type of JSP and supports 25 attributes, as shown in Table 16.3.

The <html:cancel /> tag must be nested inside the body of an <html:form /> tag.

Table 16.3 <html:cancel /> Tag Attributes

Attribute	Description
accessKey	Identifies a keyboard character to be used to immediately move focus to the HTML input component defined by this tag. (optional)
alt	Defines an alternate text string for this input component. (optional)
altKey	Defines a resources key (to be retrieved from a resource bundle) that references an alternate text string for this element. (optional)
disabled	If set to true, causes this HTML input element to be disabled. The default value is false. (optional)
onblur	Specifies a JavaScript function that is executed when the containing input component loses its focus. (optional)
onchange	Specifies a JavaScript function that is executed when this element loses input focus and its value has changed. (optional)
onclick	Specifies a JavaScript function that is executed when this element receives a mouse click. (optional)
ondblclick	Specifies a JavaScript function that is executed when this element receives a mouse double-click. (optional)
onfocus	Specifies a JavaScript function that is executed when this element receives input focus. (optional)
onkeydown	Specifies a JavaScript function that is executed when this element has focus and a key is pressed. (optional)
onkeypress	Specifies a JavaScript function that is executed when this element has focus and a key is pressed and released. (optional)
onkeyup	Specifies a JavaScript function that is executed when this element has focus and a key is released. (optional)
onmousedown	Specifies a JavaScript function that is executed when this element is under the mouse pointer and a mouse button is pressed. (optional)
onmousemove	Specifies a JavaScript function that is executed when this element is under the mouse pointer and the pointer is moved. (optional)

Table continued on following page

Attribute	Description
onmouseout	Specifies a JavaScript function that is executed when this element is under the mouse pointer but the pointer is then moved outside the element. (optional)
onmouseover	Specifies a JavaScript function that is executed when this element is not under the mouse pointer but the pointer is then moved inside the element. (optional)
onmouseup	Specifies a JavaScript function that is executed when this element is under the mouse pointer and a mouse button is released. (optional)
property	Identifies the name of the input field being processed. (optional)
style	Specifies a Cascading Style Sheet style to apply to this HTML element. (optional)
styleClass	Specifies a Cascading Style Sheet class to apply to this HTML element. (optional)
styleId	Specifies an HTML identifier to be associated with this HTML element. (optional)
tabindex	Identifies the tab order of this element in relation to the other elements of the containing Form. (optional)
title	Specifies the advisory title for this HTML element. (required)
titleKey	Specifies a resources key (to be retrieved from a resource bundle) that references a title string for this element. (optional)
value	Specifies the label to be placed on this button. The body of this tag can also be used for the button label. (optional)

<html:checkbox />

The <html:checkbox /> tag is used to render an HTML <input> element with an input type of checkbox. The<html:checkbox /> tag has a body type of JSP and supports 27 attributes, described in Table 16.4.

> **The <html:checkbox /> tag must be nested inside the body of an <html:form /> tag. Another thing to note about this tag is that, in order to correctly recognize deselected checkboxes, the ActionForm bean associated with the parent form must include a reset() method that sets the property corresponding to this checkbox to false.**
>
> **The body of this tag can also be used as the element label.**

Table 16.4 <html:checkbox /> Tag Attributes

Attribute	Description
property	Identifies the name of the input field being processed. (required)
accessKey	Identifies a keyboard character to be used to immediately move focus to the HTML element defined by this tag. (optional)
alt	Defines an alternate text string for this element. (optional)
altKey	Defines a resources key (to be retrieved from a resource bundle) that references an alternate text string for this element. (optional)
disabled	If set to true, causes this HTML input element to be disabled. The default value is false. (optional)
indexed	If set to true, then the name of the HTML tag is rendered as propertyName[indexnumber]. The [] characters surrounding the index are generated for every iteration and taken from its ancestor, the <logic:iterate /> tag. The indexed attribute is valid only when the tag using it is nested with a <logic:iterate /> tag. (optional)
name	Identifies a JavaBean to use when defaulting the value of the input field. (optional)
onblur	Specifies a JavaScript function that is executed when the containing element loses its focus. (optional)
onchange	Specifies a JavaScript function that is executed when this element loses input focus and its value has changed. (optional)
onclick	Specifies a JavaScript function that is executed when this element receives a mouse click. (optional)
ondblclick	Specifies a JavaScript function that is executed when this element receives a mouse double-click. (optional)
onfocus	Specifies a JavaScript function that is executed when this element receives input focus. (optional)
onkeydown	Specifies a JavaScript function that is executed when this element has focus and a key is pressed. (optional)
onkeypress	Specifies a JavaScript function that is executed when this element has focus and a key is pressed and released. (optional)
onkeyup	Specifies a JavaScript function that is executed when this element has focus and a key is released. (optional)
onmousedown	Specifies a JavaScript function that is executed when this element is under the mouse pointer and a mouse button is pressed. (optional)
onmousemove	Specifies a JavaScript function that is executed when this element is under the mouse pointer and the pointer is moved. (optional)
onmouseout	Specifies a JavaScript function that is executed when this element is under the mouse pointer but the pointer is then moved outside the element. (optional)

Table continued on following page

Attribute	Description
onmouseover	Specifies a JavaScript function that is executed when this element is not under the mouse pointer but the pointer is then moved inside the element. (optional)
onmouseup	Specifies a JavaScript function that is executed when this element is under the mouse pointer and a mouse button is released. (optional)
style	Specifies a Cascading Style Sheet style to apply to this HTML element. (optional)
styleClass	Specifies a Cascading Style Sheet class to apply to this HTML element. (optional)
styleId	Specifies an HTML identifier to be associated with this HTML element. (optional)
tabindex	Identifies the tab order of this element in relation to the other elements of the containing Form. (optional)
title	Specifies the advisory title for this HTML element. (required)
titleKey	Specifies a resources key (to be retrieved from a resource bundle) that references a title string for this element. (optional)
value	Specifies the label to be placed on the request if this checkbox is selected. The default value is on. (optional)

<html:errors />

The <html:errors /> tag is used to display the ActionError objects stored in an ActionErrors collection. The <html:errors /> tag has a body type of JSP and supports four attributes, described in Table 16.5.

Table 16.5 <html:errors /> Tag Attributes

Attribute	Description
bundle	Specifies a MessageResources key of the resource bundle defined in the struts-config <message-resource> element. The default key is ApplicationResources. (optional)
locale	Specifies the session attribute containing the Locale instance of the current request. This Locale is then used to select Locale-specific text messages. (optional)
name	Specifies the name of the request scope object that references the ActionErrors collection being displayed. The default value is Action.ERROR_KEY. (optional)
property	Specifies which error messages should be displayed, based on each property contained in the ActionErrors collection. The default value indicates that all error messages should be displayed. (optional)

<html:file />

The <html:file /> tag is used to create an HTML <file> element. This tag allows you to upload files that will be populated in a named ActionForm's identified property. The <html:file /> tag has a body type of JSP and supports 30 attributes, described in Table 16.6.

> **The <html:file /> tag must be nested inside the body of an <html:form /> tag.**

Table 16.6 <html:file /> Tag Attributes

Attribute	Description
property	Identifies the name of the input field being processed. (required)
accessKey	Identifies a keyboard character to be used to immediately move focus to the HTML element defined by this tag. (optional)
accept	Identifies a comma-delimited list of file types that will be accepted by this <html:file /> tag. There is no default value for this tag. (optional)
alt	Defines an alternate text string for this element. (optional)
altKey	Defines a resources key (to be retrieved from a resource bundle) that references an alternate text string for this element. (optional)
disabled	If set to true, causes this HTML input element to be disabled. The default value is false. (optional)
indexed	If set to true, then the name of the HTML tag is rendered as propertyName[indexnumber]. The [] characters surrounding the index are generated for every iteration and taken from its ancestor, the <logic:iterate /> tag. The indexed attribute is valid only when the tag using it is nested with a <logic:iterate /> tag. (optional)
maxlength	Identifies the maximum number of input characters that is accepted by this tag. The default value is unlimited. (optional)
name	Identifies a JavaBean to use when defaulting the value of the input field. (optional)
onblur	Specifies a JavaScript function that is executed when the containing element loses its focus. (optional)
onchange	Specifies a JavaScript function that is executed when this element loses input focus and its value has changed. (optional)
onclick	Specifies a JavaScript function that is executed when this element receives a mouse click. (optional)
ondblclick	Specifies a JavaScript function that is executed when this element receives a mouse double-click. (optional)

Table continued on following page

Attribute	Description
onfocus	Specifies a JavaScript function that is executed when this element receives input focus. (optional)
onkeydown	Specifies a JavaScript function that is executed when this element has focus and a key is pressed. (optional)
onkeypress	Specifies a JavaScript function that is executed when this element has focus and a key is pressed and released. (optional)
onkeyup	Specifies a JavaScript function that is executed when this element has focus and a key is released. (optional)
onmousedown	Specifies a JavaScript function that is executed when this element is under the mouse pointer and a mouse button is pressed. (optional)
onmousemove	Specifies a JavaScript function that is executed when this element is under the mouse pointer and the pointer is moved. (optional)
onmouseout	Specifies a JavaScript function that is executed when this element is under the mouse pointer but the pointer is then moved outside the element. (optional)
onmouseover	Specifies a JavaScript function that is executed when this element is not under the mouse pointer but the pointer is then moved inside the element. (optional)
onmouseup	Specifies a JavaScript function that is executed when this element is under the mouse pointer and a mouse button is released. (optional)
size	Specifies a Cascading Style Sheet style to apply to this HTML element. (optional)
style	Specifies a Cascading Style Sheet style to apply to this HTML element. (optional)
styleClass	Specifies a Cascading Style Sheet class to apply to this HTML element. (optional)
styleId	Specifies an HTML identifier to be associated with this HTML element. (optional)
tabindex	Identifies the tab order of this element in relation to the other elements of the containing Form. (optional)
title	Specifies the advisory title for this HTML element. (required)
titleKey	Specifies a resources key (to be retrieved from a resource bundle) that references a title string for this element. (optional)
value	Specifies the label to be placed on the request if this checkbox is selected. The default value is on. (optional)

Table continued on following page

<html:form />

The <html:form /> tag is used to create an HTML form. The form implicitly interacts with the named ActionForm bean to pre-populate the input fields values with the matching data members of the named bean. The <html:form /> tag has a body type of JSP and supports 13 attributes, described in Table 16.7.

Table 16.7 <html:form /> Tag Attributes

Attribute	Description
action	Identifies the URL to which this form is submitted. This value is also used to select an ActionMapping described by an <action> element in the struts-config.xml file. (required)
enctype	Identifies the content encoding of the request submitted by this form. If you are using the file tag, then this attribute must be set to multipart/form-data. If this value is not indicated, then the default value is determined by the client browser. (optional)
focus	Identifies the input field name to which initial focus is assigned. (optional)
focusIndex	An array of input element ids representing their associated tab order. (optional)
method	Identifies the HTTP request method used when submitting the form request (GET or POST). The default method is POST. (optional)
onreset	Specifies a JavaScript function that is executed if the form is reset. (optional)
onsubmit	Specifies a JavaScript function that is executed if the form is submitted. (optional)
scope	Specifies the scope of the form bean associated with this input form. (optional)
style	Specifies a Cascading Style Sheet style to apply to this HTML element. (optional)
styleClass	Specifies a Cascading Style Sheet class to apply to this HTML element. (optional)
styleId	Specifies an HTML identifier to be associated with this HTML element. (optional)
target	Specifies the frame window target to which this form is submitted. (optional)
type	Provides the fully qualified class name of the ActionForm bean to be created, if no such bean is found in the named scope. (optional)

<html:hidden />

The <html:hidden /> tag is used to render an HTML <input> element with an input type of hidden. The<html:hidden /> has a body type of JSP and supports 25 attributes, described in Table 16.8.

The <html:hidden /> tag must be nested inside the body of an <html:form /> tag.

Table 16.8 <html:hidden /> Tag Attributes

Attribute	Description
property	Identifies the name of the input field being processed. (required)
accessKey	Identifies a keyboard character to be used to immediately move focus to the HTML element defined by this tag. (optional)
alt	Defines an alternate text string for this element. (optional)
altKey	Defines a resources key (to be retrieved from a resource bundle) that references an alternate text string for this element. (optional)
indexed	If set to true, then the name of the HTML tag is rendered as propertyName[indexnumber]. The [] characters surrounding the index are generated for every iteration and taken from its ancestor, the <logic:iterate /> tag. The indexed attribute is valid only when the tag using it is nested with a <logic:iterate /> tag. (optional)
name	Identifies a JavaBean to use when defaulting the value of the input field. (optional)
onblur	Specifies a JavaScript function that is executed when the containing element loses its focus. (optional)
onchange	Specifies a JavaScript function that is executed when this element loses input focus and its value has changed. (optional)
onclick	Specifies a JavaScript function that is executed when this element receives a mouse click. (optional)
ondblclick	Specifies a JavaScript function that is executed when this element receives a mouse double-click. (optional)
onfocus	Specifies a JavaScript function that is executed when this element receives input focus. (optional)
onkeydown	Specifies a JavaScript function that is executed when this element has focus and a key is pressed. (optional)
onkeypress	Specifies a JavaScript function that is executed when this element has focus and a key is pressed and released. (optional)
onkeyup	Specifies a JavaScript function that is executed when this element has focus and a key is released. (optional)

Table continued on following page

Attribute	Description
onmousedown	Specifies a JavaScript function that is executed when this element is under the mouse pointer and a mouse button is pressed. (optional)
onmousemove	Specifies a JavaScript function that is executed when this element is under the mouse pointer and the pointer is moved. (optional)
onmouseout	Specifies a JavaScript function that is executed when this element is under the mouse pointer but the pointer is then moved outside the element. (optional)
onmouseover	Specifies a JavaScript function that is executed when this element is not under the mouse pointer but the pointer is then moved inside the element. (optional)
onmouseup	Specifies a JavaScript function that is executed when this element is under the mouse pointer and a mouse button is released. (optional)
style	Specifies a Cascading Style Sheet style to apply to this HTML element. (optional)
styleClass	Specifies a Cascading Style Sheet class to apply to this HTML element. (optional)
styleId	Specifies an HTML identifier to be associated with this HTML element. (optional)
title	Specifies the advisory title for this HTML element. (required)
titleKey	Specifies a resources key (to be retrieved from a resource bundle) that references a title string for this element. (optional)
value	Specifies the label to be placed on the request if this checkbox is selected. The default value is on. (optional)

<html:html />

The <html:html /> tag is used to render the top-level <html> element. The <html:html /> tag has a body type of JSP and supports two attributes, as shown in Table 16.9.

Table 16.9 <html:html /> Tag Attributes

Attribute	Description
locale	If set to true, then the Locale object named by the HTTP Accept-Language header is used to set the language preferences. The default value is false. (optional)
xhtml	If set to true, causes an xml:lang attribute to be rendered as an attribute of the generated <html> element. The default value is false. (optional)

<html:image />

The <html:image /> tag is used to render an HTML <input> element with an input type of image. The image URL generated for this image is calculated using the value identified by the src or page attributes. You must specify one of the src or page attributes. The <html:image /> has a body type of JSP and supports 34 attributes, described in Table 16.10.

> **The <html:image /> tag must be nested inside the body of an <html:form /> tag.**

Table 16.10 <html:image /> Tag Attributes

Attribute	Description
accessKey	Identifies a keyboard character to be used to immediately move focus to the HTML element defined by this tag. (optional)
align	Defines the image alignment of this image. (optional)
alt	Defines an alternate text string for this element. (optional)
altKey	Defines a resources key (to be retrieved from a resource bundle) that references an alternate text string for this element. (optional)
border	Defines the width, in pixels, of the image border. (optional)
bundle	Specifies a MessageResources key of the resource bundle defined in the struts-config <message-resource> element. The default key is ApplicationResources. (optional)
disabled	If set to true, causes this HTML input element to be disabled. The default value is false. (optional)
indexed	If set to true, then the name of the HTML tag is rendered as propertyName[indexnumber]. The [] characters surrounding the index are generated for every iteration and taken from its ancestor, the <logic:iterate /> tag. The indexed attribute is valid only when the tag using it is nested with a <logic:iterate /> tag. The default value is false. (optional)
locale	Specifies the session attribute containing the Locale instance of the current request. This Locale is then used to select Locale-specific text messages. (optional)
onblur	Specifies a JavaScript function that is executed when the containing element loses its focus. (optional)
onchange	Specifies a JavaScript function that is executed when this element loses input focus and its value has changed. (optional)
onclick	Specifies a JavaScript function that is executed when this element receives a mouse click. (optional)
ondblclick	Specifies a JavaScript function that is executed when this element receives a mouse double-click. (optional)

Table continued on following page

Attribute	Description
onfocus	Specifies a JavaScript function that is executed when this element receives input focus. (optional)
onkeydown	Specifies a JavaScript function that is executed when this element has focus and a key is pressed. (optional)
onkeypress	Specifies a JavaScript function that is executed when this element has focus and a key is pressed and released. (optional)
onkeyup	Specifies a JavaScript function that is executed when this element has focus and a key is released. (optional)
onmousedown	Specifies a JavaScript function that is executed when this element is under the mouse pointer and a mouse button is pressed. (optional)
onmousemove	Specifies a JavaScript function that is executed when this element is under the mouse pointer and the pointer is moved. (optional)
onmouseout	Specifies a JavaScript function that is executed when this element is under the mouse pointer but the pointer is then moved outside the element. (optional)
onmouseover	Specifies a JavaScript function that is executed when this element is not under the mouse pointer but the pointer is then moved inside the element. (optional)
onmouseup	Specifies a JavaScript function that is executed when this element is under the mouse pointer and a mouse button is released. (optional)
page	Provides the application-relative path of the image source used by this input tag. (optional)
pageKey	Specifies a resources key (to be retrieved from a resource bundle) that references an application-relative path of the image source used by this input tag. (optional)
property	Identifies the parameter names of the image tag. The parameter names will appear as property.*x* and property.*y*, with the x and y characters representing the coordinates of the mouse click for the image. (optional)
src	Specifies a URL that references the location of the image source used by this input tag. (optional)
srcKey	Specifies a resources key (to be retrieved from a resource bundle) that references a URL pointing to the location of the image source used by this input tag. (optional)
style	Specifies a Cascading Style Sheet style to apply to this HTML element. (optional)
styleClass	Specifies a Cascading Style Sheet class to apply to this HTML element. (optional)
styleId	Specifies an HTML identifier to be associated with this HTML element. (optional)

Table continued on following page

Attribute	Description
tabindex	Identifies the tab order of this element in relation to the other elements of the containing Form. (optional)
title	Specifies the advisory title for this HTML element. (required)
titleKey	Specifies a resources key (to be retrieved from a resource bundle) that references a title string for this element. (optional)
value	Specifies the label to be placed on this button. (optional)

<html:img />

The <html:img /> tag is used to render an HTML <img> element. The image URL generated for this image is calculated using the value identified by the src or page attributes. You must specify one of the src or page attributes. The <html:img /> has no body and supports 40 attributes, described in Table 16.11.

Table 16.11 <html:img /> Tag Attributes

Attribute	Description
align	Defines the image alignment of this image. (optional)
alt	Defines an alternate text string for this element. (optional)
altKey	Defines a resources key (to be retrieved from a resource bundle) that references an alternate text string for this element. (optional)
border	Defines the width, in pixels, of the image border. (optional)
bundle	Specifies a MessageResources key of the resource bundle defined in the struts-config <message-resource> element. The default key is ApplicationResources. (optional)
height	Indicates the height of the image, in pixels. (optional)
hspave	Specifies the amount of horizontal space, in pixels, between the image and the text. (optional)
imageName	Defines a JavaScript name that can be referenced by JavaScript methods. (optional)
ismap	Specifies a server-side map that this image references, if applicable. (optional)
locale	Specifies the session attribute containing the Locale instance of the current request. This Locale is then used to select Locale-specific text messages. (optional)
lowsrc	Specifies an image for clients with low-resolution graphics cards. (optional)

Table continued on following page

Attribute	Description
name	Identifies a scripting variable containing a java.util.Map object of parameters and values to be appended to the src attribute, enabling the dynamic augmentation of the image src. (optional)
onclick	Specifies a JavaScript function that is executed when this element receives a mouse click. (optional)
ondblclick	Specifies a JavaScript function that is executed when this element receives a mouse double-click. (optional)
onkeydown	Specifies a JavaScript function that is executed when this element has focus and a key is pressed. (optional)
onkeypress	Specifies a JavaScript function that is executed when this element has focus and a key is pressed and released. (optional)
onkeyup	Specifies a JavaScript function that is executed when this element has focus and a key is released. (optional)
onmousedown	Specifies a JavaScript function that is executed when this element is under the mouse pointer and a mouse button is pressed. (optional)
onmousemove	Specifies a JavaScript function that is executed when this element is under the mouse pointer and the pointer is moved. (optional)
onmouseout	Specifies a JavaScript function that is executed when this element is under the mouse pointer but the pointer is then moved outside the element. (optional)
onmouseover	Specifies a JavaScript function that is executed when this element is not under the mouse pointer but the pointer is then moved inside the element. (optional)
onmouseup	Specifies a JavaScript function that is executed when this element is under the mouse pointer and a mouse button is released. (optional)
paramId	Specifies a request parameter that is added to the generated src URL when the hosting JSP is requested. (optional)
page	Specifies the application-relative path of the image source used by this input tag. (optional)
pageKey	Specifies a resources key (to be retrieved from a resource bundle) that references an application-relative path of the image source used by this input tag. (optional)
paramName	Identifies the name of a scripting variable of type java.lang.String that references the value for the request parameter identified by paramId attribute. (optional)
paramProperty	Identifies a data member of the bean named by the paramName attribute that is dynamically added to this src URL. (optional)
paramScope	Identifies the scope of the bean specified by the paramName attribute. If the paramScope attribute is not specified, then the tag will search for the bean in the scopes, in the order of page, request, session, and application. (optional)

Table continued on following page

Attribute	Description
property	Identifies a data member of the bean named by the name attribute that contains the java.util.Map object of parameters. (optional)
scope	Identifies the scope of the bean specified by the name attribute. If the scope attribute is not specified, then the tag will search for the bean in the scopes, in the order of page, request, session, and application. (optional)
src	Specifies a URL that references the location of the image source used by this tag. (optional)
srcKey	Specifies a resources key (to be retrieved from a resource bundle) that references a URL pointing to the location of the image source used by this tag. (optional)
style	Specifies a Cascading Style Sheet style to apply to this tag's HTML element. (optional)
styleClass	Specifies a Cascading Style Sheet class to apply to this tag's HTML element. (optional)
styleId	Specifies an HTML identifier to be associated with this tag's HTML element. (optional)
title	Specifies the advisory title for this HTML element. (required)
titleKey	Specifies a resources key (to be retrieved from a resource bundle) that references a title string for this element. (optional)
usemap	Specifies a coordinate map used when hyperlinking a hotspot of this image. (optional)
vspace	Indicates the amount of vertical spacing between the identified image and its surrounding text. (optional)
width	Indicates the width of the image being displayed. (optional)

<html:javascript />

The <html:javascript /> tag is used to insert JavaScript validation methods based on the Commons Validator Plugin, which we discussed in Chapter 12, "Working with the Validator." The JavaScript methods used for validation are retrieved from the Validator definition file using the formName as the index. The <html:javascript /> tag has no body and supports eight attributes, described in Table 16.12.

Table 16.12 <html:javascript /> Tag Attributes

Attribute	Description
cdata	If true and the xhtml attribute of the <html:html /> tag is also true, then the generated JavaScript will be placed within CDATA elements (preventing XML parsing). The default is true. (optional)
dynamicJavascript	Indicates if dynamic JavaScript should be enabled. The default value is true. (optional)
formName	Represents the identifier that is used to retrieve the appropriate Validator rules. (optional)
htmlComment	If true, then the defined JavaScript elements are enclosed within HTML comment markers. (optional)
method	Allows a user of the tag to override the default method name. If not indicated, the default method name is validate. (optional)
page	Represents the current page number of a multipart form. This attribute is valid only when the formName attribute is used. (optional)
src	Names an external JavaScript resource to include in the hosting page. This attribute is valid only when the formName attribute is used. (optional)
staticJavascript	Indicates whether static JavaScript should be rendered in this page. The default value is true. (optional)

<html:link />

The <html:link /> tag is used to generate an HTML hyperlink. The URL for the generated link can be calculated using either the forward, href, or page attributes. The <html:link /> tag has a body type of JSP and supports 37 attributes, described in Table 16.13.

Table 16.13 <html:link /> Tag Attributes

Attribute	Description
accessKey	Identifies a keyboard character to be used to immediately move focus to the HTML element defined by this tag. (optional)
action	Used to create a link naming a Struts Action as its target. The name of the Action should be a defined Action name from the struts-config.xml file. (optional)
anchor	Used to append an HTML anchor to the end of a generated hyperlink. (optional)
forward	Identifies the name of the global forward element that will receive control of the forwarded request. (optional)

Table continued on following page

Attribute	Description
href	Specifies the URL of the resource to forward the current request to. (optional)
indexed	If set to true, then the name of the HTML tag is rendered as propertyName[indexnumber]. The [] characters surrounding the index are generated for every iteration and taken from its ancestor, the <logic:iterate /> tag. The indexed attribute is valid only when the tag using it is nested with a <logic:iterate /> tag. The default value is false. (optional)
indexId	Specifies a JSP scripting variable, exposed by the <logic:iterate /> tag, that will hold the current index of the current object in the named collection. (optional)
linkName	Specifies an anchor to be defined within the hosting page so that you can reference it with hyperlinks hosted in the same document. (optional)
name	Identifies a scripting variable referencing a java.util.Map object, whose collection of key/value pairs is used as the HTTP request parameter augmenting the redirected request. (optional)
onblur	Specifies a JavaScript function that is executed when the containing element loses its focus. (optional)
onchange	Specifies a JavaScript function that is executed when this element loses input focus and its value has changed. (optional)
onclick	Specifies a JavaScript function that is executed when this element receives a mouse click. (optional)
ondblclick	Specifies a JavaScript function that is executed when this element receives a mouse double-click. (optional)
onfocus	Specifies a JavaScript function that is executed when this element receives input focus. (optional)
onkeydown	Specifies a JavaScript function that is executed when this element has focus and a key is pressed. (optional)
onkeypress	Specifies a JavaScript function that is executed when this element has focus and a key is pressed and released. (optional)
onkeyup	Specifies a JavaScript function that is executed when this element has focus and a key is released. (optional)
onmousedown	Specifies a JavaScript function that is executed when this element is under the mouse pointer and a mouse button is pressed. (optional)
onmousemove	Specifies a JavaScript function that is executed when this element is under the mouse pointer and the pointer is moved. (optional)
onmouseout	Specifies a JavaScript function that is executed when this element is under the mouse pointer but the pointer is then moved outside the element. (optional)
onmouseover	Specifies a JavaScript function that is executed when this element is not under the mouse pointer but the pointer is then moved inside the element. (optional)

Table continued on following page

Attribute	Description
onmouseup	Specifies a JavaScript function that is executed when this element is under the mouse pointer and a mouse button is released. (optional)
page	Specifies an application-relative path of the image source used by this input tag. (optional)
paramId	Used to add a named request parameter to a hyperlink. The corresponding parameter value is indicated by the paramName attribute. (optional)
paramName	Identifies the name of a scripting variable of type java.lang.String that references the value to be used for the request parameter identified by the paramId attribute. (optional)
paramProperty	Used to identify a data member of the bean named by the paramName attribute that is dynamically added to this src URL. (optional)
paramScope	Specifies the scope of the bean specified by the paramName attribute. If the paramScope attribute is not specified, then the tag searches for the bean in the scopes, in the order of page, request, session, and application. (optional)
property	Used to identify a data member of the bean named by the name attribute that contains the java.util.Map object of parameters. (optional)
scope	Identifies the scope of the bean specified by the name attribute. If the scope attribute is not specified, then the tag searches for the bean in the scopes, in the order of page, request, session, and application. (optional)
style	Specifies a Cascading Style Sheet style to apply to this HTML element. (optional)
styleClass	Specifies a Cascading Style Sheet class to apply to this HTML element. (optional)
styleId	Specifies an HTML identifier to be associated with this HTML element. (optional)
tabindex	Identifies the tab order of this element in relation to the other elements of the containing Form. (optional)
target	Used to name a window target in a framed environment. (optional)
title	Specifies the advisory title for this HTML element. (required)
titleKey	Specifies a resources key (to be retrieved from a resource bundle) that references a title string for this element. (optional)
transaction	If set to true, indicates that the current transaction control token should be included in the generated URL. The default value is false. (optional)

<html:messages />

The <html:messages /> tag is used to display a collection of messages stored in an ActionErrors, ActionMessages, String, or String array object. The <html:messages /> tag has a body type of JSP and supports eight attributes, described in Table 16.14.

Table 16.14 <html:messages /> Tag Attributes

Attribute	Description
id	Identifies the scripting variable containing the current message to be displayed. (required)
bundle	Names a key, stored in the ServletContext, that will point to the ResourceBundle used when retrieving messages. If not indicated, then the default ResourceBundle is used. (optional)
locale	Indicates the Locale key to use when retrieving messages. If this value is not set, then the standard Struts method of determining the Locale is used. (optional)
name	Identifies the scripting variable containing the collection of messages to be displayed. The default value is Action.ERROR_KEY. (optional)
property	Identifies an input property for which retrieved messages should be displayed. If no value is indicated, then all messages are rendered. (optional)
header	An optional Resource key that is printed prior to the collection of messages. This is often a handy place to include list formatting. (optional)
footer	An optional Resource key that will be printed after the collection of messages. This is often a handy place to include list formatting. (optional)
message	If set to true, then the Globals.MESSAGE_KEY is used to retrieve the request scoped bean as opposed to the Globals.ERROR_KEY. (optional)

<html:multibox />

The <html:multibox /> tag is used to generate an HTML <input> element of type checkbox. The <html:multibox /> tag has a body type of JSP and supports 26 attributes, described in Table 16.15.

Table 16.15 <html:multibox /> Tag Attributes

Attribute	Description
property	Used to identify a data member of the bean named by the name attribute that contains the java.util.Map object of parameters. (required)
accessKey	Identifies a keyboard character to be used to immediately move focus to the HTML element defined by this tag. (optional)

Table continued on following page

Attribute	Description
alt	Defines an alternate text string for this element. (optional)
altKey	Defines a resources key (to be retrieved from a resource bundle) that references an alternate text string for this element. (optional)
disabled	If set to true, causes this HTML input element to be disabled. The default value is false. (optional)
name	Identifies a scripting variable referencing a java.util.Map object, whose collection of key/value pairs is used as the HTTP request parameter augmenting the redirected request. (optional)
onblur	Specifies a JavaScript function that is executed when the containing element loses its focus. (optional)
onchange	Specifies a JavaScript function that is executed when this element loses input focus and its value has changed. (optional)
onclick	Specifies a JavaScript function that is executed when this element receives a mouse click. (optional)
ondblclick	Specifies a JavaScript function that is executed when this element receives a mouse double-click. (optional)
onfocus	Specifies a JavaScript function that is executed when this element receives input focus. (optional)
onkeydown	Specifies a JavaScript function that is executed when this element has focus and a key is pressed. (optional)
onkeypress	Specifies a JavaScript function that is executed when this element has focus and a key is pressed and released. (optional)
onkeyup	Specifies a JavaScript function that is executed when this element has focus and a key is released. (optional)
onmousedown	Specifies a JavaScript function that is executed when this element is under the mouse pointer and a mouse button is pressed. (optional)
onmousemove	Specifies a JavaScript function that is executed when this element is under the mouse pointer and the pointer is moved. (optional)
onmouseout	Specifies a JavaScript function that is executed when this element is under the mouse pointer but the pointer is then moved outside the element. (optional)
onmouseover	Specifies a JavaScript function that is executed when this element is not under the mouse pointer but the pointer is then moved inside the element. (optional)
onmouseup	Specifies a JavaScript function that is executed when this element is under the mouse pointer and a mouse button is released. (optional)
style	Specifies a Cascading Style Sheet style to apply to this HTML element. (optional)

Table continued on following page

Attribute	Description
styleClass	Specifies a Cascading Style Sheet class to apply to this HTML element. (optional)
styleId	Specifies an HTML identifier to be associated with this HTML element. (optional)
tabindex	Identifies the tab order of this element in relation to the other elements of the containing Form. (optional)
title	Specifies the advisory title for this HTML element. (required)
titleKey	Specifies a resources key (to be retrieved from a resource bundle) that references a title string for this element. (optional)
value	Represents the value that will be submitted if this checkbox is selected. (optional)

<html:option />

The <html:option /> tag is used to generate an HTML <input> element of type <option>, which represents a single option element nested inside a parent <select> element. The <html:option /> tag has a body type of JSP and supports eight attributes, described in Table 16.16.

This tag is valid only when nested within an <html:select /> tag.

Table 16.16 <html:option /> Tag Attributes

Attribute	Description
value	Represents the value that is submitted if this checkbox is selected. (required)
bundle	Specifies a MessageResources key of the resource bundle defined in the struts-config <message-resource> element. The default key is ApplicationResources. (optional)
disabled	If set to true, causes this HTML input element to be disabled. The default value is false. (optional)
key	Defines a resources key (to be retrieved from a resource bundle) that references a text string to be displayed to the user as this element's text value. (optional)
locale	Specifies the session attribute containing the Locale instance of the current request. This Locale is then used to select Locale-specific text messages. (optional)

Table continued on following page

Attribute	Description
style	Specifies a Cascading Style Sheet style to apply to this HTML element. (optional)
styleId	Associates an id attribute with the rendered <option> tag. (optional)
styleClass	Specifies a Cascading Style Sheet class to apply to this HTML element. (optional)

<html:options />

The <html:options /> tag (as a child of the <html:select /> tag) is used to generate a list of HTML <option> elements. The <html:options /> tag has no body and supports eight attributes, described in Table 16.17.

> **The <html:options /> tag must be nested inside an <html:select /> tag. The <html:options /> tag can also be used n-number of times within an <html:select /> element.**

Table 16.17 <html:options /> Tag Attributes

Attribute	Description
collection	Specifies a JSP scripting variable that references a collection of beans, with each bean containing the properties property and labelProperty, which are used as the tag attribute value's property and labelProperty, respectively. (required)
filter	If set to true (the default), causes the tag to replace all HTML-sensitive characters with their encoded equivalents. (optional)
labelName	Specifies a scripting variable that references a collection of labels to be displayed to the user for the options in this option list. The object referenced by the labelName attribute can point to the collection directly or to an object that contains a data member referencing the collection. (optional)
labelProperty	Specifies the property of the object identified by the labelName attribute that references the collection of option labels. (optional)
name	Identifies a scripting variable referencing a Collection object that contains a collection of option values. (optional)
property	Used to identify a data member of the bean named by the name attribute that contains a collection of option values. (optional)
style	Specifies a Cascading Style Sheet style to apply to this HTML element. (optional)
styleClass	Specifies a Cascading Style Sheet class to apply to this HTML element. (optional)

<html:optionsCollection />

The <html:optionsCollection /> tag (as a child of the <html:select /> tag) is used to generate a list of HTML <option> elements from a collection of JavaBeans. The <html:optionsCollection /> tag has no body and supports seven attributes, described in Table 16.18.

The <html:optionsCollection /> tag must be nested inside an <html:select /> tag. The <html:optionsCollections /> tag can also be used n-number of times within an <html:select /> element.

Table 16.18 <html:optionsCollections /> Tag Attributes

Attribute	Description
property	Indicates the property of the ActionForm bean or scripting variable named by the name attribute that will contain the collection of objects to be used for each <option> element. (required)
filter	If true, then all special HTML characters will be filtered from the element. (optional)
label	Indicates the data member name of the current object in the collection that represents the <option> label. (optional)
name	Indicates the name of the JavaBean representing the contents of this input field. If not included, then the ActionForm named by the <html:form /> tag is used. (optional)
style	Specifies a Cascading Style Sheet style to apply to this HTML element. (optional)
styleClass	Specifies a Cascading Style Sheet class to apply to this HTML element. (optional)
value	Indicates the data member name of the current object in the collection that represents the <option> value. (optional)

<html:password />

The <html:password /> tag is used to render an HTML <input> element with an input type of password. The <html:password /> tag has a body type of JSP and supports 31 attributes, described in Table 16.19.

The <html:password /> tag must be nested inside the body of a <html:form /> tag.

Table 16.19 <html:password /> Tag Attributes	
Attribute	**Description**
property	Identifies the name of the input field being processed. (required)
accessKey	Identifies a keyboard character to be used to immediately move focus to the HTML element defined by this tag. (optional)
alt	Defines an alternate text string for this element. (optional)
altKey	Defines a resources key (to be retrieved from a resource bundle) that references an alternate text string for this element. (optional)
disabled	If set to true, causes this HTML input element to be disabled. The default value is false. (optional)
indexed	If set to true, then the name of the HTML tag is rendered as propertyName[indexnumber]. The [] characters surrounding the index are generated for every iteration and taken from its ancestor, the <logic:iterate /> tag. The indexed attribute is valid only when the tag using it is nested with a <logic:iterate /> tag. The default value is false. (optional)
maxlength	Determines the maximum number of input characters allowed in this input field. The default is no limit. (optional)
name	Identifies a JavaBean to use when defaulting the value of the input field. (optional)
onblur	Specifies a JavaScript function that is executed when the containing element loses its focus. (optional)
onchange	Specifies a JavaScript function that is executed when this element loses input focus and its value has changed. (optional)
onclick	Specifies a JavaScript function that is executed when this element receives a mouse click. (optional)
ondblclick	Specifies a JavaScript function that is executed when this element receives a mouse double-click. (optional)
onfocus	Specifies a JavaScript function that is executed when this element receives input focus. (optional)
onkeydown	Specifies a JavaScript function that is executed when this element has focus and a key is pressed. (optional)
onkeypress	Specifies a JavaScript function that is executed when this element has focus and a key is pressed and released. (optional)
onkeyup	Specifies a JavaScript function that is executed when this element has focus and a key is released. (optional)
onmousedown	Specifies a JavaScript function that is executed when this element is under the mouse pointer and a mouse button is pressed. (optional)

Table continued on following page

Attribute	Description
onmousemove	Specifies a JavaScript function that is executed when this element is under the mouse pointer and the pointer is moved. (optional)
onmouseout	Specifies a JavaScript function that is executed when this element is under the mouse pointer but the pointer is then moved outside the element. (optional)
onmouseover	Specifies a JavaScript function that is executed when this element is not under the mouse pointer but the pointer is then moved inside the element. (optional)
onmouseup	Specifies a JavaScript function that is executed when this element is under the mouse pointer and a mouse button is released. (optional)
readonly	If set to true, sets the input field generated by this tag to uneditable. The default value is false. (optional)
redisplay	Indicates whether an existing value should be displayed. When using a <html:password /> tag, you should consider setting this value to false; otherwise, a user can see the clear-text password by simply viewing the rendered HTML source. (optional)
style	Specifies a Cascading Style Sheet style to apply to this HTML element. (optional)
styleClass	Specifies a Cascading Style Sheet class to apply to this HTML element. (optional)
styleId	Specifies an HTML identifier to be associated with this HTML element. (optional)
size	The number of characters allowed in the rendered input element. (optional)
tabindex	Identifies the tab order of this element in relation to the other elements of the containing Form. (optional)
title	Specifies the advisory title for this HTML element. (required)
titleKey	Specifies a resources key (to be retrieved from a resource bundle) that references a title string for this element. (optional)
value	Specifies the value of this input element. If the ActionForm bean associated with the parent <html:form /> tag has a property that matches the value attribute, then the value of the ActionForm bean property is used as the value of this attribute. (optional)

<html:radio />

The <html:radio /> tag is used to render an HTML <input> element with an input type of radio. The <html:radio /> has a body type of JSP and supports 28 attributes, described in Table 16.20.

The <html:radio /> tag must be nested inside the body of a <html:form /> tag.

Table 16.20 <html:radio /> Tag Attributes

Attribute	Description
property	Identifies the property of the ActionForm bean associated with this input element. (required)
value	Specifies the value of this input element. (required)
accessKey	Identifies a keyboard character to be used to immediately move focus to the HTML element defined by this tag. (optional)
alt	Defines an alternate text string for this element. (optional)
altKey	Defines a resources key (to be retrieved from a resource bundle) that references an alternate text string for this element. (optional)
disabled	If set to true, causes this HTML input element to be disabled. The default value is false. (optional)
indexed	If set to true, then the name of the HTML tag is rendered as propertyName[indexnumber]. The [] characters surrounding the index are generated for every iteration and taken from its ancestor, the <logic:iterate /> tag. The indexed attribute is valid only when the tag using it is nested with a <logic:iterate /> tag. The default value is false. (optional)
name	Identifies a JavaBean to use when defaulting the value of the input field. (optional)
onblur	Specifies a JavaScript function that is executed when the containing element loses its focus. (optional)
onchange	Specifies a JavaScript function that is executed when this element loses input focus and its value has changed. (optional)
onclick	Specifies a JavaScript function that is executed when this element receives a mouse click. (optional)
ondblclick	Specifies a JavaScript function that is executed when this element receives a mouse double-click. (optional)
onfocus	Specifies a JavaScript function that is executed when this element receives input focus. (optional)
onkeydown	Specifies a JavaScript function that is executed when this element has focus and a key is pressed. (optional)
onkeypress	Specifies a JavaScript function that is executed when this element has focus and a key is pressed and released. (optional)
onkeyup	Specifies a JavaScript function that is executed when this element has focus and a key is released. (optional)
onmousedown	Specifies a JavaScript function that is executed when this element is under the mouse pointer and a mouse button is pressed. (optional)

Table continued on following page

Attribute	Description
onmousemove	Specifies a JavaScript function that is executed when this element is under the mouse pointer and the pointer is moved. (optional)
onmouseout	Specifies a JavaScript function that is executed when this element is under the mouse pointer but the pointer is then moved outside the element. (optional)
onmouseover	Specifies a JavaScript function that is executed when this element is not under the mouse pointer but the pointer is then moved inside the element. (optional)
onmouseup	Specifies a JavaScript function that is executed when this element is under the mouse pointer and a mouse button is released. (optional)
style	Specifies a Cascading Style Sheet style to apply to this HTML element. (optional)
styleClass	Specifies a Cascading Style Sheet class to apply to this HTML element. (optional)
styleId	Specifies an HTML identifier to be associated with this HTML element. (optional)
tabindex	Identifies the tab order of this element in relation to the other elements of the containing Form. (optional)
title	Specifies the advisory title for this HTML element. (required)
titleKey	Specifies a resources key (to be retrieved from a resource bundle) that references a title string for this element. (optional)
idName	Used if an Iterator is used to render a collection of <html:radio /> tags. The value of the attribute should be the name of the exposed variable containing the value of the tag. (optional)

<html:reset />

The <html:reset /> tag is used to render an HTML <input> element with an input type of reset. The <html:reset /> tag has a body type of JSP and supports 25 attributes, described in Table 16.21.

> **The <html:reset /> tag must be nested inside the body of an <html:form /> tag.**

Table 16.21 <html:reset /> Tag Attributes

Attribute	Description
accessKey	Identifies a keyboard character to be used to immediately move focus to the HTML element defined by this tag. (optional)
alt	Defines an alternate text string for this element. (optional)
altKey	Defines a resources key (to be retrieved from a resource bundle) that references an alternate text string for this element. (optional)

Table continued on following page

Attribute	Description
disabled	If set to true, causes this HTML input element to be disabled. The default value is false. (optional)
onblur	Specifies a JavaScript function that is executed when the containing element loses its focus. (optional)
onchange	Specifies a JavaScript function that is executed when this element loses input focus and its value has changed. (optional)
onclick	Specifies a JavaScript function that is executed when this element receives a mouse click. (optional)
ondblclick	Specifies a JavaScript function that is executed when this element receives a mouse double-click. (optional)
onfocus	Specifies a JavaScript function that is executed when this element receives input focus. (optional)
onkeydown	Specifies s a JavaScript function that is executed when this element has focus and a key is pressed. (optional)
onkeypress	Specifies a JavaScript function that is executed when this element has focus and a key is pressed and released. (optional)
onkeyup	Specifies a JavaScript function that is executed when this element has focus and a key is released. (optional)
onmousedown	Specifies a JavaScript function that is executed when this element is under the mouse pointer and a mouse button is pressed. (optional)
onmousemove	Specifies a JavaScript function that is executed when this element is under the mouse pointer and the pointer is moved. (optional)
onmouseout	Specifies a JavaScript function that is executed when this element is under the mouse pointer but the pointer is then moved outside the element. (optional)
onmouseover	Specifies a JavaScript function that is executed when this element is not under the mouse pointer but the pointer is then moved inside the element. (optional)
onmouseup	Specifies a JavaScript function that is executed when this element is under the mouse pointer and a mouse button is released. (optional)
property	Indicates the name of the input element. (optional)
style	Specifies a Cascading Style Sheet style to apply to this HTML element. (optional)
styleClass	Specifies a Cascading Style Sheet class to apply to this HTML element. (optional)
styleId	Specifies an HTML identifier to be associated with this HTML element. (optional)
tabindex	Identifies the tab order of this element in relation to the other elements of the containing Form. (optional)
title	Specifies the advisory title for this HTML element. (optional)

Table continued on following page

Attribute	Description
titleKey	Specifies a resources key (to be retrieved from a resource bundle) that references a title string for this element. (optional)
value	Specifies the label to be placed on this button. You should note that the body of this tag can also be used as the button label. The default value is Reset. (optional)

<html:rewrite />

The <html:rewrite /> tag is used to create a request URI based on the identical policies used with the <html:link /> tag but without the <a> element. The <html:rewrite /> tag has no body and supports 12 attributes, described in Table 16.22.

> **The <html:rewrite /> tag is especially useful when used to generate a String constant that is expected to be used by a JavaScript function.**

Table 16.22 <html:rewrite> Tag Attributes

Attribute	Description
anchor	Used to append an HTML anchor to the end of a generated hyperlink. (optional)
forward	Identifies the name of the global forward element that will receive control of the forwarded request. (optional)
href	Specifies the URL of the resource to forward the current request to. (optional)
name	Identifies a scripting variable referencing a java.util.Map object, whose collection of key/value pairs is used as the HTTP request parameter augmenting the redirected request. (optional)
page	Specifies an application-relative path of the image source used by this input tag. (optional)
paramId	Specifies a request parameter that is added to the generated src URL when the hosting JSP is requested. (optional)
paramName	Identifies the name of a scripting variable of type java.lang.String that references the value to be used for the request parameter identified by the paramId attribute. (optional)
paramProperty	Used to identify a data member of the bean named by the paramName attribute that is dynamically added to this src URL. (optional)
paramScope	Defines the scope of the bean specified by the paramName attribute. If the paramScope attribute is not specified, then the tag searches for the bean in the scopes, in the order of page, request, session, and application. (optional)

Table continued on following page

Attribute	Description
property	Used to identify a data member of the bean named by the name attribute that contains the java.util.Map object of parameters. (optional)
scope	Defines the scope of the bean specified by the name attribute. If the scope attribute is not specified, then the tag searches for the bean in the scopes, in the order of page, request, session, and application. (optional)
transaction	If set to true, indicates that the current transaction control token should be included in the generated URL. The default value is false. (optional)

<html:select />

The <html:select /> tag is used to render an HTML <input> element with an input type of select. The <html:select /> tag has a body type of JSP and supports 28 attributes, described in Table 16.23.

The <html:select /> tag must be nested inside the body of an <html:form /> tag.

Table 16.23 <html:select /> Tag Attributes

Attribute	Description
property	Specifies a request parameter that is included with the current request, set to the value of the selection. (required)
alt	Defines an alternate text string for this element. (optional)
altKey	Defines a resources key (to be retrieved from a resource bundle) that references an alternate text string for this element. (optional)
disabled	If set to true, causes this HTML input element to be disabled. The default value is false. (optional)
indexed	If set to true, then the name of the HTML tag is rendered as propertyName[indexnumber]. The [] characters surrounding the index are generated for every iteration and taken from its ancestor, the <logic:iterate /> tag. The indexed attribute is valid only when the tag using it is nested with a <logic:iterate /> tag. The default value is false. (optional)
multiple	If set to true, creates a <select> list support for multiple selections. The default value is false. (optional)
name	Identifies the JavaBean whose data members will be used as the pre-selected values of the <select> list. If this name attribute is not defined, then the ActionForm indicated by the <html:form /> tag is used. (optional)

Table continued on following page

Attribute	Description
onblur	Specifies a JavaScript function that is executed when the containing element loses its focus. (optional)
onchange	Specifies a JavaScript function that is executed when this element loses input focus and its value has changed. (optional)
onclick	Specifies a JavaScript function that is executed when this element receives a mouse click. (optional)
ondblclick	Specifies a JavaScript function that is executed when this element receives a mouse double-click. (optional)
onfocus	Specifies a JavaScript function that is executed when this element receives input focus. (optional)
onkeydown	Specifies a JavaScript function that is executed when this element has focus and a key is pressed. (optional)
onkeypress	Specifies a JavaScript function that is executed when this element has focus and a key is pressed and released. (optional)
onkeyup	Specifies a JavaScript function that is executed when this element has focus and a key is released. (optional)
onmousedown	Specifies a JavaScript function that is executed when this element is under the mouse pointer and a mouse button is pressed. (optional)
onmousemove	Specifies a JavaScript function that is executed when this element is under the mouse pointer and the pointer is moved. (optional)
onmouseout	Specifies a JavaScript function that is executed when this element is under the mouse pointer but the pointer is then moved outside the element. (optional)
onmouseover	Specifies a JavaScript function that is executed when this element is not under the mouse pointer but the pointer is then moved inside the element. (optional)
onmouseup	Specifies a JavaScript function that is executed when this element is under the mouse pointer and a mouse button is released. (optional)
style	Specifies a Cascading Style Sheet style to apply to this HTML element. (optional)
styleClass	Specifies a Cascading Style Sheet class to apply to this HTML element. (optional)
styleId	Specifies an HTML identifier to be associated with this HTML element. (optional)
tabindex	Identifies the tab order of this element in relation to the other elements of the containing Form. (optional)
size	Indicates the number of options to display at once. (optional)
title	Specifies the advisory title for this HTML element. (required)
titleKey	Specifies a resources key (to be retrieved from a resource bundle) that references a title string for this element. (optional)
value	Specifies the value to test for when setting the currently selected option. (optional)

<html:submit />

The <html:submit /> tag is used to render an HTML <input> element with an input type of submit, which results in a Submit button. The <html:submit /> tag has a body type of JSP and supports 26 attributes, described in Table 16.24.

The <html:submit /> tag must be nested inside the body of an <html:form /> tag.

Table 16.24 <html:submit /> Tag Attributes

Attribute	Description
accessKey	Identifies a keyboard character to be used to immediately move focus to the HTML element defined by this tag. (optional)
alt	Defines an alternate text string for this element. (optional)
altKey	Defines a resources key (to be retrieved from a resource bundle) that references an alternate text string for this element. (optional)
disabled	If set to true, causes this HTML input element to be disabled. The default value is false. (optional)
indexed	If set to true, then the name of the HTML tag is rendered as propertyName[indexnumber]. The [] characters surrounding the index are generated for every iteration and taken from its ancestor, the <logic:iterate /> tag. The indexed attribute is valid only when the tag using it is nested with a <logic:iterate /> tag. The default value is false. (optional)
onblur	Specifies a JavaScript function that is executed when the containing element loses its focus. (optional)
onchange	Specifies a JavaScript function that is executed when this element loses input focus and its value has changed. (optional)
onclick	Specifies a JavaScript function that is executed when this element receives a mouse click. (optional)
ondblclick	Specifies a JavaScript function that is executed when this element receives a mouse double-click. (optional)
onfocus	Specifies a JavaScript function that is executed when this element receives input focus. (optional)
onkeydown	Specifies a JavaScript function that is executed when this element has focus and a key is pressed. (optional)
onkeypress	Specifies a JavaScript function that is executed when this element has focus and a key is pressed and released. (optional)
onkeyup	Specifies a JavaScript function that is executed when this element has focus and a key is released. (optional)

Table continued on following page

Attribute	Description
onmousedown	Specifies a JavaScript function that is executed when this element is under the mouse pointer and a mouse button is pressed. (optional)
onmousemove	Specifies a JavaScript function that is executed when this element is under the mouse pointer and the pointer is moved. (optional)
onmouseout	Specifies a JavaScript function that is executed when this element is under the mouse pointer but the pointer is then moved outside the element. (optional)
onmouseover	Specifies a JavaScript function that is executed when this element is not under the mouse pointer but the pointer is then moved inside the element. (optional)
onmouseup	Specifies a JavaScript function that is executed when this element is under the mouse pointer and a mouse button is released. (optional)
property	Specifies a request parameter that is included with the current request, set to the value of the selection. (optional)
style	Specifies a Cascading Style Sheet style to apply to this HTML element. (optional)
styleClass	Specifies a Cascading Style Sheet class to apply to this HTML element. (optional)
styleId	Specifies an HTML identifier to be associated with this HTML element. (optional)
tabindex	Identifies the tab order of this element in relation to the other elements of the containing Form. (optional)
title	Specifies the advisory title for this HTML element. (optional)
titleKey	Specifies a resources key (to be retrieved from a resource bundle) that references a title string for this element. (optional)
value	Specifies the label to be placed on this button. You should note that the body of this tag can also be used as the button label. The default value is Submit. (optional)

<html:text />

The <html:text /> tag is used to render an HTML <input> element with an input type of text. The <html:text /> has a body type of JSP and supports 30 attributes, described in Table 16.25.

The <html:text /> tag must be nested inside the body of a <html:form /> tag.

Table 16.25 <html:text /> Tag Attributes

Attribute	Description
property	Identifies the name of the input field being processed. (required)
accessKey	Identifies a keyboard character to be used to immediately move focus to the HTML element defined by this tag. (optional)
alt	Defines an alternate text string for this element. (optional)
altKey	Defines a resources key (to be retrieved from a resource bundle) that references an alternate text string for this element. (optional)
disabled	If set to true, causes this HTML input element to be disabled. The default value is false. (optional)
indexed	If set to true, then the name of the HTML tag is rendered as propertyName[indexnumber]. The [] characters surrounding the index are generated for every iteration and taken from its ancestor, the <logic:iterate /> tag. The indexed attribute is valid only when the tag using it is nested with a <logic:iterate /> tag. The default value is false. (optional)
maxlength	Determines the maximum number of input characters allowed in this input field. The default is no limit. (optional)
name	Identifies a JavaBean to use when defaulting the value of the input field. (optional)
onblur	Specifies a JavaScript function that is executed when the containing element loses its focus. (optional)
onchange	Specifies a JavaScript function that is executed when this element loses input focus and its value has changed. (optional)
onclick	Specifies a JavaScript function that is executed when this element receives a mouse click. (optional)
ondblclick	Specifies a JavaScript function that is executed when this element receives a mouse double-click. (optional)
onfocus	Specifies a JavaScript function that is executed when this element receives input focus. (optional)
onkeydown	Specifies a JavaScript function that is executed when this element has focus and a key is pressed. (optional)
onkeypress	Specifies a JavaScript function that is executed when this element has focus and a key is pressed and released. (optional)
onkeyup	Specifies a JavaScript function that is executed when this element has focus and a key is released. (optional)
onmousedown	Specifies a JavaScript function that is executed when this element is under the mouse pointer and a mouse button is pressed. (optional)

Table continued on following page

Attribute	Description
onmousemove	Specifies a JavaScript function that is executed when this element is under the mouse pointer and the pointer is moved. (optional)
onmouseout	Specifies a JavaScript function that is executed when this element is under the mouse pointer but the pointer is then moved outside the element. (optional)
onmouseover	Specifies a JavaScript function that is executed when this element is not under the mouse pointer but the pointer is then moved inside the element. (optional)
onmouseup	Specifies a JavaScript function that is executed when this element is under the mouse pointer and a mouse button is released. (optional)
readonly	If set to true, will set the input field generated by this tag to uneditable. The default value is false. (optional)
size	Indicates the number of character positions to display. (optional)
style	Specifies a Cascading Style Sheet style to apply to this HTML element. (optional)
styleClass	Specifies a Cascading Style Sheet class to apply to this HTML element. (optional)
styleId	Specifies an HTML identifier to be associated with this HTML element. (optional)
tabindex	Identifies the tab order of this element in relation to the other elements of the containing Form. (optional)
title	Specifies the advisory title for this HTML element. (required)
titleKey	Specifies a resources key (to be retrieved from a resource bundle) that references a title string for this element. (optional)
value	Specifies the value of this input element. If the ActionForm bean associated with the parent <html:form /> tag has a property that matches the value attribute, then the value of the ActionForm bean property is used as the value of this attribute. (optional)

<html:textarea />

The <html:textarea /> tag is used to render an HTML <input> element with an input type of textarea. The <html:textarea /> has a body type of JSP and supports 30 attributes, described in Table 16.26.

The <html:textarea /> tag must be nested inside the body of a <html:form /> tag.

Table 16.26 <html:textarea /> Tag Attributes

Attribute	Description
property	Identifies the name of the input field being processed and the name of the bean property that maps to this input element. (required)
accessKey	Identifies a keyboard character to be used to immediately move focus to the HTML element defined by this tag. (optional)
alt	Defines an alternate text string for this element. (optional)
altKey	Defines a resources key (to be retrieved from a resource bundle) that references an alternate text string for this element. (optional)
cols	Indicates the number of columns to display in the generated text area. (optional)
disabled	If set to true, causes this HTML input element to be disabled. The default value is false. (optional)
indexed	If set to true, then the name of the HTML tag is rendered as propertyName[indexnumber]. The [] characters surrounding the index are generated for every iteration and taken from its ancestor, the <logic:iterate /> tag. The indexed attribute is valid only when the tag using it is nested with a <logic:iterate /> tag. The default value is false. (optional)
name	Identifies a JavaBean to use when defaulting the value of the input field. (optional)
onblur	Specifies a JavaScript function that is executed when the containing element loses its focus. (optional)
onchange	Specifies a JavaScript function that is executed when this element loses input focus and its value has changed. (optional)
onclick	Specifies a JavaScript function that is executed when this element receives a mouse click. (optional)
ondblclick	Specifies a JavaScript function that is executed when this element receives a mouse double-click. (optional)
onfocus	Specifies a JavaScript function that is executed when this element receives input focus. (optional)
onkeydown	Specifies a JavaScript function that is executed when this element has focus and a key is pressed. (optional)
onkeypress	Specifies a JavaScript function that is executed when this element has focus and a key is pressed and released. (optional)
onkeyup	Specifies a JavaScript function that is executed when this element has focus and a key is released. (optional)
onmousedown	Specifies a JavaScript function that is executed when this element is under the mouse pointer and a mouse button is pressed. (optional)

Table continued on following page

Attribute	Description
onmousemove	Specifies a JavaScript function that is executed when this element is under the mouse pointer and the pointer is moved. (optional)
onmouseout	Specifies a JavaScript function that is executed when this element is under the mouse pointer but the pointer is then moved outside the element. (optional)
onmouseover	Specifies a JavaScript function that is executed when this element is not under the mouse pointer but the pointer is then moved inside the element. (optional)
onmouseup	Specifies a JavaScript function that is executed when this element is under the mouse pointer and a mouse button is released. (optional)
readonly	If set to true, sets the input field generated by this tag to uneditable. The default value is false. (optional)
rows	Indicates the number of rows to display in the text area. (optional)
style	Specifies a Cascading Style Sheet style to apply to this HTML element. (optional)
styleClass	Specifies a Cascading Style Sheet class to apply to this HTML element. (optional)
styleId	Specifies an HTML identifier to be associated with this HTML element. (optional)
tabindex	Identifies the tab order of this element in relation to the other elements of the containing Form. (optional)
title	Specifies the advisory title for this HTML element. (required)
titleKey	Specifies a resources key (to be retrieved from a resource bundle) that references a title string for this element. (optional)
value	Specifies the value of this input element. If the ActionForm bean associated with the parent <html:form /> tag has a property that matches the value attribute, then the value of the ActionForm bean property is used as the value of this attribute. (optional)

<html:xhtml />

The <html:xhtml /> tag is used to tell other HTML taglib tags to render in XHTML. The <html:xhtml /> tag has no body and supports no attributes.

To use the <html:xhtml /> tag, you simply need to insert the tag, as shown in the following code snippet, at the top of your JSP:

```
<html:xhtml />
```

17

The Tiles Tag Library

In this chapter, we provide a reference for using the Jakarta Struts Tiles tag library. As we described in Chapter 13, "Using Tiles," the Tiles tag library (with its supporting classes) give page designers a mechanism that allows them to componentize and therefore reuse existing JSP components.

Installing the Tiles Tags

To use the Tiles tag library in a Web application, you must complete the following steps, replacing the value *webappname* with the name of the Web application that will be using this library:

1. Copy the TLD packaged with this tag library, struts-tiles.tld, to the <*CATALINA_HOME*>/webapps/*webappname*/WEB-INF directory.
2. Make sure that the struts.jar file is in the <*CATALINA_HOME*>/webapps/*webappname*/WEB-INF/lib directory.
3. Add the following <taglib> sub-element to the web.xml file of the Web application:

```
<taglib>
  <taglib-uri>/WEB-INF/struts-tiles.tld</taglib-uri>
  <taglib-location>/WEB-INF/struts-tiles.tld</taglib-
location>
</taglib>
```

You must also add the following taglib directive to each JSP that will leverage the Tiles tag library:

```
<%@ taglib uri="/WEB-INF/struts-tiles.tld" prefix="tiles" %>
```

This directive identifies the URI defined in the previously listed <taglib> element and states that all Tiles tags should be prefixed with the string *tiles*.

To fully deploy the tiles project, you must follow further configuration instructions as described in Chapter 13.

<tiles:insert />

The <tiles:insert /> tag is used to insert a Tiles template into a JSP. You must use the <tiles:put /> or <tiles:putList /> tags to substitute sub-components of the tile being inserted. The <tiles:insert /> tag has a body type of JSP and supports 14 attributes, described in Table 17.1.

Table 17.1 <tiles:insert /> Tag Attributes

Attribute	Description
template	A URI identifying a predefined template or tile that will be inserted into the current page. (Optional)
component	The relative or absolute path of a component that you want to insert into the JSP. (Optional)
page	The relative or absolute path of a JSP that you want to insert into the containing JSP. (Optional)
definition	The name of a predefined Tiles template that you want to insert into the containing JSP. (Optional)
attribute	The name of an attribute in the Tiles context. The retrieved value is passed to the entity defined by the name attribute. (Optional)
name	The name of the Tiles object being inserted into this page. (Optional)
beanName	The name of a JavaBean that will be used as the value of the name attribute. The JavaBean is retrieved from the appropriate scope, if not specified, using the PageContext.findAttribute() method. (Optional)
beanProperty	Used in conjunction with the beanName attribute to identify a JavaBean property that will be used as the value of the name attribute as opposed to the JavaBean itself. (Optional)
beanScope	The scope of the JavaBean identified by the beanName attribute. (Optional)
flush	If true, then the output stream of the containing JSP is writing to the client prior to the insertion of the template identified by this tag. (Optional)
ignore	If this attribute is true and the Tiles object identified by the name attribute is not found, then this tag is not evaluated. (Optional)
role	The required role for evaluating this <tiles:insert /> tag. If the requesting user is not in the named role, then this tag is ignored. (Optional)
controllerUrl	The URL of a Controller class that is invoked prior to the insertion of the template identified by this tag. (Optional)

Table continued on following page

Attribute	Description
controllerClass	A fully qualified class that is invoked prior to the insertion of the template named by this <tiles:insert /> tag. The named class must be an extension of an org.apache.struts.tiles.Controller, org.apache.struts.tiles.ControllerSupport, or org.apache.struts.action.Action class. (Optional)

When using the <tiles:insert /> tag, you must use the template, component, page, definition, attribute, or name attribute.

<tiles:definition />

The <tiles:definition /> tag is used to create a JavaBean representation of a Tiles template definition that is stored in the named scope bound to the identifier named by the id attribute. The <tiles:definition /> tag acts much like a runtime counterpart to the XML <definition /> found in the Tiles definitions file. The <tiles:definition /> tag has a body type of JSP and supports six attributes, described in Table 17.2.

Table 17.2 <tiles:definition /> Tag Attributes

Attribute	Description
id	The identifier that the created JavaBean will be bound to. (Required)
scope	The scope location of the created JavaBean. The default value is page. (Optional)
template	A URI identifying a Tiles component that will be associated to this component. (Optional)
page	A URL identifying a Tiles template or component that will be associated to this definition. (Optional)
role	The required role for evaluating this <tiles:definition /> tag. If the requesting user is not in the named role, then this tag is ignored. (Optional)
extends	An optional parent template definition that is used to initialize this <tiles:definition /> instance. (Optional)

<tiles:put />

The <tiles:put /> tag is used to define the equivalent of a parameter, representing a sub-component of a template, that will be passed to the Tiles object. The <tiles:put /> tag has a body type of JSP and supports eight attributes, described in Table 17.3.

Table 17.3 <tiles:put /> Tag Attributes	
Attribute	**Description**
name	Specifies the name of the parameter being passed to the tag's parent. (Optional)
value	Specifies the value of the parameter being passed to the tag's parent. (Optional)
direct	Indicates how the parameter content is to be handled. If the value is true, then the content is written immediately; otherwise, the content is included. (Optional)
type	Specifies the content type of the value being passed. The possible values are string, page, template, and definition. (Optional)
beanName	Represents an alternative to value, which allows you to use the contents of a JavaBean as the parameter value. (Optional)
beanProperty	Used in conjunction with the beanName attribute to identify a JavaBean property that will be used as the parameter value. (Optional)
beanScope	Indicates the scope location of the JavaBean identified by the beanName attribute. If the beanScope attribute is not specified, the PageContext.findAttribute() method is used to locate the named bean. (Optional)
role	Represents the required role for evaluating this <tiles:put /> tag. If the requesting user is not in the named role, this tag is ignored. (Optional)

The <tiles:put /> tag must be a sub-element of either a <tiles:insert /> or a <tiles:definition /> tag.

<tiles:putList />

The <tiles:putList /> tag is used to define a list of parameters that will be passed as attributes to the Tiles object. The list is created from a collection of child <tiles:add /> tags. The <tiles:putList /> tag has a body type of JSP and supports a single attribute, described in Table 17.4.

Table 17.4 <tiles:putList /> Tag Attribute	
Attribute	**Description**
name	The name of the list being created. (Required)

The <tiles:putList /> tag must be a sub-element of either a <tiles:insert /> or a <tiles:definition /> tag.

<tiles:add />

The <tiles:add /> tag is used to add parameters to a parameter as defined by a <tiles:putList /> tag. The <tiles:add /> tag has a body type of JSP and supports seven attributes, described in Table 17.5.

Table 17.5 <tiles:add /> Tag Attributes

Attribute	Description
beanName	Represents an alternative to value, which allows you to use the contents of a JavaBean as the parameter value. (Optional)
beanProperty	Used in conjunction with the beanName attribute to identify a JavaBean property that will be used as the parameter value. (Optional)
beanScope	Indicates the scope location of the JavaBean identified by the beanName attribute. If the beanScope attribute is not specified, the PageContext.findAttribute() method is used to locate the named bean. (Optional)
direct	Indicates how the parameter content is to be handled. If the value is true, then the content is written immediately; otherwise, the content is included. (Optional)
role	Represents the required role for evaluating this <tiles:add /> tag. If the requesting user is not in the named role, then this tag is ignored. (Optional)
type	Specifies the content type of the value being passed. The possible values are string, page, template, and definition. (Optional)
value	The value of the parameter being passed to the <tiles:add /> tag. (Optional)

<tiles:get />

The <tiles:get /> tag is used to retrieve and insert parameters previously defined from the Tiles context. With the exception of the ignore attribute being defaulted to true, this tag is functionally the same as the <tiles:insert /> tag. The <tiles:get /> tag has no body content and supports four attributes, described in Table 17.6.

Table 17.6 <tiles:get /> Tag Attributes

Attribute	Description
name	The identifier of the content being retrieved. (Required)
ignore	If this attribute is true and the Tiles object identified by the name attribute is not found, then this tag is not evaluated. The default value is true. (Optional)
flush	If true, then the output stream of the containing JSP is writing to the client prior to the insertion of the Tiles object identified by this tag. (Optional)
role	Represents the required role for evaluating this <tiles:get /> tag. If the requesting user is not in the named role, then this tag is ignored. (Optional)

<tiles:getAsString />

The <tiles:getAsString /> tag is used to retrieve the identified Tiles object, invoke that object the toString() method, and insert the results into the current JspWriter. The <tiles:getAsString /> tag has no body and supports three attributes, described in Table 17.7.

Table 17.7 <tiles:getAsString /> Tag Attributes

Attribute	Description
name	Identifies the name of the Tiles attribute being retrieved. (Required)
ignore	If this attribute is true and the Tiles object identified by the name attribute is not found, then this tag is not evaluated. The default value is false. (Optional)
role	Represents the required role for evaluating this <tiles:getAsString /> tag. If the requesting user is not in the named role, then this tag is ignored. (Optional)

<tiles:useAttribute />

The <tiles:useAttribute /> tag is used to retrieve a Tiles object from the Tiles context and expose that object as a scriptlet variable. The <tiles:useAttribute /> tag has no body and supports five attributes, described in Table 17.8.

Table 17.8 <tiles:useAttribute /> Tag Attributes

Attribute	Description
name	The name of the Tiles object being retrieved. (Required)
id	The id that the new scriptlet variable will be bound to. (Optional)
className	The fully qualified class name of the Java object being declared. (Optional)
scope	The scope of the newly created object. The default value is page. (Optional)
ignore	If this attribute is true and the Tiles object identified by the name attribute is not found, then this tag is not evaluated. The default value is false. (Optional)

<tiles:importAttribute />

The <tiles:importAttribute /> tag is used to import a Tiles object from the Tiles context into a JSP scriptlet variable, which is stored in the named scope. If the name and scope attributes are not included in the tag instance, then all Tile objects stored in the Tiles context are imported and placed in page scope. The <tiles:importAttribute /> tag has no body and supports three attributes, described in Table 17.9.

Table 17.9 <tiles:importAttribute /> Tag Attributes

Attribute	Description
name	The name of the Tiles object being retrieved. If the name attribute is not included, then all Tiles objects are retrieved. (Optional)
scope	The scope of the newly created object. The default value is page. (Optional)
ignore	If this attribute is true and the Tiles object identified by the name attribute is not found, then this tag is not evaluated. The default value is false. (Optional)

<tiles:initComponentDefinitions />

The <tiles:initComponentDefinitions /> tag is used to initialize the Tiles definition factory. This tag is evaluated only once or not at all if the factory has already been initialized by other means. The <tiles:initComponentDefinitions /> tag has no body and supports two attributes, described in Table 17.10.

Table 17.10 <tiles:initComponentDefinitions /> Tag Attributes

Attribute	Description
file	The file containing your Tile definitions. (Required)
classname	The fully qualified classname of the definition factory being initialized. This class, if specified, must implement the org.apache.struts.tiles.DefinitionsFactory. (Optional)

The initialization of the Tiles definition factory is most often done in the ComponentActionServlet. You can read about this in Chapter 14.

The Logic Tag Library

The focus of the Logic tag library is on decision making and object evaluation. This taglib contains 14 tags that can be used in a Struts application. In this chapter, we introduce you to each of these tags and show you how to use them.

Installing the Logic Tags

To use the Logic tag library in a Web application, you must complete the following steps. Be sure to replace the value *webappname* with the name of the Web application that will be using this library:

1. Copy the TLD packaged with this tag library, struts-logic.tld, to the *<CATALINA_HOME>*/webapps/*webappname*/WEB-INF/ directory.
2. Make sure that the struts.jar file is in the *<CATALINA_HOME>*/webapps/*webappname*/WEB-INF/lib directory.
3. Add the following <taglib> subelement to the web.xml file of the Web application:

```
<taglib>
  <taglib-uri>/WEB-INF/struts-logic.tld</taglib-uri>
  <taglib-location>/WEB-INF/struts-logic.tld</
taglib-location>
</taglib>
```

You must add the following taglib directive to each JSP that will leverage the Logic tag library:

```
<%@ taglib uri="/WEB-INF/struts-logic.tld" prefix="logic" %>
```

This directive identifies the URI defined in the previously listed <taglib> element and states that all Logic tags should be prefixed with the string logic.

<logic:empty />

The <logic:empty /> tag evaluates its body if either the scripting variable identified by the name attribute or a property of the named scripting variable is equal to null or an empty string. The <logic:empty /> tag has a body type of JSP and supports three attributes, described in Table 18.1.

Table 18.1 <logic:empty /> Tag Attributes

Attribute	Description
name	Identifies the scripting variable being tested. If the property attribute is included in the tag instance, then the property of the named scripting variable is tested; otherwise, the named scripting variable itself is tested. (Required)
property	Identifies the data member of the scripting variable to be tested. (Optional)
scope	Defines the scope of the bean specified by the name attribute. If the scope attribute is not specified, then the tag will search for the bean in the scopes, in the order of page, request, session, and application. (Optional)

An example of using the <logic:empty /> tag is shown here:

```
<logic:empty name="user">
  <forward name="login" />
</logic:empty>
```

In this example, we test the scripting variable user. If this variable is null or an empty string, then the body will be evaluated, which will result in the user being forwarded to the global forward login.

<logic:notEmpty />

The <logic:notEmpty /> tag evaluates its body if either the named scripting variable or property of the named scripting variable is not equal to null or an empty string. The <logic:notEmpty /> tag has a body type of JSP and supports three attributes, described in Table 18.2.

Table 18.2 <logic:notEmpty /> Tag Attributes

Attribute	Description
name	Specifies a scripting variable to be used as the variable being tested. (Required)
property	Specifies the data member of the scripting variable to be tested. (Optional)
scope	Defines the scope of the bean specified by the name attribute. If the scope attribute is not specified, then the tag will search for the bean in the scopes, in the order of page, request, session, and application. (Optional)

An example of using the <logic:notEmpty /> tag is shown here:

```
<logic:notEmpty name="user">
  Welcome to our Struts application.
</logic:notEmpty>
```

In this example, we test the scripting variable user. If this variable is not null and does not contain an empty string, then the body will be evaluated, which will result in the body of the tag being evaluated.

<logic:equal />

The <logic:equal /> tag evaluates its body if the variable specified by any one of the attributes cookie, header, name, parameter, or property equals the constant value specified by the value attribute. The <logic:equal /> tag has a body type of JSP and supports seven attributes, described in Table 18.3.

Table 18.3 <logic:equal /> Tag Attributes

Attribute	Description
value	Identifies the constant value to which the scripting variable will be compared. (Required)
cookie	Specifies an HTTP cookie to be used as the variable being compared to the value attribute. (Optional)
header	Specifies an HTTP header to be used as the variable being compared to the value attribute. (Optional)
name	Specifies a scripting variable to be used as the variable being compared to the value attribute. (Required)
property	Specifies the data member of the scripting variable to be tested. (Optional)
parameter	Specifies an HTTP parameter to be used as the variable being compared to the value attribute. (Optional)
scope	Defines the scope of the bean specified by the name attribute. If the scope attribute is not specified, then the tag will search for the bean in the scopes, in the order of page, request, session, and application. (Optional)

An example of using the <logic:equal /> tag is shown here:

```
<logic:equal name="user"
  property="age"
  value="<%= requiredAge %>">
  You are exactly the right age.
</logic:equal>
```

In this example, we test the age data member of the scripting variable user. If this data member equals the value stored in the requiredAge scripting variable, then the tag's body will be evaluated.

<logic:notEqual />

The <logic:notEqual /> tag evaluates its body if the variable specified by any one of the attributes cookie, header, name, parameter, or property is not equal to the constant value specified by the value attribute. The <logic:notEqual /> tag has a body type of JSP and supports seven attributes, described in Table 18.4.

Table 18.4 <logic:notEqual /> Tag Attributes

Attribute	Description
value	Identifies the constant value to which the scripting variable will be compared. (Required)
cookie	Specifies an HTTP cookie to be used as the variable being compared to the value attribute. (Optional)
header	Specifies an HTTP header to be used as the variable being compared to the value attribute. (Optional)
name	Specifies a scripting variable to be used as the variable being compared to the value attribute. (Required)
property	Specifies the data member of the scripting variable to be tested. (Optional)
parameter	Specifies an HTTP parameter to be used as the variable being compared to the value attribute. (Optional)
scope	Defines the scope of the bean specified by the name attribute. If the scope attribute is not specified, then the tag will search for the bean in the scopes, in the order of page, request, session, and application. (Optional)

An example of using the <logic:notEqual /> tag is shown here:

```
<logic:notEqual name="user"
  property="age"
  value="<%= requiredAge %>">
  You are not the right age.
</logic:notEqual>
```

In this example, we test the age data member of the scripting variable user. If this data member equals the value stored in the requiredAge scripting variable, then the tag's body will be evaluated.

<logic:forward />

The <logic:forward /> tag is used to forward control of the current request to a previously identified global forward element. The <logic:forward /> tag has no body and supports a single attribute name, which identifies the name of the global element that will receive control of the request. An example of using the <logic:forward /> tag is shown here:

```
<logic:forward name="login" />
```

In this example, we forward the current request to the global forward login. This resource must be defined in the <global-forwards /> section of the struts-config.xml file.

```
<global-forwards>
  <forward name="login" path="/login.jsp"/>
</global-forwards>
```

<logic:redirect />

The <logic:redirect /> tag uses the HttpServletResponse.sendRedirect() method to redirect the current request to a resource identified by either the forward, href, or page attributes. The <logic:redirect /> tag has no body and supports 12 attributes, described in Table 18.5.

Table 18.5 <logic:redirect /> Tag Attributes

Attribute	Description
anchor	Used to append an HTML anchor to the end of a generated resource. (Optional)
forward	Identifies the name of a global forward element that will receive control of the forwarded request. (Optional)
href	Specifies the URL of the resource to forward the current request to. (Optional)
name	Identifies a scripting variable referencing a java.util.Map object whose collection of key/value pairs is used as HTTP request parameters augmenting the redirected request. (Optional)
property	Identifies a bean property of the bean named by the name attribute that contains a java.util.Map reference whose collection of key/value pairs is used as HTTP request parameters augmenting the redirected request. (Optional)
scope	Defines the scope of the bean specified by the name attribute. If the scope attribute is not specified, then the tag will search for the bean in the scopes, in the order of page, request, session, and application. (Optional)
transaction	If set to true, indicates that the current transaction control token should be included in the generated URL. The default value is false. (Optional)
page	Specifies a context-relative path to a resource that will receive control of the current request. You must prepend the named resource with the / character. (Optional)
paramId	Identifies the name of a request parameter that will be added to the generated URL. The corresponding value of this parameter is defined by the paramName attribute. (Optional)
paramName	Specifies a JSP scripting variable, containing a String reference, that represents the value for the request parameter named by the paramId attribute. (Optional)
paramProperty	Identifies a bean property of the bean named by the paramName attribute; the property will be used as the value of the parameter identified by the paramId attribute. (Optional)
paramScope	Specifies the scope of the bean specified by the paramName attribute. If the paramScope attribute is not specified, then the tag will search for the bean in the scopes, in the order of page, request, session, and application. (Optional)

An example of using the <logic:redirect /> tag is shown here:

```
<logic:redirect name="login"
  paramId="companyId" paramName="company" />
```

In this example, we perform a redirect to the global forward login. This resource must be defined in the <global-forwards /> section of the struts-config.xml file. The <logic:redirect /> tag differs from the <logic:forward /> tag in that the <logic:redirect /> tag allows you to dynamically augment the request with parameters.

<logic:greaterEqual />

The <logic:greaterEqual /> tag evaluates its body if the variable specified by any one of the attributes cookie, header, name, parameter, or property is greater than or equal to the constant value specified by the value attribute. The <logic:greaterEqual /> tag has a body type of JSP and supports seven attributes, described in Table 18.6.

Table 18.6 <logic:greaterEqual /> Tag Attributes

Attribute	Description
value	Identifies the constant value to which the scripting variablewill be compared. (Required)
cookie	Specifies an HTTP cookie to be used as the variable being compared to the value attribute. (Optional)
header	Specifies an HTTP header to be used as the variable being compared to the value attribute. (Optional)
name	Specifies a scripting variable to be used as the variable being compared to the value attribute. (Required)
property	Specifies the data member of the scripting variable to be tested. (Optional)
parameter	Specifies an HTTP parameter to be used as the variable being compared to the value attribute. (Optional)
scope	Specifies the scope of the bean specified by the name attribute. If the scope attribute is not specified, then the tag will search for the bean in the scopes, in the order of page, request, session, and application. (Optional)

An example of using the <logic:greaterEqual /> tag is shown here:

```
<logic:greaterEqual name="user" property="age"
  value="<%= minAge %>">
  You are old enough.
</logic:greaterEqual>
```

In this example, we test the age data member of the scripting variable user. If this data member is greater than or equal to the value stored in the scripting variable minAge, then the tag's body will be evaluated.

<logic:greaterThan />

The <logic:greaterThan /> tag evaluates its body if the variable specified by any one of the attributes cookie, header, name, parameter, or property is greater than the constant value specified by the value attribute. The <logic:greaterThan /> tag has a body type of JSP and supports seven attributes, described in Table 18.7.

Table 18.7 <logic:greaterThan /> Tag Attributes

Attribute	Description
value	Identifies the constant value to which the scripting variable will be compared. (Required)
cookie	Specifies an HTTP cookie to be used as the variable being compared to the value attribute. (Optional)
header	Specifies an HTTP header to be used as the variable being compared to the value attribute. (Optional)
name	Specifies a scripting variable to be used as the variable being compared to the value attribute. (Required)
property	Specifies the data member of the scripting variable to be tested. (Optional)
parameter	Specifies an HTTP parameter to be used as the variable being compared to the value attribute. (Optional)
scope	Defines the scope of the bean specified by the name attribute. If the scope attribute is not specified, then the tag will search for the bean in the scopes, in the order of page, request, session, and application. (Optional)

An example of using the <logic:greaterThan /> tag is shown here:

```
<logic:greaterThan name="user" property="age"
  value="<%= minAge %>">
  You are over the minimum age <%= minAge %>.
</logic:greaterThan>
```

In this example, we test the age data member of the scripting variable user. If this data member is greater than the value stored in the scripting variable minAge, then the tag's body will be evaluated.

<logic:iterate />

The <logic:iterate /> tag is used to iterate over a named collection—which contains a Collection, Enumerator, Iterator, Map, or Array—and evaluates its body for each Object in the collection. We can identify the collection being iterated over by using a request-time expression or a scripting variable. The <logic:iterate /> tag has a body type of JSP and supports nine attributes, described in Table 18.8.

Table 18.8 <logic:iterate /> Tag Attributes

Attribute	Description
id	Specifies a JSP scripting variable, exposed by the <logic:iterate /> tag, that will hold the current object in the named collection. (Required)
collection	Used to identify a collection using a request-time expression. (Optional)
name	Specifies a scripting variable that represents the collection to be iterated over. (Optional)
property	Specifies the data member of the scripting variable, identified by the name attribute, that contains a reference to a collection. (Optional)
scope	Defines the scope of the bean specified by the name attribute. If the scope attribute is not specified, then the tag will search for the bean in the scopes, in the order of page, request, session, and application. (Optional)
type	Provides the fully qualified class name of the element being exposed from the collection. This object is referenced by the id attribute. (Optional)
indexId	Specifies a JSP scripting variable, exposed by the <logic:iterate /> tag, that will hold the current index of the current object in the named collection. (Optional)
length	Identifies the maximum number of collection entries to be iterated over. The length attribute can be either an integer or a scripting variable of type java.lang.Integer. If the length attribute is not included, then the entire collection will be iterated over. (Optional)
offset	Indicates where iteration should begin. If this value is not specified, then the beginning of the collection is used. (Optional)

An example of using the <logic:iterate /> tag is shown here:

```
<logic:iterate id="employee" name="employees">
  <tr align="left">
    <td>
      <bean:write name="employee" property="username" />
    </td>
    <td>
      <bean:write name="employee" property="name" />
    </td>
    <td>
      <bean:write name="employee" property="phone" />
    </td>
  </tr>
</logic:iterate>
```

In this example, we are iterating over the collection referenced by the employee's scripting variable. As the <logic:iterate /> tag iterates over the named collection, it exposes each object in the collection in the employee scripting variable. The result of this iteration is an HTML table row for each object in the named collection.

<logic:lessEqual />

The <logic:lessEqual /> tag evaluates its body if the variable specified by any one of the attributes cookie, header, name, parameter, or property is less than or equal to the constant value specified by the value attribute. The <logic:lessEqual /> tag has a body type of JSP and supports seven attributes, described in Table 18.9.

Table 18.9 <logic:lessEqual /> Tag Attributes

Attribute	Description
value	Identifies the constant value to which the scripting variable will be compared. (Required)
cookie	Specifies an HTTP cookie to be used as the variable being compared to the value attribute. (Optional)
header	Specifies an HTTP header to be used as the variable being compared to the value attribute. (Optional)
name	Specifies a scripting variable to be used as the variable being compared to the value attribute. (Required)
property	Specifies the data member of the scripting variable to be tested. (Optional)
parameter	Specifies an HTTP parameter to be used as the variable being compared to the value attribute. (Optional)
scope	Specifies the scope of the bean specified by the name attribute. If the scope attribute is not specified, then the tag will search for the bean in the scopes, in the order of page, request, session, and application. (Optional)

An example of using the <logic:lessEqual /> tag is shown here:

```
<logic:lessEqual name="user" property="age"
  value="<%= maxAge %>">
  You are young enough.
</logic:lessEqual>
```

In this example, we test the age data member of the scripting variable user. If this data member is less than or equal to the value stored in the scripting variable minAge, then the tag's body will be evaluated.

<logic:lessThan />

The <logic:lessThan /> tag evaluates its body if the variable specified by any one of the attributes cookie, header, name, parameter, or property is less than the constant value specified by the value attribute. The <logic:lessThan /> tag has a body type of JSP and supports seven attributes, described in Table 18.10.

Table 18.10 <logic:lessThan /> Tag Attributes

Attribute	Description
value	Identifies the constant value to which the scripting variable will be compared. (Required)
cookie	Specifies an HTTP cookie to be used as the variable being compared to the value attribute. (Optional)
header	Specifies an HTTP header to be used as the variable being compared to the value attribute. (Optional)
name	Specifies a scripting variable to be used as the variable being compared to the value attribute. (Required)
property	Specifies the data member of the scripting variable to be tested. (Optional)
parameter	Specifies an HTTP parameter to be used as the variable being compared to the value attribute. (Optional)
scope	Defines the scope of the bean specified by the name attribute. If the scope attribute is not specified, then the tag will search for the bean in the scopes, in the order of page, request, session, and application. (Optional)

An example of using the <logic:lessThan /> tag is shown here:

```
<logic:lessThan name="user" property="age"
  value="<%= maxAge %>">
  You are under the maximum age <%= maxAge %>.
</logic:lessThan>
```

In this example, we test the age data member of the scripting variable user. If this data member is less than the value stored in the scripting variable maxAge, then the tag's body will be evaluated.

<logic:match />

The <logic:match /> tag evaluates its body if the variable specified by any one of the attributes cookie, header, name, parameter, or property attributes contains the specified constant value. The <logic:match /> tag has a body type of JSP and supports eight attributes, described in Table 18.11.

Table 18.11 <logic:match /> Tag Attributes

Attribute	Description
value	Identifies the constant value to which the scripting variable will be compared. (Required)
location	Specifies where the match should occur in the named variable. The possible values are *start* and *end*. If the location attribute is not specified, then the value can occur anywhere in the variable. (Optional)

Table continued on following page

Attribute	Description
cookie	Specifies an HTTP cookie to be used as the variable being compared to the value attribute. (Optional)
header	Specifies an HTTP header to be used as the variable being compared to the value attribute. (Optional)
name	Specifies a scripting variable to be used as the variable being compared to the value attribute. (Required)
property	Specifies the data member of the scripting variable to be tested. (Optional)
parameter	Specifies an HTTP parameter to be used as the variable being compared to the value attribute. (Optional)
scope	Defines the scope of the bean specified by the name attribute. If the scope attribute is not specified, then the tag will search for the bean in the scopes, in the order of page, request, session, and application. (Optional)

An example of using the <logic:match /> tag is shown here:

```
<logic:match name="sentence" value="Bob">
  The string Bob occurs in the sentence.
</logic:match>
```

In this example, we test the scripting variable sentence. If it contains the text Bob, then the tag's body will be evaluated.

<logic:notMatch />

The <logic:notMatch /> tag evaluates its body if the variable specified by any one of the attributes cookie, header, name, parameter, or property does not contain the constant specified by the value attribute. The <logic:notMatch /> tag has a body type of JSP and supports eight attributes, described in Table 18.12.

Table 18.12 <logic:notMatch /> Tag Attributes

Attribute	Description
value	Identifies the constant value to which the scripting variable will be compared. (Required)
location	Specifies where the match should occur in the named variable. The possible values are *start* and *end*. If the location attribute is not specified, then the value can occur anywhere in the variable. (Optional)
cookie	Specifies an HTTP cookie to be used as the variable being compared to the value attribute. (Optional)
header	Specifies an HTTP header to be used as the variable being compared to the value attribute. (Optional)

Table continued on following page

Attribute	Description
name	Specifies a scripting variable to be used as the variable being compared to the value attribute. (Required)
property	Specifies the data member of the scripting variable to be tested. (Optional)
parameter	Specifies an HTTP parameter to be used as the variable being compared to the value attribute. (Optional)
scope	Defines the scope of the bean specified by the name attribute. If the scope attribute is not specified, then the tag will search for the bean in the scopes, in the order of page, request, session, and application. (Optional)

An example of using the <logic:notMatch /> tag is shown here:

```
<logic:notMatch name="sentence" value="Bob">
  The string Bob does not occur in the sentence.
</logic:notMatch >
```

In this example, we test the scripting variable sentence. If it does not contain the text Bob, then the tag's body will be evaluated.

<logic:present />

The <logic:present /> tag evaluates its body if the variable specified by any one of the cookie, header, name, parameter, or property attributes is present in the applicable scope. The <logic:present /> tag has a body type of JSP and supports eight attributes, described in Table 18.13.

Table 18.13 <logic:present /> Tag Attributes

Attribute	Description
cookie	Specifies an HTTP cookie to be used as the variable being tested for existence. (Optional)
header	Specifies a case-insensitive HTTP header to be used as the variable being tested for existence. (Optional)
name	Defines a scripting variable to be used as the variable being tested for existence. (Optional)
property	Specifies the data member of the scripting variable to be tested. (Optional)
parameter	Specifies an HTTP parameter to be used as the variable being tested for existence. (Optional)
scope	Defines the scope of the bean specified by the name attribute. If the scope attribute is not specified, then the tag will search for the bean in the scopes, in the order of page, request, session, and application. (Optional)

Table continued on following page

Attribute	Description
role	Used to determine if the currently authenticated user belongs to one or more named roles. If more than one role is listed, then they must be separated by commas. (Optional)
user	Used to determine if the currently authenticated user has the specified name. (Optional)

An example of using the <logic:present /> tag is shown here:

```
<logic:present parameter="username">
  Welcome <%= username %>.
</logic:present >
```

In this example, we test for the existence of the request parameter username. If the username parameter is part of the request, then the tag's body will be evaluated.

<logic:notPresent />

The <logic:notPresent /> tag evaluates its body if the variable specified by any one of the cookie, header, name, parameter, or property attributes is not present in the applicable scope. The <logic:notPresent /> tag has a body type of JSP and supports eight attributes, described in Table 18.14.

Table 18.14 <logic:notPresent /> Tag Attributes

Attribute	Description
cookie	Specifies an HTTP cookie to be used as the variable being tested for existence. (Optional)
header	Specifies a case-insensitive HTTP header to be used as the variable being tested for existence. (Optional)
name	Defines a scripting variable to be used as the variable being tested for existence. (Optional)
property	Specifies the data member of the scripting variable to be tested. (Optional)
parameter	Specifies an HTTP parameter to be used as the variable being tested for existence. (Optional)
scope	Defines the scope of the bean specified by the name attribute. If the scope attribute is not specified, then the tag will search for the bean in the scopes, in the order of page, request, session, and application. (Optional)
role	Used to determine if the currently authenticated user belongs to one or more named roles. If more than one role is listed, then they must be separated by commas. (Optional)
user	Used to determine if the currently authenticated user has the specified name. (Optional)

An example of using the <logic:notPresent /> tag is shown here:

```
<logic:notPresent name="username" scope="session">
  There is no username attribute in the session.
</logic:notPresent >
```

In this example, we test for the existence of the session attribute username. If the username parameter is not found in the HttpSession, then the tag's body will be evaluated.

19

The Template Tag Library

The Struts Template tags provide a simple method of defining reusable templatized it is a nerd term Views. It does this through the use of three custom tags that allow you to define JSP template files. These three tags are the <template:get />, <template:insert /> and <template:put /> tags. In this chapter, we define each of these tags and examine their use.

Installing the Template Tags

To use the Template tag library in a Web application, you must complete the following steps. Be sure to replace the value *webappname* with the name of the Web application that will be using this library.

1. Copy the TLD packaged with this tag library, struts-template.tld, to the *<TOMCAT_HOME>*/webapps/*webappname*/WEB-INF/lib directory.
2. Make sure that the struts.jar file is in the *<TOMCAT_HOME>*/webapps/*webappname*/WEB-INF/lib directory.
3. Add the following <taglib> subelement to the web.xml file of the Web application:

```
<taglib>
  <taglib-uri>/WEB-INF/struts-template.tld</taglib-uri>
  <taglib-location>
    /WEB-INF/struts-template.tld
  </taglib-location>
</taglib>
```

You must add the following taglib directive to each JSP that will leverage the Template tag library:

```
<%@ taglib uri="/WEB-INF/tlds/struts-template.tld"
  prefix="template" %>
```

This directive identifies the URI defined in the previously listed <taglib> element and states that all Template tags should be prefixed with the string template.

<template:get />

The <template:get /> tag is used to retrieve the contents of a bean stored in the request scope, with the intention of replacing the tag instance with the contents of the retrieved bean. It is used to define the actual template JSP that will be referenced by the <template:insert /> tag. The bean being retrieved is assumed to have been placed on the request by a <template:put /> tag. The <template:get /> tag has no body and supports three attributes, as shown in Table 19.1.

Table 19.1 <template:get /> Tag Attributes

Attribute	Description
name	Identifies the name of the request attribute to be retrieved. The name attribute should match the name attribute of the <template:put /> tag. (Required)
role	Specifies the role in which the user must exist for this tag to be evaluated. If the user does not exist in the named role, then the tag is ignored. If no role is named, then the tag will be evaluated by default. (Optional)
flush	If set to true, results in the flushing of the response buffer prior to the inclusion of the specified request attribute. The default value is false. (Optional)

A sample code snippet, from a JSP named catalogTemplate.jsp, is shown here:

```
<%@ taglib uri="/WEB-INF/tlds/struts-template.tld"
  prefix="template" %>

<html>
  <body>
    <table>
      <tr valign="top">
        <td><template:get name="navbar"/></td>
        <td>
          <table>
            <tr><td><template:get name="header" /></td></tr>
            <tr><td><template:get name="body" /></td></tr>
            <tr><td><template:get name="footer" /></td></tr>
          </table>
        </td>
      </tr>
    </table>
  </body>
</html>
```

This JSP defines a template with four parameterized tags: navbar, header, body, and footer. This JSP will first be evaluated, and the <template:get /> tag instances will be replaced by the named request attributes. Then, it will be inserted into a JSP that names it using the <template:insert /> tag. You will see an example of the <template:insert /> tag in the following section.

<template:insert />

The <template:insert /> tag is used to retrieve and insert the contents of the named URI. The <template:insert /> tag acts as the parent to one or more <template:put /> tags, which act as parameters to the named template JSP. The <template:insert /> tag has a body type of JSP and a single required attribute template that names the URI of the resource to include as the template. A sample code snippet using the <template:insert /> tag is shown here:

```
<%@ taglib uri="/WEB-INF/tlds/struts-template.tld"
  prefix="template" %>

<template:insert template="/catalogTemplate.jsp">

  <template:put name="navbar" content="/navbar.jsp" />
  <template:put name="header" content="/header.jsp" />
  <template:put name="body" content="/login.jsp" />
  <template:put name="footer" content="/footer.html" />

</template:insert>
```

This instance of the <template:insert /> tag will set four request attributes to the values of their content attributes, which in this case are a combination of JSPs and a single HTML document.

The content attributes in this example could just as easily have been a static string that could be stored as the value in the request attribute.

<template:put />

The <template:put /> tag is used to store the content of a particular URL or text (URIs or text) into the request scope. This tag is the parent to one or more put tags. The put tags specify the content to be inserted into the template. The layout of the content is determined by get tags placed in the template. The <template:put /> tag has no body and supports four attributes, described in Table 19.2.

Table 19.2 <template:put /> Tag Attributes

Attribute	Description
name	Identifies the name of the attribute to be stored in the request. The name attribute should match the name attribute of the <template:get /> tag being used to retrieve it. (Required)
role	Specifies the role in which the user must exist for this tag to be evaluated. If the user does not exist in the name role, then the tag is ignored. If no role is named, then the tag will be evaluated by default. (Optional)
content	Specifies the content that will be stored in the request. This value can be a URI or static text. If this value is not included, then the body of the tag will be used as the content and the direct attribute must be set to true. (Optional)
direct	If set to true, indicates that the content attribute or body is printed to the request; if set to false (the default), the content is included. (Optional)

The <template:put /> tag must be nested within a <template:insert /> tag.

A sample code snippet using the <template:put /> tag is shown here:

```
<%@ taglib uri="/WEB-INF/tlds/struts-template.tld"
  prefix="template" %>

<template:insert template="/chapterTemplate.jsp">

  <template:put name="title" content="Templates"
    direct="true" />
  <template:put name="header" content="/header.html" />
  <template:put name="sidebar" content="/sidebar.jsp" />
  <template:put name="content" content="/introduction.html"/>
  <template:put name="footer" content="/footer.html" />

</template:insert>
```

20

The Bean Tag Library

At this point, we begin our discussions of the Jakarta Struts tag libraries. In this chapter, we examine the Jakarta Struts Bean tag library. The Bean tag library provides a group of tags that encapsulate the logic necessary to access and manipulate JavaBeans, HTTP cookies, and HTTP headers using scripting variables. There are currently 11 custom tags in the Bean tag library.

Installing the Bean Tags

To use the Bean tag library in a Web application, you must complete the following steps, replacing the value *webappname* with the name of the Web application that will be using this library:

1. Copy the TLD packaged with this tag library, struts-bean.tld, to the <*CATALINA_HOME*>/webapps/*webappname*/WEB-INF/ directory.
2. Make sure that the struts.jar file is in the <*CATALINA_HOME*>/webapps/*webappname*/WEB-INF/lib directory.
3. Add the following <taglib> subelement to the web.xml file of the Web application:

```
<taglib>
  <taglib-uri>/WEB-INF/struts-bean.tld</taglib-uri>
  <taglib-location>/WEB-INF/struts-bean.tld</taglib-
location>
</taglib>
```

You must add the following taglib directive to each JSP that will leverage the Bean tag library:

```
<%@ taglib uri="/WEB-INF/struts-bean.tld" prefix="bean" %>
```

This directive identifies the URI defined in the previously listed <taglib> element and states that all Bean tags should be prefixed with the string bean.

<bean:cookie />

The <bean:cookie /> tag is used to retrieve the value of an HTTP cookie. It can be used to retrieve single or multiple cookie values. The retrieved cookie(s) are stored in a page scoped attribute of type Cookie (or Cookie[], if there is more than one HTTP cookie). If the named cookie is not found and no default value is specified, then a request-time exception is thrown.

The <bean:cookie /> tag has no body and supports four attributes, described in Table 20.1.

Table 20.1 <bean:cookie /> Tag Attributes

Attribute	Description
id	Specifies the ID of the scripting variable to be added to the request as a Cookie object. (Required)
name	Identifies the name of the HTTP cookie being retrieved. (Required)
multiple	If not null, will cause a Cookie[] containing all of the values for the named HTTP cookie to be returned as opposed to a single Cookie object. If the multiple attribute is not null and there is only a single HTTP cookie, then the first [0] element of the Cookie[] will contain the retrieved value. (Optional)
value	Specifies the default value to return to store in the javax.servlet.http.Cookie object, if no cookie is found. (Optional)

Here's an example of using the <bean:cookie /> tag:

```
<bean:cookie id="userId"
  name="userCookie"
  value="UNKNOWN_USER"/>
```

In this example, we are looking for a HTTP cookie named userCookie. If the userId cookie exists in the request, then a javax.servlet.http.Cookie object containing the retrieved value is created and stored in the page. Otherwise, a javax.servlet.http.Cookie object containing the string specified in the value attribute--UNKNOWN_USER in this example--is created and stored in the page.

<bean:define />

The <bean:define /> tag is used to retrieve the value of a named bean property and define it as a scripting variable, which is will be stored in the scope specified by the toScope attribute. The retrieved object will perform type conversion on the returned property value, unless it is a Java primitive type, in which case it is wrapped in the appropriate wrapper class (for example, int is wrapped by java.lang.Integer).

This <bean:define /> tag has a body type of JSP and supports seven attributes, described in Table 20.2.

Table 20.2 <bean:define /> Tag Attributes

Attribute	Description
id	Specifies the scripting variable that will be created and stored in a scoped attribute that will be made available with the value of the indicated property. (Required)
name	Specifies the attribute name of the bean whose property is retrieved to define a new scoped attribute. You must include the name attribute, unless you specify a value attribute. (Optional)
property	Identifies the property of the bean, specified by the name attribute, that is being retrieved. If the property attribute is not specified, then the bean identified by the name attribute is given a new reference to the object identified by the id attribute. (Optional)
scope	Identifies the scope of the bean specified by the name attribute. If the scope attribute is not specified, then the tag will search for the bean in the scopes, in the order of page, request, session, and application. (Optional)
toScope	Identifies the scope of the newly defined bean. The default scope is page. (Optional)
type	Provides the fully qualified class name of the value to be exposed as the id attribute. The default type is java.lang.String if a value attribute is specified; otherwise, the object will be of type java.lang.Object. (Optional)
value	Contains a string value to which the exposed bean should be set. You must include the value attribute, unless you specify the name attribute. (Optional)

An example of using the <bean:define /> tag is shown here:

```
<jsp:useBean
  id="user"
  scope="page"
  class="com.wrox.User"/>

<bean:define
  id="name"
  name="user"
  property="firstName"/>

Welcome: <%= name %>
```

In this example, we have user, a page-level object of type com.wrox.User. We then use the <bean:define /> tag to retrieve the user property firstName and store this value in the scripting variable named name. We conclude this snippet by printing the contents of the newly created name object.

<bean:header />

The <bean:header /> tag functions exactly like <bean:cookie />, except that it retrieves its values from the named request header. Once the tag has the header values, it creates a java.lang.String or java.lang.String[] attribute and stores it in the PageContext.

If the named header cannot be located and no default value is given, then a request-time exception will be thrown. The <bean:header /> tag has a body type of JSP and supports four attributes, described in Table 20.3.

Table 20.3 <bean:header /> Tag Attributes

Attribute	Description
id	Represents the name of the scripting variable that will be exposed as a page scoped attribute. (Required)
name	Identifies the name of the HTTP header being retrieved. (Required)
multiple	If not null, causes a String[] containing all of the header values for the named HTTP header to be returned as opposed to a single header. If the multiple attribute is not null and there is only a single HTTP header, then the first or [0] element of the String[] will contain the retrieved value. (Optional)
value	Specifies the default value to return and store in the name object, if the named header is not found. (Optional)

An example of using the <bean:header /> tag is shown here:

```
<bean:header id="headId"
  name="Cache-Control"
  value="Cache-Control Not Found" />
```

In this example, we are looking for a HTTP header, Cache-Control. If the Cache-Control header exists, then a String object containing the retrieved value is created and stored in the page; otherwise, a String object containing the String named in the value attribute--Cache-Control Not Found in this example--is created and stored in the page.

<bean:include />

The <bean:include /> tag is used to evaluate and retrieve the results of a Web application resource. The tag makes the response data available as an object of type String. The tag functions much like the <jsp:include> standard action, except that the response is stored in a page scoped object attribute, as opposed to being written to the output stream.

The resource being evaluated by the <bean:include /> tag can be identified using three different attributes: forward, href, and page.

The <bean:include /> tag has no body and supports six attributes, described in Table 20.4.

Table 20.4 <bean:include /> Tag Attributes

Attribute	Description
id	Specifies the page-level variable used to store the result of the evaluated URI condition. (Required)
anchor	Specifies an HTML anchor tag that will be added to the generated URI. You do not need to include the # character when identifying the anchor. (Optional)
forward	Used to name a global <forward /> subelement, which will be used to look up a reference to the application-relative or context-relative URI identified by the <forward /> element's path attribute. (Optional)
href	Used to include resources external to the hosting application. (Optional)
page	Used to include the value of an application-relative URI. (Optional)
transaction	If true, causes the transaction token, if available, to be included in the URI being requested. The default value is false. (Optional)

Here's an example of how we can use the <bean:include /> tag:

```
<bean:include id="navbar" page="/navbar.jsp"/>
```

In this example, the context-relative resource navbar.jsp is evaluated and its response is placed in the page-level attribute navbar. The type of page-level attribute is java.lang.String.

<bean:message />

The <bean:message /> tag is a very useful tag that we can employ to retrieve keyed values from a previously defined resource bundle. It also supports the ability to include parameters that can be substituted for defined placeholders in the retrieved string. The <bean:message /> tag has no body and supports 11 attributes, described in Table 20.5.

> **We used this tag throughout Chapter 9, "Internationalizing Your Struts Applications."**

Table 20.5 <bean:message /> Tag Attributes

Attribute	Description
arg0	Contains the first parametric replacement value. (Optional)
arg1	Contains the second parametric replacement value. (Optional)
arg2	Contains the third parametric replacement value. (Optional)
arg3	Contains the fourth parametric replacement value. (Optional)

Table continued on following page

Attribute	Description
arg4	Contains the fifth parametric replacement value. (Optional)
bundle	Specifies the name of the bean under which messages are stored. This bean is stored in the ServletContext. If the bundle is not included, the default value of the Action.MESSAGES_KEY is used. This attribute is an optional request-time attribute. If you use the ActionServlet to manage your resource bundles, you can ignore this attribute. (Optional)
key	Identifies the unique key that is used to retrieve a message from a previously defined resource bundle. (Optional)
locale	Specifies the session bean that references the requesting client's locale. If the bundle is not included, the default value of Action.LOCALE_KEY is used. (Optional)
name	Specifies the name of the object whose data member is being retrieved. If the property attribute is not specified, then the value of this bean itself will be used as the message resource key. (Optional)
property	Specifies the name of the property to be accessed on the bean identified by the name attribute. If this attribute is not specified, then the value of the bean identified by the name attribute will be used as the message resource key. (Optional)
scope	Identifies the scope of the bean specified by name attribute. If the scope attribute is not specified, then the tag will search for the bean in the scopes, in the order of page, request, session, and application. (Optional)

The following code snippet contains a simple example of using the <bean:message /> tag:

```
<html>
  <head>
    <title><bean:message key="app.title"/></title>
  </head>
  <body>

  </body>
</html>
```

In this example, we are retrieving the value stored in the resource bundle that is referenced by the key app.title. This retrieved value will be substituted for the occurrence of this <bean:message /> tag. The result is a JSP that will have an HTML <title> that matches the locale of the requesting client.

<bean:page />

The <bean:page /> tag is used to retrieve the value of an identified implicit JSP object, which it stores in the page context of the current JSP. The retrieved object will be stored in the page scoped scripting variable named by the id attribute. The <bean:page /> tag has no body and supports two attributes, as shown in Table 20.6.

Table 20.6 <bean:page /> Tag Attributes

Attribute	Description
id	Identifies the name of the scripting variable that is being made available with the value of the specified page context property. (Required)
property	Specifies the implicit object being retrieved from the current page context. The property attribute must be set to one of these implicit object values: application, config, request, response, or session. (Required)

This code snippet contains a simple example of using the <bean:page /> tag:

```
<bean:page id="sessionVar" property="session"/>
```

In this example, we are retrieving the implicit session object and storing this reference in the scripting variable sessionVar.

<bean:parameter />

The <bean:parameter /> tag is used to retrieve the value of a request parameter identified by the name attribute. The retrieved value will be used to define a page scoped attribute of type java.lang.String or String[], if the multiple attribute is not null. The <bean:parameter /> tag has no body and supports four attributes, as shown in Table 20.7.

Table 20.7 <bean:parameter /> Tag Attributes

Attribute	Description
id	Represents the name of the scripting variable that will be exposed as a page scoped attribute. (Required)
name	Identifies the name of the request parameter being retrieved. (Required)
multiple	If not null, causes a String[] containing all of the parameter values for the named request parameter to be returned as opposed to a single parameter. If the multiple attribute is not null and there is only a single parameter value, then the first or [0] element of the String[] will contain the retrieved value. (Optional)
value	Specifies the default value to return and store in the name object, if the named parameter is not found. (Optional)

An example of using the <bean:parameter /> tag is shown here:

```
<bean:parameter id="userId"
  name="username"
  value="User Not Found" />
```

In this example, we are looking for the request parameter username. If the username parameter exists in the request, then a String object containing the retrieved value is created and stored in the page; otherwise, a String object containing the String named in the value attribute—User Not Found in this example—is created and stored in the page.

<bean:resource />

The <bean:resource /> tag is used to retrieve the value of Web application resource identified by the name attribute; the tag makes the resource available as either a java.io.InputStream or a java.lang.String object, based on the value of the input attribute. The <bean:resource /> tag has no body and supports three attributes, described in Table 20.8.

Table 20.8 <bean:resource /> Tag Attributes

Attribute	Description
id	Identifies the name of the page scoped scripting variable that will contain the retrieved value of the named Web application resource. (Required)
name	Identifies the application-relative name of the Web application resource being retrieved. The resource name must begin with a / character. (Required)
input	If not null, causes the retrieved resource to be returned as an InputStream as opposed to a String. (Optional)

<bean:size />

The <bean:size /> tag is used to retrieve the number of elements contained in a reference to an array, collection, or map. The results of the <bean:size /> tag's evaluation is a scripting variable of type java.lang.Integer that contains the number of elements in that collection. You can specify the collection as a runtime expression, as a bean, or as a property of the bean named by the bean attribute. The <bean:size /> tag has no body and supports five attributes, as shown in Table 20.9.

Table 20.9 <bean:size /> Tag Attributes

Attribute	Description
id	Contains the scripting variable used to store the result of the evaluation. (Required)
collection	Identifies the runtime expression that evaluates to an array, a collection, or a map. (Optional)
name	Identifies the bean that contains the collection that will be counted. If the property attribute is specified, then the collection is assumed to be a data member of the bean; otherwise, the bean itself is assumed to be a collection. (Optional)

Attribute	Description
property	Specifies the name of the property to be accessed on the bean identified by the name attribute whose getter method will return the collection to be counted. (Optional)
scope	Identifies the scope of the bean specified by the name attribute. If the scope attribute is not specified, then the tag will search for the bean in the scopes, in the order of page, request, session, and application. (Optional)

An example of using the <bean:size /> tag is shown here:

```
<bean:size id="count"
  name="users" />
```

In this example, we are counting the collection users and storing the results in the scripting variable count.

<bean:struts />

The <bean:struts /> tag is used to copy a specified Struts internal component into a paged scoped scripting variable. The Struts components that can be retrieved include a FormBean, a forward, or a mapping object. The <bean:struts /> tag has no body and supports four attributes, as shown in Table 20.10.

Table 20.10 <bean:struts /> Tag Attributes

Attribute	Description
id	Specifies the scripting variable used to store the retrieved Struts component. (Required)
formBean	Specifies the Struts ActionFormBean object to be copied into the named scripting variable. (Optional)
forward	Specifies the Struts ActionFormBean object to be copied into the named scripting variable. (Optional)
mapping	Contains the path of the Struts ActionMapping object to be copied into the named scripting variable. (Optional)

The forward and mapping attributes for the <bean:struts /> tag are mutually exclusive: you can only use one of the attributes for any single <bean:struts /> tag instance.

Here's an example of how we can use the <bean:struts /> tag:

```
<bean:struts id="userForm"
  formBean="UserForm"/>
```

In this example, we retrieve a UserForm FormBean, as it is described by the struts-config.xml file, and store a reference to it in the scripting variable userForm.

<bean:write />

The <bean:write /> tag is used to retrieve and print the value of a named bean property. If the format attribute is encountered, then the value being written will be formatted based upon the format string represented by the format attribute. The <bean:write /> tag has no body and supports nine attributes, described in Table 20.11.

Table 20.11 <bean:write /> Tag Attributes

Attribute	Description
bundle	Represents the condition to be evaluated by the <bean:if> tag. If the <bean:if> tag is being included from the expression language tag library, then the value represented by the test attribute must evaluate to a Boolean primitive or a java.lang.Boolean. If the <bean:if> tag is being included from the runtime tag library, then the value represented by the test attribute must evaluate to a java.lang.Boolean. (Required)
filter	If set to true, causes the retrieved value to be filtered for HTML reserved characters. If an HTML specific character is found, it will be replaced by its encoded counterpart. The default value of this attribute is false. (Optional)
format	Specifies the format string to use when converting the retrieved value to a String. (Optional)
formatKey	Specifies the key to search for a format string that is stored in an application resource bundle. (Optional)
ignore	If set to true and the named bean does not exist, causes the tag to skip its processing and ignore its evaluation. The default value is false, which causes a runtime exception to be thrown, consistent with the other tags in this tag library. (Optional)
locale	Identifies the session bean that references the current Locale object. The default value is Action.LOCALE_KEY. (Optional)
name	Identifies the attribute name of the bean property that is being retrieved and printed. If the property attribute is not included, then the value of the bean itself will be printed. (Optional)
property	Identifies the name of the bean property being accessed. (Optional)
scope	Identifies the scope of the bean specified by the name attribute. If the scope attribute is not specified, then the tag will search for the bean in the scopes, in the order of page, request, session, and application. (Optional)

An example of using the <bean:write /> tag is shown here:

```
<bean:write name="employee"
  property="username" />
```

In this example, we retrieve and print the username property of the employee scripting variable. Here, because the scope attribute is not set, the tag will search for the bean in the scopes, in the order of page, request, session, and application.

21

Struts Cookbook

This chapter contains a wealth of advanced material that will enable you to get the most out of Struts. Think of it as a cookbook for recipes that will help you solve common problems in your Web application development with Struts.

Action Helper Methods

The Action class contains many helper methods which enable you to add advanced functionality to your Struts applications. Some of the functionality we'll cover in this section includes:

- Making sure that a form is not submitted twice (see the section "Action saveToken and isTokenValid").
- Display dynamic messages that are i18n-enabled (see the section "Action saveMessages and getResources").
- Allow users to cancel an operation (see the section "Action isCancelled").
- Allow users to change their locale (see the section "Action getLocale and setLocale").

Action saveToken and isTokenValid

Have you ever wanted to make sure that a user does not submit a form twice? I have. Perhaps you have even implemented your own routine that does this. The idea behind saveToken and isTokenValid is to make sure that a form has not been submitted twice. It is nice to know that this functionality is built into Struts and that it is handled by many of its internal operations.

Struts provides transaction tokens to ensure that a form is not submitted twice. A transaction token has nothing to do with Extended Attribute (XA) transactions, Enterprise JavaBeans (EJB), or Java Transaction Services (JTS). A *transaction token* is a unique string that is generated. The token is submitted with the html:form tag. Several classes and one custom tag are involved in this bit of choreography.

To use a transaction token, follow these steps:

1. Before you load the JavaServer Pages (JSP) page that has the html:form tag on it, call saveToken inside an action.
2. When the user submits the form, call isTokenValid and handle the form only if the token is valid.

The first step is to call saveToken inside an action. To do this, you have to make sure an action is called before the JSP page loads.

Let's say that before you started using transaction tokens you had a form that was associated with an action using the action mapping's forward attribute, as follows:

```
<global-forwards>
    <forward name="input" path="/input.do" />
    ...
</global-forwards>


<action-mappings>

      <action path="/input" forward="/input.jsp" />

</action-mappings>
```

Then any JSP page that links to the input form would link to it like this:

```
<html:link forward="input"> Input </html:link>
```

Therefore, no JSP links directly to input.jsp. If this is the case, it is easy to start using transaction tokens.

Now let's say that you want to make sure that the user cannot hit the back button in the browser and submit the form twice. To do this, you must change the action mapping associated with the input form to map to an action that will call the saveToken method of Action:

```
<action-mappings>

      <action
          path="/input"
          type="masteringStruts.InputAction"
          parameter="loadAddForm">
       <forward name="success" path="/input.jsp"/>
     </action>

      <action
          path="/inputSubmit"
          type="masteringStruts.InputAction"
          name="inputForm"
          scope="request"
          validate="true"
          input="/input.jsp">
```

```
            <forward name="success" path="/success.jsp"/>
            <forward name="resubmit" path="/resubmit.jsp"/>
        </action>

    </action-mappings>
```

Action's saveToken method generates and saves a transaction token and puts it in session scope under the key Globals.TRANSACTION_TOKEN_KEY. Think of a transaction token as a unique string.

Notice that the action mapping for input sets the parameter to loadAddForm. The action will use the parameter to load the form.

We already have an InputAction for this form that processes the form once it is validated. Thus, we need to modify the InputAction so that it can handle loading the form by calling saveToken:

```
public class InputAction extends Action {

    public ActionForward execute(
        ActionMapping mapping,
        ActionForm form,
        HttpServletRequest request,
        HttpServletResponse response)
        throws Exception {

        if ("loadAddForm".equals(mapping.getParameter())) {
            return loadAddUserForm(mapping, form, request, response);
        } else {
            return add(mapping, form, request, response);
        }

    }

    public ActionForward loadAddUserForm(
        ActionMapping mapping,
        ActionForm form,
        HttpServletRequest request,
        HttpServletResponse response)
        throws Exception {
            saveToken(request);
            return mapping.findForward("success");
    }
...
```

If you have been following along, you realize that we want to pass the parameter back to the action when the form is submitted. And you may think you need to add your own hidden field to the form. Actually, the html:form tag does this bit of magic for us; in fact, here is a code snippet from html:form:

```
String token =
    (String) session.getAttribute(Globals.TRANSACTION_TOKEN_KEY);

if (token != null) {
    results.append("<input type=\"hidden\" name=\"");
    results.append(Constants.TOKEN_KEY);
```

```
                results.append("\" value=\"");
                results.append(token);
                if (this.isXhtml()) {
                    results.append("\" />");
                } else {
                    results.append("\">");
                }
            }
```

Now, as you'll recall from Step 2, when the user submits the form call isTokenValid, the code should handle the form only if the token is valid. Now that we know the form will have the transaction token, we can check to see whether it exists by using isTokenValid. When the user submits the valid form, the add method is called on the InputAction:

```
public class InputAction extends Action {

    public ActionForward execute(
        ActionMapping mapping,
        ActionForm form,
        HttpServletRequest request,
        HttpServletResponse response)
        throws Exception {

        if ("loadAddForm".equals(mapping.getParameter())) {
            return loadAddUserForm(mapping, form, request, response);
        } else {
            return add(mapping, form, request, response);
        }

    }

  ...

    public ActionForward add(
        ActionMapping mapping,
        ActionForm form,
        HttpServletRequest request,
        HttpServletResponse response)
        throws Exception {

        ...
        if ( isTokenValid(request, true)){
            InputForm inputForm = (InputForm) form;
            // Do something useful with this form!
            return mapping.findForward("success");
        } else{
            // Invalid token! User tried to submit form twice.
            return mapping.findForward("resubmit");
        }

    }
```

The way the add method is implemented, it will not allow a user to submit a form, then hit the Backspace key and submit the same form again. If the token is valid, the add method will do something useful with the form and then forward to success. If the token is not valid, the user is forwarded to the "resubmit" forward.

In RC1, saveToken and isTokenValid methods were implemented in the Action class. They have been refactored, and now all they do is delegate to methods of the same name in TokenProcessor (in the Struts util package). Thus, you can use these methods in your own Web components (e.g., the Tile controller, a custom RequestProcessor, JSP custom tags).

The RequestUtils computeParameters method optionally adds a transaction token to its list of parameters. The computeParameters method is used by the html:link, bean:include, html:rewrite, and logic:redirect tags. Many tags are transaction token aware.

Take a look at the JavaDocs for TokenProcessor to learn more and to see some variations of these methods. You can check the source code for TokenProcessor to gain a good understanding of how things really work.

Action isCancelled

It is often nice to give your user the ability to cancel an operation. Struts provides a special input field called html:cancel:

```
<html:form action="inputSubmit">

  <bean:message key="inputForm.userName"/>
  <html:text property='userName'/> <br />

  <bean:message key="inputForm.password"/>
  <html:text property='password'/> <br />
  ...
  <html:cancel/>
</html:form>
```

You can use this input field to cancel a form submission. Then you just use the isCancelled method in the action handler to see whether the action was canceled:

```
public class InputAction extends Action {

    public ActionForward execute(
        ActionMapping mapping,
        ActionForm form,
        HttpServletRequest request,
        HttpServletResponse response)
        throws Exception {

        if ("loadAddForm".equals(mapping.getParameter())) {
            return loadAddUserForm(mapping, form, request, response);
        } else {
            return add(mapping, form, request, response);
        }
```

```
    }
...
    public ActionForward add(
        ActionMapping mapping,
        ActionForm form,
        HttpServletRequest request,
        HttpServletResponse response)
        throws Exception {


        if (isCancelled(request)) {
            System.out.println("this submission has been cancelled");
            return mapping.findForward("home");
        } else if ( isTokenValid(request, true)){
            InputForm inputForm = (InputForm) form;
            System.out.println(inputForm.getUserName());
            return mapping.findForward("success");
        } else{
            System.out.println("Can't resubmit the same form twice");
            return mapping.findForward("resubmit");
        }

    }
```

This action handler checks to see whether the operation was canceled. If it was, the action forwards the user to the home page.

Action getLocale and setLocale

You can dynamically set the locale for the user's session. Essentially, you let users decide what locale they want, using a form or link. Think of an automated teller machine (ATM); the first thing it often asks you is what language you speak, and you press the appropriate button. Well, you could do the same thing for your site.

To do this magic, you have an action tied to a form or link that reads the locale information from the request, creates a java.util.Locale, and stores the locale in session scope under the key Globals.LOCALE_KEY using the setLocale method:

```
public class SetLocaleAction extends Action {

  public ActionForward execute(
            ActionMapping mapping,
            ActionForm form,
            HttpServletRequest request,
            HttpServletResponse response) throws Exception {

    String language = request.getParameter("language");
       String country = request.getParameter("country");

    Locale locale = new Locale(language, country);
```

```
        setLocale(request,locale);


        if (getLocale(request).getLanguage().equals("en")){

            System.out.println("the language is set to English");
            // Do something special for those who are logged in
            // who speak English. Perhaps some features
            // are different or disabled for English.
            ...
        }
        ...

        return actionMapping.findForward("success");

    }
}
```

Notice that you can also get the locale and operate on it accordingly if needed. All of the tags (such as bean:message) respect this locale for the entire user session.

See Chapter 9, "Internationalizing Your Struts Applications," for more details on how to support the internationalization (i18n) features with resource bundles and bean:message.

Action saveMessages and getResources

Back in the primordial ooze of Struts pre-1.1, people liked ActionErrors. They started using them for tasks for which they were never intended. People started using ActionErrors as a general-purpose way to display i18n-enabled dynamic messages. Then Struts 1.1 added the concept of ActionMessages. If you recall from our ActionErrors discussion in Chapter 10, "Managing Errors," ActionErrors subclass ActionMessages. Now you can use ActionMessages to display dynamic i18n-enabled messages without feeling like a hack.

Working with ActionMessages is nearly identical to working with ActionErrors. Here is an example of adding ActionMessages that you want to be displayed inside an Actions Execute method:

```
public ActionForward execute(
    ActionMapping mapping,
    ActionForm form,
    HttpServletRequest request,
    HttpServletResponse response)
    throws Exception {

    ActionMessages messages = new ActionMessages();



    ActionMessage message = new ActionMessage("inputForm.greet");
    messages.add(ActionMessages.GLOBAL_MESSAGE, message);

    ...
    saveMessages(request,messages);
    ...
```

Then to display the messages in the JSP, you use the html:messages tag as follows:

```
<ul>
<font color='green' >
<html:messages id="message" message="true">
  <li><%= message %></li>
</html:messages>
</font>
</ul>
```

The html:messages tag will iterate over all of the messages. Notice that the message attribute of html:messages is set to true. This forces html:messages to get the messages from Globals.MESSAGE_KEY in request scope. If you do not set the message attribute, the html:messages tag will display the errors instead (Globals.ERROR_KEY).

What if you want to display an arbitrary number of messages—and it could vary by locale? In that case, you use getResources to get the number of messages for that locale:

```
public ActionForward execute(
    ActionMapping mapping,
    ActionForm form,
    HttpServletRequest request,
    HttpServletResponse response)
    throws Exception {

    ActionMessages messages = new ActionMessages();



    ActionMessage message = new ActionMessage("inputForm.greet");
    messages.add(ActionMessages.GLOBAL_MESSAGE, message);

    String num =
        this.getResources(request).getMessage("inputForm.messageNum");

    int messageCount = Integer.parseInt(num);
    for(int index=0; index<messageCount; index++){
        String messageKey="inputForm.message" + index;
        message = new ActionMessage(messageKey);
        messages.add(ActionMessages.GLOBAL_MESSAGE, message);
    }
    saveMessages(request,messages);

    System.out.println(Globals.MESSAGE_KEY);
    if (messages ==
         request.getAttribute(Globals.MESSAGE_KEY)){
       System.out.println("its there can't you see it");
    }
   ...
```

The previous code corresponds to the following resource bundle entries:

```
inputForm.greet=Hello Welcome to Trivera Technologies
inputForm.messageNum=2
inputForm.message0=Please be sure to fill out your phone ...
inputForm.message1=Pick a user name and password you can remember
```

The inputForm.messageNum method specifies the number of messages for the inputForm. The for loop iterates up to the count of messages, grabbing each message for inputForm—that is, inputForm.message0, inputForm.message1, and so on.

These examples cause the messages in the resource bundle to display in an unordered list at the top of the input JSP page.

The RequestUtils class has a method called getActionMessages() that is used by logic:messagePresent and html:messages. The getActionMessages method allows you to retrieve the messages saved by Action.saveMessages and Action.saveErrors. The messages look like the one shown in Figure 21.1.

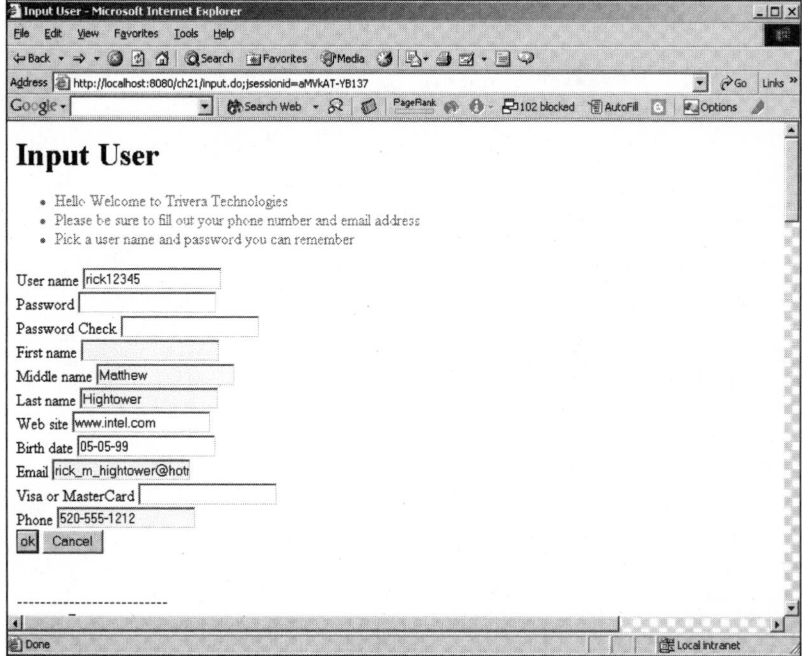

Figure 21.1 The getActionMessages method allows you to retrieve messages.

Populating ActionForms with Domain Objects

To populate an ActionForm with a domain object so that it can be displayed on an input JSP with html:form, you first have to create an action that is called before the form:

```
<action path="/readUser"
        type="rickhightower.ReadUserAction"
        name="UserForm" scope="request" validate="false">
    <forward name="success" path="/userForm.jsp"/>
</action>
```

Notice that we mapped in the form that the userForm will display. This form will be created and passed to the execute method of ReadUserAction before the userForm.jsp service method is called. This gives the code an opportunity to populate the form and put it into scope so that the userForm.jsp's html:form tag can display it.

Here is an example of the ReadUserAction's execute method:

```
public ActionForward execute(
    ActionMapping mapping,
    ActionForm form,
    HttpServletRequest request,
    HttpServletResponse response)
                           throws Exception {

        //Get the user id of
    String id = request.getParameter("id");

        //Obtain the default DAOFactory
    DAOFactory factory = DAOFactory.getDefaultfactory();

        //Obtain the DAO for users
    UserDAO userDAO = factory.getUserDAO();

        //Retrieve the user from the database
    UserDTO user = userDAO.getUser(id);

        //Cast the form to a UserForm
    UserForm userForm = (UserForm)form;

        //Copy over the properties from the DTO to the form.
    BeanUtils.copyProperties(userForm,user);

        //Many struts developers add this next code segment, but it is
        //not necessary because it is done by the RequestProcessor
        //if ("request".equals(mapping.getScope())) {
        //request.setAttribute(mapping.getAttribute(), form);
        //} else {
        //request.getSession().
        //setAttribute(mapping.getAttribute(), form);
        //}

    ...
```

Notice that the action does not create a new UserForm. It did not need to because the action mapping caused a form to be created. The code looks up the user based on an ID that was passed as a request parameter. Then it uses BeanUtils.copyProperties (org.apache.commons.beanutils.BeanUtils) to copy the domain objects properties to the userForm. The userForm properties should all be of type String (Strings are best for validation). The domain objects properties can be any primitive type or wrapper objects (BeanUtils will perform the type conversion automatically).

However, BeanUtils does not convert dates well. This means that you cannot have properties that are dates with the same property name as the form. If you do, you will have to use the BeanUtils.describe method in combination with the BeanUtils populate method. The describe method converts a bean into a Map, where the name/value pairs in the Map correspond to the properties in the bean. The populate method populates bean properties with name/value pairs from a Map. Therefore, you would describe the domain object. Remove the offending property from the Map and then use the populate method. For simple form-to-domain object mapping, it is easy to use form.setXXX(domainObject.getXXX()); for more complex forms, BeanUtils saves the day.

It is probably best just to avoid property name type mismatches by having different names, as follows:

```
SimpleDateFormat sdf = new SimpleDateFormat("yyyy-MM-dd");
String dateString = sdf.format(user.getHireDate());
userForm.setDateHire(dateString);
```

Note that userForm's property is called dateHire and that the domain object user date property is called hireDate. A third option is to create and register a custom Converter; see the JavaDocs for org.apache.commons.beanutils.converters to learn more. Using converters to do this is a best practice.

Uploading Files

Let's say that you want users to be able to upload a picture of themselves. To do this, you must enable file upload in your Struts application. Of course, you don't want them to upload a 1GB image of themselves, so you have to put some limits on the pictures that users upload.

First, set up two areas for enabling the uploading of files: enable the user to supply the file with an HTML form, and enable the Struts application to process the file upload.

To enable the user to upload a file, set the encoding type of html:form to multipart/form-data and use the html:file tag as follows:

```
<html:form action="/UserUpdate"
           method="post"
           enctype="multipart/form-data">

   <html:file property="userImage"/> <br />
  ...
```

The property userImage in the userForm is of type FormFile (org.apache.struts.upload.FormFile). FormFile represents the file sent by the client. FormFile has a method called getInputStream, which returns an InputStream. The action handler for this form uses FormFile to access the file:

```
public ActionForward execute(ActionMapping mapping,
                             ActionForm form,
                             HttpServletRequest request,
                             HttpServletResponse response) throws Exception {
    UserForm userForm = (UserForm) form;

    InputStream inputStream =
         userForm.getUserImage().getInputStream();
    // Do something with the inputStream, it is the file data.
    ...
  }
```

To set up the Struts application to restrict file size and to specify the directory location, you could set up a controller element:

```
<controller maxFileSize="200K" tempDir="/temp/struts/user/uploads/"/>
```

This code snippet states that the temporary files will be put into a directory provided by your servlet container in the directory /temp/struts/user/uploads/ and that users are allowed to upload files up to 200KB only.You can also specify the size of the input buffer and other parameters; see Chapter 15, "The struts-config.xml File," for more details.

At eBlox, we allowed users to upload product data using this Struts feature. When you compare this code to the way we used to have to do it, you can easily see that the Struts approach is much easier than the alternatives.

Context-Sensitive Error Messages

If you have a form with a lot of properties and something goes wrong, you want to give the user more cues than just error messages at the top of the page. For example, you may want to turn the label red by field. You can do this by using logic:messagesPresent:

```
<logic:messagesPresent property="userName">
    <font size="4" color="red">
</logic:messagesPresent>
<bean:message key="inputForm.userName"/>:
<logic:messagesPresent property="userName">
    </font>
</logic:messagesPresent>
<html:text property='userName'/> <br />
```

By specifying the property attribute as userName, we are checking to see whether there are any error messages for the userName property. If there are, we turn the font of the userName red. This snippet contains a lot of repetitive JSP code. You may want to either write a visual component with a Tile layout (see Chapter 13, "Using Tiles," to learn more) or write a custom tag. The following is a custom tag that does the job:

```
package trivera.tags.html;

import java.util.Iterator;

import javax.servlet.jsp.JspException;
import javax.servlet.jsp.tagext.BodyTagSupport;

import org.apache.struts.Globals;
import org.apache.struts.action.ActionErrors;
import org.apache.struts.util.RequestUtils;
import org.apache.struts.util.ResponseUtils;

/**
 *
 * @jsp.tag name="redIfError"
 *          body-content="JSP"
 */
public class RedIfErrorTag extends BodyTagSupport {

    private String property;

    private boolean isError() throws JspException{
        ActionErrors actionErrors =
          RequestUtils.getActionErrors(pageContext,Globals.ERROR_KEY);


        if (actionErrors == null){
            return false;
        }

        Iterator iter =  actionErrors.get(this.getProperty());
        if (iter==null) return false;
        if (iter.hasNext()==false)return false;
        return true;
    }


    /** Getter for property property.
     * @return Value of property property.
     * @jsp.attribute required="false"
     *                rtexprvalue="false"
     *                description="The property attribute"
     */
    public String getProperty() {
        return property;
    }

    /**
     * @param string
     */
    public void setProperty(String string) {
        property = string;
    }

    /* (non-Javadoc)
```

```
     * @see javax.servlet.jsp.tagext.IterationTag#doAfterBody()
     */
    public int doAfterBody() throws JspException {
        boolean wasErrors = isError();

        StringBuffer buffer = new StringBuffer(50);
        if (wasErrors){ //For real projects, use CSS
            buffer.append("<font color=\"red\" size='4'>");
        }

        buffer.append(this.bodyContent.getString());

        try{

            this.bodyContent.clear();
        }catch(Exception e){
            throw new JspException(e);
        }


        if (wasErrors){
            buffer.append("</font>");
        }

        ResponseUtils.writePrevious(pageContext, buffer.toString());
        return SKIP_BODY;
    }

}
```

Notice the liberal use of Struts utility classes. Now we can use that code as follows:

```
<thtml:redIfError property="userName">
<bean:message key="inputForm.userName"/>:
       </thtml:redIfError>
```

> **In a future release of Struts, look for a tag called html:label. This tag is under development by Erik Hatcher, and will likely be in a future release of Struts. This tag also integrates with the Validator framework to find the labels. It is similar in concept to redIfError but more advanced. Erik's html:label uses CSS instead of <font>. Using CSS is a best practice.**

So how did we know how to write this custom tag? Easy! Just look at the Struts source code for the tags that are most like the tag you want to write. Don't be afraid of the code!

Another thing you may want to do is put the message right next to the field. You can do that with <html:messages>:

```
<html:text property='userName'/>
 <html:messages id="message" property='userName'>
 <font color="red">
 <%=message%>
```

```
</font>
</html:messages>
```

The problem with this code is that you would have to type it out for each property in the form. Notice in Figure 21.2 how that code would put the image right by the field.

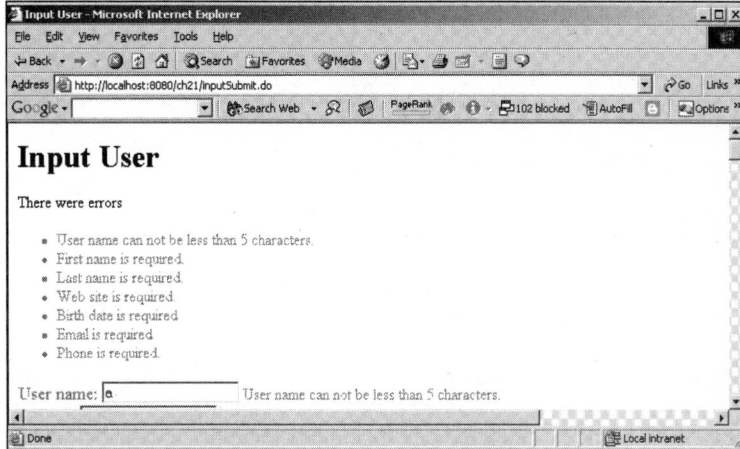

Figure 21.2 The message appears next to the field.

You can write your own custom tag or Tile layout component that does a similar thing so that you don't have to repeat the code for each field:

```
import java.util.Iterator;

import javax.servlet.jsp.JspException;

import org.apache.struts.Globals;
import org.apache.struts.action.ActionError;
import org.apache.struts.action.ActionErrors;
import org.apache.struts.taglib.html.TextTag;

import org.apache.struts.util.RequestUtils;
import org.apache.struts.util.ResponseUtils;

/**
 *
 * @jsp.tag name="text-ext"
 *          body-content="JSP"
 *
 */
public class TextTagExt extends TextTag {

    /*
     */
    public int doAfterBody() throws JspException {
        ActionErrors actionErrors = (ActionErrors)
```

```
                pageContext.getRequest().getAttribute(Globals.ERROR_KEY);
        if (actionErrors!=null){

            Iterator iter =  actionErrors.get(this.getProperty());
            while (iter.hasNext()){

                ActionError error =  (ActionError) iter.next();
                String key = error.getKey();
                Object [] values = error.getValues();
                String message = RequestUtils.
                        message(pageContext, null, null, key, values);

                ResponseUtils.write(pageContext,message + "    ");
            }
        }
        return SKIP_BODY;
    }

}
```

The previous tag subclasses the tag handler for form:text. It then uses RequestUtils.message to retrieve the message for the property out of the ressource bundle. To subclass TextTag, we had to study it so we could figure out where it could be extended. We find extending the customs tags makes them a bit fragile; the extentions points are not well documented and there is not much consistency of implementation from tag to tag. Therefore, to use the tag

```
<thtml:text property="userName" />
```

without our custom tags, the following would turn the label red and put the error text by the field (where thtml is our own tag library):

```
<logic:messagesPresent property="userName">
    <font size="4" color="red">
</logic:messagesPresent>
<bean:message key="inputForm.userName"/>:
<logic:messagesPresent property="userName">
    </font>
</logic:messagesPresent>
 <html:text property='userName'/>
 <html:messages id="message" property='userName'>
 <font color="red">
 <%=message%>
 </font>
 </html:messages>
 <br />
```

By developing our own custom tags, we can rewrite the above as follows:

```
<thtml:redIfError property="userName">
           <bean:message key="inputForm.userName"/>:
</thtml:redIfError>
<thtml:text property="userName" />
```

Best Practices

At this point in the book you have a thorough understanding of how sophisticated a tool Struts really is. This section addresses a range of best practices that, when adhered to, will help you use Struts to its fullest.

i18n Best Practices

If you know the history of Struts, then you know it was built from the ground up to support i18n. If there is a way to do something in an un-i18n way, there is usually also an i18n way to do the same thing. For example, this is how you format a String with bean:write:

```
<bean:write name="employee" property="salary" format="$#.##"/>
```

This code is great—unless of course you are supporting more than one locale, and one of the locales does not support the $ sign. A better way to do that would be:

```
<bean:write name="employee" property="salary" formatKey="patterns.Currency"/>
```

Now instead of hard-coding the way we do formatting, we grab the format key out of the i18n-enabled resource bundle.

Every time you can use a static string with the html:* tag library, you can also use a key to the resource bundle instead. For example:

```
<html:image pageKey="icons.exit"

  altKey="icons.exit.alternate"  titleKey="icons.exit.title"/>
```

The image tag has page, alt, and title attributes, but if you use those you mess up your i18n support. Always use the ${attributeName}Key version of the attribute instead. The previous code snippet grabs the alternative text from the image out of the resource bundle and also takes the title text out of the resource bundle. And (what may not appear to be as intuitive) it grabs the icon path (pageKey) out of the resource bundle. It does this because iconography is not the same from locale to locale. In addition, some images have text in them, which would vary from locale to locale.

In addition to the custom tags, both the Validator framework and the Tiles framework support i18n in their configuration files. Use this support liberally to vary things such as lists of links (Tiles) and different types of validation based on locale.

Read the DTDs

There are all kinds of golden nuggets and comments in the document type definition (DTD). You should have a copy of the source for whatever release you are using to develop your applications; the DTDs ship with the source. Read the DTDs for all of the configuration files (struts-config.xml, validation.xml, tiles-def.xml). It is time well spent.

Read the Source

You'll find all kinds of golden nuggets and comments in the source as well. You should have a copy of the source for whatever release you are using to develop your applications. If you want to develop a routine or custom tag, look for a custom tag or routine that does something similar in the Struts API, and then study how the creator implemented it. Also, when something does not work the way you think it should, you have the source (the ultimate documentation) to refer to. Keep the source handy. You will need it.

Understand MVC, Model 2, Sun's Blueprints for J2EE, and J2EE design patterns

To get the most out of Struts, you should have a background with Model-View-Controller (MVC) and Java 2 Enterprise Edition (J2EE) design patterns, such as the data transfer object (DTO), the front controller, and so forth. You should also understand Sun's vision for J2EE Web applications as explained in the Blueprint documentation. This includes a good understanding of MVC and Model 2 architecture. Also, get yourself a good book on J2EE design patterns. Struts will not prevent you from creating a large mess of an application. You need the requisite background in architecture and design of J2EE Web applications.

Don't Use Java Scriptlets in JSP (<% %>)

I hope that I am preaching to the choir. You should limit your Java scriplets to zilch. This does not apply to Tile layouts that are visual components (stand-ins for custom tags), but it does apply to Tile layouts that are site layouts. In my opinion, this does not include simple Java expressions in JSP (<%=%>).

I don't see much difference between

```
<html:messages id="errorMessage">
  <p class="error"><%= errorMessage %></p>
</html:messages>
```

and

```
<html:messages id="errorMessage">
  <p class="error"><bean:write name="errorMessage"/></p>
</html:messages>
```

except that the latter is more verbose. The purpose of getting rid of Java scriplets (<% %>) is to reduce the logic in your page, not for you to be more verbose. Be pragmatic, not dogmatic.

Limit the Logic in Your JSPs

I've seen some developers ban simple expressions (<%= errorMessage%>) yet litter their JSPs with Struts logic tags (logic:present, logic:empty, logic:notEmpty, logic:match, core:if, and so forth). They are rigid about the details but miss the principle behind the rule. The point is to limit your logic as much as possible in your JSP whether you implement that logic with JSP Standard Tag Library (JSTL) or Struts logic tags. If possible, try to limit your logic to iteration (logic:iterate and core:forEach regularly) and see if an object is present before displaying it.

There are several ways to limit the logic in your JSPs. You can use the logic:present tag to see whether model objects are mapped into scope. If they are, then you display them (otherwise, you do not display them). This way, you move the logic while it is in scope to the Controller (the action). If you change the rules and map them into scope for different reasons, the JSP never knows the difference. Keep the logic in your JSPs thin.

Another approach to limiting the logic in the page is to use Tiles and forward to Tile definitions. This is a powerful approach. You can use it to eliminate a lot of logic in your JSPs. For example, if a user is logged in as a manager versus a regular user, you can forward that user to a definition that specifies parameter Tiles that only a manager can use. The manager's definition can extend the regular uses definition and define attributes that include areas only for the manager. The two types of users can even use the same Tile layout if the layout uses the insert tag with the ignore attribute (to clarify areas that are unavailable if the person is logged in as a user but available in the manager's definition). The action could select the correct forward, and you would not have to use a logic:* tag at all. Getting logic out of your JSPs and into the Controller is a step in the right direction and is so much easier when you are using Tiles.

If you see yourself writing the same three custom tags over and over, either create a Tile layout that acts a visual component or write a custom tag. See the earlier section "Context-Sensitive Error Messages" and Chapter 13 for more details.

Create Multiple Resource Bundles per Module

You spent all of this time making your application object oriented, modular, and well designed. You've mastered MVC, and you've limited the logic in your JSPs. Your actions never talk directly to the database using Java Database Connectivity (JDBC); they always talk to the model to get DTOs and choose the next view. Yet you have a resource bundle that has 5000 messages!

Break up your resource bundle by configuring more than one bundle in your module. (Even if you are not using modules, you get a default module). You might have a bundle for just form labels, and another bundle that is just for patterns, and so forth. Remember that the bean:message tag takes a bundle parameter so that you can specify a bundle.

Break Up Your struts-config.xml File

Your struts-config.xml file is huge! Did you know that you can break it up without creating a new module? The config init-parameter of the Action servlet takes a comma-delimited list of files. This means that you can break up your struts-config.xml file into several smaller, more manageable files (e.g., struts-config.xml, struts-config-forms.xml). Perhaps you could group similar action mappings into one configuration file. Every configuration file in the comma-delimited list can be in the same module.

Break Your Application Up into Modules

You've noticed that you can break up your application into nearly stand-alone modules. Well, you can break up your application into modules. See Chapter 4, "Actions and the ActionServlet" for more details.

The nice thing about breaking your application up into modules is that each module can have its own configuration—for instance, its own RequestProcessor. Also, modules are nice if you have several teams working on the same site and you are tired of stepping on each other's toes. Divide and conquer!

Use html:messages instead of html:errors

The problem with html:errors is that you have to put markup in your resource bundle. Yuck! The nice thing about html:messages is that it iterates over the messages and allows you to leave the markup in the JSP where it belongs.

Remember that when you use html:errors you have to define the following in your resource bundle:

```
errors.header=<ul>
errors.footer</ul>
errors.prefix=<li class="error">
errors.suffix=</li>
```

Now you can do the same with html:messages in the JSP:

```
<ul>
<html:messages id="errorMessage">
  <li class="error"><bean:write name="errorMessage"/></p>
</html:messages>
</ul>
```

This helps you keep the i18n text in the resource bundle and the markup in the JSP page. By default, html:messages works with errors. If you want to work with message, set the message attribute to true. See section "Action saveMessages and getResources" earlier in this chapter for more details.

Develop Your Own Custom Tags

Learn how to develop custom tags. It will help you to create more maintainable JSPs. See the section "Context-Sensitive Error Messages" for a more in-depth discussion. The ability to write custom tags is definitely something you want to add to your repertoire. Many good books and resources are available that describe how to write custom tags, including *Mastering JSP Custom Tags and Tag Libraries*, also written by James Goodwill.

Declaratively Handle Exceptions

One of the major additions to Struts 1.1 is the ability to declaratively define exception handlers in the Struts configuration file. This is nice because it allows you to separate your go code from your exception-handling code. The go code is located in your actions, and the exception-handling code is located in exception handlers. The Struts Framework can handle "uncaught" application exceptions in two ways: by specifying global exception handlers and by specifying a local exception handler per action mapping (as follows):

```
<action path="/addUser"
        type="richhightower.UserAction"
        input="/userForm.jsp" name="userForm"
        scope="request" validate="true">
  <exception key="exception.user.exists"
```

```
              type="rickhightower.UserExistsException"
              path="/exceptions/user_exists.jsp"/>
  <forward name="success"
           path="/userAdded.jsp"/>
</action>
```

You can use html:errors or html:messages in the user_exists.jsp page to display the error message corresponding to the message associated with the exception.user.exists key in the resource bundle. The previous code uses the default exception handler (org.apache.struts.action.ExceptionHandler). If you need an exception handler to take a certain action or perform a certain task, then you could override the exception handler and configure your own using the className attribute:

```
<action path="/addUser"
        type="richhightower.UserAction"
        input="/userForm.jsp" name="userForm"
        scope="request" validate="true">
  <exception key="exception.user.exists"
             type="rickhightower.UserExistsException"
             path="/exceptions/user_exists.jsp"
             className="rickhightower.CustomExceptionHandler"/>
  <forward name="success"
           path="/userAdded.jsp"/>
</action>
```

Here is an example of defining your own custom exception handler:

```
public class CustomExceptionHandler extends ExceptionHandler {


    public ActionForward execute(Exception exception,
                                 ExceptionConfig econfig,
                                 ActionMapping mapping,
                                 ActionForm form,
                                 HttpServletRequest request,
                                 HttpServletResponse response)
        throws ServletException {

         if (exception instanceof rickhightower.UserExistsException){
            //do something special
            ...
         }

         return super.execute(exception, econfig, mapping,
                              form, request, response);
    }
...
```

This code does something special with the exception and then delegates the rest of the flow to the basic exception handler (super class).

For Visual Components, Use Tile Layouts

If you have a visual component and it uses a lot of HTML markup, you should probably implement it as a Tile layout instead of a custom tag. It is okay to use Java scriptlets in this type of JSP. If the JSP is meant as a visual component—that is, a Tile layout—then you can use some Java scriptlets. Try to reduce the scriptlets as much as possible by using a Tile controller. It is not wise to use scriptlets with Tile layouts that are used as site layouts (page layouts). There is no hard-and-fast rule when a Tile layout is a visual component or a page layout. Strive to keep visual components in a directory separate from your other JSPs. See Chapter 13 for more details.

Start Using Tiles

If you are not using Tiles in your Struts projects, you are missing out. Learn how to use Tiles as soon as possible; it will help you separate your logic from your pages and help you reuse markup and custom tags that you would otherwise repeat over and over. See Chapter 13 to learn more.

Start Using the Validator Framework

If you are not using Validator framework in your Struts projects to validate code, start as soon as possible. The Validator framework allows you to reuse validation code on many forms. For example, suppose you have a user login form and a user registration form. Both of these forms have a field called userName, and the userName is validated the same way on both forms. By using the Validator framework, you can define the validation for userName in one place. See Chapter 12, "Working with the Validator," for more information.

Group Related Actions

Actions are often too small, and this ruins the cohesiveness of your application. You can group related actions using DispatchAction or LookupDispatchAction or by using the parameter and writing your own dispatch. Let's look at an example that uses the parameter attribute of the action mapping to implement your own dispatch.

First, we use the same action handler in two action mappings, as follows:

```
<action-mappings>

    <action
        path="/input"
        type="masteringStruts.InputAction"
        parameter="loadAddForm">
     <forward name="success" path="/input.jsp"/>
   </action>

    <action
        path="/inputSubmit"
        type="masteringStruts.InputAction"
        name="inputForm"
        scope="request"
        validate="true"
        input="/input.jsp">
```

```
            <forward name="success" path="/success.jsp"/>
            <forward name="resubmit" path="/resubmit.jsp"/>
        </action>

    </action-mappings>
```

Then we use the parameter attribute as the pivot point to decide which method to invoke (each method is like an action):

```
public class InputAction extends Action {

    public ActionForward execute(
        ActionMapping mapping,
        ActionForm form,
        HttpServletRequest request,
        HttpServletResponse response)
        throws Exception {

        if ("loadAddForm".equals(mapping.getParameter())) {
            return loadAddUserForm(mapping, form, request, response);
        } else {
            return add(mapping, form, request, response);
        }

    }

    public ActionForward loadAddUserForm(
        ActionMapping mapping,
        ActionForm form,
        HttpServletRequest request,
        HttpServletResponse response)
        throws Exception {
    }

    public ActionForward add(
        ActionMapping mapping,
        ActionForm form,
        HttpServletRequest request,
        HttpServletResponse response)
        throws Exception {

        ...
}
...
```

The execute method invokes the loadAddUserForm method if the parameter is set to loadAddForm; otherwise, it executes the add method. This is simple and straightforward, and unlike DispatchAction, it is completely hidden from the client in the confines of the Struts configuration file.

To learn more about DispatchAction and LookupDispatchAction, see Chapter 5, "Advanced Action Classes."

Never Link to a JSP

Never link directly to a JSP page from a JSP page. This breaks the MVC model. An Action (part of the Controller) should always be executed before a JSP displays. For a complete discussion of this topic, see Chapter 5 (read the section "Linking to JSP Directly: More than Just Bad Design").

Extend Actions with Action Chaining

Let's say that you have an action that is a lot like another action. In fact, it does everything the first action does along with a few other things. At first, you might consider subclassing it, but subclassing adds a lot of coupling from your new action to the old action. Instead, you can extend the action using action chaining, as shown here:

```
<action-mappings>

     <action
          path="/old"
          type="masteringStruts.OldAction"
          >
       <forward name="success" path="/success.jsp"/>
     </action>

     <action
          path="/extendedOld"
          type="masteringStruts.OldAction"
          >
       <forward name="success" path="/new.do"/>
     </action>

     <action
          path="/new"
          type="masteringStruts.NewAction"
          >
       <forward name="success" path="/success.jsp"/>
     </action>

</action-mappings>
```

The extendedOld action mapping does everything the old action mapping did along with everything the new action mapping does—and we did not have to subclass the old action. You can extend other actions in the same manner.

Don't Use DynaActionForms without the Validator Framework

Don't use DynaActionForms without the Validator framework; otherwise, you will have to handle all of your form validation in your actions (using saveErrors). You'd be circumventing the Struts validation mechanism and workflow for not much benefit. To see how to integrate DynaActionForms with the Validator framework, see Chapter 12.

Use JSTL instead of Struts-Equivalent Tags

Use JSTL in place of the built-in Struts tags whenever their functionality overlaps. JSTL consists of four tag libraries: core, format, xml, and sql.

The core tag library is similar to the Struts bean and logic taglibs in that it provides custom actions for managing data through scoped variables, as well as iteration and logic based on the page content. The core library also has some aspects of the Struts html library in that it provides tags for generating and operating on URLs for URL rewriting (for session management).

The format taglib has tags for formatting numbers and dates. It also provides support for i18n similar to Struts' bean:message custom tag in the bean taglib.

The xml taglib provides tags for manipulating XML via XPath and Extensible Stylesheet Language (XSL)-like support. The sql taglib defines actions for manipulating and updating relational databases.

You can define JSTL custom tag Attribute values using the JSTL expression language (EL). The EL provides identifiers, accessors, and operators. It allows you to retrieve and manipulate values in JSP scopes (session, request, page, application), headers, cookies, and parameters. It takes the place of many of the bean:* tags (bean:header, bean:parameter, bean:define, bean:cookie).

The EL syntax resembles a combination of JavaScript and XML Path Language, with an emphasis on looking up beans and their properties and performing operations on them.

Use core:out instead of bean:write

EL expressions are delimited using a dollar sign ($) and curly braces ({}) as follows:

```
<core:out value="${employee.firstName}"/>
```

The previous snippet prints out the firstName property of the employee bean. It is similar in purpose to the following scriptlet:

```
<%
 Employee employee (Employee) = request.getAttribute("employee");
 out.println( employee.getFirstName());
%>
```

Unlike with Struts' bean:write, you can use many expressions in the same string:

```
<core:out value="Employee Record: ${employee.firstName}
${employee.lastName}"/>
```

Compare this snippet with doing the same thing using bean:write:

```
Employee Record:
<bean:write name="employee" property="firstName"/>
<bean:write name="employee" property="lastName"/>
```

Use core:set instead of bean:define

The <core:set> custom tag defines beans similar to the struts custom tag bean:define. The following defines the bean companyName with the value Intel in session scope:

```
<core:set var="companyName" scope="session" value="Intel"/>
```

Think of how you would do the bean:define equivalent. Also remember that the value can be any JSTL expression. The JSTL expression does not have to be simple; they can be fairly complex.

The following defines a bean called sum in request scope by multiplying the numeric equivalent of the request parameters dailySalary and numberOfDays:

```
<core:set var="sum"
   value="${param['dailySalary'] * param['numberOfDay']}"
   scope="request"/>
```

The expression param['dailySalary'] is equivalent to request.getParameter("dailySalary").

The param object is a built-in JSTL object that refers to request parameters. Think of it as a HashMap of request parameters.

There are many other built-in objects. Many of them are the same as the implicit objects of JSP pages with the addition of the following map-like objects: pageScope, requestScope, sessionScope, applicationScope, param, header, and initParam.

The JSTL EL negates the reason behind many of the Struts logic tags.

Use JSTL core:if and core:forEach instead of Struts logic:*

You can use the core:forEach tag in place of logic:iterate. For example, use

```
<core:forEach items="${results}" var="currentCD">
    <core:out value="${currentCD.ID}"/> <br />
</core:forEach>
```

instead of:

```
<logic:iterate name="results" id="currentCD" scope="request">
      <jsp:getProperty  name="currentCD" property="ID"/> <br />
</logic:iterate>
```

The core:if tag checks to see if an expression is true. It has the following syntax:

```
<core:if
    test="expression"
    var="name"
    scope="scope">
          body content
</core:if>
```

When you use the power of JSTL EL, the core:if tag takes the place of bean:equal, bean:notEqual, bean:greaterEqual, bean:lessEqual, bean:greaterThan, bean:lessThan, bean:present, and so on.

Covering all of the capabilities of JSTL and the JSTL EL is beyond the scope of this book, but you've got a glimpse of why you should use JSTL. Some tags in Struts have no JSTL equivalent. But when an equivalent is available, you should almost always use the JSTL version.

Use JSTL EL in Your Custom Tags

You want to start developing custom tags that support JSTL EL. How can you do this? It is actually quite simple. The Jakarta Taglibs project ships with an API for the JSTL EL so that you can use the same Expression Parser that the reference implementation of JSTL uses; namely, the ExpressionEvaluatorManager (org.apache.taglibs.standard.lang.support.ExpressionEvaluatorManager).

The ExpressionEvaluatorManager is easy to use because it has only one method:

```
public static Object evaluate(
                                        String  attributeName,
                                        String expression,
                                        Class expectedType,
                                        Tag tag,
                                        PageContext pageContext)
```

Here is an example how the core:if tag uses the ExpressionEvaluatorManager:

```
Object r = ExpressionEvaluatorManager
.evaluate("test",
test,
Boolean.class,
this,
pageContext);
```

As you can see, this code is pretty straightforward. The attribute is called test, so we pass test as the attributeName. The expression is from the test attribute, so we pass the test property from the custom tag. The core:if tag expects a Boolean (true or false), so we specify Boolean.class as the expectedType. If we did not know the expected type, we could pass Object.class. We know that the EL has access to all of the implicit objects of JSP, so we pass it the pageContext.

In addition to providing EL support to custom tags, JSTL provides Tag classes that simplify the lifecycle of tags, which makes them easier to write.

The class ConditionalTagSupport (javax.servlet.jsp.jstl.core.ConditionalTagSupport) facilitates development of conditional tags—that is, tags like <core:if>. The body of this tag is a conditional executed based on one single overridable condition() method.

Thus, to use this class you just need to subclass and override one method. The condition method returns true or false, and it represents the condition that the subclass uses to drive behavior. You don't have to implement doStartTag, doEndTag, or doAfterBody—you just have to implement condition(). Whew! It makes developing tags like this so much easier.

Here is an example of a JSTL-style tag that uses ConditionalTagSupport (it is similar to the tag we defined earlier without the JSTL API):

```
public class IfErrorTag extends ConditionalTagSupport {

    private String property;

    public boolean condition(){
    try{

        ActionErrors actionErrors =
RequestUtils.getActionErrors(pageContext,Globals.ERROR_KEY);


        if (actionErrors == null){
            return false;
        }

        Iterator iter =  actionErrors.get(this.getProperty());
        if (iter==null) return false;
        if (iter.hasNext()==false)return false;
        return true;
    }catch(Exception e){
        throw new RuntimeException(e);
    }
    }


    /** Getter for property property.
     * @return Value of property property.
     * @jsp.attribute required="false"
     *                rtexprvalue="false"
     *                description="The property attribute"
     */
    public String getProperty() {
        return property;
    }

    /**
     * @param string
     */
    public void setProperty(String string) {
        property = string;
    }

}
```

The condition() method of this tag checks to see if the property (specified by the property attribute) has any errors associated with it. The LoopTagSupport() method facilitates the development of iteration custom tags. LoopTagSupport defines default logic for iteration tags to subclass.

Most iteration tags behave in a similar way with regard to the looping functionality, so LoopTagSupport implements this behavior. That way, you don't have to reinvent the wheel. All you need to do is subclass LoopTagSupport and override the next() and hasNext() methods.

The hasNext() method returns true if there are more items. The next() method advances the iteration and returns the object at the current iteration. The beautiful thing is that you don't have to implement doStartTag, doEndTag, doAfterBody, and so forth—you only have to implement next() and hasNext().

Useful Related Utilities

No tool, framework, or programming language is an island. One of the arts of software development is assembling a set of complementary tools that, together, enable you to create better software faster. This section discusses several tools that are ideal for use with Struts.

Cactus

Cactus is a framework that extends JUnit. It allows you to test Web components inside the J2EE container. If you haven't already, you should adopt a process in which you test all of your code.

Some experts advocate a test-driven approach in which you write your tests before you write your code. I think that this approach helps you write better code. Testable code implies that the code has cleaner interfaces, with improved cohesion and coupling held to a minimum. Spaghetti code is difficult to test; clean code is easy to test.

If you've used JUnit before, then getting started with Cactus is easy. Cactus runs on both the client and the server. The test*XXX* runs on the server. Several methods are involved in the test: setUp, begin*XXX*, test*XXX*, end*XXX*, and tearDown (where *XXX* is the name of the test).

The begin*XXX* method is executed before test*XXX* and is executed on the client. This gives you an opportunity in the begin*XXX* method to set up request parameters. After begin*XXX*, Cactus "calls" ServletRedirector remotely over HTTP. ServletRedirector is a component on the server that starts tests.

Cactus sends parameter data to ServletRedirector, tells the engine which test to run on the server, and passes along any request parameter you set up in the begin*XXX* method. ServletRedirector instantiates a new copy of test case copies container objects to test case. Then it calls the setUp method (on the server), calls test*XXX* (on the server), and calls tearDown (on the server).

The end*XXX* method runs on the client and is passed a WebResponse object that contains the output of the Web component. The end*XXX* method executes on the client so that you can test the response.

Let's say we have a simple servlet to test:

```
public class MapperServlet extends HttpServlet{

  public void doGet(HttpServletRequest request,
                    HttpServletResponse response)throws IOException{

    Map paramMap =  SessionMapper.mapRequestToSession(request);
    PrintWriter writer = response.getWriter();

    Set mapEntries = paramMap.entrySet();
    Map.Entry e = null;
    for(Iterator iter = mapEntries.iterator(); iter.hasNext();){
```

```
          Map.Entry entry = (Map.Entry)iter.next();
          String entryStr = entry.getKey() + "=" + entry.getValue();
          if(useAllCaps()){
            entryStr = entryStr.toUpperCase();
          }
          writer.println(entryStr);
        }
      }

...
}
```

This servlet is simple; it takes request parameters and maps them into session scope. It then prints the parameter data out to the browser (optionally capitalizing the data based on servlet config parameters). Let's say we want to write a test that does the following: It makes sure items are mapped into session on the server with test*XXX* and makes sure items are sent to the browser with end*XXX*. We also want to send some setup data in begin*XXX*.

You first extend ServletTestCase:

```
import org.apache.commons.cactus.*;
import junit.framework.*;

public class MapperServletTest extends ServletTestCase{
private MapperServlet servlet;
public MapperServletTest(String name) {
        super(name);
}
```

Next you want to override the setUp method and create an instance of Servlet under Test:

```
public void setUp()throws Exception{
        this.config.setInitParameter("ALL_CAPS","true");
        servlet = new MapperServlet();
        servlet.init(config);
    }
```

Next you need to write the tests for doGet (notice the addition of begin*XXX*, end*XXX*, and test*XXX*, where *XXX* is the name of the test):

```
   public void beginDoGet(ServletTestRequest request){
        request.addParameter("foo","manchu");
    }

    public void testDoGet() throws Exception{
        servlet.doGet(request, response);
        /*maps the parameters into the session as a side effect*/
        String value = (String)session.getAttribute("foo");
        assertEquals("request param mapped into session", "manchu", value);
    }

    public void endDoGet(WebResponse response) throws Exception{
        String responseString = response.getText();
```

```
        boolean paramInResponse =
                    responseString.indexOf("FOO=MANCHU") > -1;
        assertTrue("param not found in response", paramInResponse);
    }
```

If your are not familiar with HttpUnit, you may want to become familiar with it. You can use it in combination with Cactus by using it with a specialized end*XXX* method, as follows:

```
public void endDoGet(com.meterware.httpunit.WebResponse theResponse) {
       WebTable table = theResponse.getTables()[0];
       assertEquals("rows", 4, table.getRowCount());
       assertEquals("columns", 3,
                        table.getColumnCount());
       ...
}
```

HttpUnit, unlike Cactus, does not extend the JUnit framework. HttpUnit provides simplified access to the HTML Document Object Model (DOM). It has a set of helper methods that make dealing with HTML responses easy.

HttpUnit can be found at http://www.httpunit.org/. Cactus is a Jakarta project and can be found at http://jakarta.apache.org/cactus/index.html.

Our example so far covers how to test a servlet. Of course, if you are developing with Struts you will not be testing many servlets; you could, however, use Cactus to test a JSP:

```
public class SalesReport extends JspTestCase {
...
//Setup session in setUp method if needed
//Setup request parameters in beginXXX if needed
public void testSalesReport() {
    RequestDispatcher rd =
         theConfig.getServletContext().
          getRequestDispatcher("/salesreport.jsp");

    rd.forward(theRequest, theResponse);
   //Check Session scope variable
}

public void endTestSalesReport(
         com.meterware.httpunit.WebResponse theResponse) {
     //Use HttpUnit to verify the HTML
}
```

If you have adopted MVC, you realize that JSPs should not really do much. It might make more sense to test the JSP through the action. This gives the action a chance to map in model items into scope so that the JSP can use them (otherwise, you would have to set up the model items in the setUp method):

```
public class SalesReport extends JspTestCase {
...
//Setup session and request scope in setUp method (need?)
//Setup request parameters in beginXXX (if needed)
public void testSalesReport() {
    RequestDispatcher rd =
```

```
            theConfig.getServletContext().
             getRequestDispatcher("/generateSalesreport.do");

        rd.forward(theRequest, theResponse);
       //Check Session scope variable
    }

    public void endTestSalesReport(
             com.meterware.httpunit.WebResponse theResponse) {
         //Use HttpUnit to verify the HTML with HttpUnit
    }
```

In addition to testing JSP and actions, you can test custom tags that you write. Suppose you have a tag that looks up an entity bean and prints out a cmp field. This is similar to bean:write except that it works with entity beans:

```
public class EJBWriteTag extends WriteTag {

    public int doStartTag() throws JspException {
        doStartTagPrecondition();

        Object bean = null;
        Object primaryKey = getPrimaryKey();

          ...
            /* Look up the bean */
        bean =
              LocalFinderUtils
                  .findByPrimaryKey(primaryKey, name);

            /* Get the value from the bean */
        String output =
                BeanUtils.getProperty(bean, property);

            /* Write out the value */
        ResponseUtils.write(pageContext, output);
    ...
```

The test you write will simulate the custom tag lifecycle. You will need to populate the attributes of the custom tag. Finally, you check the output to see if the correct value appears:

```
public class EJBWriteTagTest extends JspTestCase {
    public final static String DEPT_NAME = "TESTZZZ";
     ...
    public void testEJBWriteTag ()throws Exception{

        EJBWriteTag tag = new EJBWriteTag();
        tag.setPageContext(pageContext);
        Integer id = Util.createDept(DEPT_NAME);

        request.setAttribute("id", id);
        tag.setIdName("id");
        tag.setName("DeptBean");
        tag.setProperty("name");
```

```
            tag.doStartTag();

            Util.killDept(id);
        }

        public void endEJBWriteTag (WebResponse response){
            String output = response.getText();
            assertEquals(DEPT_NAME, output);
        }
    }
```

We did not cover Cactus in detail in this book. For more information on using Cactus and JUnit in your projects, check out *Java Tools for Extreme Programming*, also by Rick Hightower, et al.

StrutsTestCase

Like Cactus, StrutsTestCase extends the JUnit framework. StrutsTestCase is geared for testing Struts components. It provides two ways to test actions: a mock object approach and a Cactus approach. If you have adopted a test-centric development process and you are developing in Struts, you should start using StrutsTestCase. Here is an example using StrutsTestCase to test an action mapped under the path /listDepartments:

```
import servletunit.struts.CactusStrutsTestCase;

public class DeptListingActionTest
                extends CactusStrutsTestCase {

    public void testDeptListingAction(){
        setRequestPathInfo("/listDepartments");
        actionPerform();
        verifyForward("listing");
        verifyNoActionErrors();
    }

}
```

This code test ensures that the action is forwarded to "listing" and that no action errors are mapped into scope. You can find StrutsTestCase at http://strutstestcase.sourceforge.net/.

XDoclet

If you are a J2EE development veteran, you know that keeping code in sync with deployment descriptors and configuration files can be tedious. Often you may need to reuse components with other applications or in other environments, such as other application servers or with other database systems. You need to keep a separate deployment descriptor for each application/environment combination, even if only one or two lines of the large deployment descriptor changes. This can really slow down development. At times you may feel you spend more time syncing deployment descriptors than writing code.

XDoclet facilitates automated deployment descriptor generation. As a code-generation utility, it allows you to tack on metadata to language features such as classes, methods, and fields using what looks like JavaDoc tags. Then, it uses that extra metadata to generate related files, like deployment descriptors and source code. This concept has been coined *attribute-oriented programming* (not to be confused with aspect-oriented programming, the other "AOP").

XDoclet generates these related files by parsing your source files in a way similar to the method the JavaDoc engine uses to parse your source to create JavaDoc documentation. In fact, earlier versions of XDoclet relied on JavaDoc. XDoclet, like JavaDoc, not only has access to these extra metadata that you tacked on in the form of JavaDoc tags to your code, but also has access to the structure of your source—that is, packages, classes, methods, and fields. It then applies this hierarchy tree of data to templates. It uses all of this (along with templates that you define) to generate what would otherwise be monotonous manual creation of support files.

XDoclet ships with an Ant task that enables you to create web.xml files, ejb-jar.xml files, and much more. Note that XDoclet Ant tasks do not ship with the standard distribution of Ant. You will need to download the XDoclet Ant tasks from the XDoclet site at http://xdoclet.sourceforge.net/.

You can also use XDoclet to generate Struts configuration files such as validation.xml and struts-config.xml. Using XDoclet simplifies tasks like adding validation support; for example, the following XDoclet-enabled version of inputForm uses XDoclet tags to mark up the user form field:

```
/**
 * @author rhightower
 * @struts.form    name="inputForm"
 *
 */
public class InputForm extends ValidatorForm {

    private String userName;
...

    public String getUserName() {
        return userName;
    }

    /**
     * @struts.validator type="required"
     * @struts.validator type="mask" msgkey="inputForm.userName.mask"
     * @struts.validator type="minlength" arg1value="${var:minlength}"
     * @struts.validator type="maxlength" arg1value="${var:maxlength}"
     * @struts.validator-var name="minlength" value="5"
     * @struts.validator-var name="maxlength" value="11"
     * @struts.validator-var name="mask" value="^[a-zA-Z]{1}[a-zA-Z0-9_]*$"
     */
    public void setUserName(String string) {
        userName = string;
    }
...
```

The class tag @struts.form denotes that this is a Struts ActionForm. The @struts.validator tag is a method-level tag, and it is used four times to associate the corresponding userName property (form field) with the required, mask, minlength, and maxlength rules. The @validator-var tag sets up the variables needed by the rules. Our XDoclet-enabled form generates the following validation.xml file entries:

```
<formset>
    <form name="inputForm">
            <field property="userName"
                   depends="required,mask,minlength,maxlength">
                <msg
                  name="mask"
                  key="inputForm.userName.mask"/>

                <arg0 key="inputForm.userName"/>
                <arg1
                    name="maxlength"
                  key="${var:maxlength}"
                    resource="false"
                />
                <arg1
                    name="minlength"
                  key="${var:minlength}"
                    resource="false"
                />
                <var>
                  <var-name>minlength</var-name>
                  <var-value>5</var-value>
                </var>
                <var>
                  <var-name>maxlength</var-name>
                  <var-value>11</var-value>
                </var>
                <var>
                  <var-name>mask</var-name>
                  <var-value>^[a-zA-Z]{1}[a-zA-Z0-9_]*$</var-value>
                </var>
            </field>
    </form>
```

You will find the Validator framework much easier to use with XDoclet support. The XDoclet templates and tasks for the Validator framework were created by famed Struts, Ant, and XDoclet expert Erik Hatcher.

You can also use XDoclet to generate Struts configuration files. You do this by marking up the action as follows:

```
/**
 * @author rhightower
 * @struts.action path="/inputSubmit" name="inputForm"
 *                validate="true" input="/input.jsp"
 *                attribute="employeeForm"
 *
 * @struts.action-forward name="success" path="/success.jsp"
```

```
 * @struts.action-forward name="resubmit" path="/resubmit.jsp"
 *
 * @struts.action path="/input" parameter="loadAddForm">
 * @struts.action-forward name="input-success" path="/input.jsp"/>
 *
 */
public class InputAction extends Action {

    public ActionForward execute(
        ActionMapping mapping,
        ActionForm form,
        HttpServletRequest request,
        HttpServletResponse response)
        throws Exception {
```

This code generates the following entries in your struts-config.xml files:

```
<action-mappings>
 <action
   path="/inputSubmit"
   type="masteringStruts.InputAction"
   name="inputForm"
   scope="request"
   input="/input.jsp"
   unknown="false"
   validate="true"
 >
   <forward
     name="success"
     path="/success.jsp"
     redirect="false"
   />
   <forward
     name="resubmit"
     path="/resubmit.jsp"
     redirect="false"
   />
   <forward
     name="input-success"
     path=""
     redirect="false"
   />
 </action>
 <action
   path="/input"
   type="masteringStruts.InputAction"
   unknown="false"
   validate="true"
 >
   <forward
     name="success"
     path="/success.jsp"
     redirect="false"
   />
```

```
    <forward
      name="resubmit"
      path="/resubmit.jsp"
      redirect="false"
    />
    <forward
      name="input-success"
      path=""
      redirect="false"
    />
  </action>
```

I find that generating action mappings works best for simpler actions (actions that don't have more than one mapping associated with them). You can keep your more complex action mappings along with your global forwards, global exception handling, and more in merge files. Merge files are merged into the final Struts configuration file during XDoclet generation.

Another problem with mapping actions is that you end up hard-coding the forward and input path into the action (albeit as a comment). At first blush, this defeats the purpose of separating all of this within the Struts configuration file to begin with.

You can alleviate this problem by using Ant properties. Any value can be replaced by an Ant property. Because XDoclet runs inside Ant, it has access to Ant properties. For example, notice the value of the success forward's path:

```
/**
 * @author rhightower
 * @struts.action path="/inputSubmit" name="inputForm"
 *                validate="true" input="/input.jsp"
 *                attribute="employeeForm"
 *
 * @struts.action-forward name="success" path="${input.success}"
 * @struts.action-forward name="resubmit" path="/resubmit.jsp"
 *
 * @struts.action path="/input" parameter="loadAddForm">
 * @struts.action-forward name="input-success" path="/input.jsp"/>
 *
 */
public class InputAction extends Action {
```

It is now set to ${input.success}, which means whatever value ${input.success} is set to when you run the Ant build script is the value that is generated output for the path of the success forward to the Struts configuration file. This gives you the benefits of both worlds and allows you to vary the paths at build time.

Tto run XDoclet from Ant, you need to import the XDoclet task into your build script as follows:

```
<path id="xdoclet.classpath">
    <fileset dir="/tools/xdoclet/lib" includes="*.jar"/>
</path>

<path id="web.compile.classpath">
  <fileset dir="${j2ee.libs}">
```

```
            <include name="**/*.jar" />
        </fileset>
        <fileset dir="web\WEB-INF\lib">
            <include name="**/*.jar" />
        </fileset>
    </path>

...
        <taskdef
             name="webdoclet"
             classname="xdoclet.modules.web.WebDocletTask">
             <classpath>
                 <path refid="xdoclet.classpath"/>
                 <path refid="web.compile.classpath"/>
             </classpath>
        </taskdef>
```

Then to start using the XDoclet, you use the webdoclet task inside a target, like this:

```
        <webdoclet destdir="meta-data/web"
             force="true"
             mergedir="meta-data/web">
             <fileset dir="src">
               <include name="**/*Form.java"/>
               <include name="**/*Action.java"/>
             </fileset>
             <strutsconfigxml validatexml="true" version="1.1"/>
             <strutsvalidationxml omitdtd="true"/>
        </webdoclet>
```

A full discussion and coverage of XDoclet is beyond the scope of this book. As you can see, it is a powerful tool that can help simplify your J2EE and Struts development efforts. Excellent online resources for XDoclet are available. There is a multipart tutorial on XDoclet written by Rick Hightower on IBM developerWorks. You'll find a series of example applications built with XDoclet at http://xpetstore.sourceforge.net/. In addition, Erik Hatcher provides an example application (which comes with documentation on how to use XDoclet) at http://www.ehatchersolutions.com/JavaDevWithAnt/.

If you are doing Struts development, you should seriously consider using XDoclet to generate your configuration files.

Index

A

B

F

G

H

L

M

N–O

P

R

S

T

U–V

W

X

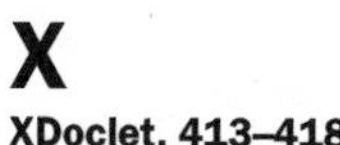